A Study of Generations

presented to

Lutheran congregations, colleges, and seminaries

in the United States and Canada

by

Lutheran Brotherhood
a fraternal benefit society

whose interest and financial support

made this study possible

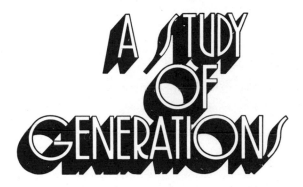

A STUDY OF GENERATIONS

Merton P. Strommen · Milo L. Brekke · Ralph C. Underwager · Arthur L. Johnson

Report of a Two-Year Study
of 5,000 Lutherans
Between the Ages of 15-65:
Their Beliefs, Values, Attitudes, Behavior

AUGSBURG PUBLISHING HOUSE
MINNEAPOLIS, MINNESOTA

A STUDY OF GENERATIONS

MANUFACTURED IN THE UNITED STATES OF AMERICA

Contents

3

FIGURES

5

TABLES

Foreword

It is not surprising that Lutherans would be the first American denomination to sit for their portrait, now unveiled with this volume. Since they are perfectly clear that personal salvation and the vitality of God's church and mission do *not* depend on such things as contemporary church architecture, or the communications media, or empirical research, Lutherans are thereby freed to develop such devices of contemporary culture to the fullest for what they *are* good for; Lutherans have been magnificently in the forefront of the church's effort to make appropriate use of such tools.

What is the use of a portrait, such as this book presents? If "portrait" suggests a picture to be admired in a museum or a memorial to the retired and the dead, then the portrait may not seem very useful and perhaps the picture presented by this book should be called, instead, an "x-ray." It provides a penetrating, diagnostic appraisal that probes below surface impressions and gives sounder basis for judgment and decision. For example, one surface impression, encouraged by many journalistic writers, authors of best sellers, and even some prominent theoreticians, is that of a generation "gap" in which the young are alleged to hold very different religious and moral values from their elders. Some Lutherans might be tempted to decisions about the place of youth in the church's ministry on the basis of such surface impressions. But the more penetrating portrait presented here shows us something quite different from this surface impression and makes us realize that any decision based on it would be quite misguided.

The research portrait does confirm quite dramatically, however, a distinction that Lutherans have learned to talk about rather easily, so easily that some persons might suppose the distinction to be only a surface impression; this is the distinction between the religious posture associated with a sense of justification by faith and that associated with reliance on "law." The penetrating look shows these to be not just slogans but deeply entrenched alternatives in the kinds of religious postures of which men are capable. These, then, are some of the underlying contours revealed by the portrait/x-ray these researchers have completed. At the same time that the report shows us these patterns, it also makes another character-istic perfectly clear: there is a great diversity among Lutherans; different patterns can be identified by this picture, and it would be wrong to sup-pose that Lutherans as a whole are characterized by any single pattern.

Or, if not an x-ray, perhaps we should say that this portrait has the usefulness of a "mirror," especially the kind of verbal mirror that can be offered by a discerning and trusted friend, someone who can graciously show us things about ourselves that we never noticed but are helped by seeing. "You are coming to me this way," he may say, or, "You seem to be wanting to say such and such," or, "Have you ever noticed how certain circumstances seem to bring out particular traits in you?" With such "reflections" as these, a counselor helps us to know ourselves more truly. And with such self-understanding, we may be able to live more effectively and more responsibly. Such are the kinds of "reflections" the portrait recorded in this book provides, saying to Lutherans, with con-cern and objectivity, "Here is how we see you. Make the most of it." This is the kind of insight the skillful portrait painter conveys when at last, sometimes to our dismay but almost always to our profit, he lets us come around behind the easel and look at the canvas on which he has recorded his insights.

Lutherans can be assured that their portrait has been drawn here sensibly and responsibly by a skilled team. This first thorough denomi-national portrait has set high standards for others to follow. A portrait is not easy to paint because the artist sets out to show us subtle inner nuances that elude a conventional photographer or a more casual ob-server. Some features are easy to represent: the shape of the nose, the color of the eyes (for the portrayer of an individual); the number of church members and their distribution among age groups or geographic regions or social class categories (for the portrayer of a church). These can be recorded mechanically, by a camera or by a computerized tabu-lation of data. The portrait must be accurate about these features, and the report here is accurate; such mapping of the more obvious features has been done with care and thoroughness. But the portrait artist must also discern and portray for us qualities of mind and spirit that require much more sensitivity and subtle study. The authors of this volume have brought such requisite sensitivity to their task as well. They have devised methods of research and of analysis, with energy and resourcefulness, that have raised the perceptivity and precision of their work to a high order.

How would you give a portrait of the religion in your own church or community? If a visitor comes to your town or city and asks, "Tell me about the religion here," how do you answer? You can point to the church buildings and tell how many people attend there and how much money they give and how large a staff they employ and how many activities go on in the building during the week. This is not a bad way to give an account of the religion of a church or community. Certainly it is the most common way. Newspapers and chambers of commerce, denominational officials and sociological researchers most often give us their portrait of religion by showing us the church buildings and the activities and the people connected with them. (If such things as commitment and conviction, service and healing, love and trust are found outside the precincts of the church building, the news magazine classifies the report on other pages, in some other portrait, not under "religion.") Most research on religion gives us building-centered portraits. Your visiting inquirer might be satisfied with such a portrait. But he might not, and perhaps neither are you.

He might ask, "Tell me about religion in the lives of the people, in their daily comings and goings, in their attitudes toward the life they find around them, in its big and small dimensions. What posture do they take toward the ultimate and the intimate aspects of their life? What beliefs? What manner of life?" You will admit that these are valid questions. Any complete portrait of religion ought to include answers to such searching questions. But if you are like most of us, you will feel stymied and not be able to do more than stammer out a few general responses: "Well, people believe in God, and the creeds, and read the Bible, and try to live Christian lives and be good neighbors." Previous research portraits of religion have hardly succeeded in answering such questions any more precisely than that, either. Such general answers are hardly very illuminating and are bound to be disappointing to one who takes seriously the kinds of searching questions posed above. Religion in the lives and thoughts of people may be so central and so fundamental that it becomes most difficult to locate and identify. The researchers whose work is recorded here have succeeded admirably in finding authentic and reliable ways of helping us discern these elusive fundamentals.

A good portrait requires a sense of active collaboration between artist and subject. The research reported here has resulted from a remarkable and rare degree of collaboration between the principal researchers and their fellow churchmen who have served as respondents to the questionnaires, their advisers, consultants, interviewers, and now their readers and respondents to the report. In more conventional, and unfortunately, far more typical research, church people are pressed into the service of the researcher; they are his research "subjects" much as medieval people were "subjects" of a king. But the researchers who have produced this volume have self-consciously put themselves into the service of the church and its people. They have not abdicated their responsibility—their vocation—for rigorous conceptualization and interpretation, for scrupulous collection and sophisticated analysis of the data. But they have not excluded their fellow churchmen from serious participation in this enterprise. Questionnaire items have been assembled and tried out and modified with the active cooperation of churchmen. The items have been presented to respondents in an ingenious format that made the respondents' task seem less like the meaningless, arduous chore that questionnaires often are, and more like a serious yet pleasant encounter with ideas. In the analysis of the data, preconceived categories have not been imposed rigidly by the researchers, but rather respondents' own answers have been allowed, with sophisticated computational methods, to generate the categories of analysis. Especially remarkable and admirable is the way that the researchers' fellow churchmen have been invited to participate in the report itself. Preliminary drafts have been tried out on prospective readers, and the final drafts have profited much from their reactions. The readers will be grateful that the sophisticated statistical analysis which underlies this report has been matched by the effort and imagination that has gone into making this final presentation intelligible and useful. These chapters let the readers share the drama of the researchers' discoveries.

It seems to me that these researchers have done their work as an offering to the church. Their research is one more way—their way—of participating in the life of the church; research for them is not a way of standing aloof and judgmental. Far from compromising the "scientific" value of their work, this spirit has enhanced its value. It is through this extra dedication and self-involvement, this co-labor with fellow churchmen, this sense of mutual service and mutual assistance that the research has come to render such a faithful portrait of Lutherans in the United States.

JAMES E. DITTES
Yale University

Preface

The family portrait of Lutherans in the United States that we present here differs from the usual portrait in that we use words, statistical analyses, and charts rather than paints, brushes, and canvas. It is different, too, because it deals with that which is often unseen: the attitudes, values, beliefs, opinions, and personal circumstances of the lives of its subjects.

The purpose of this book is to help us think together into the life, work, and mission of a local congregation. It is an attempt to show the structural framework that underlies the common life and religious practices of Lutherans. And it is an effort to identify what church members believe, value, aspire to, and do.

To do research that is worthy of the church is a very demanding task. Our research team can appreciate the conviction of Leonardo da Vinci who believed that one essential preparation for the painting of portraits was a precise education in anatomy; therefore, before he took up portrait painting, he undertook a painstaking analysis of the skeletal and muscular systems of the human body. With a similar conviction, *A Study of Generations* research team approached this group portrait of Lutherans. In preparing to present this massive picture, we have made a serious effort, using complex statistical procedures, to go beneath the surface and arrive at an understanding of the structural form of what Lutherans value, believe, and do, and what effect that structure has on more visible behavior.

13

This commitment has forced us beyond the scope of an opinion poll to the type of research that probes deeper levels of how a person's thoughts and feelings are organized.

We found 78 dimensions relating to what Lutherans believe, value, aspire to, and do. And we found that Lutherans range from one extreme to the other on every dimension. It would be misleading, therefore, to use averages only and say Lutherans are *this* or Lutherans are *that*. We cannot paint a portrait of an "average Lutheran," though at times we must describe what is true of "most" Lutherans. It is far more accurate to emphasize the diversity of the Lutheran church by identifying subgroups of people and by showing how one type differs from another. To continue our analogy, we found that though the same basic skeleton underlies all of Lutheranism, the outward forms vary a great deal. In this book we will describe the members of the Lutheran church in a way that shows both the framework and the outward expressions of its people.

This report comes at a significant time for several reasons. First of all many people are questioning whether there is vitality and life in the church. We have all heard the "God is dead" argument, and we may have seen cover stories of major magazines with such headlines as, "Has the Church Lost Its Soul?" For people with less extreme claims, there is still a quiet but urgent concern for the life of the church.

A new willingness to allow the spotlight of research to focus on the church is a second advantage. Once considered an institution beyond public scrutiny, the church now has leaders who believe that openness to realities of life and faith will help the church. They believe that Christianity will be better understood and church members will be better informed through a study such as this. This kind of openness has not always been the characteristic of church leaders. Prior to 1960 several major denominations, which had spent millions of dollars in research, chose to keep their research findings as private information.

The renewed interest of social scientists in the study of religion also makes this a timely study. A case in point is the publication, *Research on Religious Development: A Comprehensive Handbook* (1971), which well over 50 scholars shared in writing. This *Handbook* summarizes and critiques 40 years of research in which religion is a variable. The volume also makes strong recommendations for future research in the area of religion, several of which are incorporated in this study.

We took seriously the critique that much past research has been "mindless research." Therefore, we prepared several working papers before beginning our study. One gave a schema of conceptual categories of beliefs, values, attitudes, and behavior, and specified the interrelationships that we anticipated between them. This conceptualization, presented as a 68-page document to a conference of advisors on 30 January

1970, served as a guide to the development of the survey instrument and later to interpretation of survey data. A second document spelled out the assumptions of the research team and how they understood the nature of man. A third paper served as a scaffolding for organizing and understanding generations.

Another recommendation made in the *Handbook* called for the use of a complex form of data analysis where many variables are examined simultaneously to determine their relative effects. This method of analysis shows the relative contribution of a number of important variables. We found that as a result of this form of analysis, some of our preliminary findings, where we examined our data one variable at a time, lost some of their importance. We describe the process in Chapter 3 for anyone who is interested.

As the four of us on the research team were writing this book, we were faced with several dilemmas. One was that we wished we could have had more time to produce the book. But there was a sense of urgency to report the findings while interest was high and the data were current. In responding to this sense of urgency, we experienced the frustrations that plague any effort to rush a manuscript into print. But we are convinced that our decision to share data now, rather than take the customary years to report a study, was a good one.

We struggled, also, with the question of whether to use an inductive or deductive approach. Should we lead the reader through the process and drama of discovery, telling everything we as scientists did, and finally tell what we found? Or should we respond to our excitement over the findings, scream "Eureka!" and tell you immediately what we found? As the chapters well illustrate, we followed the example of the scientist Archimedes who called attention to his findings with the words, "I have found it!" Readers who need to know the "how" before they read about the "what" are advised to begin with Appendix A which describes the scientific process that underlies the findings.

Our third dilemma related to selection of data. When we have such immense numbers of data from interviews, items, scales, and factor analyses, what do we report in our first book? We resolved this dilemma by going back to the questions we were asked when the study began. They provided our focus and, as you will see, most of them were answered. Unanswered questions will be picked up in the paperbacks which follow this publication.

Overview of the Book

This book is organized into four sections. Before reading the chapters in each section, the reader is advised to read the introductions. These give background information that will enhance the meaning of the chapters which follow.

Section One begins with an orientation to how the study was carried out. The second chapter describes the object of our study by comparing Lutherans with Americans in general and with each other. The third chapter introduces readers untrained in research to the concepts and procedures used in this study.

The introduction to Section Two enters the world of research with its specialized jargon. The reader is invited to look at the many dimensions of thought and feeling and see how they combine to form a dynamic structure that underlies a person's attitudes and opinions. The chapters of this section give in-depth descriptions of Lutherans in many intriguing areas—values, beliefs, attitudes toward mission and ministry, life styles, and feelings about themselves and others.

Section Three helps the reader stand back for a look at group differences among Lutherans. One chapter is devoted to the generational tension that finds its source in differing world views of young and old. Another chapter focuses on the diversity within and among church bodies and between clergy and laity. Differences due to education, regional impact, sex, and size of congregation are reported also. The section concludes with a summary of findings and a series of basic conclusions.

The final section is important to social scientists who must know the details of a research before accepting its findings. The essentials of the study are reported in sufficient detail to account for how the research team carried out this complex and highly involved study.

Inasmuch as this book is team-written, variation in writing style can be expected from chapter to chapter. One advantage may be to provide variety and change of pace, as well as greater breadth of insight.

It should be understood, also, that this volume, a research report, is intended to serve as the basic source document for a subsequent series of interpretive paperbacks. The "where-do-we-go-from-here" type of commentary will follow in five paperbacks.

Considering that this is a study of the church, in a day when serious questions have been raised about the church's vitality, even its survival, a fitting overview of this book is expressed in the words of Mark Twain, "The reports of my death are grossly exaggerated."

As the data will show, the Lutheran church is not only alive but eager.

Acknowledgments

It will be evident that this study is a product of the work of many people. As Principal Investigator, I can say that major credit for this study must go to my colleagues, Milo Brekke and Ralph Underwager. They and

Arthur Johnson, who later joined the team, are largely responsible for the quality and depth of what is reported here. Though the research team carried the major load, hundreds of other people gave necessary help.

Commendation goes to eight seminarians who for nearly a year were a part of the research team. They well represented the study during the three summer months of 1970 when they collected the research data. From Northwestern Theological Seminary were Gary Hopson, James Schoenrock, and John Sjoblom. From Luther Theological Seminary were Paul Forde, Howard Fosser, Lauren Johnson, Hugh Mechesney, and Clifford Schmidt.

Appreciation is extended to the Steering Committee (listed in Chapter 1) and especially to E. Clifford Nelson whose interest and initiative sparked the study.

Our special thanks go to Lutheran Brotherhood for its sponsorship of the study and to its Board of Directors for their supportive interest in the life and welfare of the Lutheran church.

We also acknowledge with thanks the work of our consultants in the social sciences and theology who offered invaluable help in shaping and evaluating the research methods and survey content, and in many cases in criticizing early manuscripts. They are:

Dr. May Brodbeck, University of Minnesota

Dr. James E. Dittes, Yale University

Rev. Brady Y. Faggart, Jr., Assistant to the President,
Lutheran Church in America

Dr. Francis C. Gamelin, The Central States College Association

Dr. Thomas J. Kiresuk, Hennepin County Mental Health Center,
Minneapolis

Dr. Kent S. Knutson, President, The American Lutheran Church

Dr. Frederick Meuser, Evangelical Lutheran Theological Seminary

Rev. Norbert Mueller, Theological Commission, Lutheran Church—
Missouri Synod

Dr. Alvin Rogness, Luther Theological Seminary

Dr. Richard Sommerfeld, Capital University

Dr. Bernard Spilka, University of Denver

Dr. John Tietjen, Concordia Seminary

Dr. Barbara Varenhorst, Palo Alto Schools

Dr. Raymond Willis, University of Minnesota

We make grateful acknowledgment of the 316 pastors who opened their homes and congregations to our research visitors. Their gracious assistance in gathering the data and later reacting to the preliminary findings made this book possible.

Many colleagues and coworkers have assisted along the way. Gordon Solomonson helped gather and analyze presurvey data; Ram Gupta and Peter Braun (University of Alberta, Edmonton) kept the project on schedule during the laborious stages of data analysis. Marilyn Graves assisted in the painstaking detail of instrument development, data analysis, and manuscript reading. Elaine Springsted served as coordinator of arrangements for the seven regional conferences which, in the spring of 1971, drew together 698 pastors, laymen, and church leaders. Ernest Thompson, systems analyst, shepherded the data processing through the summer and fall of 1971, assisted by Vernon Suhr, Dennis Bornes, and Bonnie Barnum. Shelby Andress, my assistant, and Dorothy Williams gave invaluable aid on the writing and rewriting of manuscripts. Finally, through the entire period, and at times assisted by other members of the Youth Research Center staff, Katherine Rouzer served as executive secretary for the study.

To all these important people we give public acknowledgment of our thanks.

MERTON P. STROMMEN

1. A Study of Generations

What do Lutherans believe?

How do they assign priorities and make choices in their day-to-day living?

Where are they ready to act out their convictions?

What are their opinions on

— the mission and ministry of the church?

— the necessity of maintaining a continuing loyalty to the institutional church—specifically, the Lutheran church?

— their relationships with other human beings?

In what kinds of life styles do they operate?

Who are they?

Where do they live?

A Study of Generations reports the results of a survey designed to supply the answers to these and other related questions. This book reports the beliefs, values, attitudes, opinions, and religious life styles of a representative sample of 4,745 adults between the ages of 15 and 65. These people were members in 1970 of a representative sample of congregations in the three major Lutheran bodies in the United States: The American Lutheran Church (ALC), the Lutheran Church—Missouri Synod (LC-MS), and the Lutheran Church in America (LCA).

A great deal of negative criticism of the church has been published recently, some of it the result of research of various kinds. When you want people to hear what you have to say, there is always a temptation to make dramatic use of the negative: "The schools are ruining our children!" "God is dead!" "The church cannot survive the century!" And a good many people have given in to that temptation.

A Study of Generations has no intention of making exaggerated statements of either a positive or a negative nature to produce "a story." There is solid, lasting drama of a quieter sort in facts, and this quieter drama of facts is the story which this book reveals. This is the story of what 6,000,000 adult Lutherans are doing, thinking, believing, and choosing in the living out of their responses to the questions of life. It is a huge drama, far too vast to grasp. But by bringing the techniques of social science to bear on a representative part of the stage, we can show what a sample of these 6,000,000 Lutherans replied to *A Study of Generations* questions about matters that touch their lives.

Our objective is to determine reality behind the facts. This is not completely available, of course. All knowledge is tentative; we assume our conclusions to be true until further information makes our present knowledge obsolete.

No one is more aware of the tentative nature of knowledge than a conscientious research team. They have memories long enough to recall times when information once accepted as true has now, in light of later information, proved only partly true, or downright wrong. Present research techniques are far more sophisticated, capable of producing far more refined and accurate results than were accessible with the techniques used 15 years ago. Fifteen years from now (or will it be five?) we assume that today's knowledge will be superseded.

Underlying all the statements made in the chapters that follow is this basic assumption: by use of the most sophisticated research techniques now available, this has been found to be true. More refined techniques, additional discoveries, new data, may one day produce research results that will necessarily revise what is said now. But one cannot wait for tomorrow. Today's work must be done today. The perspectives that this study make available to the church present opportunities for rethinking her ministry that are unique in the history of American Lutheranism.

We call this *A Study of Generations*, and you may wonder why.

During the first months of our project, we interviewed many people for the purpose of determining what issues should be faced through the study. One concern that came through loud and clear was a concern about youth. Men in positions of responsibility were asking questions like these:

Will today's youth support and help maintain the church in the years ahead? Or, to be very practical,

Can we expect declining memberships and budgets because today's youth will no longer want to be members of a church?

Lurking behind these questions was a fear that a radical break had occurred in society—a fear that today's youth were adopting a style and philosophy of life that is basically anti-institutional.

If one is going to assess a break between generations—a break in beliefs, values, life styles, and attitudes—then a study of generations is required.

But what is a generation?

How does one identify Lutheran generations?

Some authorities believe that generations are formed by societal events that are of dramatic intensity. Such tragic episodes, they claim, significantly shape the nature of the entire population. Some insist that a new generation of youth was formed in the late 1960s as a result of the heart-rending experiences of that period: three public heroes were assassinated; cities erupted in riots and violence; the Vietnam War became a national tragedy; and students took possession of universities. These and similar episodes in the life of a country, they say, helped to shape a new generation.

In line with this concept of generations, the research team, before collecting its data, chose the two major World Wars as occurrences that likely marked the boundaries of generations. It was decided that at least three generations would be studied: those born before the end of World War I (ages 50-65); those born between World War I and World War II (ages 30-49); and those born after World War II (ages 15-29).

The question which naturally arises is this: did the wars change our national life drastically enough to demark demonstrably different generations within these age groupings?

A major test of the assumption that world wars *did* provide boundaries for distinct generations was carried out through a highly complex form of data analysis called factor analysis. It is sufficient to say that all nondemographic answers from each person of each age (15-year-olds, 16-year-olds, etc.) were compared with answers of persons of every other age, through age 65. (*Demographic* is used throughout the book in the broad sense of population descriptors such as age, education, region, and the like; therefore, *nondemographic*, by contrast, refers to psychological, theological, and behavioral information including beliefs, values, attitudes, opinions, and actions.) The purpose of this analysis was to determine whether or not there was enough in common among people of various ages; that is, whether or not people of one age level answered similarly to people of another age level. If this were found to be so, we might say that they share enough common characteristics so that we can classify them as a generation.

Three different factor analyses were made of the same data with similar results. Factor analysis is a delicate technique susceptible to the effects of arranging data. That the findings survived is a sign of their stability and likelihood to represent truth.

One generation of responses included people between the ages of 15 and 29. The cut-off age of 29 was not precise and could just as well, we discovered from the data, be set at age 27. The next generation included ages 30-39, though a cut-off point of 37 or possibly 41 could also be used. Another generation was formed by a cut-off point of 49 or 51. In spite of the overlap of two or three years, four distinct age groups emerged from the data: 15-29, 30-39, 40-49, and 50-65. However, the slightly differing factor analytic results became available at quite widely separated times during the processing of data. Because of this and because of the resultant overlap at each cut-off, slightly differing age groupings will be reported from time to time throughout the book where generational comparisons are being made.

One naturally wonders why persons between the two World Wars (ages 30-49) form two distinct generations (ages 30-39 and 40-49). Why did one major factor in the computer analysis unite people between the ages of 30 and 39 and another factor unite persons between the ages of 40 and 49? What would account for this? We are suggesting that events occurring at the midpoint between the two World Wars (1930) had a sufficient impact to form these two distinct generations.

The event which did occur half-way between World War I and World War II was the financial crash and its resulting Depression in the 1930s. Without question this difficult period did produce changes in the lives of many people. It may have made an impact sufficient to form two generations.

Factors other than historical and cultural pressures, however, may account for this division into four generations. One such factor is a person's position in the family life cycle. The pervasive changes that occur for youth, once they have assumed the responsibilities of marriage and parenthood, may account for the break between ages 27 and 29 (e.g., in the sample only 15% of youth ages 24-29 are still single). Likewise, the changes that occur for adults who face an "empty nest" and waning physical vitality may account for the break around the age of 49. It may be that the results of factor-analyzing by age reflect periods in the life cycle that usually end around ages 29, 39, and 49, irrespective of the period in history. Notwithstanding, we do know that events as momentous as the World Wars and the Depression do leave their impact on what people believe, value, think, and do. Hence, cultural and historical pressures, though possibly not a sufficient explanation, have undeniably helped shape the generations.

How about the wide span of age between 15 and 29? Is this generation span too broad?

A factor analysis of ages 15 through 29 yields subgenerations that roughly approximate the high school, college, and post-graduation years: 15-18, 19-23, and 24-29. As will be seen later, these smaller generational units do differ enough to warrant a separate classification of data, and so we arrive at four major generations and three subclassifications in this study of generations.

Four Major Generations reported variously as follows:

Ages 50-65	Ages 50-65	Ages 49-65
Ages 40-49	Ages 42-49	Ages 39-48
Ages 30-39	Ages 30-41	Ages 29-38
Ages 15-29	Ages 15-29	Ages 15-28

Three Subgenerations of Youth:
Ages 24-29
Ages 19-23
Ages 15-18

Church leaders and social scientists, both at the outset of the study and when preliminary results were reviewed in conferences, showed great concern for such detailed information and comparisons about youth alone. Therefore, no additional factor analyses were performed to identify possible subgenerations of the other major generations (30-39, 40-49, or 50-65).

At times throughout the book a distinction will be made between comparisons by *generation* and comparisons by *age*. The age groupings outlined above will be used for comparisons by generation. Two-year age groupings (i.e., 15-16, 17-18, etc.) will be reported most frequently when the possible association of chronological age to some variations in beliefs, values, or attitudes is being investigated.

Who sponsored and guided the study?

Financial undergirding for *A Study of Generations* was provided entirely by Lutheran Brotherhood of Minneapolis, Minnesota. Only two requirements were set by Lutheran Brotherhood when providing the nearly $300,000 required for this massive undertaking. They were that the study be *(a)* scientifically sound and in keeping with the highest standards of scientific research, and *(b)* maximally beneficial and relevant to the mission and ministry of the church.

The study was launched after the presidents of the three Lutheran bodies to be surveyed knew of it and concurred. A Steering Committee of seven recognized leaders in the three church bodies was formed at the outset and met regularly, often monthly, to give counsel and direction in the conduct and policy of the study. The members of this Steering Committee were:

Norman D. Fintel, Executive Director, Board of College Education, The American Lutheran Church

Luther O. Forde, Vice President and Director of Research and Development, Lutheran Brotherhood

Arthur L. Johnson, Ph.D., Professor, University of Minnesota

Kent S. Knutson, Ph.D., President, The American Lutheran Church (President of Wartburg Theological Seminary at the time of the formation of the Steering Committee)

Adalbert R. Kretzman, D.D., Pastor, The Evangelical Lutheran Church of Saint Luke, Chicago, Illinois

Malvin H. Lundeen, D.D., Assistant to the President, The Minnesota Synod, Lutheran Church in America

E. Clifford Nelson, Ph.D., Professor, St. Olaf College

In addition, some 75 theologians, educators, pastors, and administrators were asked what they would like such a study to include, describe, and attempt to answer. Fifty-four of this same group attended a special conference in January 1970 to discuss the general form and direction of the study and the proposed content of the questionnaire. The following spring, laymen in a variety of widely scattered congregations gave their reactions to a preliminary version of the questionnaire.

Who conducted the research?

Youth Research Center of Minneapolis was charged with the responsibility of conducting the research. The Center is a non-profit corporation whose stated purpose is:

> to provide opportunities for study and development of theoretical positions interrelating the social sciences, religion, and education; to conduct research in these areas; and, based upon these activities, to disseminate findings and offer services—with special reference to youth—to society, its institutions and movements.

Persons who made up the research team were:

Principal Investigator, Merton P. Strommen, Ph.D., President, Youth Research Center; author, *Profiles of Church Youth* (1963); editor, *Research on Religious Development: A Comprehensive Handbook* (1971); ordained pastor of The American Lutheran Church.

Research Associate, Milo L. Brekke, Vice President for Research Analysis, Youth Research Center; ordained pastor of The American

Lutheran Church; experience as parish pastor; researcher for the ALC Division of Parish Education; completing a doctoral program in empirical research at the University of Minnesota.

Research Associate, Ralph C. Underwager, Ph.D., Research staff of Youth Research Center; certified clinical psychologist; experience as parish pastor; Wheat Ridge Fellow in Pastoral Care; ordained pastor of the Lutheran Church—Missouri Synod.

Associate Analyst and Writer, Arthur L. Johnson, Ph.D., Professor of Sociology, Graduate School, University of Minnesota; layman of the Lutheran Church in America.

Executive Secretary, Katherine A. Rouzer, Staff, Youth Research Center.

How was the information for the study acquired?

The survey questionnaire—the central instrument by which the findings reported in this book were collected—was developed by the research team during the first nine months of the study (September 1969 through May 1970). The questionnaire consists of 740 multiple-choice statements and questions. Each respondent replied by pencil-marking his choices of answer on three precoded answer sheets that could be read by machine for electronic data processing.

Hundreds of previous studies were examined for possible questions or sets of questions that would be useful in the survey. In addition to those so selected, new items concerning areas not covered in any existing survey were written. Over a period of months all these items were considered, compared, sorted, and compiled into a 932-question survey which was then tried out and evaluated in the spring of 1970 in about 20 graciously willing congregations. ("Graciously" because their answers didn't "count" in the survey; and because, in addition to answering the 932 questions, they supplied helpful criticism on the clarity of instructions and expressed their feelings about the items.) The results from this pretesting enabled a further sorting and modification process which produced the final 740 items used in the survey.

The survey questions were printed in three booklets: Book I is entitled *Your Beliefs, Values, and You;* Book II, *How You See Yourself and Others;* and Book III, *Your Attitudes and Way of Life.* Every respondent used all three books, and, as the survey was administered, books were presented in such a way that one-third of each group surveyed began with Book I, one-third with Book II, and one-third with Book III. This eliminated the probability of everyone's being fresh and eager on Book I and jaded and fatigued by the end of Book III.

In the summer of 1970 eight carefully trained Lutheran seminarians fanned out across the United States from Caribou, Maine, to Los Angeles,

California; from Fort Lauderdale, Florida, to Port Angeles, Washington. Each in his assigned territory, the seminarians visited 316 Lutheran congregations to conduct interviews and to administer the survey. The result was a collection of roughly 7,000,000 items of information from and about Lutheran church members.

In addition to their group administration of the printed surveys, the eight seminarians conducted individual oral interviews on a predetermined schedule of topics with at least three persons (one of the three being the pastor) in each of the 316 congregations visited.

The interview schedule concentrated in two areas: (a) What do people think and feel when they hear certain words which not only are associated with the faith but are used in ordinary language as well? and (b) What are people's images, expectations, hopes, dreams, and disillusionments about the church?

Data from these interviews are at times reflected in interpretations offered in this book, but the complete findings are not included here; they will be included in subsequent publications.

How were the people who took the survey chosen?

At the same time as the survey questionnaire was being prepared, the sample of persons to be surveyed was being selected.

There are approximately 6,000,000 adult Lutherans belonging to about 15,000 congregations in the United States. A census of all of them was not taken. Rather, only 378 congregations were selected at random and invited to participate (though only 376 were actually available, since one congregation lost its identity in merger, and another disbanded before time of data collection). Of those invited, 85% (316 congregations) agreed to do so; no substitutions were made for congregations who rejected the opportunity. From each of the participating congregations individual members were randomly chosen from membership lists.

"Random," when used in the statistical sense employed here, is not at all the hit-or-miss, here-a-few-and-there-a-few sense that the word carries in ordinary conversation. With a specific congregation, it worked like this: Each of the 316 congregations supplied Youth Research Center with a list of the total confirmed membership of that church, first eliminating the names of all persons under age 15 and over age 65. All of the listed names were numbered in sequence. A table of random numbers (a standard reference in statistical work) was used to select people from the numbered list solely according to their numerical placement in the alphabetical sequence. For a given congregation the table might dictate that persons numbered 76, 321, 4, 208, etc., on the list be invited to participate. No substitutes for the persons so selected were knowingly permitted. Congregations invited to be a part of the study were chosen by this random process also. By this means every person in every congregation in all three Lutheran bodies had an equal chance (one in 667) of being selected for the survey. Of those selected, 73%, a total of 4,745 persons, actually took the survey.

Church members as well as some pastors have expressed puzzlement over the reason for employing this painstaking but seemingly mechanical process. It seemed strange to single out men away from home in military service, persons known to be antagonistic to the present pastor, college students away from home, or people who hadn't attended church in years. Why were such persons selected along with a sprinkling of familiar faces such as, possibly, one or two Sunday school teachers or a choir member?

The reason for using this elaborate selection process is that it is the only way to obtain a true picture of the *whole* population of the Lutheran church. To give the survey to those who volunteered, or to the 15 persons who came first to the pastor's mind, would be to limit the sample to representing parts of the church, but not the whole. In order to have a true picture of the church, people taking the survey must represent all levels of interest in the church, all levels of commitment to the faith.

Pastors often expressed surprise on seeing which invited people did in fact turn up to take the survey, at how many of their inactive members came. One hypothesis is that nonattendance at regular church activities cannot be assumed to indicate a total lack of interest in the church.

A serious effort was made, with considerable success, to reach people who did not come for the survey administration and to have them take the survey at another time. There was, however, a remaining number who were invited to take the survey and who did not. Nonrespondents were studied later and were found to differ only slightly from participants. (See Section IV, Appendix A, "How the Study Was Conducted.")

How valid is the sample? Is it possible that the information secured from 4,745 persons in 316 congregations can tell us about all 6,000,000 Lutherans in approximately 15,000 congregations? The answer is Yes. Not with absolute certainty, of course, but with a very high degree of probability, not only because of the random process of choice just described but because of a number of other research and statistical processes designed to minimize the factor of error as much as possible. (If you are interested in further elaboration of the research process, see Section IV, Appendix A.)

Because of the care with which the survey has been taken and interpreted, it is possible to use the information secured from the few to speak with considerable certainty about *all* Lutherans in the United States.

Who is involved?

A great deal has already been invested in this study. The financial investment was, of course, a basic necessity and an indispensable ingredient. But beyond that, people, once drawn into the study, have invested themselves and their time—which is an irreplaceable part of their life —with a vigor sometimes bordering on recklessness.

The church members who took the survey generally showed a heart-warming willingness to take their part of the responsibility seriously. An over-the-road trucker arranged his run with a break in the middle; his truck waited in the church parking lot while he completed the survey, and then truck and driver went on their way. A blind member brought his wife to go through the laborious process of reading and marking the answer sheets for him, through the entire 740 sometimes-lengthy items. A girl working 250 miles away arranged a trip home on the appointed night to take the survey. One woman postponed surgery in order to participate. People rearranged vacations, social events, work schedules, leisure, so that they might make their contribution to the survey.

The study had its effect on the eight seminarians who personally administered the survey. All wrote a summary report of their experiences. Here is what one said:

> Of the 40 congregations I visited, I would say that the church is seeing itself as having a mission and is trying to move in that direction. Any doubts in my mind that would have hindered my entering the parish aspect of the ministry have been settled, and I am firmly convinced that this is where the action is and this is where the answer will be found.

There has been a general undercurrent of excitement among the people working on this study because they have become convinced that it can be of overwhelming importance to the future of the Lutheran church.

Unless you are accustomed to reading a good deal in sociological and psychological research, and in theological and philosophic thought, what is to come in this book will not be uniformly easy reading. A good many of the concepts are complex, and we were not always willing to sacrifice the complexity of statement that precision demands in order to achieve simplicity. But we have done our best to make it as readable as possible.

2. A Social Profile of Lutherans

This chapter describes the social characteristics of Lutherans. In short, it says that Lutherans

- *are racially homogeneous (98% white).*
- *are native born (96%).*
- *attend church more frequently than other American Protestants do.*
- *claim Scandinavian and German backgrounds for most members over 50 years of age.*
- *have been church members in their present congregation (70%) for five years or more.*

When compared with the United States population, it can be said that Lutherans are:

- *average in occupational status; white and blue collar occupations are represented equally.*
- *above average in educational level; one-third have been to college.*
- *slightly above average in family income; 31% have incomes over $15,000, and 76% have incomes over $9,000.*
- *less mobile.*
- *more highly concentrated in the Midwest than other geographical regions.*
- *less frequently raised in farm areas or large metropolitan centers.*

The survey data show that the local congregation is not the primary nucleus around which friendship clusters of Lutherans form. However, Lutherans do tend to marry exclusively within their own groups. Three out of four report no non-Lutherans in their immediate families.

Only 18% have held prior membership in a non-Lutheran church body. About one-half are participants in some community organization. Two out of five declare a preference for the Republican party and one out of four for the Democratic party. One out of four heads of household is in a professional or managerial position; only 9% are in farming.

The three major Lutheran church bodies find their strength in different regions of the country. Lutheran Church in America is strongest in the East; Lutheran Church—Missouri Synod in the East North Central region; and The American Lutheran Church in the West North Central region. The church bodies also differ in their relative proportion of youth and in their level of education. Largest congregations are found more frequently in The American Lutheran Church.

Approximately one in five homes knows serious home difficulties. Frequent illness is reported by more Lutherans in the oldest (50-65) and the youngest (15-18) age brackets. Lutherans over age 24 tend to give high evaluations of their work, church, and family. Three out of four felt they are as religious as their parents, or more religious.

In this chapter we will present an elaboration of this overview in two general areas: how Lutherans are different from other Americans, and how Lutherans differ among themselves.

Lutherans Compared with Other Americans

ARE LUTHERANS DIFFERENT IN RACIAL AND NATIONALITY BACKGROUND?

Race. The answer is Yes. *A Study of Generations* found 98% of Lutherans to be white, whereas whites constitute 87% of the total United States population. One percent of Lutherans are black, and 1% are of other or mixed racial background. Blacks make up 11% of the total United States population.

Nationality. Ninety-six percent of Lutherans are native-born United States citizens. Two percent were born in Northern and Central Europe, and 2% were born elsewhere. The pattern changes substantially as we ask about where their parents were born. For Lutherans under 30 years of age, the typical pattern is having parents who also were born in the United States. As the age of Lutherans increases, a rising percentage had parents born in another country. Figure 2.1 shows this familiar trend for fathers. Although not shown, mothers of respondents have a similar pattern.

Figure 2.1 Percent of Fathers Born Outside the United States, Compared by Generation and Subgeneration

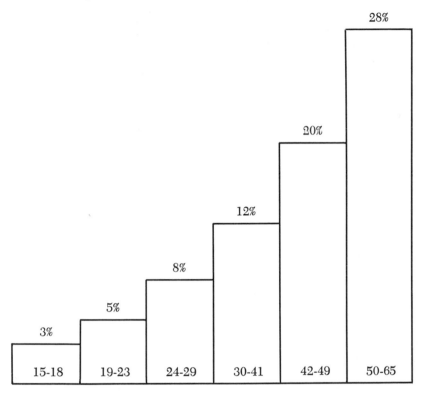

Generational Groups of Lutherans

A Study of Generations limited its scope to persons between the ages of 15 and 65. It should be obvious that among the Lutherans over 65 years of age a rising proportion were foreign-born, which is a typical pattern for our total population. The great waves of immigration to this country subsided drastically after the end of World War I. Therefore the data show the trend toward more Lutherans born in the United States after that period. In the total white population of the United States, 79% were born in this country, compared with 96% of Lutherans ages 15-65. Thus one might say that Lutherans are "more American" in nationality background than the average resident of the United States.

We can get a glimpse of national background by noting that among the older Lutherans (ages 50-65) whose fathers were foreign-born, 12% were born in Northern Europe, 10% in Central Europe, and 6% elsewhere. We can infer from this a predominant Scandinavian and Germanic background for these older Lutherans. Making the same generalization for Lutherans under 50 years of age would be less valid.

ARE LUTHERANS DIFFERENT IN THEIR COMMUNITY AND EDUCATIONAL BACKGROUND?

Community. Lutherans do differ remarkably from other Americans in the size of community in which they were raised, as revealed by Figure 2.2.

Figure 2.2 Size of Community Where Lutherans Were Reared, Compared with United States Population

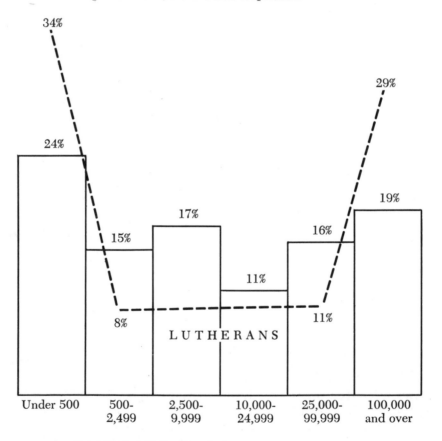

— — — — Total United States Population

Lutherans display a pattern of uniformity; they are about evenly divided in all sizes of communities where they were reared. This stands in contrast to the total population, indicated by the dotted line. This figure on the percentage of Americans living in different size communities uses averages of the 1910-1950 census, which includes the years when most of our sample members were born. Fewer Lutherans come from farm areas and fewer from large metropolitan centers. A higher proportion were reared in small or medium-sized communities.

What is even more remarkable is that this pattern generally holds true for *all* age groups of Lutherans (see Figure 2.3). A slightly larger percentage of older Lutherans came from communities with populations under 2,500 than did youth, which is to be expected. The noteworthy pattern is that only 17-21% of all age groups of Lutherans were reared in cities with populations over 100,000. National census figures indicate

Figure 2.3 Size of Community Where Lutherans Were Reared, Compared by Generation and Subgeneration

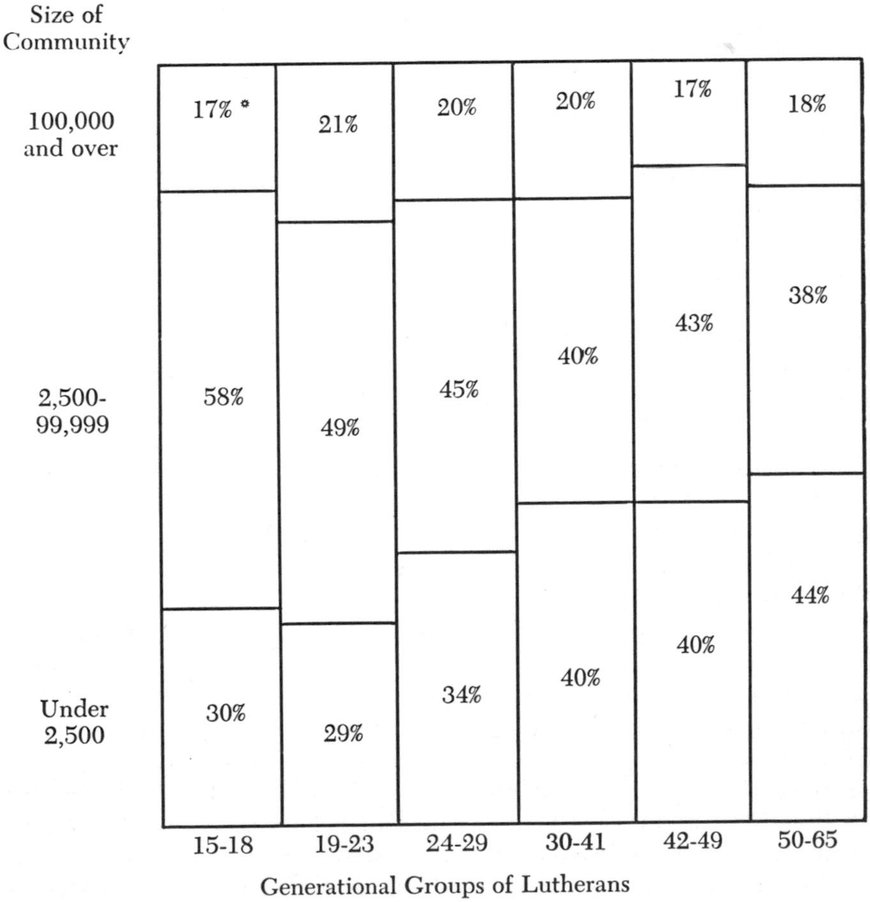

Size of
Community

Size of Community	15-18	19-23	24-29	30-41	42-49	50-65
100,000 and over	17% °	21%	20%	20%	17%	18%
2,500- 99,999	58%	49%	45%	40%	43%	38%
Under 2,500	30%	29%	34%	40%	40%	44%

Generational Groups of Lutherans

° All percentages rounded to the nearest whole percent.

that this is true for about 30% of the total population and is even higher for younger persons.

Education. The majority of previous generations of Lutherans had an eighth grade education or less. They are now a dwindling minority in the older age categories. The parental sacrifices made in order to enrich the educational lives of their children is dramatically portrayed in the number of these children going on for additional training beyond high school. In the 50-65 age group, 30% report some college training, whereas 50% of those ages 24-29 have had some college training. This figure reaches 65% of those ages 19-23. We can expect even higher figures for Lutherans ages 15-18 as they continue to complete their education. Compared with all persons between the ages of 25 and 64 in the United States, Lutherans have completed more education for each comparable age group. One-third of all Lutherans have been to college. (Details can be found in Chapter Note 1.)

WHERE DO LUTHERANS LIVE?

Compared with the total population, there is unmistakable evidence that Lutherans are more concentrated in some areas than in others. To illustrate we can note the relative strength of Lutherans, using standard census regions of the country. This is done in Figure 2.4, where we can see on the map that Lutherans are heavily concentrated in the Midwest —58% of all Lutherans are in this geographical area. That is, the East North Central and West North Central regions contain 30% and 28% respectively of the members of the three Lutheran church bodies covered by this study.

What about relative strength by church body? Each church body constitutes approximately one-third of the total sample of Lutherans; however, their respective numerical strength varies from region to region.

Of the 18% of all Lutherans living in the East, 13% are members of the Lutheran Church in America, 3% are members of the Lutheran Church—Missouri Synod, and 2% are members of The American Lutheran Church. Conversely, the LC-MS shows greatest strength (13%) in the East North Central region, followed by 9% in the West North Central, a region where the ALC has its greatest strength (12%). In the West, the ALC and LC-MS share equal strength, with the LCA lightly represented. All three church bodies have relatively light representation in the South. Of the 11% of Lutherans in the South, half belong to the LCA (largely in the Atlantic coastal states), whereas southern members of ALC and LC-MS congregations are more likely to be found in urban centers in border states, and in the Southwest.

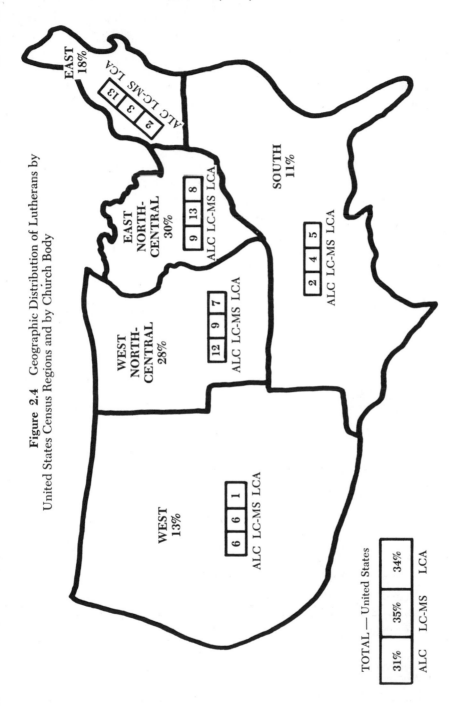

Figure 2.4 Geographic Distribution of Lutherans by United States Census Regions and by Church Body

A natural question arises at this point: how similar or how different
are Lutheran regional patterns from those of the general population?
A direct and simple answer is possible. Our sample has been compared
with 1970 United States census data for comparable age groups, and
also with a series of 1970 Gallup polls (Gallup and Davies, 1971) involving over 16,000 respondents. Lutherans differ substantially from
the population at large in regional concentrations, a fact uniformly
shown in both the A *Study of Generations* sample and the samples used
by Gallup. The comparison is provided in Table 2.1. Both A *Study of
Generations* and the Gallup Poll find Lutherans over-represented in the
Midwest (East and West North Central) and under-represented in
other regions, particularly the South. Differences in samples for A *Study
of Generations* and Gallup surveys are due primarily to differences in
how Lutherans were identified (Gallup uses *religious preference,* and
this study uses *actual membership)* and differences in what age groups
were included. (See Chapter Note 2.)

Table 2.1   Comparison of Surveys Showing Geographic Distribution of
Lutherans in the United States, 1970 (Using United States
Census Regions)

REGION	% of Total Population	% of Lutherans	
	U.S. Census	Study of Generations	Gallup Poll
East	25% °	18%	21%
East North Central	20	30	
	⟩ 28	⟩ 58	⟩ 56
West North Central	8	28	
South	31	11	10
West	17	13	14
Total United States	100%	100%	100%
Sample Size		4,444 °°	16,532

° All percentages rounded to the nearest whole percent; therefore, total may vary
slightly from 100%.

°° Lay people only, as is the case for all data reported in this chapter.

ARE LUTHERANS DIFFERENT IN THEIR MOBILITY PATTERNS?

Neighborhood. A number of indicators of mobility are found in the study, some of which can provide rough comparisons with the total population. Americans in general are a very mobile people. Studies and census surveys for decades have shown that approximately 20% of Americans change their place of residence *each year.* From the days of initial white settlement and on through periods of massive immigration, followed by equally massive migrations from rural to urban to metropolitan centers, there has been a restless and relentless movement from place to place. In addition, with improved transportation there has been a vast movement to and from place of residence for work and other activities.

Census studies indicate that approximately 18% of the people in the United States changed residence during the year 1969-1970. Twelve percent moved within the same county and 6% moved to a different county.

Figure 2.5 Length of Lutherans' Residence in Same Neighborhood, Compared by Generation and Subgeneration

Length of
Residence

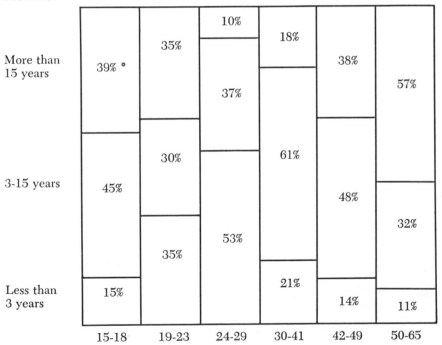

Generational Groups of Lutherans

° All percentages rounded to the nearest whole percent.

How do Lutherans compare in mobility? Lutherans were asked how long they had lived in their present *neighborhood,* a question which allowed them to change residences without changing neighborhoods. Eight percent of Lutherans had changed neighborhood during the year 1969-1970. A total of 23% have lived in their present neighborhood less than three years. An unknown additional percentage have changed addresses but still live in the same neighborhood. It does appear that Lutherans are less mobile than the general United States population.

What is more significant about mobility patterns is not the rate of mobility but the age of those most likely to move. Figure 2.5 shows that the most mobile group of Lutherans are persons ages 24-29. This finding conforms with most studies which show young adults in the family formation years as most mobile. (Comparisons of mobility patterns among Lutherans ages 20-29 and the general population of the same age groups are found in Chapter Note 3.)

Figure 2.6   Length of Lutherans' Membership in Same Congregation, Compared by Generation and Subgeneration

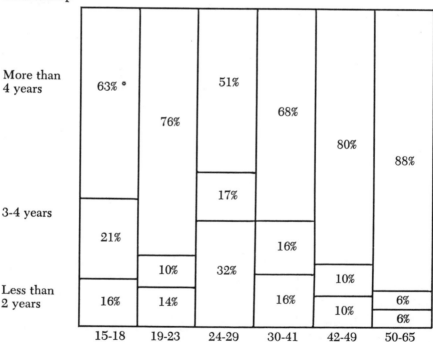

Length of
Membership

More than
4 years

3-4 years

Less than
2 years

Generational Groups of Lutherans

* All percentages rounded to the nearest whole percent.

Congregation. Length of residence in the neighborhood is associated with length of membership in one's present congregation, as seen by comparing Figures 2.5 and 2.6. Mobility rises to a peak in the twenties and then gradually subsides. Except for recently confirmed youth, ages 15-18, and those ages 24-29, there is a firm pattern of long-term membership reported by respondents. Seventy percent of Lutherans have been church members in their present congregation for five or more years; the percentage reaches 80% when one excludes the two age groups just noted (15-18 and 24-29). Lutherans were asked if they had belonged to any other denomination prior to joining their present denomination. Twenty-five percent indicated they had prior membership in another church body. Percentages by denomination are 7% another Lutheran body, 6% Methodist, 4% Baptist, 4% Catholic, 3% Presbyterian, and fractional percentages from a variety of other church bodies.

Figure 2.7   Occupational Status of Lutheran Heads of Household

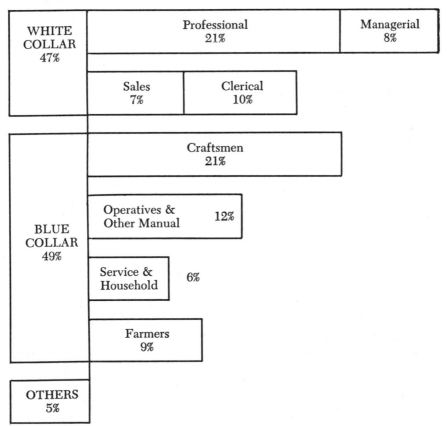

Do LUTHERANS DIFFER FROM OTHERS IN OCCUPATIONAL
AND ECONOMIC STATUS?

Occupational status of heads of household is shown in Figure 2.7. It indicates that 47% are white collar workers and 49% are blue collar, with 5% other. This coincides very closely with the current occupational break-down of general population, which shows about an even split between white collar and blue collar workers.

It might surprise some that only 9% of Lutheran heads of household are farmers. Other data confirm this as a realistic figure. This percentage would likely be higher if the sample included persons over age 65, since a larger proportion of the general population over age 65 are farmers.

The data clearly reveal over one-fourth (29%) of heads of household engaged in professional or managerial activities. This would imply no shortage of potential leadership within Lutheranism when such a large percentage are in white collar occupations engaged in service and man-agerial activities.

Income. Lutherans tend to be near the middle in occupational status among Americans, and they tend to be about average in family income. Median family income in 1970 was slightly in excess of $11,000; incomes under $3,000 were concentrated in families of the youngest (15-18) and the oldest (50-65) age groups. Paradoxically, those ages 15-18 reported *both* high and low incomes as being more prevalent. Greatest homo-geneity of income was reported for ages 24-29 where young couples are struggling to get established in career and/or parenthood.

Government sources indicate that median family income for white families not living in the South (which would be most comparable for our total Lutheran population) was $10,930 in 1970. This places Lutheran median income at slightly above the national average. Thirty-one percent have family incomes over $15,000; 76% over $9,000. If at one time Lu-therans were likely to be below average in educational, occupational, and income status, these data indicate they have closed the gap.

WHAT ARE THE COMMUNAL BONDS OF LUTHERANS?

Some social scientists have indicated in recent years that a distinguish-ing feature of religious identification is that members of a given religious body do more than worship together. It is observed that their communal lives are also intertwined by means of friendships, intermarriage, and formal group participation. In this connection we have data that pro-vide rich enlargement of the social dimension to Lutheran lives.

We might ask first if Lutherans are friendly, and second, if their close friends are people within their own congregations. Figures 2.8 and 2.9 provide the answers. Most Lutherans, especially those of older ages,

Figure 2.8 Number of Close Friends, Compared by Generation and Subgeneration

Close
Friends

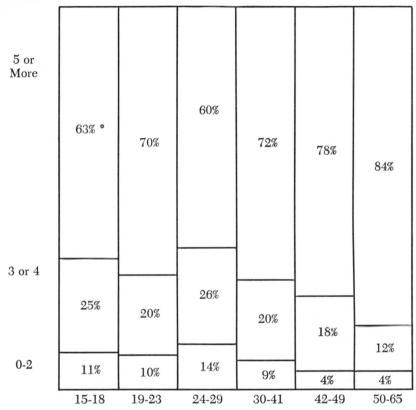

Generational Groups of Lutherans

° All percentages rounded to the nearest whole percent.

report that they do have close friends. Yet 4-14% of each age group report fewer than three close friends who really care about them, and those in the most mobile age group (24-29) report the fewest close friends.

The failure of and opportunity for the church become apparent when Lutherans are asked how many of their five closest friends are also members of their own congregation. A surprisingly large percentage of Lutherans in all age brackets indicate that *none* of their five closest friends is a member of their own congregation. Thirty-six percent said, "None"; only 29% said, "Three or more." This might be interpreted in many ways. One interpretation could be that Lutherans get along with

Figure 2.9   Number of Close Friends in Congregation, Compared by Generation and Subgeneration.

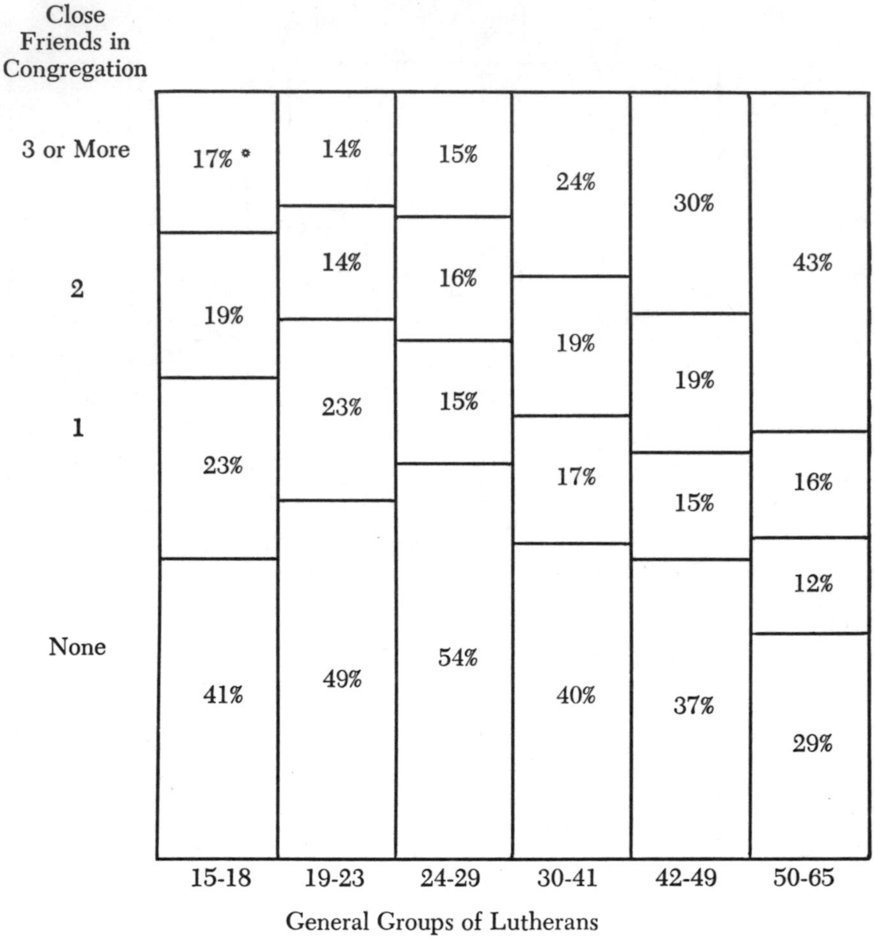

Close
Friends in
Congregation

	15-18	19-23	24-29	30-41	42-49	50-65
3 or More	17% *	14%	15%	24%	30%	43%
2	19%	14%	16%	19%	19%	
1	23%	23%	15%	17%	15%	16%
None	41%	49%	54%	40%	37%	12% / 29%

General Groups of Lutherans

* All percentages rounded to the nearest whole percent.

others better than they get along with each other; this would be the testimony of some who have observed annual church meetings! Another interpretation could be that close friends made at one time in life have the distressing habit of also moving about the country, so that the friendship network is far-flung. A third interpretation could be that Lutherans are not particularly clannish, huddling within their own little enclave. However communally oriented Lutherans might be, and these data are not definitive, it does appear that the local congregation, at least, is not the primary nucleus around which their friendship clusters form.

A more sensitive and discriminating indicator of the strength of communal bonds within Lutheranism is reflected in Figure 2.10. This indicates the extent to which Lutherans are endogamous, that is, tend to

Figure 2.10   Non-Lutheran Family Members, Compared by Generation and Subgeneration.

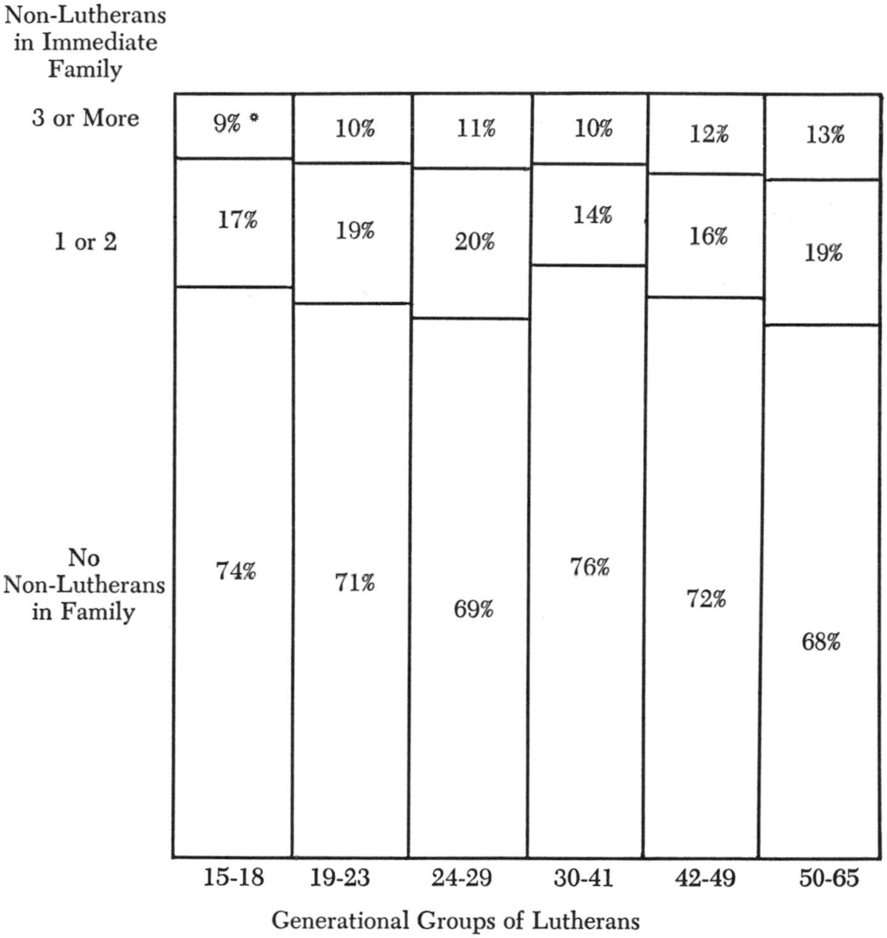

Non-Lutherans
in Immediate
Family

3 or More 9% *	10%	11%	10%	12%	13%
1 or 2 17%	19%	20%	14%	16%	19%
No Non-Lutherans in Family 74%	71%	69%	76%	72%	68%
15-18	19-23	24-29	30-41	42-49	50-65

Generational Groups of Lutherans

* All percentages rounded to the nearest whole percent.

marry exclusively within their own group. Of all Lutherans, 73% report no non-Lutherans among their immediate family, 16% indicate one or two, and 10% indicate three or more.

Recent trends have indicated more intermarriage across religious bodies than in the past. This finding is not confirmed here for Lutherans because the age groups display an unexpected uniformity of response. Apparently Lutherans have close friends outside their congregations but marry Lutherans—or convert them!

Two other pieces of information conclude the portrait of broad social patterns of Lutherans. One refers to their involvement in organized community activities (18 types, to be specific) such as service clubs, labor unions, professional organizations, etc., and the frequency with which they attend meetings of these organized groups.

Our findings for each age group show that about half are members in some organized group activity in the community, with lowest proportions in membership reported by youth ages 19-23 and persons over age

Figure 2.11   Frequency of Worship Attendance, Compared by Generation and Subgeneration.

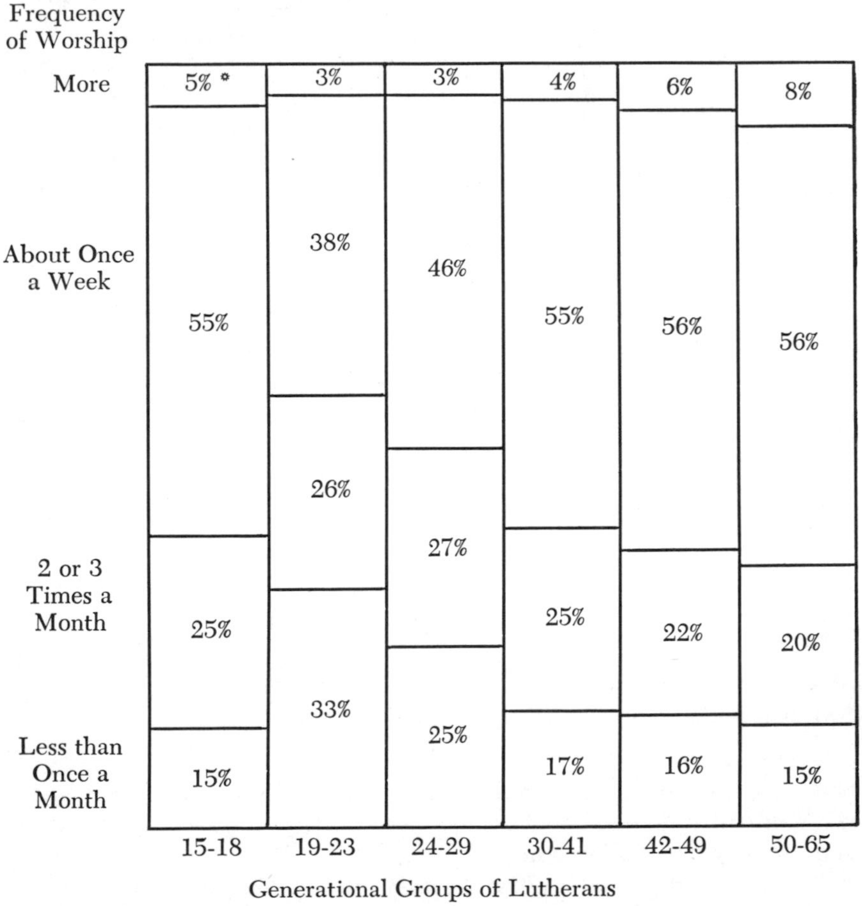

Frequency of Worship

	15-18	19-23	24-29	30-41	42-49	50-65
More	5% °	3%	3%	4%	6%	8%
About Once a Week	55%	38%	46%	55%	56%	56%
		26%				
2 or 3 Times a Month	25%		27%	25%	22%	20%
		33%				
Less than Once a Month	15%		25%	17%	16%	15%

Generational Groups of Lutherans

° All percentages rounded to the nearest whole percent.

50. Relatively small percentages attend nonchurch meetings on a weekly (17%) or even a bimonthly (34%) basis.

Self-reports of Lutheran church members on the frequency of their attendance at worship are shown in Figure 2.11. A pattern of uniformity cuts across all age groups, except those ages 19-29 where fewer frequencies are reported.

Compared with national surveys of church attendance, our data indicate a higher frequency of attendance than is typical of American Protestants in general. Gallup surveys (Gallup and Davies, 1971) show a steady drop in weekly church attendance for all religious bodies from a high of 49% in 1955 to a low of 42% in 1970. Protestants reported 38%

Figure 2.12 Length of Sunday School Attendance, Compared by Generation and Subgeneration.

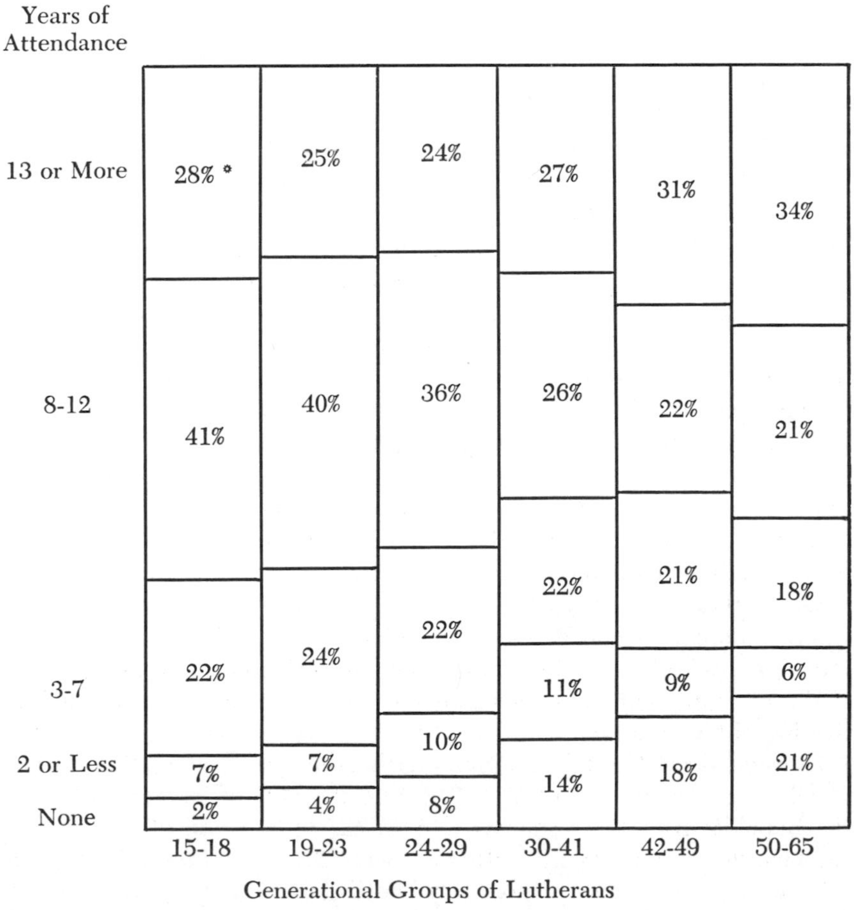

Years of Attendance

	15-18	19-23	24-29	30-41	42-49	50-65
13 or More	28% °	25%	24%	27%	31%	34%
8-12	41%	40%	36%	26%	22%	21%
3-7	22%	24%	22%	22%	21%	18%
				11%	9%	6%
2 or Less	7%	7%	10%	14%	18%	21%
None	2%	4%	8%			

Generational Groups of Lutherans

° All percentages rounded to the nearest whole percent.

attending worship in 1970, and Lutherans alone reported 43%. In this study 54% responded, "About once a week or more," to the statement, "If not prevented by unavoidable circumstances, I attend worship services."

Accepting the fact that Lutheran church members are more likely to attend worship than those merely indicating a Lutheran religious *preference*, we should expect the reports of worship attendance in *A Study of Generations* to be higher than Gallup surveys. Again the two data sources mutually support one another.

For youth and some adults there is another indicator of church participation: their involvement in the Sunday school activity of the church. For some youth this may supplant worship attendance; for others it supplements it. Practically all youth report some experience with Sunday school with rising proportions of adults indicating no Sunday school experience (See Figure 2.12).

In summary, these data suggest that for a large number of Lutherans the church is the major, if not exclusive, organized group activity in which they participate on a regular basis.

How Do Lutherans Differ from Others in Their Political Loyalties?

Two indicators of Lutheran political allegiance and behavior were included in the study. One question asked for their political party preference, and a series of questions asked about their voting record in previous presidential elections. Forty-two percent of Lutherans prefer the Republican party; 25% give a Democratic preference; and 33% give an independent or other party preference (or a response indicating no interest in politics). Solid evidence of Lutheran preference for the Republican party is revealed by comparing their voting record in the 1968 presidential election with the actual results. Whereas Nixon had 1% more votes nationally than did Humphrey, Lutherans gave to Nixon 34% more votes than they gave to Humphrey. Regional analysis showed that Nixon outdrew Humphrey in Lutheran support by 27% in Humphrey's home territory (West North Central) and by 43% in New England, where Humphrey gained 18% more votes than Nixon. The conclusion seems inescapable: despite small regional variations, Lutherans voting in the 1968 presidential election showed an overwhelming loyalty toward the Republican party.

How do these findings compare with other surveys? Gallup surveys (Gallup and Davies, 1971) in 1970 found that 40% of Lutherans favored the Republican party as compared with 42% in *A Study of Generations*. Democratic preferences by Lutherans were 31% and 25% for Gallup and *A Study of Generations* respectively. Both sources agree that Lutherans favor the Republican party.

How Lutherans Differ Among Themselves

The focus in the preceding pages has been on comparisons of Lutherans with other Americans. The following comparisons will focus on differences among Lutherans with respect to church body affiliation, age group, and other characteristics.

DIFFERENCES AMONG CHURCH BODIES

We have already noted a striking difference in the regional strength of each church body. This is evident in Table 2.2. None of the regions comes close to portraying the cross-section of church body proportions that is available from the total sample. For this reason substantial analysis is required before one is sure that an observed regional difference between Lutherans is due to regionality and not to differences in church body or vice versa.

There are also church body differences in congregational size. For instance, the largest congregations (1000 and over in membership) are more frequently found in The American Lutheran Church. The same is true of congregations size 500 to 999. The Lutheran Church—Missouri Synod has the largest proportion of congregations size 250-499. It is between these two church bodies that the contrast is the greatest. In The American Lutheran Church, 59% of the respondents come from congregations over 500 in size compared with 33% in the Lutheran Church—Missouri Synod.

The three Lutheran church bodies are less strikingly different by sex, age, and education. Each group has about the same proportion of males and females. Sample differences do exist in age composition; for example, note that 62% of respondents in the Lutheran Church—Missouri Synod are under age 42 as compared with 54% of Lutheran Church in America respondents. Educational differences are also smaller: LCA has 5% more respondents who have had college experience than LC-MS. These differences need to be noted insofar as other differences may appear to be related to church body but in fact may simply reflect age, educational, or regional differences.

DIFFERENCES AMONG LUTHERAN GENERATIONS

A central pivot or axis which permeates much of the data in A *Study of Generations* is that identified with the time dimension and reflected by such terms as age, age group, or generation. The age dimension is inescapable for this study and has an impact on many of the subsequent analyses. Thus it is crucial to describe correlates of age groupings as carefully as possible.

Table 2.2   Church Body Differences Among Lutheran Laymen.

	CHURCH BODY			TOTAL LUTHERAN LAYMEN 100% n = 4,444
	ALC 31% of total laymen	LC-MS 35% of total laymen	LCA 34% of total laymen	
REGION				
East	4%	9%	38%	18%
East North Central	31	38	22	30
West North Central	39	26	20	28
South	7	10	16	10
West	19	17	4	13
CONGREGATION SIZE				
1000+	26	12	17	18
500-999	33	21	27	26
250-499	15	40	34	31
Under 250	26	28	23	25
SEX				
Male	42	43	41	42
Female	58	57	59	58
AGE				
50-65	24	22	26	24
42-49	18	17	18	18
30-41	25	25	21	24
15-29	32	37	33	33
EDUCATION				
Graduate Degree / Some Graduate School	9	8	11	9
College Graduate / Some College	26	24	26	25
High School Graduate / Some High School	41	40	42	41
Eighth Grade or Less / No Response	24	28	22	24

Differences among Lutheran generations are shown in Table 2.3. The American Lutheran Church shows a uniform frequency across each age group. Lutheran Church—Missouri Synod is stronger in the younger age groups, and the Lutheran Church in America has proportionately more

Table 2.3   Age Differences Among Lutheran Laymen

	AGE GROUPS				All
n = 4,444	15-29 33%	30-41 24%	42-49 18%	50-65 24%	Ages 100%
CHURCH BODY					
ALC	32%	25%	18%	24%	30%
LC-MS	37	25	17	22	35
LCA	33	21	18 ·	26	34
REGION					
East	18	14	20	19	17
East North Central	29	34	29	29	30
West North Central	28	27	27	29	28
South	12	11	10	10	11
West	13	14	14	13	13
CONGREGATION SIZE					
1000+	17	17	17	20	17
500-999	25	28	28	26	26
250-499	32	29	31	30	30
Under 250	27	27	24	24	25
SEX					
Male	42	43	40	43	42
Female	58	57	60	57	58
EDUCATION					
Graduate Degree } Some Graduate School }	7	12	10	9	9
College Graduate } Some College }	32	27	21	17	26
High School Graduate } Some High School }	38	49	48	35	42
Eighth Grade or Less } No Response }	23	12	21	39	24

respondents in the older age categories. Therefore, the East has more persons ages 42-49, and the East North Central region has more persons ages 30-41.

No substantial variation in age groups exists by congregational size. What is most significant is the interrelationship of age and education. College training is most conspicuous among younger age groups; conversely, eighth grade or less education is almost the exclusive property of persons over age 50. If this age group should be found to differ substantially from the others, the difference *could* be due to a variety of factors other than age itself.

It should be noted that there is a shift in the sex composition of the sample from ages 15-29. Males are in closer balance with females at the younger ages (46% versus 54%) and are disproportionately represented in the age group 24 to 29 (37% versus 63%). The harder-to-involve male of this age is under-represented in the sample, and this fact must be recognized in subsequent discussions of data from the 24-29-year-old age group.

Comparisons of church bodies also reveal substantial age differences. In the LC-MS our sample shows 9% more in age group 24-29 than in 19-23; the pattern in somewhat less extreme form is reversed for the LCA. These otherwise hidden differences need to be kept in mind in interpreting the subsequent data. As one would expect, the 15-18-year-old group is overwhelmingly single and in school. The 19-23-year-olds are moving into marriage and full-time employment, with some starting families (females primarily). The 24-29 age group have completed school, are married, and 72% are also parents. These represent the basic social roles identified with the age groups here separated.

OTHER COMPARISONS

What troubles have Lutherans experienced? How do they feel about their lives, their families, and their church? What do they see as influential in their lives?

Lutherans were asked a few simple questions about whether they had been hospitalized during the past five years and, if so, for how long; if they had experienced any serious difficulties in their home during the past year; if they had ever sought help for emotional problems; and if they or an immediate family member were now receiving welfare aid. A digest of these data is shown for each age group in Figure 2.13. Between 3% and 11% of respondents report being on welfare, frequently ill, or seeking counseling for emotional problems. Frequent illness is most often reported by the older persons, followed somewhat surprisingly by the 15-18 age group.

Higher percentages of respondents indicate hospitalization for two weeks or more during the past five years. Perhaps most significant for this study is the percent (19-25%) in every age category who report serious difficulties during the past year.

Lutherans were asked also to tell how they feel about their school, family, marriage, work, and the church. (Chapter Note 4 discusses the

Figure 2.13 Personal Difficulties as Reported by Generations and Subgenerations

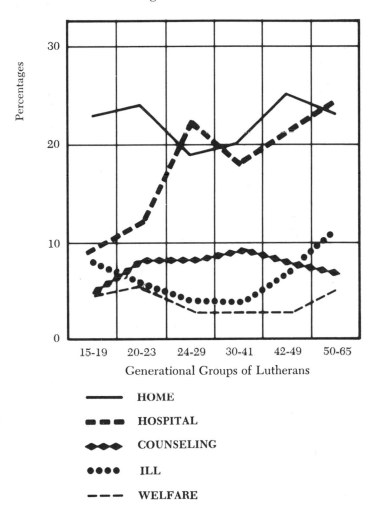

choice possibilities.) Personal unhappiness with role relationships is noted in Figure 2.14. The evidence is very clear that Lutherans age 24 and over give very high evaluations of work, church, and family. Highest dissatisfaction with *all* basic role relationships is reported by high school age youth (15-18), followed by those ages 19-23.

A simple way of illustrating influences in the lives of Lutherans is to take their own self-reports to the question, "Which of the following have had the greatest influence in making you what you are today in terms of your personality and approach to life? Choose only two." The

Figure 2.14   Personal Unhappiness with Role Relationships
                   as Reported by Generations and Subgenerations

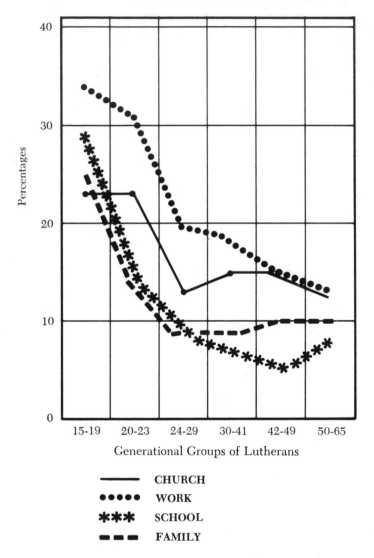

Generational Groups of Lutherans

—————— CHURCH

●●●●● WORK

✱✱✱ SCHOOL

■ ■ ■ FAMILY

response possibilities were: church, father, mother, brother(s) or sis-
ter(s), larger family, friends other than family, teachers or school, my
country, and God. The responses are presented in Figure 2.15.

Mothers consistently receive the highest response within each age
group. Fathers receive higher ranking among youth than among older
Lutherans who generally use the "God" answer. Likewise, youth more

Figure 2.15 Two Greatest Influences on "What You Are Now"
as Reported by Generations and Subgenerations

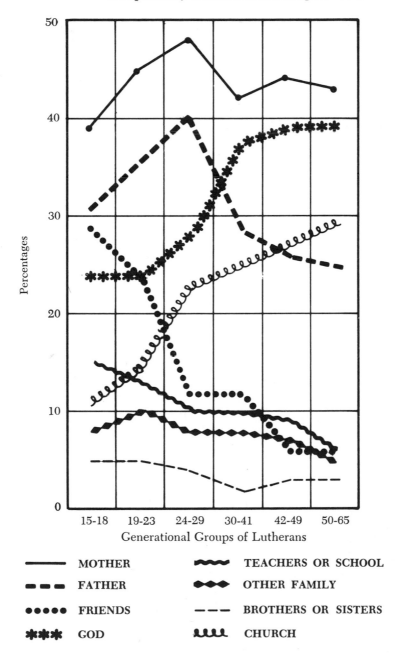

MOTHER ———   TEACHERS OR SCHOOL

FATHER – – –   OTHER FAMILY

FRIENDS ●●●●●   BROTHERS OR SISTERS – – –

GOD ✱✱✱   CHURCH

than older persons tend to rank friends as more influential. The older ones in turn are more likely to feel the influence of the church.

Of the paired choices, the mother-father combination was chosen most frequently (20%), followed by mother and God (13%), God and church (9%), mother and church (8%). All other choice combinations make up the remaining 50% of the paired choices.

Inasmuch as parents, God, and church are deemed important for shaping personalities and lives of Lutherans, it is important to identify the direction of these influences. Hence, Lutherans were asked how active their parents were in church during the respondent's youth. They were asked also whether they consider themselves to be more active or less active in church than their mother and father.

About three in five Lutherans (62%) remember their mother as having been active in church during their youth, and 45% remember this as having been true of their fathers. When comparing their own religiosity with that of their parents, 26% saw themselves as more religious than their mothers, and 31% as less religious. Forty-two percent saw themselves as more religious than their fathers, and 23% as less. This means that about three out of four Lutherans see themselves as or more religious than their parents.

CHAPTER NOTE 1

A comparison of completed education of Lutherans and somewhat comparable age groups for all persons in the United States, ages 24-65, is as follows:

LUTHERANS			
	Percentage Completing		
Age	8th Grade or Less	Some High School or H. S. Grad.	Some College or More
24-29	6%	45%	50%
30-41	12	49	39
42-49	21	48	31
50-65	39	35	27

TOTAL UNITED STATES POPULATION			
	Percentage Completing		
Age	8th Grade or Less	Some High School or H. S. Grad.	Some College or More
25-29	9%	60%	31%
30-34	12	62	26
35-44	18	58	24
45-54	25	56	19
55-64	40	44	16

CHAPTER NOTE 2

Differences in samples for *A Study of Generations* and Gallup surveys (Gallup and Davies, 1971) need to be kept in mind. The *A Study of Generations* sample was drawn randomly from rosters of *church members* on the rolls of randomly selected congregations. Gallup polls, on the other hand, interview persons in the community who identify their *religious preference* as Lutheran. Gallup interviewed all adults over 21 years of age; our study focused on the age group 15-65. As most churchmen are well aware, there is a floating percentage of our population who indicate a religious preference as Lutheran, Protestant, or Catholic who nonetheless belong to no church, never attend a church service, and never contribute to the survival of a church.

Both studies include persons ages 21-65, with Gallup adding those over age 65 and *A Study of Generations* adding persons ages 15-20. Differential responses by these two age groups could easily account for any minor discrepancies reported by the two independent surveys (though in sampling one always expects a variation of 1-2%). It seems reasonable to conclude that the two studies corroborate one another, showing over-representation of Lutherans in the Midwest, strongest under-representation in the South, and some slight under-representation in the East and West.

CHAPTER NOTE 3

We have shown that the most mobile group of Lutherans are persons ages 24-29. This finding conforms with most studies which show young adults in the family formation years as most mobile. Yearly residence changes for the total population, according to the United States census, are highest for the age group 20-24, with 46% moving yearly. They are followed by the age group 25-29, of which 38% move yearly. Likewise the data on Lutherans show highest mobility within these age groups but with the higher group reversed. Two plausible interpretations are offered: one is that for census purposes even a temporary residence such as a college dormitory indicates change of residence, whereas most respondents who are young and unmarried would report their parental home as their residence if perchance they were away at college on 1 April 1970 when the decennial census was taken. Another factor which could contribute to this discrepancy is that the high mobility among the age group 20-24 also makes it more difficult to track them down if they are single and hence under-represented in the survey.

CHAPTER NOTE 4

Lutherans were asked: "How do you feel about your (church) (spouse) (family life) (school life) (work)?" Seven choices were provided for each question, ranging from "happy" through "neutral" to "unhappy," plus a response, "This isn't a part of my experience at present." Of those responding to these questions, the following two choices were combined: "There are many things which I do not like about it, but in some ways I am happy with it," and "I am not happy about it." The combined percentages for each question are portrayed by age groups in Figure 2.14.

3. Orientation to Research Concepts and Procedures

At this point, readers will no doubt sort themselves into three categories. Category One is thoroughly familiar with the methods and terminology of research in the social sciences. All Category Ones should feel free to skim rapidly or even to skip the next pages and proceed to Chapter Four without fear of having missed anything.

Category Two has no background in research but is willing to take his chances at understanding the technical language without which research of this kind cannot be readily reported. Skip the next few pages, if you like. The explanations of "reliability," "scales," "weights," and the rest will still be here, waiting, if you get to the point where you really want to know what they mean.

Category Three also has little or no background in social science research, but is prepared to do whatever learning of terminology and method he needs before entering on a study of the data presented here. Category Three wants to understand what it means the first time he encounters a cryptic "reliability .61." Category Three, we salute you! Read on.

Research Concepts

MAKING GENERALIZATIONS FROM SAMPLE DATA

Because information from a sample of persons is being used to *infer* conclusions about all Lutherans, the task that faces the researcher in preparing his findings is one of sorting out the difference between what is true of the sample alone and what is very likely true of the entire

population studied. For example, if 30% of our sample clergymen agree
with a statement about the Lord's Supper, and 40% of the sample laymen
agree with it, are we reasonably sure that if all Lutherans, clergy and
lay, were asked that question there would still be 30% of clergymen
agreeing and 40% of laymen agreeing?

In order to answer this question, statistical tests based on laws of
probability are used. *Probability* is expressed by a sign like this: p =
< .001. The symbol is a short way of saying "probability (p) is less
than (<) one in a thousand (.001)," which means, "The probability is
less than one in a thousand that the results we are reporting are due
to chance alone, and not due to the fact that our results are an accurate
representation of what is true for the whole population."

"*Significant* at .001" (which is another way of saying p = .001) is a
merely shorthand way of saying, "There is only one chance in a thousand of our getting these responses to a given item from our 4,745 respondents, and a different response pattern to the same item if we ques-
tioned the entire membership of the Lutheran church."

Reliability (which is abbreviated Rxx) refers to the accuracy and precision of a measurement. Putting it another way, high reliability is the
relative certainty that if we were to survey the same people again with the
same instrument, we would get the same results.

To base one's conclusions upon people's answers to just one question
is very unreliable, as we all know from experience. But to draw conclusions from answers to a large group of questions, all bearing on the
same issue, can be reliably enlightening. It is for this reason, among
several others, that a survey as long as 740 items was prepared. Using
that many items allowed for several of them to raise approximately the
same question in a variety of ways.

Reliabilities are expressed in the form of a decimal from 0.00 (a
measure with no precision at all) to 1.00 (a perfectly reliable measure
with no error whatever). In social scientific research, experience has
shown that for measuring characteristics of individuals, scores with
reliabilities below .75 are unstable. However, for measuring the average
characteristics of groups even as small as 25 to 50 people, scores with
reliabilities as low as .50 may be serviceable. For much larger groups,
such as the sample used in the study, even lower reliability coefficients
are frequently useful. We have tended, however, not to report any
measures with reliability lower than .50, and most of them are well
above .70.

Organizing Data by Scales

We make frequent references in this book to *scales*. Seven million data
can be organized in almost an infinite number of ways. How, then, can

we present a simple summary of so many data in manageable form? In groups of items, rather than singly, to begin with. But how are the groups to be formed?

The constant temptation facing the researcher is to organize the items into groups that seem to him reasonable and logical. But in doing so he would be forcing his personal perspective on the data. And then the resulting interpretation might well be more a reflection of the researcher than of the persons from whom the data were collected. Twenty researchers organizing the same data according to their own personal frames of reference might come up with 20 different interpretations. Some other less subjective way to do the job must be used.

As the survey was being prepared, we kept accurate records of those items that formed each set of interrelated questions, all bearing on the same issue. But we did not analyze the data primarily in terms of these preconceived groupings, for fear of limiting what people were saying about themselves to the boundaries of our ways of thinking. Nor did we arbitrarily put items together into scales after the fact, that is, after having collected our data and taken a first look at them. At no point was there anything like, "Well, these 11 items all deal with negative attitudes toward Jews, so we'll put them together and call them an anti-Semitism scale." Rather, our analyses and interpretations of the data have utilized a variety of scientific methods *giving the data freedom to organize themselves* into groups and sets—*scales*—of items across which Lutherans tend to give consistent responses. We used methods that identified sets of items which, if persons agreed with one, they tended to agree with all; if they marked "never" to one in the set, they tended to mark "never" to all. This consistency, of course, was not perfect. If it had been, all scales would have had perfect reliability of 1.00. Across sets of items that formed scales *most* people gave consistent responses as just described. The few who were erratic account for the difference between the actual reliability of a given scale of perhaps .80, and ideal reliability of 1.00 for a scale where everyone responded consistently across all items in the scale. But if the vast majority of all persons did not respond consistently to a given group of items, those items would not form a scale.

Homogeneous keying, one of the several methods used, works something like this: From a group of about 200 items the computer selects the three items that people answer the most consistently; that is, in whatever way they respond to one item, they respond to all three. Then, without any consideration of the content, only to the ways people responded, items are added one at a time to the set of three, but only if by each added item the reliability (internal consistency) of the set is increased. When no more items will increase the reliability, that set is complete, and the process is begun again.

WEIGHTING ITEMS IN A SCALE

Within scales, each possible response to each item in the scale is *weighted*. Weighting is achieved by running the answers to a set of items through the computer a number of times in a number of different ways so that it is possible to take a simultaneous comparative look at all the responses of all individuals to that set of items, as well as the response patterns of each individual person to that set. Weights are not assigned according to the researcher's subjective judgment; the complex mathematical method used allows the data to determine what weight each answer should be given.

To reiterate, scales form because the response patterns tell us that from the way people answer a group of items, those items all measure roughly the same thing. Weights within scales tell us *(a)* how strongly people feel about their answer to a given item (that is, whether the agreement or disagreement expressed in the response, if it had been spoken, would have been given in a normal tone of voice, or shouted), and *(b)* of a set of items that form a scale, which of the items come closest to measuring the central issue of that scale.

Weights come in the form of numbers from 1 to 9. If the response possibilities are "strongly agree," "agree," "disagree," and "strongly disagree," an item on which people feel strongly one way or another, and which clearly relates to the issue without being muddied by secondary or extraneous factors, will probably come out with a weight of 9 for "strongly agree," perhaps 6 for "agree," 3 for "disagree," and 1 for "strongly disagree." If people feel lukewarm about an issue, or if it is muddied by extraneous factors, that item may emerge with a weight of 5 for "strongly agree," 4 for "agree," 3 for "disagree," and 2 for "strongly disagree."

Secondary or extraneous factors can muddy responses, and much of a researcher's effort in preparing a survey instrument is directed toward finding or constructing items that avoid this problem. On an item such as "I like my present pastor," with possible responses of "strongly agree," "agree," "disagree," and "strongly disagree," the responses may be muddied by the fact that what was going through some respondent's head was, "Yes, but I can't stand his wife," which caused some to waver between "strongly agree" and "agree." Or perhaps the respondent puzzles, "Is 'like' the right word? I respect him; I think he does a good job as a pastor. But 'like'?" The weights would show this question to be less useful in measuring congregational approval of a pastor than one worded, "Do you respect the ministry your pastor offers your congregation?" which would rule out such muddying factors as wives, personal liking, and so on.

The weights maximize the relationship between the score or value that a person gets for his response to a single item and the score or value that he gets for the whole set.

Weights on an item and the total scores on a set might look like this:

Pattern of response (Systematic ways of answering)	Typical single item weight for this person's answer	Typical score for this person on a set of 10 items
a. A person who strongly agrees with the item and also strongly agrees with all the rest of the items in the set.	9	85
b. A person who agrees with the item and generally agrees or strongly agrees with most of the other items in the set.	6	68
c. A person who agrees or disagrees with the item and has a mixed pattern of agreement-disagreement with the rest of the items in the set.	3 or 6	45
d. A person who disagrees with the item and generally disagrees or strongly disagrees with most of the other items in the set.	3	27
e. A person who strongly disagrees with the item and strongly disagrees with all the rest of the items in the set.	1	13

In making physical measurements of a box in inches or feet, dozens and dozens of measurements can be taken in all directions around and through the box. But from experience dating back at least as far as Aristarchus and Euclid, we have learned that for regular objects just three dimensions are important—length, width, and depth—for a full description of the object. If we know accurately the extent of those three dimensions, we can explain (or we have summarized) all of the dozens of other measurements we might take.

In at least an analogous sense, groups of items formed into scales, as described oversimply above, provide measurement or assessment of certain dimensions that run through the millions of individual data we have in *A Study of Generations.* Scales, therefore,

1. Summarize the data doing a minimum of violence to the structure and internal organization of people's answers and the frames of reference in which they think and express themselves.

2. Reflect the natural organization of the data and thus the existing, though not necessarily otherwise apparent, characteristics of the persons surveyed.

3. Reflect the limits of the questions and answer choices in the survey questionnaire.

4. Provide for accurate estimate of the precision (reliability) with which the dimensions of people's beliefs, attitudes, opinions, values, and life styles are being measured.

Understanding the Concept of Dimension

We have already used the term in this introduction, and in order to get as much benefit as possible from *A Study of Generations* it is vital to understand the concept of *dimension*. What is a dimension? To start with, in a survey like this one, we assume the following:

1. People do possess and hold to a very complex system of beliefs, values, attitudes, opinions, and behaviors.

2. Groups of people hold such systems pretty much in common. Therefore there is enough regularity among people so that we can legitimately hope to find that regularity. And it will likely be expressed in similar dimensions that appear across people and along which individuals may vary.

3. The psychological space representing such complex systems is multidimensional with an unknown number of dimensions.

Because the dimensions are unknown we use the technical methods described above to isolate groups of items where people tended to show a consistent pattern of responses. (If they answered in a given fashion on one item, they tended to answer in the same fashion to all the items in that group.) When we have found such a consistent pattern of responses for a given group of items and they form a scale, we feel we have an indication of a dimension of which all items are a part. A scale, then, is a set of items which together indicate or measure a *single* dimension.

Suppose we find a consistent pattern of response in an experiment on the meaning of words that isolates and pulls together these words:

exquisite	gorgeous
lovely	glamorous
beautiful	pretty
fair	comely

Because of the consistent pattern of response we know that psychologically all the words have a common attribute. There are a number of attributes we could look at. We could count the letters in the words, or look at the vowel-consonant ratio, or check out many other possible variables. But our interest is not in the attributes of the words themselves, but rather in the underlying variable, namely, the stimulus that led people to respond to the items the way they did.

It is clear that all of the words have something to do with the general concept of beauty. It is this attribute of the words that is the *dimension* that ties the words together in the observed consistent response pattern. To be sure each single word has an individual meaning of its own. Though we can differentiate each word from the others, it is cumbersome to say every word if we want to talk about beauty. It's much easier, and, in fact, does a better job of communicating, if we can talk about beauty using the single word "beauty."

That's the way it is with the scales to be reported in the next chapters. Each individual item has meaning of its own, and we could talk about each separate item. But because the items form a scale we know that something about each item is in common with the other items. It is that common element, we assume, which makes people respond to the items in a consistent pattern. What we want to look at and work with is the common element that ties the group together in people's minds.

It's something like working a jigsaw puzzle. Most people will begin solving a 1000-piece puzzle by putting the frame together. That defines the boundaries of the puzzle. The frame here is the 740-item questionnaire. It establishes the boundaries. The next step in solving a jigsaw puzzle is to look for some feature that is common to several pieces. Let's say you have a face in the puzzle. Several individual pieces have portions of the face, as well as other features—leaves, a wall, or a hat. You pay attention to the portions of the face and fit 11 pieces together to complete the face. Now you go on to find another feature which cuts across several pieces and assemble that. You continue this process until you have all 1000 pieces assembled. Note that in putting pieces together what helped you was not what was individual to the piece—size, shape, thickness—but what was common—parts of the face. Also you did not need to pay much attention to what was unique to each piece—leaves, wall, or hat.

The techniques used fit together the pieces for us. Now we know there is a common thread that ties a group of items together. Our problem is to identify and understand that common thread, the dimension. If we do that we have summarized a lot of awkward and cumbersome data. We can talk more readily and communicate more effectively by using the dimension than by using each individual item and each person.

In reading all the chapters that follow, keep in mind the concept of dimension and look for the common thread that ties each group of items together. This step is vital, for in later chapters you will be given information about how the dimensions reported in this section fit together to form groups of dimensions that will help you understand much more about the church and groups of people within the church. (See Section IV, Appendix B, for names and descriptions of the 78 scales derived in this study.)

One further point needs to be clear. It is *not the size* of a group which makes a scale form. It is the degree of *consistency* of response pattern. In some cases it appears some of our scales formed because a group of about 100 people responded very consistently. That a scale forms says nothing about where most people are on the dimension represented by that scale. To find out where the majority of the people in the sample are on any given scale-dimension, we need to look at the scores of everybody and how those scores are distributed along the range of possible scores for the scale.

Technical Terms and Procedures

Sometimes we attempt to summarize the information in such a *frequency distribution* of the scores of everybody or some smaller group. To do so we may use terms like the *mean* and *standard deviation*. The mean of the scores of a group of people on a given scale is nothing more than the arithmetic average of their scores. Add up all the scores, divide by the number of people, and you get the average (mean) score, or, putting it another way, the score of the "average" person. The standard deviation is the average amount that the other people's scores differed from the mean. If we refer to the *mode*, we are identifying the most common score. The *median* is the score both above and below which exactly 50% of the people scored on a given scale or dimension.

At times we will use the following symbols or abbreviations for some of these terms:

N — number of people in the group.

$\bar{X}$ — mean for our sample of 4,745 or some subgroup of them.

$\bar{Y}$ — estimate of the mean for all Lutherans in the U.S. or some subgroup of them like the subgroup of our sample we are reporting about.

s — standard deviation of some distribution of scores with mean = $\bar{X}$.

σ — standard deviation of some distribution of scores with mean = $\bar{Y}$.

s ^{2} — variance in a group of scores (standard deviation squared).

p — probability (usually that some difference between groups being compared is due purely to chance).

Rxx — reliability.

r — correlation, which here is usually an estimate of degree to which a group of people's answers to one item coincide with or resemble their answers to another item (or the same for scales or dimensions). Correlations range from +1.00 (perfect agreement) through 0.00 (no relationship) to –1.00 (perfect disagreement or inverse relationship).

CONTROLLING A VARIABLE'S EFFECT

When considering relationships between groups of people with differing characteristics, another concept that is helpful to understand is "controlling," as in the sentence, "These results may change when *controlled for* age." To control the data is a kind of detective work used to discover whether the results are being affected by a single variable or more than one. (A variable is any single category of information in which there are two or more possibilities. Sex is a variable; age is a variable; marital status is a variable. There are thousands of variables.)

Let us say that you find a strong positive response in a group to a set of items (a scale) about civil rights. It may be useful to know whether this interest in civil rights is affected by the age or by the sex of the persons responding, or whether it is affected by a combination of both. You might first control for sex by examining all the answers of only the males, age by age. That would tell you whether, among males, there is any difference in interest in civil rights according to age. You might also examine the answers, by age, of only the females, controlling for gender again. Then you might control for age by looking at the responses of both males and females 15 years old. To control for a variable means, then, analyzing the data as you hold that one variable constant and let one or more others vary.

Supposing that in analyzing Lutherans' scores on some measure of interest in civil rights, one controlled for age and sex as just described and found that *both* the age and the gender of the respondents did seem to be related to, or did affect, their scores. Let us say that on the average, if a person is over age 27, his score is about 10 points higher, and if the person is male he will tend to get a scale score about five points higher on the average. Can one assume that these apparent effects of age and gender are additive? Will a person who is *both* over 27 and male tend on the average to have a scale score that will be 15 points (10 + 5) higher? Not necessarily. Maybe the combined effects of being male and over 27 will only be on the order of 7 points higher instead of 15. If so, both of the variables of gender and age are said to be related to interest in civil rights, not *additively,* but in some sort of special interaction.

DETERMINING HOW VARIABLES INTERACT

When testing for this possibility of interaction we used a more sophisticated method of data analysis called *analysis of variance.* In such an analysis in the above example, three tests would be involved: (1) for effects of people's sexes on their interest in civil rights, (2) for effects of people's ages on that same interest, and (3) for the effects of both their sexes and ages. The last test is called a test of additivity or interaction. Therefore the results of such an analysis of variance would be reported as follows:

(Additivity)   Interaction $p = .000036$

                  Sex $p = .000100$

                  Age $p = .000210$

This is just a shorthand way of saying (loosely speaking):

1. There are only 36 chances in a million that the age and sex of respondents are related additively to interest in civil rights. Rather, both age and sex have a combined interaction effect on interest in civil rights.

2. There is only one chance in 10,000 that a person's sex is *not* related to his/her interest in civil rights.

3. There are only 21 chances in 100,000 that a person's age is *not* related to his interest in civil rights.

Since, however, in the real world a person cannot be male or female without also being of a certain age, and vice versa, the results of the first test are the only test results of importance here. You would then find the author discussing just how *both* the age and sex of Lutherans relate to higher or lower interest in civil rights. (This entire example, of course, is fictitious.)

In a study such as this the choice of a *significance level* is very important. A significance level is a level below which the probability for one's statistical test results must fall before one can reject the possibility of no significant relationship between the variables in question, and decide that the data support the conclusion that different values of one variable (in this case, interest in civil rights) are systematically related to values of another variable (here, sex or age). A significance level of $p = .01$ is customary, or $p = .001$ in extreme situations. Because of the large number of people surveyed in *A Study of Generations,* a significance level of $p = .0001$ was selected for tests dealing with the entire sample in order to avoid the error of reporting relationships (or subgroup differences) that are statistically significant but are too weak (or small) to be of any practical consequence. Therefore, in the above example, probabilities greater than one in 10,000 ($p = > .000100$) would be interpreted as reason for concluding no relationship. Specifically, if it made sense to examine the results of testing for a systematic relationship between age alone and interest in civil rights, in this case one would properly conclude there is no relationship; i.e., age is *not* related to interest in civil rights, because the probability of getting the test results reported for age was .000210 which is greater than $p = .0001$.

ANALYZING MANY VARIABLES AT ONCE

One final matter. Any analysis of data in terms of the possible *simultaneous* relationships between at least two variables (such as where one lives, size of congregation, belief in the divinity of Jesus) on some third matter (such as degree of personal witnessing, or sense of alienation) is a *multivariate* analysis of the data. In a study such as this each person surveyed has hundreds of characteristics all of which are present simultaneously. A person is 35 years of age, at the same time he lives in New York, at the same time he values self-development, etc. The more variables analyzed for their possible simultaneous relationships to the way persons vary on some one other dimension, the more interesting, informative, and valuable the conclusions that can be reported from a study such as this.

In the analysis of *A Study of Generations* data the simultaneous effects of as many as 39 variables at a time were analyzed in a special technique called AID, or Automatic Interaction Detection (Sonquist and Morgan, 1964). In the reports of such analyses in all the chapters that follow, the 39 variables (like age and sex in the above example) being examined at once in their simultaneous effect on how people scored on one scale or dimension (like interest in civil rights in the above example) are called *predictors.* Results of AID analyses have made it possible to report such information as the following about dozens of dimensions of belief, value, attitude, and behavior in succeeding chapters:

1. In order of importance, or strength of relationship, which of the as many as 39 predictors are significantly related to the dimension being described.

2. How the several significant predictors are related to the dimension or characteristic being described and explained.

      a. Whether singly and additively related to the dimension, or jointly and interactively related.

      b. How the predictors are related to each other in terms of the dimension.

3. Identification of significant subgroups of Lutherans who, because of several clearly identified characteristics they have in common (several predictors), have also in common much higher or much lower scores on a given scale or dimension.

      a. How much higher or lower on the average those scale scores are (how much more or less of the characteristic under consideration they will likely exhibit).

      b. What percent of Lutherans are most probably in each such group, or are of each type so identified.

With the above information, of course, one may find clues and detailed insights for deeper understanding, more relevant help, and hopefully wiser and more effective ministry to people.

The research concepts that have just been introduced and briefly discussed will appear throughout the chapters that follow. They are an assumed foundation for the findings and how they are reported. Those who desire deeper understanding of these and related concepts should next read Section IV, Appendix A, "How the Study Was Conducted."

Section II

Introduction

There are two organizing principles for Section II. First, the six chapters of the section are organized in keeping with the original conceptualization of the study as research about Lutherans' values (Chapter 4); beliefs (Chapter 5, and misbelief, Chapter 6); opinions and attitudes concerning institutional loyalty, mission and ministry (Chapter 7), as well as selves and others (Chapter 9); and life styles or self-reported behaviors (Chapter 8).

The second organizing principle is based on the interrelationships of all answers to all questions—a structure within the data discovered only after it was collected. This consists of a number of primary characteristics of people, that we shall call dimensions; and an even smaller number of major themes running through the data, that we shall call factors.

If we can summarize the answers to 740 questions from each of 4,745 people under only 64 properties or dimensions that run through the data, things have been simplified considerably. But have they been condensed enough?

By the empirical methods described in Chapter 3 and in Section IV, Appendix A, all answers to 553 of the items did organize into 64 basic (or parent) scales and 14 subscales. Each scale consisted of a set of items that Lutherans tended to answer consistently in given ways. Each scale (set of items) represented a dimension of people's beliefs, values, opinions, attitudes, or life styles. They were not organized according to some preconceived notions of the researchers. They formed because of the ways in which Lutherans answered all of the items involved. If another group of social scientists were to take the same data and use the same methods of analysis, the probability is very high that they would identify most of the same dimensions that organize or give structure to A *Study of Generations* data.

The 64 basic dimensions could now be described and discussed as a summary of findings. But who would read through all of them with interest and understanding? (They are listed with a brief description in Section IV, Appendix B.) Surely there must be a way of organizing these 64 dimensions under a considerably smaller number of topics without doing violence to the natural organization, structure, and patterns of the answers people gave.

Essentially the same analytic methods used to group items empirically into scales representing an underlying dimension were also used to identify the major factors running through or across the dimensions like themes. (See Section IV, Appendix A, for the details of how this was done.) Most of A *Study of Generations* data can now be presented in terms of just 14 factors that demonstrate the natural organization or structure of the information provided by the entire sample of Lutherans.

The next six chapters (4 through 9), then, are also organized around the 14 factors identified from the interrelationships of the 64 dimensions particularly within the data from the 4,444 lay people. Each chapter is organized around one or more factors. Though a few dimensions are significantly related to more than one factor, each dimension is usually presented and discussed only in connection with the one theme-like factor to which it is most highly related.

The degree to which a given dimension is related to a given factor is shown by a number called a factor loading. The higher the factor loading the closer the relationship, or, stating it another way, the higher the factor loading the more that that particular dimension reflects, coincides with, or assesses whatever the factor really is. Factor loadings can be any decimal from +1.00 through 0.00 to −1.00. A loading of +1.00 means the dimension and factor are, for practical purposes, identical, while −1.00 means they are exact opposites. A loading of 0.00 means they are unrelated.

Summarizing thus far:

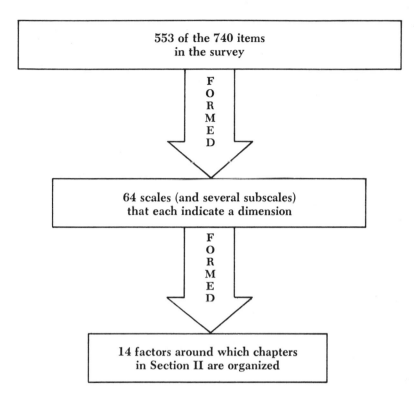

If you want a better understanding of what a given dimension is all about as you meet it in the following chapters, study the brief description of the researchers' conception of it as given in Appendix B, Section IV, or better yet, the items that form or indicate it as given in Appendix C, Section IV. If you want to form your own idea of a given factor, study the dimensions that load heavily upon it and the relative strength of the factor loading of each dimension. The 14 factors and the chapters in which they receive fullest discussion are listed below. Each dimension is listed only with the factor where it had the highest positive or negative loading, except in a few cases where a dimension loaded approximately equally on more than one factor.

Chapter 4:   Values

FACTOR 1

(Only the two dimensions that identify the positive and negative poles are discussed in Chapter 4. Otherwise see Chapter 5.)

FACTOR 10

Load	Scale	Dimension Title
Positive		
.75	53	Desire for a Controllable World
.65	54	Desire for Detachment from the World
.58	52	Desire for a Dependable World

Chapter 5: The Heart of Lutheran Piety

FACTOR 1

Load	Scale	Dimension Title
Positive		
.80	28	Transcendental Meaning in Life
.74	14	A Personal Caring God
.73	66	Emotional Certainty of Faith
.72	44	Fundamentalism—Liberalism
.67	46	Importance of Christian Practices in My Life
.65	71	Attitude Toward Life and Death
.55	41	Personal Piety
.54	19	Religious Experience
.52	58	Awareness of the Immanent Trinity
.52	6	Divinity of Jesus
.48	16	The Exclusive Truth Claim of Christianity Exaggerated
.44	36	Christian Utopianism
Negative		
−.29	15	Salvation by Works
−.32	29	Values of Self-Development

FACTOR 14

Load	Scale	Dimension Title
Positive		
.44	70	Gospel-Oriented Life
.38	5	Humanity of Jesus
.30	8	Biblical Knowledge
Negative		
−.32	69	Horatio Alger Orientation

Chapter 6: Law-Oriented Lutherans

FACTOR 2

Load	Scale	Dimension Title
Positive		
.76	37	Need for Unchanging Structure
.70	43	Need for Religious Absolutism

Load	Scale	Dimension Title
.69	34	Generalized Prejudice
.69	56	Social Distance—Radical Life Styles
.65	57	Social Distance—Racial and Religious Groups
.53	67	Self-Oriented Utilitarianism
.49	16	The Exclusive Truth Claim of Christianity Exaggerated
.47	26	Mutual Support Among Church, Society, and Individuals
.44	36	Christian Utopianism
.38	15	Salvation by Works
.36	69	Horatio Alger Orientation
.32	35	Pessimism

Negative

Load	Scale	Dimension Title
−.34	42	The Role of Pastors in Social Action
−.35	65	Church Involvement in Social Issues
−.36	5	Humanity of Jesus
−.42	55	Family Education Level

Chapter 7: Mission and Ministry

FACTOR 3

Load	Scale	Dimension Title
Positive		
.69	78	Openness to Change Within the Church
.66	65	Church Involvement in Social Issues
.61	12	The Church, Me, and Social Justice
.60	42	The Role of Pastors in Social Action
.59	64	Power Orientation to Social Issues
Negative		
−.30	56	Social Distance—Radical Life Styles
−.32	34	Generalized Prejudice

FACTOR 4

Load	Scale	Dimension Title
Positive		
.64	60	Individual Christian Responsibility
.56	59	Social Utility of Christianity
Negative		
−.52	62	Service Without Proclamation
−.63	35	Pessimism
−.67	61	Image of Lutherans as Different

FACTOR 8

Load	Scale	Dimension Title
Positive		
.59	18	Identification with Parents
.56	13	Family and Congregational Caring Life

Negative

−.52	63	Peer Orientation
−.55	27	Disappointment with the Church

Chapter 8: Lutheran Life Styles

FACTOR 6

Load	Scale	Dimension Title
Positive		
.69	40	Congregational Activity
.63	45	Organizational Memberships
.61	47	Personal Involvement in Church and Community
.29	74	Personal Initiative on Church and Public Issues

FACTOR 5

Load	Scale	Dimension Title
Positive		
.86	22	Neighborliness
.78	20	Supporting Others in Crises
.66	21	Personal Evangelism
.29	74	Personal Initiative on Church and Public Issues

FACTOR 11

Load	Scale	Dimension Title
Positive		
.54	9	Biblical Ignorance
.42	23	Questionable Personal Activities
.36	29	Values of Self-Development
.33	15	Salvation by Works

FACTOR 12

Load	Scale	Dimension Title
Positive		
.53	51	Acceptance of Authority
.49	72	Orientation to "Doing" Influenced by the Church

Negative

−.21	70	Gospel-Oriented Life
−.31	29	Values of Self-Development
−.35	73	Drug Culture Orientation

Chapter 9: How Lutherans Feel About Themselves and Others

FACTOR 7

Load	Scale	Dimension Title
Positive		
.70	68	Life Purpose
.30	50	Acceptance of Middle-Class Norms

Negative

-.68   17   Feelings of Isolation and Pressure

-.70   49   Anxiety over My Faith

Factors 4 and 8 are discussed from the perspective of mission and ministry in Chapter 7. They are discussed again from the perspective of personal and interpersonal attitudes in Chapter 9.

Two factors are not discussed in any of the chapters of Section II. Both are rather obvious and simple. Factor 13 concerns only about 3% of Lutherans, and the issue it raises has already been described in Chapter 2 of Section I. In effect, we learn from this factor that having previously been a member of any other denomination distinguishes an individual more than what particular denomination it was.

FACTOR 13

Load   Scale   Dimension Title
   Positive

.80   10   Prior Denominational Membership—Larger Bodies

.79   11   Prior Denominational Membership—Smaller Bodies

Factor 9 shows (1) the voting for Democratic presidential candidates is a phenomenon that has arisen among Lutherans mostly since World War II, and (2) that Lutherans tend to vote for presidential candidates rather consistently by party affiliation.

FACTOR 9

Load   Scale   Dimension Title
   Positive

.89   75   Post World War II Presidential Voting

.76   77   Democratic Presidential Voting

Negative

-.55   76   Republican Presidential Voting

Some additional unexpected findings appeared when the research team studied the dimensions of the various factors. For example, these are not mentioned in the next six chapters:

1. Notice that ignorance of the Bible, or misinformation about it, is significantly related to belief in salvation by works, high evaluation of self-development goals, and participation in questionable personal behaviors (Factor 11, Chapter 8).
2. Conversely, knowledge of the Bible is significantly related to belief in the true humanity of Jesus and applying the gospel in one's interpersonal relationships (Factor 14, Chapter 5).
3. Acceptance of authority is inversely related to being oriented to use of drugs and participating in the drug culture (Factor 12, Chapter 8).

    4. Identification with one's parents, by contrast with being oriented only to one's peers, is related to perceiving one's own parents, family, and congregation as really caring about and for people in their need and diversity (Factor 8, Chapter 7).

Occasionally single items from the survey are discussed, usually as supplementary information in succeeding chapters. Some are items that did not form scales. A more well-rounded understanding of others may come from examination of those items in the context of the scale set of which they are a part and that together form a dimension of belief, value, or the like.

Notice also that there appear to be two types of factors. Factors 3, 5, 6, 9, 10, and 13 are of one type that is more simple and, from certain perspectives, probably less interesting but no less important. Most, if not all, of the dimensions of each of these factors are of one kind such as assessment of attitudes in Factor 3 and self-reported behaviors in Factor 6. Possibly these factors have drawn attention in each case to groups of slightly different facets of much the same one characteristic that is being assessed just a little differently but with considerable overlap by each of the dimensions of the factor. In effect, each of these factors may be a case of identification of a series of somewhat different but cross-validating measures of the same thing.

By contrast, the rest of the factors (4; 7, 8, 11, 12, 14, and especially 1 and 2) are very comprehensive, much more subtle, and profoundly more interesting. The dimensions of each are variously belief, value, attitude, opinion, and behavior in one factor or a conglomeration of several of these in a single dimension. The number of facets (dimensions) per theme (factor) is generally greater. The identity and meaning of each of these factors is much less apparent and requires more sophisticated interpretation. This second type (particularly in the case of Factors 1 and 2) comes much closer to being, if it is not actually, a representation of a way of life, or a worldview, or a type of Lutheran. As a result, for everything stated in the next six chapters, there is equally as much unstated but that nevertheless is apparent and interesting in the interrelationships of items with dimensions and with factors.

. . . the very world which is the world
Of us all—the place where, in the end,
We find our happiness, or not at all.

—Wordsworth

4. Values

*This chapter explores two questions: What meaning do Lutherans find
in life? and What kind of "good life" do Lutherans dream about?*

*The first question is answered by showing that two dimensions of
value characterize the entire population of Lutherans. The majority
accept a transcendental worldview and find their source of meaning in
relationships with God and with others. A minority reject the transcendental dimension of life and show a preoccupation with values of self-
development. These two dimensions of value are important indicators
of two quite contrasting ways of believing, thinking, and doing. Inasmuch as these two dimensions of value are strongly identified with different types of Lutherans, one can view them broadly as watershed
dimensions.*

*The second half of the chapter answers the next question by describing
three systems of value that emerged from the analyses. These systems
of value, or visions of the "good life," center in a desire for a dependable world, a desire for a controllable world, and a desire for a life of
detachment from the world. Cross-cultural studies show that the same
three visions of the "good life" could be called value universals inasmuch as they are found among the people of many countries and cultures
of the world. These value universals emerge as significant desires that
appear to be more personal and more basic than specific social or cultural
values.*

One of the problems that has faced the church is the persistent appearance of attitudes of prejudice. This chapter introduces information on where sources of prejudice may be found.

The dimensions of value described in this chapter anticipate and lay the groundwork for the chapters which follow. Transcendental Meaning in Life and Values of Self-Development serve as polarities for the factor discussed in Chapter 5. One of the systems of value, Desire for a Dependable World, is part of Chapter 6.

People are talking and doing a lot to preserve what they call the "good life." They campaign to save trees, they set up rural communes, they try to stop the building of new factories.

If I have an idea of the "good life," what is it for? What does it all mean? How do my visions of the "good life" and my idea about "what it all means" fit with the way I see myself and other people? How do I relate myself and my visions of life to the world I know? What kind of "good life" do Lutherans dream about?

Fortunately, we *can* answer these questions because Lutherans told us a great deal about their values in *A Study of Generations.* Values are ideas people have about the "good life" and about what life means. They are the ideas we use to tell whether we like something or not; whether it is important or unimportant to us; whether we are frightened of or feel good about an object, an event, a course of action, or a person. Everything that happens inside us or outside us is graded by our values.[1] Values lead me to choose one job over another, one house rather than another, one person to marry out of several who may have wanted to marry me.

The topic of values has attracted much attention among social scientists in recent years.[2] Unfortunately the increased attention has not brought about any gain in conceptual clarity nor consensus among social scientists. Too many different things are labeled "values." Concepts called values range from the abstract utilities of mathematical decision theory [3] to core-attitudes that set preferences,[4] to the real criteria of mental health.[5] With such confusion evident, we have to make clear what we mean by values.

There are two main poles in the discussion of values and valuing— the person and the object. Some locate values in the object, in its intrinsic or useful properties. We choose to locate values in the person doing the valuing.[6] Out of the variety of theories and ideas regarding personal values we have chosen as an unequivocal core meaning the following definition of value:

> Values are beliefs held by persons. These beliefs ascribe relationships between objects and abstract concepts that sum up to a positive or negative evaluation of a given object that may be physical, social,

or ideal. These evaluations guide selective attention or behavior and impart moral quality to the process of interaction with the objects.

We hold that all values come from the one fundamental idea: good and evil. All people may not agree on *what* good and evil are, but all seem to agree that good and evil are real.[7]

We get our idea of good–evil from the way we exist. From the beginning of life we are conscious that there is "me" and there is everyone else "out there," apart from me. There is my internal self-consciousness and there is the demand of external reality. I get my fundamental idea of good–evil from the meeting of these two experienced realities.[8] Everything outside of me demands that I make choices. The only way I can make choices is to have some idea of good and evil.

Our concept of good and evil is the basis we use to rank everything else, including all other values, beliefs, abstract ideas like truth, scientific theories, people, even God. Of course, nothing human is ever *all* good or *all* evil. There are different mixtures of good and evil. Values are how we grasp the mixture of good and evil in any combination of circumstances involving interaction between ourselves and external reality. How we evaluate ourselves and other people is part of the set of values we use to mark out the meaning of life.

Two Dimensions of Value

What is life for? Why do I exist? Why does the universe exist? Why is there anything at all? These are old, familiar questions. They can all be seen as two major questions—one about me and one about the universe. Most of us don't separate the two but rather see them as a single issue—the meaning of life, particularly the meaning of *my* life. Since this is a question of relationships among myself, the external world, and ends or goals, the way in which the question gets answered is by systems of value.

Transcendental Meaning in Life

We have two dimensions to report here. The items in the first dimension are given in Scale 28. This dimension is called Transcendental Meaning in Life. It has three items that Glock and Stark (1966) call an "Orthodoxy" index and seven "Terminal Personal Values." Two of these "Terminal Personal Values" are those Rokeach (1969) called "the most distinctively Christian." They are "salvation" and "forgiving" (Items 185 and 187). The three Glock and Stark "Orthodoxy" items are those dealing with beliefs about miracles, eternal life, and the devil (Items 89, 90, and 91). (See Appendix C, Section IV, for all items in Scale 28.)

"Orthodox" or Transcendent? Glock and Stark claimed that orthodox belief, measured by these items, indirectly caused anti-Semitism. That claim has led others to the specific suggestion that the church cease teaching that Jesus is Lord and Savior. Rokeach said that the unique Christian values were connected with lack of social compassion. Therefore he suggests abandoning or changing the values of Christianity.[9]

We have a situation where items said to measure orthodoxy of belief and items said to be unique Christian values form, by our methods, a single dimension with other items. Now we must ask, "What is this dimension?" Because of the seriousness of the charges made, and because this dimension is a very powerful one in *A Study of Generations* data, we will pay careful attention to this question.

What do the items regarding miracles, eternal life, and the devil assess? We reject the claim of Glock and Stark that they assess "orthodoxy" of belief of Christians. Every religion the world has known has included belief in miraculous events, a life after death, and a personification of evil. Even as allegedly materialistic a system as communism can be said to include these three elements. Surely the Talmud, a compilation of the teachings of Judaism, includes acceptance of miracles, a life after death, and a devil. Contemporary witchcraft includes these beliefs, as does ancient Zoroastrianism, Buddhism, and the animism of the New Guinea tribes.

It is naive to say that what is "orthodox" about Christianity is that which it has in common with all other religions. Furthermore, this does not correspond in any meaningful way with what Christianity itself defines as orthodoxy. For our purposes the three ecumenical creeds (Apostles, Nicean, Athanasian) serve as a definition of the content of what has been believed "everywhere, always, by all." Doctrines such as those of the Trinity, justification, redemption, creation, and the divinity and humanity of Jesus are much closer to the church's own understanding of orthodoxy. Admittedly what makes up orthodoxy is vigorously debated within the church today. However, those who want to change the doctrinal content of credal statements know that they are changing what was clearly orthodoxy for over a thousand years.

Our results show that belief in miracles, eternal life, and the devil form a single dimension with value statements such as "service," "ethical life," "religion," and other items. The dimension is meaning in life found in relationships with others and with God. All ten items reflect value judgments which answer the question, "What is it for?" Glock and Stark's three items (miracles, eternal life, the devil) get at the same question, "Is there something other than myself and what I can touch, taste, hear, see, and smell?" It is the value judgment of choosing the supernatural over the natural, the spiritual over the material, dualism over monism.

Philosophers discussing the question of meaning in life have long maintained that *any* man, Christian or not, in searching for meaning has to confront the three basic issues of relationship to nature, mortality, and good and evil. Tertullian, writing in the second century A.D., describes these three beliefs as the testimony of the simple soul of all men.[10]

Immanuel Kant's *Critique of Practical Reason* argues that rational men must believe in God and a future life in order to conceive of the possibility of good as a goal of their decisions for action. Man's rationality creates a problem: he must have meaning for his life. A problem is not met by contemplation but by decision. In order for man to pursue the decision his reason has marked out for him, reason requires speculative belief in God, immortality, and good and evil. Man has to believe there is something beyond his immediate experience so that his actions make sense. These same three beliefs define the "boundary conditions" described as absolutely crucial for twentieth-century man by Jaspers.[11]

The contemporary discussion of meaning in life still centers around this issue.[12] The question of belief in God, the fact of death, and the question of good and evil are central to meaning in life for contemporary men.[13] The same question of the transcendent is at the root of the debate about the mind–body problem and the struggle about freedom versus determinism. This makes it clear why the three items dealing with miracles, eternal life, and the devil form a single dimension with the terminal personal values of love, family, happiness, etc. The dimension measures the decision to believe in a transcendent dimension of something other than the self and the world in order to give meaning to life. The inclusion of these items in a single dimension confirms the philosopher's insight that meaning in life is bound up with the questions of mortality, of good and evil, and of a reality beyond ourselves and our universe.

What is the common note running through all the items on this dimension? Every item contains a relationship-with-other element. The individual endorsing all items is declaring a sense of being related to the transcendental "other" in the items dealing with miracles, eternal life, the devil, religion, and salvation. He is also saying he places most importance on values that deal with relationship with other persons: service, ethical life, love, forgiveness, and family happiness. In short, the person consciously endorses a value system whereby meaning in life is found *in relationship* with the divine and the human "other."

For Lutherans "salvation," "forgiveness," "religion," and "belief in eternal life and miracles" are among the values that contribute the most discriminating power to this dimension. They also tend to be endorsed by the highest percentages. Ranking all the value statements on this dimension as of "extreme importance" and saying that one definitely believes in miracles, eternal life, and the devil results in a theoretical score of 87. Ranking all the values as "least important" and rejecting belief in miracles, eternal life, and the devil gives a theoretical score of 39. The average for all laity is 75.81. This places the weight of Lutherans definitely in the direction of accepting transcendental meaning in life as a basic system of value. Lutherans as a whole are highly committed to valuing religion, salvation, forgiveness, service to others, an ethical responsible life, love, and family happiness. They also value the supernatural over the natural.

Seven out of ten say biblical miracles happened just the way the Bible describes them. Seven out of ten definitely believe in life after death. Over half (53%) assert that the devil actually exists. Religion, love, salvation, and family happiness are ranked among the value concepts as extremely important by most Lutherans. Farther down in rank are ethical life and service. Of the value concepts, the one that contributes the most to this dimension—religion—contains the explanatory phrase "meaning in life."

VALUES OF SELF-DEVELOPMENT

The second dimension to come out of the value items included in *A Study of Generations* is given in Scale 29. It is called Values of Self-Development. The percentages of response show that a small proportion of Lutherans (approximately 10%) place high importance on these values. About one in four ranks this dimension of values as relatively important. Ranking all items on this dimension as extremely important gives a score of 65; least important, a score of 13. The average for all laity, 22.33, puts the weight of Lutherans at the point of ranking these value concepts as of some importance (the theoretical score is 19). Personal power is the item that most sharply discriminates between those who do and those who do not highly value self-development. The item concerning personal freedom has the largest proportion ranking it extremely important (20%). Beauty has the smallest proportion ranking it highly (4%).

The 10 items making up this dimension deal with the satisfaction of personal needs. The needs lying behind these values include social needs connected with a sense of self-worth, i.e., personal power, recognition, skill, achievement, physical appearance, and personal freedom. Beauty is an aesthetic need. Adventure, pleasure, and money are most closely linked to needs having a biological base in drives for "creature comforts," curiosity or exploratory drives, and gratification of instinctual drives.

The common thread running through all items is satisfaction of the self. This contrasts with the dimension of Transcendental Meaning in Life. The Values of Self-Development come close to representing that favorite whipping boy of countless preachers—materialism. However, young people consistently place more importance on these values than do older people. Consequently this dimension might well be viewed less as a negative, self-centered value system and more as a normal system of need in the process of development. Adolescent and young adult years are the periods when personal identity and a place in society must be hammered out. Finding a place for oneself in the world requires a certain amount of satisfaction of self-needs in order to develop self-worth and a sense of individual identity. Nevertheless, these values are associated with a rejection of a transcendental view of life, with a negative attitude towards life, and with an involvement in questionable forms of behavior.[14]

THE VALUE DIMENSIONS AND PREJUDICE

The relationship of these two dimensions of meaning in life—Transcendental Meaning in Life and Values of Self-Development—to prejudice is important for the church and the nation. Transcendental Meaning in Life contains items which two previous researchers have used as a base for asserting that orthodox Christian beliefs and uniquely Christian values indirectly *cause* prejudice and rejection of others.[15]

Many in the church and the society have uncritically accepted this claim. The causal claim has led to the explicit suggestion that the church should no longer teach either its historic doctrine or the unique values of salvation and forgiveness. Must the church change its doctrine and its values to conform to society's pressure to eliminate prejudice?

Change in theology and values of the church may well occur and may well be desirable. History demonstrates that both theology and values of the church shift across the centuries. We are not asking whether there should be or should not be change. Rather, the question is whether change is mandatory *in order to* decrease the level of prejudice in national life.

Do the data of *A Study of Generations* support the claim that the doctrines and values of the church cause prejudice? The question we can answer at this point is whether or not there is a *direct* relationship between prejudice and values, particularly Transcendental Meaning in Life which contains the items used in previous research. Our data show that there is *no significant direct* relationship between Transcendental Meaning in Life and prejudice.[16] Rather, there is a direct relationship between a need for structure, religious absolutism, and prejudice. We will demonstrate (in Chapter 6) that it is a law orientation or misbelief among Lutherans that is associated with prejudice. We will also discuss what our data allow us to infer about the causes of prejudice. Our conclusion is that rather than changing orthodox doctrine in order to decrease prejudice, it is misbelief that needs to be changed.

CHARACTERISTICS RELATED TO VALUES OF MEANING IN LIFE

Age is important in understanding how Lutherans find meaning in life. Figure 4.1 presents the average scores of two-year age groups on the

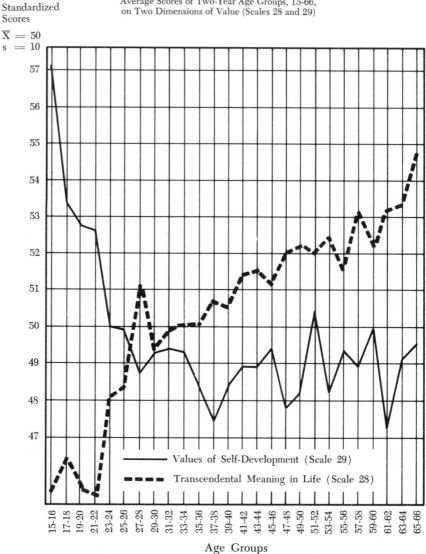

Figure 4.1
Average Scores of Two-Year Age Groups, 15-66,
on Two Dimensions of Value (Scales 28 and 29)

Standardized
Scores

$\overline{X} = 50$
$s = 10$

Values of Self-Development (Scale 29)

Transcendental Meaning in Life (Scale 28)

Age Groups

two dimensions of value. There is a steady rise in scores on the transcendental view as age increases. Older Lutherans are more likely to hold a transcendental value system than do younger Lutherans. Conversely, young Lutherans favor values of self-development most with a plateau in scores beginning about age 22 that remains fairly constant until retirement years of 65 and over.

Multivariate Analyses. We used a technique of multivariate analysis to find out more about the persons who choose or reject these two dimensions of value. (See Chapter Note 17 for more detailed discussion.) We can describe one group of persons who value a transcendental view. They are above 24 years old with two or more close personal friends in their congregation, living anywhere in the country outside of the East. A group that places less importance on Transcendental Meaning in Life says they are much less religious than their mothers and are under 24 years old.[17] This analysis used 31 characteristics like age, education, and income.

A second analysis added characteristics of beliefs and attitudes to those that had shown some effect in the first one. A second group of persons who value Transcendental Meaning in Life hold a conservative doctrinal belief system. They also feel certain about their faith in God and in Jesus. They report a high level of personal piety, such as reading Scripture, praying, and meditating. A group that does not value a transcendental view as highly tends to reject a conservative doctrinal belief and to have doubts about their faith in God and Jesus.[18]

In this analysis characteristics like age, region, etc., were shown to be less powerful than measures of belief in predicting the values a person will hold. Whether or not a person holds a conservative doctrinal belief system, is certain of his faith, and practices personal piety tells us much more about whether or not he will value Transcendental Meaning in Life than his age, income, social class, and the like.[19]

Those who prefer meaning in life as found in self-development are primarily male, part-time workers, students, or unemployed, who show little interest in a transcendental view and favor using religion and society to satisfy personal desires. A second group who prefer values of self-development are the 15-20-year-olds with little interest in a transcendental view. Values of self-development are clearly most attractive to young people.[20]

The liking youth express for values of self-development need not be seen as an indictment of young people as a group. It is a commonplace of history that youth tend toward self-identity seeking of one sort or another. The data of *A Study of Generations* cannot tell whether young people change their values as they grow older. However, most adults testify to changing from self-interest seeking to a different set of values as they grew older.

Persons rejecting self-development values also decisively reject an instrumental use of religion and society and strongly favor a transcendental view.

SUMMARY

Two dimensions of value that show where people tend to find meaning in life have been described. One finds meaning in life outside the self in relationship with the transcendental and with other persons. The other at least finds meaning in life in the self—in meeting the needs of the self. Logically they are polar opposites. Our data show that these two reflect separate dimensions. The dimensions developed separately out of the 24 value statements from which persons could choose those most important to them. One dimension, Transcendental Meaning in Life, also drew in items reflecting a value orientation to the supernatural. Most Lutherans hold this system of value. Values of self-development are held by a small proportion, mostly youthful Lutherans.

In our definition of value we said that values impart a moral quality to the process of interaction. We are well aware of the basic claim of moral relativism—that there is no logical way to get from a description of what "is" to what "ought" to be. We are also well aware of the fact that all men continue to act as if "ought" were real, not nonsense.

Values are the bridge by which people cross the gap between "is" and "ought." [21] Values define the theoretically desirable, the preferable, rather than what is actually desired or preferred at any given moment in a particular situation. They are the standards by which specific choices are tested. That a given man has a certain set of values does not predict absolutely what his specific choices are going to be. Nevertheless, in these two systems of value regarding the meaning of life, we do have indications about the kinds of choices men are most likely going to make.

VALUES AND VISIONS OF THE "GOOD LIFE"

"I didn't mean to . . . , " a phrase we have all learned to use, makes sense only because of a shared value that intentions are more important than acts. Intentions, what is aimed at, depend upon values that define the desirable, the preferable. While we can make a logical distinction between the desirable and the desired, we can safely assume that for most people there is a consistency so that what is valued as desirable is also desired. On that basis if we ask people to tell us what kind of life they prefer or desire, we can assume that we have an expression of a value choice by which attention and behavior are selectively guided.

Lutherans told us what kind of life they preferred by responding to 13 complex and widely different descriptions of "Ways of Life." [22] By our methods three dimensions came out of these 13 items. The three dimensions we found are *a desire for a dependable world, a desire for a controllable world,* and *a desire for detachment from the world.*

DESIRE FOR A DEPENDABLE WORLD

A dependable world is one that is stable, orderly, and predictable. The person who scores highly on this dimension (Scale 52) is primarily interested in morality. He is aware of his world. He knows he must exercise intelligent and reasonable restraint over his own desires. He believes that the best way to have a good life for the most people is for most people to practice self-discipline. At the same time he is committed to "sympathetic concern for other persons." Acceptance of others is better than aggression. He likes to preserve what is good from the past. He is not opposed to change but wants change to occur in an orderly fashion. A note of passivity is also included.[23]

The average for all laity on this dimension means that Lutherans as a whole are inclined to favor a dependable world, but not strongly so. The average is close to the theoretical score obtained if one answers, "I like it *slightly*" to all items. The most popular individual way of life envisions a person who is actively involved in the social life of his community.[24] He does not withdraw but works for an orderly process of gradual change. While gradual change is going on, maximum return to him comes from orderliness, predictability, and discipline. Change must not destroy the past but rather preserve it.

We do not know how well Lutherans feel their lives match this vision of a dependable world. We do know that this vision is a standard by which many judge their lives. If there is a large gap between this vision and what is really happening to them, anxiety, fear, frustration, and anger are the most likely responses. Affairs of the world and our society are rapidly changing. For those whose system of value places high importance on dependability, these are agonizing times.

Active, Open Exuberance in a Controllable World

The second dimension is the desire for a controllable world (Scale 53).[25] The main quality of this dimension is preference for a world I can help shape. The person who likes these five "Ways of Life" prefers vigorous, robust action. He likes an open, exuberant attitude toward the world. He enjoys comfortable surroundings and lives with passionate intensity. He is confident of man's ability to meet problems. Change is accepted as valuable; there is not much interest in preserving the past. Ever upward and onward, with gusto!

The average for laity places desire for a controllable world at about the same place as desire for a dependable world. There is a slightly greater tendency for Lutherans to prefer a controllable world more than a dependable one.

The second most popular individual "Way of Life" is in this dimension.[26] It sees enjoyment in relaxed possession of the "good things of life" —creature comforts. It adds a note of sensuality to the picture of an exuberant activist. There is a pleasant place to come home to after a rigorous day spent changing the world.

This dimension fits the image of the American as an energetic, brash doer. The person holding this vision of the "good life" may not experience as great a gap between his vision and reality as the person who likes a dependable world. However, recent emphasis on negative growth, ecology, and losing a war for the first time may be increasing a feeling that there is "trouble in River City."

If an individual values a controllable world subject to his actions and feels a large gap between his vision and reality, he will experience a sense of failure and depression rather than of fear or anger. He can only conclude he failed to be energetic enough to succeed in manipulating the environment. He may respond by trying even harder to assert control over both his own life and the lives of others.

DETACHMENT FROM THE WORLD

The final vision of the "good life" is detachment from a demanding, pushing world (Scale 54).[27] The chief desire is for a rich internal life of self-awareness. The self rather than the world or society is the focal point. The person who wants to live this way values passivity, non-involvement, but openness to any experience. He isn't aiming for crass self-indulgence but rather for increased insight into the self. He believes that is the way to greater openness and receptivity to the external world.

The "Way of Life" that shows the most power to distinguish between people on this dimension sets up the ideal of retreat from a hostile world.[28] True humanity comes from self-awareness. The goal is to abandon the world and absorb the self into communion with all there is. This is close to Eastern religious mysticism.

Lutherans as a whole don't like detachment from the world as a way of life, but there is a minority that do. About 5% consistently said, "I like it very much," to all items representing detachment from the world. The average for all laity is close to the score obtained if all answers are "I dislike it slightly." An average of 33% consistently expressed extreme dislike for all items envisioning detachment from the world as the "good life." There is not likely to be much support among Lutherans for experimentation with alternative societies, communes, or mysticism in the Eastern form.

SIGNIFICANCE OF THESE SYSTEMS OF VALUE

Our results show three different visions of the "good life" among Lutherans. They are the same three systems of value that earlier research found in Mainland China, Japan, India, Norway, Canada, and the United States. Morris developed the "Ways of Life" items and theory over a number of years. He carried out an extensive research program in several countries representing widely divergent cultures. Using factor analysis he found that people in different cultures share a common structure of values: desire for a dependable world, desire for a controllable world, and desire for detachment from the world. We have found the same basic systems of value among Lutherans in the United States.

We now know that a member of the Lutheran church in this country and a Hindu in India can share a common desire for the kind of life they want for themselves, for their families and their children. Let's say it is the desire for a dependable world. The Lutheran and the Hindu will be looking at events, forces, and other persons in their lives from the same basic value stance. What does this do to my world? Does it help to keep it orderly and predictable? Is it a threat? Does it mean my life or world has to change? Given roughly similar events, both are likely to respond in a similar fashion. There is a commonality and regularity in basic values across cultures.

This supports Morris's statement, "The strongest impression . . . is one of orderliness, of structure, in the domain of values." [29] Human values have a structure. That structure can be dimly perceived and can be investigated. The importance of this replication and confirmation of Morris's earlier work is great indeed. We have added to the strength of support for the concept of value universals.[30] We have our hands on three systems of value that appear to be part of the set of value universals.

In changing societies, like ours, where traditional social values no longer work in defining and dealing with circumstances and situations, we can expect personal values to become more salient, more powerful, and more rigid. The combined effect of our work and Morris's is to show these three systems of value to be basic, more personal, and deeper than social or cultural values. In our changing society, then, we can expect that much of the conflict and tension will center around these value universals.

Ideally, we may think it possible and desirable that a person "ought" to be able to hold his personal values in the face of criticism and without any support other than his own conscience. Unfortunately, very few of us are like Nietzsche's superman. We are human. We need support from other people to remain convinced that our values are valid.[31] We will try to get that support from other people who believe as we do, or we will try to convert others. The end result will be an increase of ethnocentrism, of reliance upon the "group" like us. Our data show that within the Lutheran church at least, if not the nation, three major types of groups will be present: those serving to reinforce and validate the values of desire for a dependable world, for a controllable world, and for detachment from the world.

VISIONS OF THE "GOOD LIFE" AND OTHER DIMENSIONS

We have assumed that what people say they desire at a given time and place reflects what they hold to be the desirable generally because most people are relatively consistent. The relationships between the three visions of the "good life" and other dimensions in our data show that there is a consistent picture. Table 4.1 gives all correlations above .25 between the three visions of the "good life" and other dimensions.[32] (A discussion of the other dimensions will appear in later chapters.)

Table 4.1   How Three Value Systems Relate to Other Dimensions in Rank Order by Correlations (Lay People Only)

Dimension Number	Dimension Name	Correlation with Desire for a Dependable World Scale 52
37	Need for Unchanging Structure	.31
43	Need for Religious Absolutism	.31
36	Christian Utopianism	.31
26	Mutual Support Among Church, Society, and Individuals	.28
41	Personal Piety	.27
16	The Exclusive Truth Claim of Christianity Exaggerated	.25
55	Family Level of Education	−.26
		Correlation with Desire for a Controllable World Scale 53
67	Self-Oriented Utilitarianism	.27
15	Salvation by Works	.26
		Correlation with Desire for Detachment from the World, Scale 54
67	Self-Oriented Utilitarianism	.27
15	Salvation by Works	.27
35	Pessimism	.26

Desire for a dependable world is positively related to every dimension that reflects a need for firm, rigid structures in life or an attitude favoring a closed, encapsulated stance. It is also positively related to every measure reflecting prejudice at a level between .20 and .25. It is negatively related to family level of education. This suggests that those most likely favoring a dependable world are the persons at the bottom of the social structure, the least advantaged, the most burdened, and the first to get crunched in times of rapid social change because their range of options and alternatives is the most limited.

Desire for a controllable world is related positively to two dimensions. One shows an exploitative, controlling stance toward both religion and society. The other emphasizes achievement orientation in relationship with God. The consistency of these dimensions relating to desire for a controllable world is evident. If I value a life in which I can manipulate my world, I must be oriented to manipulating society and religion. I must also believe that achievement is possible and that it is rewarded. This is close to what has been called generalized American cultural religion.

Desire for detachment from the world is positively related to the same two dimensions as desire for a controllable world and to a third: pessimism. If I believe in manipulation and achievement but find that it doesn't work, then what? I may begin to value detachment, withdrawal into self, and introspection. That world out there is just too much for me.

VISIONS OF THE "GOOD LIFE" AND OTHER CHARACTERISTICS

Desire for a Dependable World. Age is important in the dimension of need for a dependable world. There is a steady rise as age increases. The older we get the greater our desire for a stable and predictable life. (See Figure 4.2.)

When this dimension was analyzed by comparing age and education, education proved to have *no* effect.[33] In other words, the amount of education we have does not slow down our increasing need for a dependable world as we grow older. Other variables that showed no effect on this scale are sex, region of country, size of congregation, and church body affiliation. Desire for a dependable world is not affected by these characteristics which are usually considered quite important. It is more basic in the system of value than many other values or external characteristics.

Multivariate Analysis. When we simultaneously compared a large number of characteristics, including age, education, etc., to this dimension we found that persons who most like a dependable world are over age 39. They also want a perfect society, without problems, built upon religion. They believe in moral achievement as a way of pleasing God. Those who don't feel a strong need for a dependable world tend to be under 39. They don't show much agreement with trying to build a perfect, problem-free society through religion.

Morris's work establishes that desire for a dependable world is found in widely divergent cultures. Our results show a powerful effect of age but not of education. We have also demonstrated a connection between this dimension and prejudicial attitudes. We may be much closer to

Figure 4.2
Average Scores of Two-Year Age Groups, 15-66,
on Three Views of "The Good Life" (Scales 52, 53, 54)

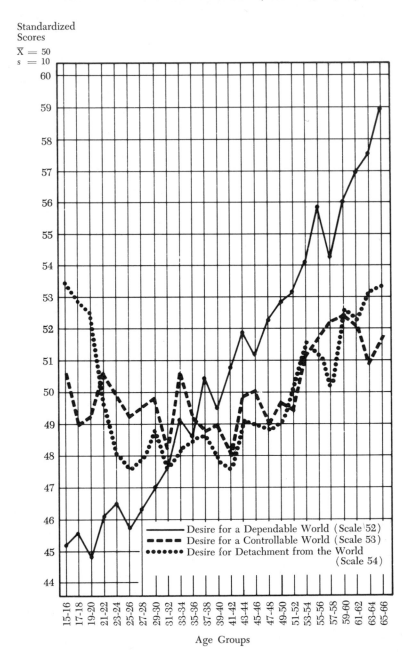

Age Groups

understanding the dynamics of prejudiced and critical attitudes toward others, which are found in *all* cultures, not only our own, by beginning to think of values like this one as playing crucial roles in the presence or absence of prejudice. If it should develop that such deep and basic human values are involved in prejudice and we can understand the human quality of the needs reflected by the values, we may be able to figure out ways of partially satisfying such needs. We may no longer have to "beat the air," limited to shouting and blaming those who reject others, but rather can do something effective in reducing the amount of rejection in the society.

Desire for a Controllable World. Generally, as the level of education rises, there are more who desire a controllable world.[34] Wanting to be an active, achieving person is independent of age, sex, region, size of congregation, and church body affiliation. A person may be most any age, male or female, living in any region of the country, etc., and still have a vision of the good life that values active control and manipulation of the world. Among these variables only higher levels of education are associated with higher levels of desire for a controllable world.

Multivariate Analysis. When the desire for a controllable world is simultaneously compared to a large number of characteristics, including age, education, etc., persons who like this way of life can best be described as those who have a strong exploitative stance toward religion and a strong conviction that doing "right and good" things will make God treat them right. Those who reject both pleasing God by works and instrumental religiosity exhibit little desire for control of their world.

Desire for a controllable world shows up a value position that is important in the religious life of Lutherans and in the life of the church. Desire for control over the world is a value reflecting American "religion-in-general," one of the principal forces in confusing Lutherans about the central trust of the gospel. These findings suggest that if the Lutheran church is successful in communicating its theological message of salvation by grace through faith in Christ, desire for a controllable world may decrease in importance. However, this requires that the theologians of the church carefully work through the meaning of the message of God's grace for a value orientation to the world. Does knowing the grace of God mean that I value a dependable world, or does it mean that I withdraw from the world, or does it mean something entirely new and different?

Which value orientation to the world is in keeping with the life of grace? None of the three found in our data fits well. Does the man who knows grace need worldly structures to buttress up his life? He is free, not bound. He knows that achievement and manipulation of the world do not earn points with God. He knows that manipulation for personal satisfaction alone does violence to God's creation. He knows that he is called to be a faithful steward in the world, not to withdraw from it. Well, then, what value does he hold? What is the vision of the good life under grace?

Desire for Detachment from the World. The majority of Lutherans don't like detachment from the world. However, emphasis upon withdrawal from the world and exploration of inner space is significantly more popular among the youngest and the oldest Lutherans. The sharp drop of interest in self-exploration happens at age 20-21 (see Figure 4.2). A marked increase in desire for detachment from the world begins to take place again about ages 40-51. Both of these breaks occur at ages established by our data as marking off separate generations. While the contemplative life is attractive to both groups, it is likely that the younger group is striving to find and identify the self in preparation for the years of active vigorous productivity in society. The older group faces a different problem—death—that requires an identification of the self.

Multivariate Analysis. Is detachment positively valued for itself, or is it rather a defense against a sense of futility and despair? When a number of characteristics are compared with detachment, those most powerfully associated with liking detachment are a high degree of resistance to change, both in youth (15-19/20) and older ages (50-65), and a high degree of instrumental religiosity, using religion for personal satisfaction. Disliking detachment is associated with early adulthood and middle age (21-50) and a low degree of interest in religion for personal gain.

Stages in life development, youth and old age, and resistance to change are associated with the preference for detachment from the world and devotion to internal feelings. It may be that when a high value is placed upon internal feelings, religious experience and practice is judged by how much it contributes to good or bad feelings. Then the tendency toward instrumental use of religion is strengthened.

Other characteristics show up affecting detachment. Young men are more inclined to detachment than young women, but older women like it more than do older men. Young members of the ALC are more likely to prefer detachment than those in the LCA and LC-MS. Older members in large congregations are more likely to envision the detached life as the good life than those in small congregations. Older members of the LCA like detachment more than do older people in the ALC and LC-MS. The farther west you go in the country, the more detachment is liked by youth. The farther east you go in the country, the more detachment is liked by older persons.

Summary

The values most Lutherans hold are "transcendent meaning in life" and "desire for a stable, dependable world," or "desire for a controllable world." Events, programs, ministry, and persons are going to be ranked by most Lutherans in terms of support or threat to these values.

Small groups of Lutherans prefer values of self-development or prefer exploration of the inner self.

Choosing a transcendent view and valuing relationships with God and men is associated with conservative doctrinal belief, a high level of certainty of faith, and considerable practice of personal piety. It is not directly related to prejudice. Desire for a dependable world consistently reflects a need for structure and rigidity. Desire for a controllable world is related to a general achievement-orientation. Detachment is associated with pessimism and a general achievement-orientation.

We cannot tell from our data whether values change over time. However, valuing is a dynamic, continuous process. We know from observation and personal experience that values do change. It seems reasonable and true to life to expect that the changing process of valuing is reflected in our data, but in a static, still portrait. We don't have evidence that values change in a given direction with age, nor do we have evidence that they do not.

Higher commitment to a transcendental view is associated with older ages, while an emphasis upon values for self-development is associated with younger ages. Desire for a dependable world is associated with older ages. Desire for a controllable world is found at all ages but is associated with higher levels of education. Desire for detachment is most popular among youth and older ages.

Our research cannot answer the question, "What are the values Lutherans *should* hold?" Whether or not a desire for a dependable world or perception of transcendental meaning in life is in accord with the gospel cannot be answered by empirical research alone. Whether the "mind of the church" is revealed by research is a debatable question. If it is, what status does it have? These are hard questions and require earnest thought and work. Those called to be teachers of the church have the responsibility to search out what "should" be.

We know there is orderliness and structure in the field of human values. We know there is a diversity and richness of values. We know there are many distinct value stances among Lutherans. Is it appropriate to say some are "right" values and others "wrong"? Does the church consciously try to change "wrong" values to "right" ones? What standards are to be used to judge values?

Notes

1. For a theoretical treatment of the construct "value," the research team has available Theoretical Appendix D, written in October 1969.
2. Albert, E. M. and Kluckhohn, C. K. M., 1960.
3. Edwards, W., 1954, pp. 380-417.

4. Allport, G. W., 1937.
5. Smith, M. B., 1961, pp. 299-306.
6. Spranger, E., 1928.
   Katz, D. and Stotland, E., 1959.
7. Bakan, D., 1966.
8. Freud spoke of this dual experience in his concepts of "death wish" and "life principle." Lutheran theology talks about the duality of human experience in saying law–gospel are opposing poles of the fundamental religious dimension of human life. See Bakan (1966) and Kelley (1955) for psychological discussion.
9. Rokeach, M., 1969, pp. 3-39.
10. Roberts, A. and Donaldson, J. (Eds.), 1963.
11. Jaspers, K., 1957.
12. Hepburn, R. W., 1966, pp. 125-140.
13. Concordia Theological Seminary, Graduate Study Number III, 1958.
14. Scale 29 correlates with Scale 28 $r = -.34$, Scale 35 $r = .25$, and Scale 23 $r = .28$.
15. Claims of a causal connection based upon typical social science data are suspect on the basis that the kinds of data and techniques available can never demonstrate causation but only association. *A Study of Generations* data cannot be used to answer the question of causation but can address the issue of association. Are the doctrines and values of the church associated with prejudiced attitudes? For an example of authors who seem both to accept the causal claim and to make explicit recommendation that the church change its teaching or practice because of it, see Gilbert (1967), Littell (1971), and Wahlberg (1971).

	Scale 32, Punitive Attitudes Toward Disadvantaged Persons	Scale 33, Negative Image of Jews	Scale 34, Generalized Prejudice	Scale 56, Social Distance— Radical Life Styles	Scale 57, Social Distance— Racial and Religious Groups
16. Scale 28, Transcendental Meaning in Life	$r = .05$	.01	.02	.09	.15
Scale 29, Values of Self-Development	.09	.14	.13	.09	.13
Scale 37, Need for Unchanging Structure	.55	.46	.59	.47	.44
Scale 43, Religious Absolutism	.42	.32	.41	.41	.38

17. Throughout this chapter and succeeding chapters the results of the multivariate analysis technique, Automatic Interaction Detection (AID), will be reported. This procedure is described more fully in Appendix A, pp. 354-357, also giving

the statistical criterion used for significance. This is the first reporting of AID results. We will report more fully at this point to provide information on the technique, illustrate the kind of information available, and show the basis for statements made as a result of interpretation of AID results. There will be no further reporting in depth. Those who wish specific data may have it upon request.

The AID program results in segregation of subgroups within the sample. Each subgroup is able to be described by the characteristics which separate it from the sample. In reporting the results of AID we comment upon the highest and lowest scoring groups, omitting comment upon intermediate groups. For each analysis there may be from six to twenty groups separated. Only those two groups at the extremes are described.

Example· The multivariate analysis reported here simultaneously compared 31 predictor variables to the dependent variable, scores on Scale 28, Transcendental Meaning of Life, across all 4,444 lay people of the sample. The 31 predictor variables were all of the kind called "status," or "nuisance," or "demographic" variables. This includes characteristics like age, education, region of country, income, social class, sex, and the like.

The process separated out seven final subgroups. Of these seven groups the one that has the highest average score on Scale 28 can be described as follows:

High Group: a) over age 24

b) say they have *more* than two close friends in their congregation

c) live in regions of the country *other* than the East

Out of the 4,444 lay people, 1,499 can be described by these three characteristics. That group of 1,499 has an average score on Scale 28 of 79.2, standard deviation of 6.4. The average of 79.2 is higher than the average for all 4,444 of 75.8. Therefore this subgroup is higher, on the average, in expressed commitment to Transcendental Meaning than the sample taken as a whole.

Out of the seven groups the one that has the lowest average score on Scale 28 can be described as follows:

Low Group: a) say they are much less religious than their mothers

b) under age 24

One hundred seventy-two people are described by these two characteristics. Those 172 persons have an average score on Scale 28 of 65.7 and standard deviation of 6.4. They are considerably lower, on the average, than the entire sample in expressed level of commitment to Transcendental Meaning in Life.

When we have more than one AID analysis reported on a single dependent variable, an indication of the relative effectiveness of the predictors on each run is available. That is the percentage of the total variance accounted for by the set of predictors in any single run. For example, the characteristics separating groups on this run of 31 status type variables accounted for 13.9% of the total variability of all 4,444 persons across the whole range of scores on Scale 28. The next analysis accounts for 48.7% of the total variability. This means that the second set of predictive characteristics is relatively more powerful in telling about scores on the dependent variable than the first set.

A very important matter in understanding AID results is the nature and content of the set of predictor variables used in any given analysis. In reporting literally hundreds of AID runs we are not going to list for each run the specific set of predictors included. Rather the text will contain a brief description of the type of predictors included in each analysis. Further specific information is available upon request.

However, because each individual analysis is limited to the set of predictors used, it must be understood that one cannot simply add together the results of several AID runs to get a composite picture of groups or individuals likely to be high or low scoring on the dependent variable. For example, it would be incorrect to add the two analyses reported here and to conclude that the group saying they are less religious than mother and are under age 24 are *also* liberal theologically and doubt their faith. The two groups are completely distinct, segregated out by separate analyses.

18. We will repeat once more the basic information available from AID analysis to describe subgroups. After this no further AID information will be reported. It is available upon request.

High group:　Q3 and 4　　Scale 44　　Q3 and 4　　Scale 66
　　　　　　　Q4　　Scale 41
　　　　　　　N= 764　　$\overline{Y}$ (on dependent variable) = 82.2　　s = 3.8

Low group:　Q1　　Scale 44,　　Q1　　Scale 66
　　　　　　　N = 656　　$\overline{Y}$ (on dependent variable) = 64.4　　s = 8.4

Percentage of variance explained in this analysis = 48.7.

19. Percentage of variance explained in Analysis #1 = 12.7; in analysis #2 = 48.7. Characteristics like age, region, and sex that had shown effect in analysis #1 were included in analysis #2. The second AID program did not select any of them at any step. AID analysis is something like a horse race. It picks the "winner" in each step. The "winner" is the single characteristic in the set that accounts for the greatest amount of variance.

20. Percentage of variance explained in analysis #1 = 17.3; analysis #2 = 10.3.

21. Heider, F., 1958, pp. 218-222.

22. Morris, C. M., 1956. The 13 "Ways of Life" used in *A Study of Generations* were developed by Morris. They were used by permission of University of Chicago Press.

23. Due to their length the items on this dimension and the others from the "Ways of Life" will not be reproduced. A representative "Way" will be given. Morris (1956) gives text of all "Ways" in full. This dimension includes Ways 1, 3, 10, and 13 by Morris's original numbering. They are items 147, 149, 156, and 159 in the *A Study of Generations* questionnaire. The reliability of the scale is Rxx = .53. The complex nature of the items and response categories beclouds the reliability of the three scales. We expect further technical work would sharpen the scoring procedure and increase the reliability of the scale.

24. WAY 1: In this "design for living" the individual actively participates in the social life of his community, not to change it primarily, but to understand, appreciate, and preserve the best that man has attained. Excessive desires should be avoided and moderation sought. One wants the good things of life but in an orderly way. Life is to have clarity, balance, refinement, control. Vulgarity, great enthusiasm, irrational behavior, impatience, indulgence are to be avoided. Friendship is to be esteemed but not easy intimacy with many people. Life is to have discipline, intelligibility, good manners, predictability. Social changes are to be made slowly and carefully, so that what has been achieved in human culture is not lost. The individual should be active physically and socially, but not in a hectic or radical way. Restraint and intelligence should give order to an active life.

25. The items on this dimension are Ways 5, 6, 7, 8, and 12 by Morris's (1956) original numbering. They are items 151, 152, 153, 154, and 158 in *A Study of Generations* questionnaire. The reliability of the scale is Rxx = .53.

26. WAY 8: Enjoyment should be the keynote of life. Not the hectic search for intense and exciting pleasures, but the enjoyment of the simple and easily obtainable pleasures: the pleasures of just existing, of savory food, of comfortable surroundings of talking with friends, of rest and relaxation. A home that is warm and comfortable, chairs and a bed that are soft, a kitchen well stocked with food, a door open to the entrance of friends—this is the place to live. Body at ease,

relaxed, calm in its movements, not hurried, breath slow, willing to nod and to rest, grateful to the world that is its food—so should the body be. Driving ambition and the fanaticism of ascetic ideals are the signs of discontented people who have lost the capacity to float in the stream of simple, carefree, wholesome enjoyment.

27. The items on this dimension are ways 2, 4, 9, and 11 by Morris's (1956) original numbering. They are items 148, 150, 155, and 157 in *A Study of Generations* questionnaire. The reliability of the scale is Rxx = .52.

28. WAY 11: The contemplative life is the good life. The external world is no fit habitat for man. It is too big, too cold, too pressing. Rather, it is the life turned inward that is rewarding. The rich internal world of ideals, of sensitive feelings, of reverie, of self-knowledge is man's true home. By the cultivation of the self within, man alone becomes human. Only then does there arise deep sympathy with all that lives, an understanding of the suffering inherent in life, a realization of the futility of aggressive action, the attainment of contemplative joy. Conceit then falls away and austerity is dissolved. In giving up the world one finds the larger and finer sea of the inner self.

29. Morris, 1956, p. 198.

30. Kluckhohn, C. K. M., 1954, pp. 921-976.

31. Festinger, L., Riecken, W., and Schachter, S., 1956.

32. We recognize that the correlations of Scales 52, 53, and 54 with other scales are not very strong. We attribute this in part to the low reliability of these three scales. As mentioned in note 23 we expect the reliability could be raised by further technical work. We could use a difference score for each individual rather than his raw score on the seven point rating scale. What we are drawing attention to in presenting the correlations is the consistency of the pattern and the theoretical implications of that consistency.

33. This statement is based upon the results of two-way analysis of variance in which age and level of education were compared against all 78 scales. The criteria set for reporting significant results from analysis of variance, that will also likely have practical significance, are given in Appendix A, p. 354. All analysis of variance results reported here and in subsequent chapters have met those criteria. If further specific information is desired, it is available upon request.

34. Two-way analysis of variance. See note 33.

There is no longer a Christian mind. It is commonplace
that the mind of modern man has been secularized. For
instance, it has been deprived of any orientation towards
the supernatural. Tragic as this factor is, it would not
be so desperately tragic had the Christian mind held out
against the secular drift. But unfortunately the Christian
mind has succumbed to the secular drift with a degree
of weakness and nervelessness unmatched in Christian
history.

—Harry Blamires, *The Christian Mind*

5. The Heart of Lutheran Piety

*This chapter discusses the 15 dimensions that form the heart of Lu-
theran piety. They are a combination of beliefs, values, attitudes, opinions, and behaviors. They describe the Lutheran who values a transcendent dimension of life, knows a personal, caring God, is relatively
certain of his faith, is biblically-oriented, considers his faith important,
and takes a positive attitude toward life and death. The underlying
quality that binds the 15 dimensions together into a single factor is a
quality of life that could be called a gospel-orientation.*

*The dimensions in this chapter are unfolded in a way that can answer
questions asked of the research team when they began the study.*

    *Do Lutherans know the gospel? How would you classify them
theologically? What is their view of God? Do many feel that only
the Lutheran church has the truth?*

In short, the data have lead the research team to these conclusions:

    *About three out of five Lutherans hold the values, beliefs, attitudes,
and feelings that are embodied in this factor. About this many
Lutherans apparently know and understand the gospel.*

    *Most Lutherans reject a fundamentalist or a liberal stance, choosing
rather a conservative theological position and reflecting this in
their reports of what they believe.*

    *Though most Lutherans agree to the exclusive truth claim of the
Christian faith, they are not rejecting in their attitudes toward*

> *others. On the contrary, they both acknowledge their oneness with other Lutherans and express a desire to experience the catholicity of the Christian church.*
>
> *More of the younger Lutherans are conscious of a trinitarian God who is both immanent and transcendent, whereas older Lutherans tend to recognize his transcendence only.*
>
> *Most Lutherans fail to recognize rightly the unity of the two natures of Christ—both his divinity and his humanity.*
>
> *Some Lutherans equate their church organization with the truth claim of Christianity and cling to the ideal of a Christian Utopia. These, however, are a minority.*

The massive and decisive struggle in the last quarter of the twentieth century is going to be about beliefs. In every area of human activity the decisive questions are narrowing down to issues of belief. The whole body of science, all branches, is now known to rest upon belief.[1] In medicine *how* to do healing is no longer crucial. *What* to do is where the agony is. Synthesis of life, abortion, euthanasia, transplants—beliefs, not techniques, will decide these issues. Physics, chemistry, engineering, biology, and space-science are in the same condition. It's not *how* but *what? whether? What is it for?* Belief will decide, not *truth,* not *wisdom,* not *justice.*

The failures of social planners and social engineers force a reexamination of hidden beliefs about the nature of man. Welfare, housing developments, racial justice—name the game, and the real issue emerging in all of them is belief.

Economists say that what blocks economic progress in underdeveloped countries is belief.[2] Sociologists have long treated belief as crucial for understanding human behavior but today even more so.[3] Psychiatrists and psychologists recognize that a major cause of emotional difficulty today is lack of a coherent belief system.[4] Some openly acknowledge that a major cause of change for the better in psychotherapy is the adoption by the patient of the therapist's belief system.[5] B. F. Skinner's latest pronouncement that we must give up the idea of human freedom has already divided the mental health professions.[6] The division is on belief about man, not on empirical data.

As we move into this era where beliefs are going to be all-important, we can know what Lutherans believe. The benchmark established in *A Study of Generations* will let Lutherans in years to come know where they were in 1970 and where they have come in what they believe.

What is a Lutheran? What do Lutherans believe? about God? about Jesus Christ? Do Lutherans know what it means to be saved? Do they understand and feel the gospel? Is there understanding of justification by faith alone? What is the relationship between belief and prejudice? These are the questions we shall respond to in the next chapters.

LAW AND GOSPEL

The proper distinction between law and gospel is a highly prized goal for Lutheran theology. It is possible to understand the whole history of Lutheran theology to the present day as a continuous struggle for clarification of the law–gospel relationship. To every move in the theological debate across the centuries the best of Lutheran theology has always responded out of the resources of the distinction between law and gospel. Our data show that this debate is not merely an abstract theological exercise but that law and gospel are deeply embedded realities in the *faith* and *misbelief* of Lutherans. Within the Lutheran community of faith, the struggle of faith against misbelief, in all of its existential starkness for each man, is the gospel yearning to be born anew each day, reaching for a firm grip on the fact of redemption in Christ.

When Lutherans are asked about belief, sooner or later it comes down to law and gospel. In the last quarter of this century, when men cry out for belief, Lutherans will respond with law and gospel as they have always done in the past, because this is reality for them. This chapter and the next present two factors which emerged from our data. The first, to be discussed here as *the heart of Lutheran piety*, shows that the gospel is a present reality and is known and believed among Lutherans. The second, to be discussed in Chapter 6 as misbelief or a law orientation among Lutherans, shows that the law of God in all of its accusing and judging power brings about the kind of misbelief long predicted by Lutheran theologians.[7] In preparing to study these two chapters bear in mind this summation by Gerhard Forde, representing the insight of theologians:

> What faith should do, however, is to enable man to make the distinction between law and gospel. Apart from faith man is bound to look for his own 'gospel' in the law and thus refuse to accept law for what it is. In faith man learns to distinguish law from gospel and thus to allow law to be used in its proper manner. Faith sees that man apart from faith *misuses* the law, which then becomes for him the source of either despair or presumption. Faith sees that man's real problem with the law is that in unfaith he attempts to use what knowledge he has to gain heaven for himself, or to tyrannize his fellow man, or perhaps even to attempt to bring in a 'heaven' on earth in the form of some sort of utopia. Faith, because it trusts totally in God's grace, sees that all of these uses are in fact misuses of the law because they are presumptuous.[8]

The empirical reality we have found in *A Study of Generations* fits that description of law and gospel in men's lives. Now we turn to the first of the second order factors that emerged from the data, the heart of Lutheran piety.

Do Lutherans Know the Gospel?

When we look at all the dimensions of this first factor, both the positive and negative ones, the total impression is that the factor describes the type of Lutheran who has a grasp of the gospel (see table 5.1). This is the most cohesive and powerful thrust among Lutherans. For these reasons we speak of the first factor as describing the heart of Lutheran

Table 5.1   Factor 1: The Heart of Lutheran Piety
Lay People Only (Parent Scales)

Load	Dimension	Title
Positive		
.80	28	Transcendental Meaning in Life
.74	14	A Personal Caring God
.73	66	Emotional Certainty of Faith
.72	44	Fundamentalism—Liberalism
.67	46	Importance of Christian Practices in My Life
.65	71	Attitude Toward Life and Death
.55	41	Personal Piety
.54	19	Religious Experience
.52	58	Awareness of the Immanent Trinity
.52	6	Divinity of Jesus
.48	16	The Exclusive Truth Claim of Christianity Exaggerated
.44	36	Christian Utopianism
.25	8	Biblical Knowledge
Negative		
−.29	15	Salvation by Works
−.32	29	Values of Self-Improvement

piety. This does not say that a majority of Lutherans typify this belief system. A rough estimate shows that about 60% of Lutherans tend to believe in this way. Three out of five likely have at least a rudimentary grasp of the gospel.

The dimension that contributes the most to the heart of Lutheran piety is Transcendental Meaning in Life (Scale 28). This dimension of value has been discussed fully in the preceding chapter. The "type" of Lutheran who knows the gospel of justification by faith accepts a transcendental dimension as basic in his life. He is oriented toward the "spiritual" rather than the "material," the "sacred" rather than the "secular," the "supernatural" rather than the "natural." He knows there is more to life than what he can feel, see, smell, hear, or taste. He knows he is in a larger cosmos than what is immediately evident, and he accepts responsibility for his behavior in that larger cosmos. He puts the vertical dimension of his relationship with God together with the horizontal dimension of his relationship with men. (See Scale 28 in Appendix C, Section IV.)

The importance of the transcendent dimension is highlighted by the negative association of the dimension of values of self-development with this factor. As mentioned in Chapter 4 the transcendent view and the focus upon self-development are logically polar opposites. They show up as opposites in real life also. The person who typifies the heart of Lutheran piety also tends to reject the idea that his life has primary meaning in values limited to this world.

Given commitment to that transcendental dimension, Lutherans who understand the gospel tend to reject belief in salvation by works. That is to say, belief in salvation by works is negatively associated with the heart of Lutheran piety. Many Lutherans recognize the grace of God clearly enough to reject a rather simple, crass statement of "works righteousness." There may be some confusion or lack of clarity about the whole range of significance of God's grace, but it is subtle and difficult to trace. It is clear that the obvious statements of "religion-in-general" folk religiosity that hold "doing right" to be all that counts before God and men, are rejected by those Lutherans who typify the beliefs, values, attitudes, and behaviors of this factor.

Following are the remaining dimensions that extend our understanding of the Lutherans who live in a gospel-orientation.

KNOWING A PERSONAL, CARING GOD

The doctrine of divine providence, that is, the belief that God personally guides my life and rules all of creation in a meaningful way, has not been very popular in theology recently. Nevertheless, Lutherans as a group show a very strong awareness of God's providential care. The dimension (Scale 14) comes through most sharply in two items (19 and 20) dealing with God's caring for me and my accountability to him. These two items are the best discriminators on the dimension. I know about God's care through Scripture (Item 22). I also know God answers my prayers (Item 24). I am convinced that there is a divine plan and purpose for my life (Item 49). The remaining items show belief in Jesus as Savior and as present in my life (16, 33, 57, and 58). He reveals God to me. I know I am saved and forgiven. I am aware of hell as a real possibility (Item 27). I live my life as a faithful steward, striving to follow biblical principles (Items 23, 25, 50, and 52).

The overwhelming endorsement of these items by Lutherans indicates that this dimension is crucial to the "folk piety" of Lutherans. From 80-95% agree with all items except the statement about the reality of hell (65% agree) and the statement that all property really belongs to God (69% agree). Agreement with all items produces a score of 135. The average for all laity ($\bar{X} = 128.23$) is very close to that maximum. Clearly almost all Lutherans agree with the content of this dimension. Britton calls this the traditional Protestant view of the meaning of life.[9] God has a beneficent plan for the world as a whole which can be carried out fully only if each person is faithful to his responsibility.

This dimension (Scale 14) includes items which show a knowledge of the gospel of Jesus Christ (16, 29, 33, 57, 58), at least in the verbal form of these statements. They are not as close to the heart of the dimension as those items which show belief in providence, but they are a part of the sense of God's caring for me. The gospel is known. Christ's work of forgiveness is one with God's care for me. This is the simple man of faith walking humbly with his God.

Multivariate Analysis. Only God knows the total amount of human effort spent through the centuries trying to find for oneself or others this kind of simple faith. Our work shows that a strong sense of God's personal caring for me is associated with commitment to transcendental meaning in life (Scale 28) and with a moderate, conservative, or fundamentalist doctrinal position (Scale 44) for one group with high awareness of God's care. Identification with the model of religious belief set by mother and having a father highly active in congregational service describes a second group. It is mother's belief but father's activity that combine to support development of belief in a loving, caring God. Rejection of belief in a personal, caring God is part of a broader rejection of traditional beliefs regarding God (Scales 28, 66, 44, 16). A given person apparently does not reject parts or pieces of the belief system of Christianity but rather tends to turn away from the entire system in a consistent pattern.

It is the presence or absence of other dimensions of belief that is most important in predicting whether or not a person believes in providence. A person can be 15 or 65, have a graduate degree or less than an eighth grade education, be a man or a woman. If he rejects the supernatural, doubts the existence of God, and rejects the church, he is not very likely to have a strong sense of God's providential care.

AN EMOTIONAL CERTAINTY

Emotional certainty about faith in God and Jesus together with warm feelings about liturgical worship, family worship, talking about the faith, and prayer, make up one pole of the next dimension, Emotional Certainty of Faith (Scale 19). Doubt and rejection of religious practices is the other extreme. As a group Lutherans express certainty of faith and good feelings about the practice of worship, prayer, and sharing the faith. The average for the whole group is 51.04, very close to the highest possible score, 54, obtained by strong agreement with all items. Three out of four Lutherans are quite certain about their faith and generally feel positive about expressing it in worship, prayer, and conversation.

Seven out of ten Lutherans say they have no doubts about the divinity of Jesus. Somewhat less than six in ten claim the same degree of certainty about the existence of God. There is more certainty of belief in Jesus than in God.

Those who are sure of their faith also tend to be those who feel best about worship, prayer, and sharing. A high level of certainty and effective religious practice go together.

Multivariate Analysis. For the kind of decisions the church must make in terms of program, direction, but above all in its theological task, the hierarchical nature of the belief system must be understood. All researchers in the area of beliefs, values, and attitudes have recognized the complex, network-like, hierarchical nature of belief systems. Of course everything in the "mind" is correlated with everything else in the "mind." There is no other way it can be as long as we remain human beings.

Without necessarily performing a mentalistic reductionism slight-of-hand trick, we can understand variables such as age, sex, and education as proxy variables for mental or "mind" events. What is age? a measure of time? of physical deterioration or development? of passage through life stages? Just what is age a measure of? The same questions can be asked of other such variables. All are related in some fashion to man's conscious self-awareness.

This being the case we feel it is a legitimate use of social science techniques to unravel some of the complexities of belief systems in terms of the hierarchical ordering of dimensions of belief. What are the most central dimensions of belief? If some insights into that question and its answers can be obtained by research, then practical information is made available for the practical decisions which the church must make. The multivariate analysis tells us about age, sex, education, and the like. It can also suggest what are the most central dimensions of belief.

From age 15 to 22 there is more doubt and questioning of faith and practice though not actual rejection of them. When education, sex, age, church body, size of congregation, region, education, occupation, family status, and employment status are simultaneously compared to this scale, we identify women over 24 years old as showing considerably more centainty of faith and males under 24 as showing considerably less. However, age and sex do not tell as much about certainty of faith as do beliefs and values. The averages of groups divided by sex and age are considerably closer to the average for everybody than the groups singled out by beliefs and values in further analyses.

If I know only a person's age and sex, I really don't know much at all about whether he or she is going to be fairly certain about faith or have doubts. Further analysis shows that if I know whether a person accepts or rejects transcendental meaning in life (Scale 28), is or is not interested in personal piety (Scale 41), is or is not happy with the church, whether he thinks he is more or less religious than his mother, then I know much more about what level of certainty of faith he is likely to show. I don't need to know his age or sex. Anyway there really isn't much I can do about his age or sex. If I should want to increase the level of certainty of faith, I at least have a chance to bring about a change of belief regarding the transcendent dimension or a change in pious behaviors.

FUNDAMENTALIST OR LIBERAL?

Most Lutherans are neither fundamentalists nor liberals. A dimension of fundamentalism-liberalism composed of 13 items emerged from the data (Scale 44). Each item first gives a statement of belief couched in traditional doctrinal language. Then there are five choices for response. The content of items and response choices are provided in Scale 44. (See Appendix C, Section IV.)

In each case, the first response stresses strong agreement with the initial traditional belief statement and adds the provision that if a person doesn't believe exactly the same, he is not true to the Christian faith. The second response expresses agreement with the belief statement but does not require exact agreement in order to be true to the Christian faith. The next two responses move slightly away from the belief statement or change it into nontraditional language. The final response is a denial of the original statement and an expression of a humanistic view of the subject of the item.

The items are based upon previous research that established them as a measurement of fundamentalism–liberalism. The first response is consistently chosen by fundamentalist groups and the last response by liberal groups.[10]

Research in religion provides powerful support for the recognition of a dimension of fundamentalism–liberalism.[11] Individuals and groups are located along this dimension by a large number of studies. We find this dimension on the factor which we claim points to a gospel-orientation among Lutherans. Inevitably this raises a most difficult and sensitive question: What is the relationship between "knowing the gospel" and the content of specific doctrinal claims? Does "knowing the gospel" mean that one *must* have either this or that doctrinal position? We do not wish to give the appearance of trying to answer that question by our data. That is an issue that empirical research cannot address directly. We will report the data fully, interpreting it as objectively as possible. Others must determine what, if anything, it says to this question. However, we feel that the matter that needs the closest scrutiny is the degree to which this factor as a whole reflects a gospel-orientation.

On the fundamentalism–liberalism dimension the average for all laymen, 93.33, places most Lutherans at the second response, tending to agree with the initial statement but not requiring that another person agree exactly in order to be a true Christian. The weight of Lutheranism is on a conservative belief system, neither fundamentalist nor liberal.

More Lutherans *describe* themselves as conservative rather than fundamentalist, neo-orthodox, or liberal. A single item asked Lutherans to describe their theological position. The choices were Fundamentalist, Conservative, Neo-Orthodox, or Liberal. The results are given in Table 5.2.

Table 5.2   Percentage Distribution for Clergy and Laity Combined
on Item 718

Item 718.	Which of the following theological positions is nearest your own?	Percentage Response
A.	I believe all things in Scripture are literal and historical (Fundamentalist).	14%
B.	I hold or retain the essential beliefs of the Christian faith (Conservative).	44%
C.	I retain the basic faith but reinterpret it in the light of today's situation (Neo-Orthodox).	10%
D.	I am willing to change some aspects of the faith in the light of new understanding (Liberal).	26%

The largest group, 44%, chose to call themselves conservative. This self-
description supports interpretation of the results on the fundamentalism–
liberalism dimension as showing Lutherans to be conservative. However,
we can ask what the label conservative apparently means to Lutherans.

Lutherans retain an historic, traditional system of beliefs but don't
insist on it for others. That is the major difference between the first and
second response on all items. For Lutherans the idea of heresy—that
false beliefs *within the church* can be identified—would be a difficult one
to accept. There is an unwillingness to label other Christians as false
believers, or to require exact agreement with the doctrinal statements.
However, there is recognition of unbelief and rejection of non-Christian
concepts. The fourth and fifth responses are chosen by an average of 10%
of the respondents.

Positively stated, this means that most Lutherans accept other Lutherans and other Christians as fellow Christians. Several individual items
show this clearly. They are given in Table 5.3. Lutherans want fellowship
with each other (Item 510). Two out of three Lutherans agree that
merger into one Lutheran church is desirable.

Most Lutherans (68%) do not see themselves as more strict doctrinally
than members of other church bodies (Item 308). Most (74%) deny
that they are more narrow-minded or exclusivistic than other Christians
(Item 319). This may be either accurate self-description or it may show
an intense desire not to be different from other Christians. Seven out of
ten Lutherans reject statements that they have different beliefs (Item
332), different worship practices (Item 361), different ethnic back-

Table 5.3 Lutheran Ecumenicity as Expressed in Percentages of Response to a Variety of Items (Lay and Clergy Combined)

Item	Strongly Agree	Agree	Disagree	Strongly Disagree
308. Lutherans are more strict in what they believe than members of most other church bodies.	4%	25%	61%	7%°
317. Lutherans are more like Roman Catholics than like Southern Baptists.	9	59	23	2
319. By comparison with other Christians, Lutherans are more narrow minded and keep more to themselves.	2	20	64	10
329. Lutherans are not different from other Christians.	10	67	18	1
332. A Lutheran is different from other Christians because he has different beliefs.	2	22	64	7
336. Lutherans believe more strongly in salvation by faith alone than other Christians do.	7	36	49	3
359. Their German or Scandinavian origin makes Lutherans different from other Christians.	1	10	72	12
361. A Lutheran is different from other Christians because he has different worship practices.	2	24	64	6
510. A merger of all Lutheran groups in the United States into one organization is desirable.	19	48	23	6

Item	Agree	Disagree	?
40. Unity among Christians can come only after complete doctrinal agreement.	34%	52%	12%

° Percentages of nonresponse account for the difference between 100% and total of percentages for each item.

grounds (Item 359) that make them stand out, or that they are distinctive because of some unusual quality to their spiritual lives. Many (52%) do not believe that complete agreement on all doctrinal matters is necessary for unity (Item 40). A slight majority (52%) also deny that they are different because they believe more strongly in salvation by faith alone than other Christians do.

The general picture which emerges is that most Lutherans do not think they are different from other Christians. They are willing to allow for divergence and variety within the large framework of the faith. This subject will be dealt with again in Chapter 12 where we will look at church body affiliation and clergy–lay differences. At this point we wish to clarify what a conservative belief stance is. Most Lutherans do not wish to require others to believe exactly the same way they do. For most Lutherans this is the major difference between a fundamentalist and a conservative position.

BIBLICAL CONTENT OF LUTHERAN CONSERVATISM

As a group, most Lutherans say they believe in the historical truth of the birth of Jesus of a virgin, his death, and his actual resurrection from the tomb. They believe in the Bible as God's Word, in the law of God as a guide and judge of men's lives. They believe in Christ's death as an atonement for sin. They believe in the gifts of the Spirit, Baptism, the reality of the Eucharist, the return of Christ, and God's response to intercessory prayer. They do not accept a simple categorical view of human nature, that man is totally depraved, but rather prefer a more complex understanding. They do not hold a simple view of the Office of the Ministry and the power to forgive sins but rather prefer a more complex idea. They do not hold a view that the theory of evolution is contrary to the Christian faith. In short, Lutherans maintain the historic quality of the faith, basing it upon the reality of Christ's birth, death, and resurrection, and believing it to be the way of salvation. They are unwilling to say that there is one true visible church to which every Christian must belong.

DOCTRINES FIRMLY AND LOOSELY HELD BY LUTHERANS

If Lutherans tend to turn away from a concept of heresy and do not see themselves as different from other Christians, what doctrines do they hold? Some sort of classification of doctrines into fundamental–nonfundamental, pure or mixed, has long been present in Lutheran theology as a practical necessity.[12] However, these classification schemes have all been attempts at a normative rule: what doctrines must be held in order to be a Christian and what doctrines can be confused or rejected by persons who are still Christians?

Our data cannot answer that question but they do tell us which doc-trines Lutherans hold to most firmly and which are more variable.[13] The doctrines Lutherans hold most firmly are belief in the virgin birth of Jesus (Item 77), the historical resurrection of Jesus (Item 78), the vicarious atonement of Jesus (Item 81), the real presence of Jesus in the Eucharist (Item 85), and the Ten Commandments as God's law (Item 86). These are the doctrines which most Lutherans are inclined to see as essential to the Christian faith. The emphasis is heavily Christo-logical, not an unexpected find in the light of the long history of Lu-theran theology. To believe and know Christ is to believe and know the gospel. Lutherans feel that to reject Christ and his work is to reject the Christian faith.

Those doctrines about which Lutherans are most inconsistent are the return of Jesus (Item 80), contemporary miraculous intervention by God (Item 82), and Baptism (Item 84). Here they are willing to express a wide range of positions, excluding only the scientific-humanistic denial of these doctrines.

Some Lutherans insist that certain doctrines are the most basic and most essential to the faith and regard persons who disagree as outside of the church. The average of the percentages of response to the first (fundamentalist) choice for five doctrinal items is 14%. It is fair to say that one out of seven Lutherans is likely to hold these five doctrines very firmly. This identifiable group takes a firm and exclusive position on the verbal inspiration of Scripture (Item 76); insists that charismatic gifts, including speaking with tongues, are essential to the faith (Item 79); and believes man is totally evil (Item 88). They insist upon stringent discipline of sinners (Item 87) and rejection of the theory of evolution (Item 83) in order to be a true Christian. Together with a high stress upon the importance of Baptism,[14] this exclusivistic position reflects a charismatic Lutheran fundamentalism.

The authority of Scripture is a most crucial and perplexing problem for all Christians today. The appearance of the item (76) dealing with Scripture on a subdimension of charismatic Lutheran fundamentalism suggests that for Lutherans at least the strongest commitment to a doc-trine of verbal inspiration of Scripture exists among those likely to hold fundamentalist views. Lutherans who are not willing to insist upon charismatic gifts, the total depravity of man, an anti-evolution stance, and stringent spiritual discipline may maintain the authority of Scrip-ture without insisting upon verbal inspiration.

Multivariate Analysis. Characteristics that do the best job in telling whether or not a person is highly conservative, leaning toward fundamentalism, or more liberal are, of course, the convictions he reflects on other dimensions of belief. High commitment to transcendental meaning in life (Scale 28) and high commitment to identification of a visible church body with the exclusive truth of Christianity (Scale 16) are associated with a tendency toward fundamentalism. Being more liberal is best predicted by rejection of the exclusive claim of Christianity that salvation is found only in Christ (Scale 16).

Church body membership makes a difference but not as much as the two beliefs mentioned above. Within the subgroup highly committed to transcendental meaning in life (Scale 28) but more moderate regarding the exclusive truth claim of Christianity (Scale 16) members of the LC-MS are slightly more conservative than members of the ALC and LCA. Here again, having a father active in church work predicts a more conservative direction. Apparently the model presented by an active father is a rather potent force in affecting religious commitment in a positive direction.

CHRISTIAN PRACTICES

Ninety-five percent of Lutherans state that faith, prayer, Baptism, and Communion are important to them. Only 5% indicate that they are of little or no importance to them. Only 1% state that "faith" is unimportant. These four items form Scale 46, Importance of Christian Practices in My Life.

There is one surprise in the percentages. When the percentage of persons rating prayer, Communion, and Baptism as "very important" is examined, 54% state their Baptism is "very important." This compares with 45% who see prayer and Communion as "very important." Baptism has a stronger pull on people's emotions than either prayer or Communion. "Faith" is "very important" to 68%. Almost unanimously Lutherans state that they feel their religion is important to them.

With almost every one saying faith, sacraments, and prayer are important, this dimension does not tell us much. The most we can say is that the appearance of this scale on the factor of the heart of Lutheran piety tells us that Lutherans with a gospel orientation also feel that faith and the sacraments are important to them. That is not inconsequential. It does mean that Lutherans value the sacraments, prayer, and faith. They have not rejected the sacramental emphasis of Lutheran theology.

ATTITUDES TOWARD LIFE AND DEATH

A complex dimension of 13 items adds attitudes toward life and death to the heart of Lutheran piety (Scale 71). The strongest component is acceptance of death as a friend, as the beginning of a new life (Items 69b and 71b). Several items reject the idea of death as something unknown or as simply the end (Items 69a, 69c, 71a, 71c, and 71d). The individual scoring highly on this dimension says that God is the greatest influence on his life and rejects "friends" as major influences on his life and personality (Items 205f and 205i). He does not accept a pessimistic view of human nature (Item 60a). He rejects a legalistic, rigid, controlling stance toward interpersonal relationships (Item 70a). Finally, he places considerable importance on family devotions as an ideal and as a source of strength (Items 730a and 730b).

The average for all laity ($\overline{X} = 90.7$) places most Lutherans close to the highest score possible, 101. A view of death that is calm, serene, and hopeful, and a view of life tending toward pious optimism is most characteristic of Lutherans.

Multivariate Analysis. Analysis of this dimension by simultaneous comparison of many characteristics shows that when there is certainty of faith (Scale 66), belief in a personal, caring God (Scale 14), and personal practice of piety (Scale 41), there is generally also serenity regarding death.

AGE AND THE HEART OF LUTHERAN PIETY

A common pattern is evident when age is compared to all of the above dimensions contributing to the heart of Lutheran piety. Beginning at age 15, there is a drop in scores to the lowest average score on all dimensions at age 21-22. Following that age, there is a sudden, sharp increase in scores to about age 30. Then the curve flattens out but continues a gradual, steady rise to age 65.

Our data alone do not say whether this common pattern reflects a process. We can't say that the 21-22-year-olds of 1970 will become more like the older Lutherans of 1970 as they grow older themselves. However, many studies done years ago showed precipitous declines in religious belief for the college age group, 18-22.[15] If that generation of, let's say 1950, had maintained a rejection of religion, and if Lutherans of roughly ages 38-42 reflected that influence, we would not expect to find them scoring consistently higher on dimensions of belief.

Only a longitudinal study of the same persons for a long period can answer whether people who experience a decline in religious belief between ages 15-22 tend to return to a more religious stance as they get older. Our data would fit that hypothesis, yet it's not the right kind of data to really answer the question. We can only raise the question, say our data do not contradict that idea, and hope for further research to answer it.

COMMON PATTERN OF INFLUENCE

When the dimensions of belief reported thus far were compared to large numbers of other external and internal characteristics, in each case the most powerful characteristic influencing these dimensions of belief was commitment or lack of commitment to the value of Transcendental Meaning in Life (Scale 28). This underscores the significance of that dimension. Once the basic commitment to acceptance of a supernatural dimension to life is made, relationships to other persons, to the world, other beliefs and values, attitudes and behavior, flow from that root choice.

Lutherans' commitment to the supernatural is evident. The strength and power of that commitment is supported by the data of A *Study of Generations*. We are beginning to see the shape of the answers to the questions put at the beginning of this chapter. Another answer is also beginning to take shape. Our data say there is yet among us a "Christian mind." That "Christian mind" is the entire system of thought and activity which holds the source of all things to be in the divine reality which is outside of this world. It sees life in this world as deriving from that other world. The final destiny of man lies outside of this world beyond physical death. This world is governed by a beneficent God who preserves and keeps it and men. The meaning of the world is to be found outside of it. Lutherans reject a secularism that finds the meaning of the world only within the world itself.

How Do Lutherans View God and Jesus?

Two dimensions that contribute to the heart of Lutheran piety deal with Lutherans' view of God and Jesus. The first, View of God (Scale 58), could be named Immanent Trinity. It shows belief in God as a trinitarian God, "three persons, yet one God," who is deeply involved in human life both through control of grand design and through other people. The second, View of Jesus as Divine (Scale 6), shows a belief in the divine nature of Jesus as distinct from his humanity.

VIEW OF GOD

The dimension combines views of God which are likely to be accepted, rejected, or to be quite controversial. Three out of four Lutherans agree that God is "three persons, yet one God" (Item 226), that he is "at work in my life" (Item 223), and that he is "friendly and loving" (Item 231). On the other hand, about four out of five Lutherans reject the statements that God is "met only in His Word and Sacraments" (Item 227) and that he "works in the world only through Christians" (Item 233). Three out of four reject the statement that God is "revealed only by the Holy Spirit" (Item 234).

Lutherans are almost evenly divided on whether God "comes to me through other people" (Item 221), "makes things work out all right" (Item 228), and "tests people" (Item 230). These are likely to be the most controversial views of God among Lutherans.

The three items rejected by most Lutherans are statements which have in common the word "only." They are not willing to declare that God has limited himself to any *one* way of being in contact with people.

This fits the findings on the fundamentalism–liberalism dimension. Most Lutherans tend to reject exclusive or limiting statements of religious belief.

The three items that divide Lutherans almost evenly deal with belief that God is actively involved in my life, either through other people or by his control of what happens to me. Many Lutherans agree that God is "at work in my life" but are not very sure just how.

The person who agrees with all items in this scale is expressing an expanded traditional view of God, adding a strong emphasis upon God's immanence to the traditional view of God as transcendant.

Multivariate Analysis. Persons who see the triune God as intimately involved in their lives tend to be those who believe strongly in *both* the divinity and humanity of Jesus or believe most strongly in the divinity of Jesus and less strongly in his humanity. They are more commonly from 15 to 44 years old. Persons who reject a view of the triune God as intimately involved in their lives tend to hold either a sharply limited view of Jesus' divinity and humanity or a limited view of his divinity and emphasize Jesus' humanity. They also more frequently reject commitment to a transcendental dimension (Scale 28) and do not engage in personal practice of piety (Scale 41).

Figure 5.1 gives scores on this dimension plotted by age. While we again see a dip at age 21-22, the most startling characteristic is the decline of the curve as it moves to age 65. Younger Lutherans are most likely to have a strong belief that the triune God is directly involved in their lives, combining the transcendent and immanent activity of God. Older Lutherans are more likely to limit their view of God to the transcendent dimension alone.

Does this finding reflect a change in the view of God taking place within Lutheranism? Will younger Lutherans of today change their view of God as they get older? We can only say that as it is now younger Lutherans tend to have a different idea of God than older Lutherans do. Possible long range effects of this fact could prove to be far ranging in the life of the church. If an idea of God as immanent *and* transcendent prevails, changes in worship, education, preaching, congregational structure, and relationship to the world would have to take place. The emphasis of the recent past has been largely a reflection of God's transcendence—his holiness, glory, honor. A widespread change in consciousness of God would require adaptation at all levels of Christian life.

VIEW OF JESUS

What do Lutherans believe about Jesus? The heart of Lutheran piety includes a strong conviction that Jesus is the divine Son of God. Two dimensions formed out of a group of items designed to assess belief in the divine and human natures of Jesus. Lutherans hold separate dimen-

Figure 5.1   View of God
Average Scores Plotted by Two-Year Age Groups
Immanent Trinity (Scale 58)
Divinity of Jesus (Scale 6)

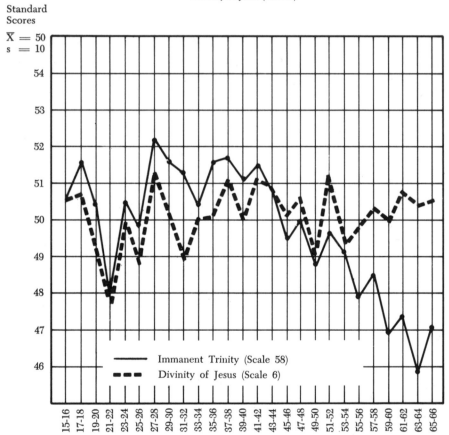

Standard
Scores

$\overline{X} = 50$
$s = 10$

Immanent Trinity (Scale 58)

Divinity of Jesus (Scale 6)

Two-Year Age Groups   15-66

sions of belief regarding Jesus' divinity and humanity. The dimension of belief in Jesus as divine (Scale 6) is part of the heart of Lutheran piety while belief in the human nature of Jesus (Scale 5) is not.[16]

This does not mean that the humanity of Jesus is repulsive or foreign to Lutheran piety. Rather, the divinity of Jesus is strongly emphasized while Jesus' human nature is underemphasized.[17] However, in terms of gross percentage of response to the items, a minority of Lutherans fully acknowledge the humanity of Jesus. These two dimensions of belief are essentially unrelated ($r = -.03$). That is, knowing that a person believes in the divinity of Jesus tells you nothing about his belief in the humanity of Jesus. Knowing a person believes in the humanity of Jesus tells you nothing about whether or not he believes in the divinity of Jesus. Knowing that a person clearly endorses all of the positive dimensions and rejects all of the negative dimensions of this factor tells you nothing about whether or not he believes in the humanity of Jesus.[18]

In theological language this finding says that Lutherans as a group are Nestorians, that is, they reflect the ancient heresy of separating the two natures of Jesus Christ. Lutherans have not learned the doctrine of the Union of the Two Natures of Christ. If that doctrine were understood and believed there would be at least some positive relationship between the two dimensions. If the heart of Lutheran piety reflected an understanding of the union of the two natures there would be some positive loading of the humanity scale on the factor. The declaration of the Council of Chalcedon (451 A.D.), "We confess one and the same Jesus Christ, the Son and Lord only-begotten, in two natures without mixture, without change, without division, without separation," has been forgotten by most Lutherans.

The content of the Divinity of Jesus dimension shows most Lutherans committed to a traditional catechetical view of Christ's divinity, including omniscience (knowing everything), omnipotence (having all power), omnipresence (present everywhere), and perfection. He is also known as a creator, a catechetically correct view, but by less than half of the respondents. The highest percentage of agreement is given to two items (12 and 14) that suggest a utilitarian view of Jesus as primarily a crisis intervention mediator.

Several findings suggest that for most Lutherans the Christian faith is largely faith in Jesus. There is a higher level of certainty of faith in Jesus than in God. The doctrines Lutherans hold most firmly are those concerning the person and work of Jesus. On the divinity of Jesus there is a higher general level of agreement as well as greater consistency than on the dimension of Immanent Trinity. The main thrust of Lutheran piety is clearly on the Second Article of the Creed. Belief in God's providence and acceptance of the Spirit and his gifts shows that Lutherans are not ignorant of the First and Third Articles. Nevertheless, it is Christ who is most basic and fundamental. Lutheran theology has been heavily Christ-centered. Lutherans have heard that message. If some of the notes of the full range of the symphony of God's grace have been missed, it may be due to the shape of Lutheran theology as it is reflected in Lutheran piety.

Multivariate Analysis. The divinity of Jesus is most emphatically endorsed by young (ages 15-24) members of the LC-MS, who are also committed to Transcendental Meaning in Life (Scale 28) and are conservative doctrinally (Scale 44). Those who are liberal doctrinally (Scale 44) and reject the exclusive truth claim of Christianity (Scale 16) are least likely to believe Jesus is divine. Degree of conservatism in belief affects the middle range of belief in Jesus' divinity. The more conservative, the higher the score on this dimension. Within LC-MS, but not ALC and LCA, age is related to belief in Jesus as divine. The youngest LC-MS members are highest in affirming divinity. Within ALC and LCA, it is not age but rather degree of certainty or doubt of faith which is most related to belief in Jesus' divinity. Acceptance or rejection of the exclusive truth claim of Christianity affects the lower range of belief in divinity. The basis of the church's exclusive truth claim is Jesus and his history. It follows that rejection of his divinity is related to rejection of the exclusive truth claim.

Do Religious Experiences Strengthen a Gospel Orientation?

So far in reporting the heart of Lutheran piety, we have dealt with dimensions that are largely cognitive, intellectual, or substantive belief. What about feelings? Do Lutherans have any? Yes, they do. The dimension of religious experience (Scale 19) tells about the feelings Lutherans report.

To experience, to feel God, has long been an important part of the total Christian experience for many persons. Luther spoke in glowing emotional terms of his experience of God's grace that thrust him into the activity of reformer. Wesley spoke of his experience. Paul's experience on the road to Damascus is one of the many biblical reports of experiences which were direct contacts with God. For many, experiences like that have the effect of erasing doubts and giving the kind of certainty that enables Paul or Luther or Wesley to stand firmly for God no matter what happens.

In human psychology, there is no difference in the quality of emotional experience between religious and nonreligious "peak experiences." We know that powerful emotional peaks change people whether the experience is religious or not. The meaning of the experience, however, is different. In the religious experience the effect is to "know God," to feel him. "Knowing God" directly changes the person's feelings toward himself and other people. God is now the major guiding, shaping connection to other persons.

Three items most clearly indicate this dimension (608, 609, and 611). They deal with a person's emotional contact with Father, Son, and Holy Spirit. Close to half of the respondents state they have felt the "presence of God," "a sense of being saved in Christ," and "assurance of having received the Holy Spirit." Two items (618 and 619) reflecting attitudes toward other people are here, too. One out of three says that loving and doing good for your neighbor is absolutely essential for salvation. This might be confusion about justification by *faith alone,* but set in the context of emotional experience of God, it can show the changes that spiritual experience makes in the way a person feels towards others.

Items dealing with the experience of speaking in tongues (612) and spiritual healing (613) are also on the dimension. This shows that there is a single dimension of religious emotional experience. Speaking in tongues and healing are not different in quality but rather in degree of intensity of the spiritual experience.

The charismatic movement has had an impact on Lutheranism. Six percent are sure they have had an experience of speaking in tongues and 12% think they have. This compares with 12% who were willing to say that anyone who did not believe speaking in tongues should be practiced today was not a true Christian. An additional 15% agree that speaking in tongues should be practiced but aren't willing to say that a person who disagrees isn't a true Christian (Scale 44, Item 79). A significant minority of Lutherans are either involved in the charismatic movement or fairly receptive to it.

Emotion by itself can result in feelings that ought to concern a pastor. One out of four says he has felt fear of being punished by God because of specific actions of his. The willingness to make statements (Items 618 and 619) which contradict the Lutheran Confessions' stand on justification is associated with emotional experience. On the other hand, emotional experience is not necessary for persons to express a feeling of certainty about their faith. The proportion saying they have had spiritual experiences is significantly less than the proportion who say they are certain of their faith (cf. Scale 66).

Feeling God as punishing and having confusion about justification are on a single dimension together with reporting religious experience. This suggests that the church would be wise to examine carefully the consequences of the present experience-emotion emphasis in the society.

Can feeling or experience *alone* lead to knowing a gracious, forgiving God? The empirical evidence of the formation of this dimension answers No. Emotional experience needs added to it the truth of revelation in order to contribute to a full and complete knowledge of a gracious and forgiving God.

Multivariate Analysis. Persons who are highest in reporting emotional spiritual experiences are those who also report the highest level of personal practices of piety (Scale 41). Practices like Bible reading, private meditation and devotion, conversation about spiritual matters, and a high commitment to the supremacy of religion in life are more powerfully associated with having spiritual experiences than other characteristics or behaviors.

Surprisingly, high commitment to transcendental meaning in life is associated only with the middle range of reported spiritual experience. The extremes of spiritual experience are not necessarily associated with a transcendental view. Strong emotional certainty of faith (Scale 66) also operates only in the middle range. Again this indicates that certainty of faith does not require intense spiritual experiences.

In summary, the heart of Lutheran piety includes a dimension of religious spiritual experience. This shows that there is an experimental, emotional element in Lutheran piety. It is an important contributor to the sense of faith, devotion, and practice of piety. The contribution it makes to Lutheran piety is not at the extreme of intense, special experiences but rather in the sense of feeling God's presence and having assurance of salvation.

Do Some Lutherans Exaggerate the Truth Claim of Christianity?

The Christian church has been and still is a missionary church. It claims to be commissioned, a "sent" church. It claims the command to tell *all* men, in *all* lands, in *all* cultures, in *all* conditions about God's acts of salvation in Jesus Christ. It claims the command to show *all* men, in *all* lands, in *all* cultures, in *all* conditions how to live in bonds of peace and love in the new community of Christ's body.

That means that the church makes a truth claim. Very simply, the church says it knows the truth that supersedes, transforms, and judges all other truth by which men live. It claims to show the falseness, error, and distortion of all human thinking and feeling, even the most noble. Jesus said it to the church, "I am *the* Truth."

When the church makes that claim today it is in the same situation as the early church. It is surrounded by a diverse religious and philosophical world culture with one common goal: to guarantee and continue the existence and well-being of the society. To a world community characterized by pluralism, where the ritual acknowledgment and celebration of pluralism and diversity is judged the absolute necessity for maintenance of society, the exclusive truth claim of the Christian church must be the highest offense possible.

The dimension of the truth claim of Christianity (Scale 16) is named the Exclusive Truth Claim of Christianity Exaggerated. The dimension runs from one end of rejection of the exclusive truth claim of Christianity (lowest score = 45) through an historic and theologically sound truth claim, to the other end of an exaggerated truth claim that identifies the truth claim with the organization and institution of the church (highest score = 94).

The numerical weights assigned to responses to the items by the process of reciprocal averaging clearly shows which items reflect the two extreme ends of the dimension.[19] This feature of the dimension is diagrammed in Figure 5.2. This figure graphically shows that one end of the exaggerated truth claim includes beliefs that the Lutheran church is the only true visible church (Item 21), that the Pope is *the* anti-Christ (Item 46), and that God is punishing Jews (Item 36). The other end includes rejection of belief that salvation is only through faith in Christ (Item 420). In the middle is acceptance of belief that salvation is only through Christ along with acceptance of personal responsibility for doing evil (Item 39), a conviction that doctrinal agreement must precede unity (Item 40), and the conviction that Christians can be identified (Item 37).

The rest of the items help to define the exaggerated end. They add a legalistic view of salvation (Item 56), the claim that only Christians do good works in God's sight (Item 38), the belief that Jews can't be forgiven for crucifying Jesus until they believe he is their Savior (Item 41), the belief that a person must be a member of one's own faith to be saved (Item 421), and the conviction that not knowing about Jesus prevents salvation (Item 422).

High scores on this scale tell that a person has a belief that the church organization and structure embodies the truth claim, thus enemies are clearly and readily identified, and that the way a person becomes a part of the known group that has "the truth" is by moral and spiritual achievement. Low scores show rejection of the truth claim in all forms.

The average for all laity places most Lutherans in the middle range, neither rejecting the truth claim nor endorsing the exaggerated truth claim. The weight of Lutherans is in the direction of an historic and theologically supported exclusive truth claim. They avoid the heretical notions at both ends. This is the contribution which this dimension makes to the heart of Lutheran piety.

Multivariate Analysis. Further understanding of the meaning of high and low scores on this scale is available from several analyses comparing a large number of characteristics simultaneously to find those that give us the best information about the people who scored high or low. Because of the significance of this dimension we will report each analysis fully.

When we compare 19 characteristics with peoples' scores on this scale,

Figure 5.2   Ranges of Weights for Items of The Exclusive Truth Claim of Christianity Exaggerated (Scale 16)

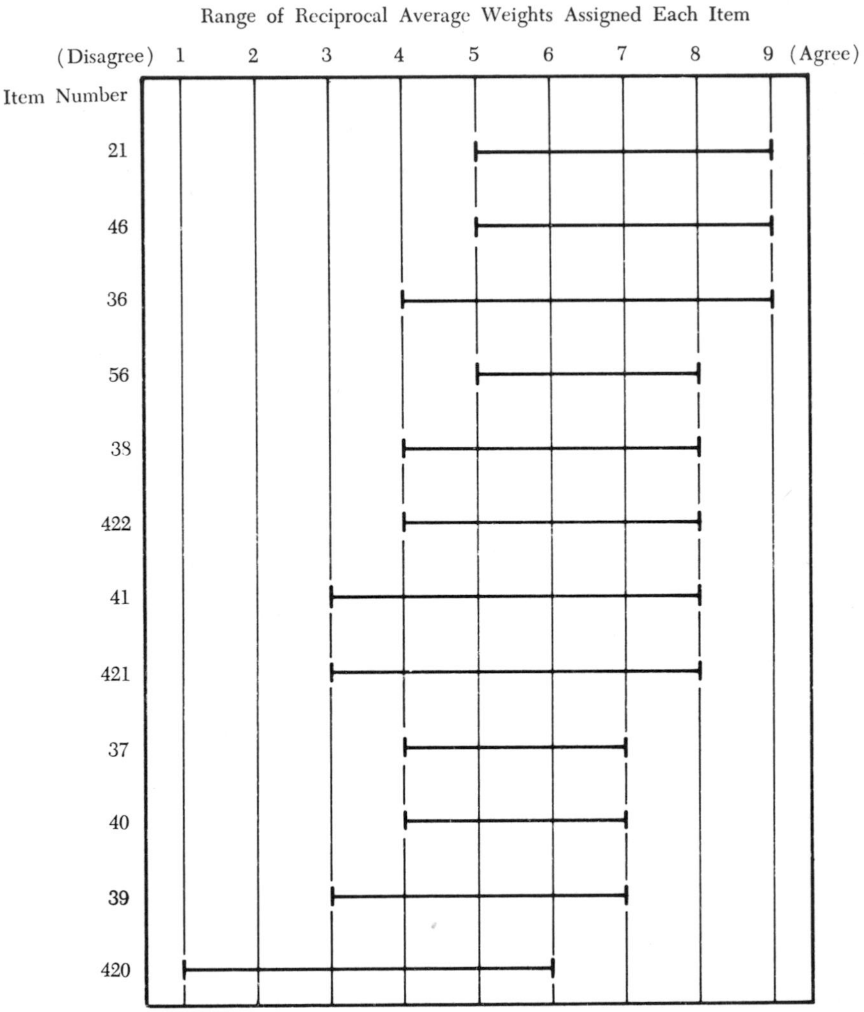

Range of Reciprocal Average Weights Assigned Each Item

we find that higher scores are associated with being a member of the LC-MS and over age 41, excluding the 45-46 year age group. Lower scores are associated with being in either the ALC or LCA, under 34 years old, and having more education than high school.

When more characteristics were added for the second analysis we found more powerful predictors. Persons who score even higher are characterized by expressing a moderate to strong desire for a rigid, unchanging structure of family life and social institutions (Scale 37) and endorsing a transcendental view (Scale 28), who are a variety of ages. Most of them are older ages, but the high scoring group also includes young adults and some middle ages. Those who score lower than average tend to be persons who reject an unchanging structure for family life and society (Scale 37) and reject transcendental meaning in life (Scale 28). When we then added some additional characteristics to the above sets and again compared them all simultaneously, we found other even more powerful characteristics. Persons who are more likely to make an *exaggerated* exclusive truth claim are those who are highly oriented to a need for rigid authoritarian rituals (Scale 43) and are highly fundamentalist in belief (Scale 44). Those scoring lower are persons who range from conservative to liberal in belief (Scale 44) and who deny a need for rigid authoritarian rituals (Scale 43). In these analyses whether belief is fundamentalist or liberal, whether a transcendental view is accepted or rejected, adding the dimension of need for rigid authoritarian rituals or the need for unchanging structures raises scores toward the exaggerated end of the exclusive truth claim.

Persons who identify the church's truth claim—salvation only in Christ —with the structure of the church reflect an underlying personality need for structures external to themselves which can offer support, security, and identity in the face of perceived threat and anxiety. Human needs are involved in systems of beliefs, values, and attitudes. This means that persons who may differ in beliefs, values, and attitudes are not being capricious, evil, or stupid. They are meeting their world with an entire bundle of needs, visions, fears, hopes, tragedies—real and imagined—and doing the best they can to make sense out of what happens to be their life.

In this section we have learned that the heart of Lutheran piety maintains the exclusive truth claim of Christianity while not going to the extreme of identifying that truth with the structures of the church. Lutherans, as a whole, have not abandoned the scandalous claim of the Christian faith.

CHRISTIAN UTOPIANISM

Utopian visions and experiments periodically pop up throughout the history of Western civilization. Plato's grand scheme for the perfect society, *The Republic,* is the first of many similar proposals. This is a time of revival of interest in utopias. The communal living movement stirs interest in young, middle-aged, and older persons alike. Television specials, books, articles, and movies set the idea of a perfect society before all of us.

Another dimension of belief that contributes to the heart of Lutheran piety reflects what Lutherans think about a Christian Utopia (Scale 36). Items like "if one will only grasp God's grace and trust in his love, all doors will be opened . . ." show a strong element of "magic-motif" in Lutherans' ideas about a Christian Utopia. The ideal is a completely happy life, free from worry or trouble. Aggressive evangelism (Items 331, 352, and 353) that will convert everyone to Christianity (Item 326) will solve all the problems and establish the perfect society. If need be, compulsion is seen as a legitimate way to educate people so they will fit in (Item 304). Sacrifice and dedication (Items 301 and 324) to make it work are willingly offered.

This dimension of Christian Utopianism is associated with Exclusive Truth Claim of Christianity Exaggerated ($r = .50$). Given the readily identified group that embodies truth, if everyone is brought into that group, the perfect life in the perfect society is assured. Christian Utopianism, at either extreme end, represents rejection or exaggeration of the claims Lutheran theology has made. To the extent Lutheran theology concerns itself with this issue, it has not accepted a utopian vision of uniting church and society. Lutheran theology could not approve the kind of theocracy that Calvin set up in Geneva. The theological tradition of the doctrine of the Two Kingdoms—the Kingdom of Grace and the Kingdom of Law—insists on maintaining a separate existence for church and state. They relate to each other in dynamic tension. The presence of this dimension in Lutheran piety points to that theological tradition as an important resource for our time when many want to merge the two kingdoms.

At the same time, Lutheran theology has consistently emphasized that being a Christian does have an effect upon one's life. There are real consequences of believing in salvation by grace through faith. Lutherans hold that to be true. Nine out of ten say that a Christian has joy and peace from knowing he is forgiven (Item 333). Seven out of ten want more personal evangelism programs (Item 331). Slightly more than half agree that a man should be prudent (Item 301), should tithe (Item 324), and that knowing Christ's grace brings happiness (Items 335 and 360).

However, most Lutherans reject the idea of a Christian Utopia. The average for the whole group is midway between agreement and disagreement with all items.[20] The majority of Lutherans agree that faith has consequences in a private, personal sense, but reject statements that would try to build a whole society around those consequences.

Multivariate Analysis. Persons likely to cling to the ideal of a Christian Utopia are those who are highly committed to a transcendental view and have a high need for rigid, unchanging structures in family life and society. Persons who reject both views tend to show little interest in a perfect Christian society. A second group of persons even more highly interested in a Christian Utopia are those who are highly committed to an exaggerated exclusivism (Scale 16), are highly involved in personal practices of piety (Scale 41), and also have a high need for rigid unchanging structures in family life and society (Scale 37). Lutherans who have a more moderate view of the exclusive truth claim and more moderate commitment to transcendental meaning in life are not inclined to have much interest in a Christian Utopia.

The characteristic that contributes the most to utopianism is the need for rigid and unchanging structure in family life and society. In the subgroup of those who are high in exaggerated exclusivism but low in personal practices of piety, the need for religious absolutism (Scale 43) is associated with higher interest in a Christian Utopia. For the subgroup highly committed to transcendental meaning in life (Scale 28) but low in need for rigid structures of family life and society (Scale 37), feelings of alienation and pessimism (Scale 35) are associated with higher interest in a Christian Utopia.

The general picture we can draw of those who are most likely to want to build a perfect society based upon Christianity is of persons who feel frightened and anxious about their world and life. They want to have sure and firm institutions all around them to help keep things calm and peaceful. Tranquillity is essential so that personal life can be secure and stable.

The Gospel and Life

Throughout the discussion of the heart of Lutheran piety we have drawn attention to the question of the relationship between knowing the gospel and the way a man lives. We have claimed that this first factor points to a gospel orientation present among Lutherans, acknowledging that the degree to which it reflects an integration of gospel into life warrants discussion. We have further acknowledged that there are various stages of growth in the tension within each man between law and gospel.

To attempt to measure the impact of the gospel upon a man's life is a difficult task. Many may object upon theological or theoretical grounds. Nevertheless we tried. A series of five items (70, 72, 73, 74, and 75) were developed that presented life situations, i.e., finding your spouse has committed adultery, and four possible responses. One of the four responses to each question was constructed to reflect behavior judged to be in keeping with integration of the gospel into life. The elements of behavior included were: (1) individual confrontation with a person wronging you, (2) confession of your personal guilt and responsibility to the party wronging you, and (3) declaration of forgive-

ness given by you to the offending party.[21] These responses formed
a dimension (Scale 70) that is called a Gospel-Oriented Life.[22] In turn,
this dimension is the strongest one on a separate factor. This factor is
given in Table 5.4.

Table 5.4   Factor 14: The Gospel and Life

Load	Scale	Dimension Title
Positive		
.44	70	Gospel-Oriented Life
.41	18	Identification with Parents
.38	5	Humanity of Jesus
.30	8	Biblical Knowledge
Negative		
−.32	69	Horatio Alger Orientation

If it is agreed that choosing to respond to an adulterous spouse, a
thief, a disobedient child, a pastor preaching false doctrine, and one's
own error in disciplining a child with these three elements of behavior
reflects one way of integrating the gospel into life, we have a gospel and
life factor in addition to a gospel and life dimension. This has significance in two directions. One, it says that it appears possible to get some
empirical assessment of the effect of the gospel on a man's life. Two, it
says that among some Lutherans there is a consistent pattern of recognizing these three behavior elements as most preferable for a Christian.
An average of three out of ten Lutherans chose these five gospel-oriented
responses.

We cannot go into full detail discussing the other dimensions that
comprise the factor. They present a consistent and highly interesting
picture. Reflecting this mode of integrating gospel and life is associated
with a close sense of identification with one's parents and their values
(Scale 18), a knowledge of the full-orbed humanity of Jesus (Scale 5),
and a knowledge of correct biblical facts (Scale 8). It is also negatively
associated with a subtle measure of achievement orientation (Scale 69)
stressing culturally approved striving, competing, industrious labor.

This finding has powerful meaning for the church. Its teaching has
an effect. Some Lutherans do have a consistent vision of a uniquely
Christian way to respond to troublesome interpersonal situations. Some
do tend to reject the values of a competitive, striving culture in favor
of a more personal, compassionate relationship. When the church teaches
Scripture, provides for fuller knowledge of Jesus, and supports love and
respect for parents, it can have hope that it is helping to make human
relationships more honest, tender, and accepting.

Furthermore, the fact that this finding is based upon our total lay sample, living in all kinds of situations, places, and conditions, suggests that the ministry of the church does have an impact independent of the surrounding culture—a significant suggestion.

Summary

We know that most Lutherans hold to transcendental meaning in life. The heart of Lutheran piety includes knowledge of a personal, caring God who loves men in Jesus Christ. There is a sense of certainty in faith. The content of belief runs toward a conservative, traditional doctrinal stance with most emphasis upon the person and work of Jesus.

There is an accepting, hopeful attitude toward death. There is an emotional dimension that accepts religious experience but does not emphasize it highly. The exclusive truth claim of Christianity is accepted and upheld while an exaggerated identification of truth with the church is rejected. While faith has consequences in personal feeling and life, a Christian Utopia is not terribly attractive. Salvation by works is rejected. Values focused on self-development are rejected. The gospel is known. Christ is the center of faith. There is still a Christian mind among us.

Notes

1. Popper, K. R., 1959.
   Polanyi, M., 1958.
   Kuhn, T. S., 1962.
   Lakatos, I. and Musgrave, A. (Eds.), 1970.
2. Myrdal, G., 1968.
3. Berger, P. and Luckmann, T., 1966.
4. Hammer, E. F. (Ed.), 1968.
5. Frank, J. D., 1962.
6. Skinner, B. F., 1971.
7. The two factors understood to reflect a gospel and law orientation have been derived by empirical methods from the responses of 4,745 Lutherans. In that sense they reflect reality. However, the factors should not be identified with the constructs of gospel and law. Living a gospel-oriented life is surely broader and more complex than what is contained in our first factor. Likewise a life under the law is more than our second factor. However, the factors point to these two modes of life and sharpen our understanding of them.
8. Forde, G. O., 1969.
9. Britton, K., 1969.
10. Gustafson, C. V., 1956.
11. Dittes, J. E., 1969.
12. Preus, R. D., 1970.
13. From the 13 items of the fundamentalism–liberalism scale three subdimensions developed. Each is technically satisfactory and interpretable. The weights assigned by the reciprocal averaging process indicate which subdimension is most firmly held, which most variable in the sense of allowing greater latitude.

14. The third subdivision, identified as a charismatic Lutheran fundamentalism, included Item 194 dealing with the importance of Baptism. Those persons who consistently chose the first response to these five items also consistently reported that their Baptism was very important to them.

15. Strommen, M. P. (Ed.), 1971.

16. Factor loading of Scale 5 on Factor 1 = −.09. This means that the dimension of belief in the full humanity of Jesus is essentially unrelated to the factor we identify as the heart of Lutheran piety.

17. It can be said that the items comprising Scale 5 reflect a full view of the humanity of Jesus that may be foreign to most Lutherans, or it may be that the items reflect an heretical view of the humanity of Jesus. Items describing Jesus' humanity in less extreme form were included in a pretesting of instrumentalism (see Appendix A, pp. 313-316). They proved unsatisfactory while the items in the present Scale 5 were effective. We can also claim that the items in Scale 5 present an acceptable full view of the humanity of Jesus on the basis of the scores of clergymen on the scale. The lay average on Scale 5 is 13.4. The clergy average is 26.0, two standard deviations greater than the lay mean. If the clergy are accepted as a group that reflects what is acceptable, this shows clergymen supporting the items in Scale 5 as reflecting a full view of the humanity of Jesus. Lutheran clergymen, then, tend neither to underemphasize nor to separate the two natures of Christ. The fact that on the basis of the same items clergymen affirm the union of the two natures of Christ makes the tendency of laymen toward Nestorianism all the more clear.

18. As shown above (Note 16), factor loading of Scale 5 on Factor 1 = −.09.

19. The process of reciprocal averaging, described in Appendix A (pp. 340-341) assigned weights on a nine point scale to the response possibilities for all items. An item that measures well across the full range of the underlying dimension will receive weights from one through nine. An item that discriminates across only a portion of the dimension will receive weights across only a portion of the one to nine range, e.g., one to six for the low end of the dimension, or four to nine for the high end only, or three to seven for the middle range of the dimension only. Persons scoring at either extreme of the dimension must have taken comparable positions at the extremes *particularly* on the items that measure *only* at those same extremes.

20. The average for all laity is $\overline{X} = 40.8$. Agreement with all items brings a theoretical score of 49. Disagreement with all items brings a theoretical score of 26. The range from strong agreement to strong disagreement is from 20-84. The actual range of scores is from 21-84.

21. In addition to the gospel-oriented response, the other three responses were written to reflect a humanistic, democratic, and authoritarian response to the life situation described in the initial statement. The respondent chose the course of action he felt it best to take. An example of the items is given below.

> 73. DISOBEDIENCE: Assume you are a parent and for some time you have been concerned that your 13-year-old has been disobeying you and has now begun to talk back when you have tried to give direction. Which of the following comes closest to what you think would be the best course of action to take?
>
> *Percentage Choosing*
> *This Response*
>
> *Response Choice*
> (Democratic)   12%
> a. Call the family together and talk through the feelings of each member about the best way for parents and children to get along together. Try to reach a family decision about what each member can do to improve the situation.

(Humanistic)   28%

b. Talk privately with the child and try to reason with him so that he can understand what is really involved in being a good member of the family, a fine citizen and a good example to those younger, so that he can responsibly choose more helpful and cooperative ways to get along.

(Authoritarian)   32%

c. Make it clear to the child that you will not tolerate such disrespect because it is important for a child to learn to do what he ought, even though he doesn't like it, because there will always be someone to whom he is responsible. Besides that, God's Law says he ought to honor his parents. To help the child learn this important lesson, you let him know what punishments are likely to come.

(Gospel)   27%

d. Go to the child and let him know that you understand that this is very human behavior but that nevertheless you are bothered and offended by it. Tell the child that you are sorry if you have hurt him or provoked him in any way and that you forgive him for hurting you. Let him know that you will try not to hold this against him.

22. Procedures used in deriving Scale 70 are described in Appendix A, pp. 342-343. Statistical information is given in Appendix A, Table IV.7.

He who does not have faith is cast down below all creatures, nor is there any creature that could console him.
For he who has God as his enemy also has all God's creatures opposed to him. These never stand still.

—Martin Luther, *Psalm 90*

6. Law-Oriented Lutherans

*This chapter rivals Chapter 5 in importance because it deals with
the second of the two major factors in this study. It discusses the 16
dimensions that form the profile of people who cannot tolerate change,
have a need for religious absolutism, are prejudiced, are threatened by
people different from themselves, are self-seeking in their relation to
religion, and believe in salvation by works. Or we could say that the
dimensions presented in this chapter describe people who prefer form
over spirit, the letter over the word, the note over the music, the part
over the whole, authority over freedom. Because these characteristics
parallel the classic theological descriptions of the law-oriented person,
an inference to that effect is being made. We assume that the underlying quality uniting these dimensions can be called, in theological
terms, a law orientation. Whatever the quality, it is a way of perceiving
life that leads a person to distort Christian truth and to misbelieve what
he is taught. The result is a type of religiosity that is like what has been
defined in past research as "consensual" or "extrinsic" religion.*

*As the content of this second factor is reported, the reader will find
answers to some important questions that have long plagued the church:*

*How can we locate resistance to change and the insistence some
people have on maintaining the status quo?*

Why do we find prejudice within the church? What is its source?

How do we account for members who care only for their own advantage and the preservation of their institution?

The answers that emerge are powerful and sobering. Resistance to change is found among the two out of five Lutherans who have a need for unchanging structures and a need for religious absolutism. Prejudice, which is so often blamed on religion, finds its roots primarily in the rigid and absolutizing qualities of a need for unchanging structures. The Lutheran who exalts form over spirit is the one most likely to be prejudiced.

The seriousness of the chapter is found in the fact that such Lutherans do exist. The 16 dimensions unhappily reflect such qualities as self-seeking, conformity to the status quo, a theology of salvation by works, and a distorted view of Christ. A composite of these characteristics, and others reported in this chapter, gives an orientation to life that contrasts with the gospel orientation of Chapter 5.

Lutheran theology recognizes one basic form of false religion: living under the law without knowledge of the gospel. This may be the condition of men within the church or outside of it. Early Lutheran theologians described "practical atheism" found within the church as "denial of God's providence"; "doing what pleases oneself"; "the mixing and confusion of religions and worship that springs from fleshly motives and in the interest of outward peace." Practical atheism, then, begins when religious indifference and syncretism (holding that all religions are basically the same) are the beliefs of people. The end result is consummate atheism, holding that every man can be saved by his own religion.[1]

Underneath all forms of false religion lies a misappropriation of God's law by man apart from faith. The creature external to man is exalted and identified as God. Luther maintains that it is the identification of God with the environment that depresses and frightens man without Christ. All creatures become "God's whips and weapons," whether it is the "sea, sickness, hunger, fire, war, government, family." [2] The environment terrifies, not because man can't control it—he can—but because it accuses, condemns, and kills by demanding judgment and evaluation of self. Life lived under the law is life lived under demand. Trying to meet that demand man attempts to impose his will upon the environment and make it stand still, firm, and rigid to satisfy his needs for peace and place.[3]

The heart of Lutheran piety described in the preceding chapter represents a gospel-oriented Christian belief system. In this chapter we present a distinct contrast: a law-oriented *misbelief* system. Through our data analyses we find that the second factor fits the description of "false religion," of a law-oriented life given by Lutheran theologians.

The law-oriented belief system shows the attempt to fix every structure of environment in static, rigid form. It shows the exploitation of religion and society for personal peace and pleasure. It shows the efforts to tyrannize man, impose a utopia, and win heaven by doing the works of the law. In short, this factor is the practical atheism within the church described by Lutheran theologians.

The fact that this is the second factor to emerge from our data tells us that this is no small problem for the Lutheran church. The heart of Lutheran piety is the most cohesive and coherent view among Lutherans, and a law-oriented life is a close second. A rough estimate of the proportion of Lutherans likely to reflect law orientation is 40%. This figure is based upon averaging the percentages of response for all items on all dimensions of the factor.

More important than the size of the proportion is the demonstration that a real and basic polarity within the Lutheran church lies between a gospel-oriented life and a law-oriented life.[4] These are the two most cohesive and powerful systems of belief, value, attitude, and behavior to be found among Lutherans. Lutherans have known this for a long time but never before has it been as clearly and empirically demonstrated as in the data of A Study of Generations.

There are tensions within the church between clergy and laity; between national church bodies; between distinct ideas about the church's role in social issues, the place of women in the church, youth in the church, doctrine, and a host of other problems. They are important issues, and A Study of Generations provides a great fund of information about them. However, none of them can be dealt with apart from the basic polarity between gospel orientation and law orientation disclosed by the emergence of these two factors. Here is the fundamental reality of life within the church. Every move, every program, every rhythm of church life is affected by this polarity. No response to an issue, problem, or program is complete unless it is set against this polarity first and framed in the light of this reality.

While our results show that there are persons typifying these two factors clearly enough to make them emerge as distinct factors, it is the insight of the theologian that reminds us that the same polarity exists within each of us. No man can claim to be wholly one or the other. Each man lives in precarious wobbling between law and gospel. It is the grace of God alone that moves a man toward gospel.

Rigid and Absolutizing Qualities of a Law Orientation

The most potent thrust in the law orientation of Lutherans is in the direction of absolutizing and depending upon structures external to the individual. By structures we mean repeated patterns of behavior, social systems composed of persons interacting according to set rules, and social organization where persons are clearly stratified.[5] As examples, the factor contains a dimension emphasizing repeated ritualistic behavior in worship following a rigid pattern (Scale 43). There is a dimension defining the roles of persons in a family setting by clear-cut rules and demands (Scale 37). There are three dimensions stressing assignment of persons to social strata much like the layers of rock regarded as geological strata (Scales 34, 56, and 57). (See Appendix C, Section IV.)

What is common to the dimensions on this factor (given in Table 6.1) is the absolute and rigid quality tendered to external structures and the dependence upon that static, frozen quality for satisfaction of

Table 6.1 Factor 2: Law Orientation

Factor Loading (Lay People Only)	Scale Number	Dimension Name	Rxx
Positive			
.76	37	Need for Unchanging Structure	.78
.70	43	Need for Religious Absolutism	.70
.69	34	Generalized Prejudice	.86
.69	56	Social Distance–Radical Life Styles	.90
.65	57	Social Distance–Racial & Religious Groups	.89
.53	67	Self-Oriented Utilitarianism	.53
.49	16	The Exclusive Truth Claim of Christianity Exaggerated	.68
.47	26	Mutual Support Among Church, Society, & Individuals	.64
.44	36	Christian Utopianism	.74
.38	15	Salvation by Works	.79
.36	69	Horatio Alger Orientation	.64
.32	35	Pessimism	.67
.29	52	Desire for a Dependable World	.53
Negative			
−.34	42	The Role of Pastors in Social Action	.86
−.35	65	Church Involvement in Social Issues	.65
−.36	5	Humanity of Jesus	.61
−.42	55	Family Level of Education	.70

personal needs. Life under the law experiences "all God's creatures opposed" and in enmity. But that is all there is. It is all "in the world." Misappropriation of the law limits life to the structures of this world, and so they become all important. Their form and shape, the rules and directions that orient and guide, are life itself. For the law-oriented person there is no more.

NEED FOR UNCHANGING STRUCTURE

The strongest dimension in law orientation is named Need for Unchanging Structure. The three strongest items (433, 443, and 449) express fear of the future and a desire to proceed cautiously while maintaining the past (Scale 37). Four additional items (428, 434, 437, and 441) strengthen the thrust of resistance to change and add the content of what must particularly remain unchanged: traditional, authoritative family structure. The remainder of the items focus on family life and societal life. In each item there is an implicit demand that sets up rules for performance in family life or society that must be met.

Agreement with all items shows a need for the structures of family life to be rigid and unchanging. The male is supreme. The woman is expected to serve and to meet the demands of both husband and society. A repressive strain is evident in the need for children to conform, to be respectful, and to be kept ignorant of sex so that their base, primitive instincts won't get out of control. Respect, obedience, and duty characterize the system of relating to each other in family life.

The kind of society which is to be kept intact is one which depends upon individual responsibility within a rigid code. There is sensitivity to what others might think, so conformity to society's norms is highly valued. That's a good way to live, so it doesn't need any changing.

Eight out of ten Lutherans do not agree with the statements that add rigidity and conformity to the structures (Items 288, 314, 427, 432, and 435). Seven out of ten want order in family life and society but do not emphasize rigidity and conformity (Items 341, 428, 429, and 448). The majority want to have roles in family life fit a traditional model of authority but apparently see the possibility of a more open and flexible stance within that role differentiation.

The average for the laymen (100.83) is midway between agreement with all items (score = 121) and disagreement with all items (score = 73). The average of clergymen (91.11) places them closer to disagreement. Apparently clergymen as a group are more likely to be open to change and less interested in rigid family life than laymen, a possible source of tension between pastor and people that has been little recognized.

Multivariate Analysis. Several analyses have been made of what might help describe persons likely to have high need for unchanging structures and persons who don't show that need. The first analysis included characteristics like age, sex, and education. Age and education are related to need for unchanging structures. Those over age 59 who are high school graduates or less score somewhat higher than the average. Those under 49 years old with some college experience or a college degree tend to score lower than the average.

A second analysis included these characteristics and added characteristics of beliefs. Persons high in belief in the exaggerated exclusive truth claim (Scale 16) and high in belief in salvation by works (Scale 15) are high in need for unchanging structures. Persons who are more moderate about the exclusive truth claim of Christianity (Scale 16), reject the idea of a Christian Utopia (Scale 36), and deny feeling pessimistic (Scale 35) are likely to reject the idea of unchanging structures.

A third analysis included the characteristics described above plus attitudes toward others. Persons highest in prejudiced attitudes (Scale 34) and expressing high need for religious absolutism (Scale 43) are highest in need for unchanging structures. In this analysis the dimension of need for religious absolutism operated at all levels to tell most about the need for unchanging structures. The two internal characteristics of high generalized prejudice and high need for religious absolutism account for 40% of the variability in need for unchanging structures. That is a very high level of predictive ability. In other words, if I know only those two things about persons and nothing else, I will likely be accurate in predicting where each stands on need for unchanging structure 40% of the time.

A fourth analysis including beliefs and attitudes toward social justice identified persons who are exploiting both religion and society for their own purposes (Scale 67), are highly committed to an exaggerated exclusivism (Scale 16), and are highly concerned with building a Christian Utopia (Scale 36), as having great need for unchanging structure. Persons who deny using society and religion for personal ends (Scale 67) and are highly committed to the church's involvement in issues of social justice (Scale 65) are not very concerned about maintaining unchanging structures.

The general picture from the analyses which include beliefs shows that in the presence of those dimensions which clearly reflect a law-oriented life as described by theologians (Scales 16, 15, 43, and 36), there is also generally going to be a high need for unchanging structures. The need for unchanging structures is part and parcel of a law-oriented life. The most intense resistance to change of any sort is likely to be associated in the church with those whose lives are yet generally under the demand of the law.

The general picture that shows is the consistent choice of external form over spirit, the letter over the word, the note over the music, the part over the whole, authority over freedom.

Effect of Age. In comparing age, sex, region of country, size of congregation, church body affiliation, and education two by two, the one consistent significant effect was that of age.[6] From age 15 to approximately the college sophomore period, ages 19-20, there is a decline in need for unchanging structure followed by a rise in need to age 65. The general pattern is that the older Lutherans are, above age 20, the greater their expressed need for unchanging structures of family and societal life. However, age is not as powerful a predictor of need for unchanging structures as the dimensions reflecting a law orientation.

NEED FOR RELIGIOUS ABSOLUTISM

A powerful dimension in the law orientation of Lutherans is the Need for Religious Absolutism (Scale 43). The key items (533, 530, and 527) show a strong desire for uniform, worldwide liturgical practices together with the feeling that Christ is more real in worship. Once again form is exalted into reality. The other items add an authoritarian, rigid cast to the form of liturgy and dogma. Religion is defined as "authority and obedience" (Item 524). The "purpose of worship is to find out what God" wants done (Item 523). The belief commitment is certain and firm (Items 283 and 292). Lutherans have "pure and true doctrine" (Item 354). The form of worship is crucial and is the source of meaning (Item 543). All of this gives security (Item 705). Two items (529 and 542) add a concern for moral and social reform and caring for people's physical and spiritual needs.

On the average, Lutherans tend slightly more toward agreement than disagreement with all items. The average for all laymen is 70.35. Agreement with all items would score 79. However, only two out of five Lutherans agree with the items that most clearly add the absolute and rigid quality to the dimension (354, 524, 530, and 543). Two out of three Lutherans tend to agree with the remainder of the items.

The average for clergymen (67.29) shows more disagreement. Lutheran laymen have more desire for a formal, stable liturgical community than do pastors. Tension is inevitable if laymen are looking for sure, definite pronouncements and a stable liturgy while pastors want more ambiguity and openness.

Multivariate Analysis. We made five analyses of this scale to find what characterizes persons high or low in their need for religious absolutism. The first analysis used nine characteristics like age, sex, education, and region. It identified persons over age 42 with less education than high school as showing a greater need for religious absolutism. These two characteristics of age and education account for 13% of the total variability across the whole range of scores of all laymen in the sample. Another analysis including 31 characteristics like employment level, income, size of community, etc., did not add to understanding a high and low need for religious absolutism.

Three analyses included various combinations of belief and attitude characteristics and those characteristics which had effects in the first two analyses. When a person has a moderate to high need for unchanging structure (Scale 37) and believes in salvation by works (Scale 15), he tends to have a greater need for religious absolutism. These two characteristics account for 32% of the total variability across the whole range of scores.

The fifth analysis included a slightly different set of characteristics. From this analysis emerged the most extreme groups we found. Persons high in need for unchanging structure and high in belief in a Christian Utopia are highest in need for religious absolutism. Those with a low need for unchanging structure who are unhappy with the church are lowest in expressing a need for religious absolutism. This analysis accounted for 36% of the total variability of all scores.

A strong expression of need for religious absolutism fits into the developing picture of law orientation for Lutherans. Once again the elevation of form over spirit, law over gospel, emerges as a cohesive system. Need for religious absolutism is closely associated with misbelief about salvation (Scale 15), the misbelief of mixing the Kingdom of Grace with the Kingdom of Law (Scales 36 and 16), and a strong desire for unchanging structures (Scale 37).

Effect of Age. While age does not affect religious absolutism as much as do the characteristics above, it does show up on the first analysis. Also when age, sex, church body affiliation, region, education, and size of congregation are compared two at a time with this scale, age is consistently significant.[7] The curve goes down from age 16 to ages 19-20, the low point. It rises until age 65 with slight dips between ages 29-32 and 41-44. The general picture is that older Lutherans tend to have more desire for rigid rituals and symbols than do younger Lutherans. Education, sex, church body affiliation, region, and size of congregation do not show consistent significant effects.

Prejudice and Two Types of Religion

In addition to the two dimensions emphasizing need for unchanging structures and religious absolutism, the law orientation factor includes three dimensions of prejudiced attitudes (Scales 34, 56, and 57). These dimensions of prejudice are discussed in detail in Chapter 9. However, we will discuss the meaning and significance of the presence of prejudiced attitudes in the factor of law orientation at this point. To do so fully and in an integrated and cohesive fashion we will have to refer back to the factor of gospel orientation and discuss both factors against a summary of social science research in religion.

Social science research in religion and in the relationship between religion and prejudice strongly supports four general conclusions: [8]

1. There are two types of religion. One is a committed, internalized, more intense, more personal religious stance. The other is consensual, external, instrumental, and self-oriented.

2. There is a negative relationship between prejudice and the committed, internalized religion. However, the committed type of religion is much less clearly conceptualized in the literature than the consensual. The lack of an adequate conceptualization of committed religion is related to the single greatest problem encountered in the definition and measurement of religion. The obvious and

immediately available indications of religion, like church attendance, do not clearly separate these two types of religion. There is also a shortage of theoretical constructs available to give coherent shape to the contradictory and often confused data which exists in the literature.

3. There is a positive relationship between the second type of religion and prejudice. Persons who exhibit the characteristics of a consensual, instrumental religiosity are very likely to be highly prejudiced.

4. Most researchers have recognized a relationship between personality characteristics, consensual religiosity, and prejudice. A composite theoretical picture of that personality type is given by Dittes:

    a. A person threatened or overwhelmed by one or another external circumstance or internal impulse;

    b. A person therefore responsive to and reliant upon controls, structures, self-supports, and identity clues, especially as these may be provided externally, clearly, and unambiguously;

    c. Thus, a person possessing a wide range of characteristics serving this latter function, including those described as suggestibility, rigidity, intolerance of ambiguity, need for definiteness, closure seeking, manipulativeness, reliance on social or institutional or other authorities, moralism, and other conventional indices of a severe super-ego.[9]

Our results support these four general conclusions and add clarity to the points of uncertainty. Our data also bring together the theoretical constructs of theology and social science. Hopefully the union of theology and social science will be beneficial to both and to the subject of their common concern: people.

GOSPEL ORIENTATION AND COMMITTED RELIGION

We have found two types of religion among Lutherans: gospel orientation and law orientation, as described by Lutheran theologians from the sixteenth century to the present time. These two types of religion also fit closely the theoretical constructs of the social scientists and agree for the most part with the empirical data. There are two important differences, however.

In all previous work involving both definition and investigation of the committed, internalized, more personal and genuine type of religion, researchers have found a positive relationship with education and a negative relationship with doctrinal conservatism. This means that the committed type of religion has been thought of as doctrinally liberal and limited to those with higher levels of education.

Our factor of gospel orientation reflects a basically conservative doctrinal view, contains most of the individual items used by previous researchers to identify the committed type of religion, and is slightly negatively associated with family level of education.[10] Knowing the gospel and living under the gospel are not limited to those with high levels of education. The committed type of religion identified by social scientists is not necessarily liberal doctrinally. The factor of gospel orientation is unrelated to attitudes of prejudice.[11]

The fact of different intellectual abilities is difficult for most equality-minded Americans to accept. Nevertheless, some people are smart and some are not so smart. One of the strongest findings in research on prejudice is that lower levels of education are associated with higher levels of prejudice. If genetically endowed intellectual ability is reflected in level of education attained, the logical conclusion is that only smart people have much chance of being tolerant while those whose genes limit their intellectual ability can only remain prejudiced. The educational process as it is now cannot overcome the limits imposed by genetic inheritance.

Unless a society embarks upon a stringent eugenic control program to produce only super-smart citizens, it will always have a large group of citizens whose intellectual ability is genetically limited. Unless an effective means is found other than an educational process dependent upon differential ability, as it now stands, that group will constitute a large reservoir of prejudice, hostility, and potential social disruption.

Our results suggest that *knowing and living under the gospel of Jesus Christ is not limited to those with superior intellectual ability.* However, knowing and living under the gospel *is* associated with decrease in level of prejudice. This suggests that knowing and living under the gospel may constitute an educational and spiritual process of development that is not dependent upon differential ability levels for positive effect upon both individuals and society. The church has long maintained that before God the one-talent and ten-talent men are equal both in need for grace and in God's giving of grace. To the extent that the church truly incorporates within its life men of different abilities it is serving well both God and man.

LAW ORIENTATION AND THE CONSENSUAL TYPE OF RELIGION

Our data fit exactly both the definitions of consensual religion and the theoretical picture of the personality type holding both consensual religion and attitudes of prejudice. In one sense our data do not supply anything new in this regard. Most of the individual items appearing on the dimensions of our factor of law orientation have come from previous research which had already clearly established the positive relationship between consensual religion and prejudice.

However, the new element which our results add is the identification of a theological construct—law orientation—as a meaningful theoretical variable. It explains both the correlation between consensual religion and prejudice and the difficulty in finding ways of distinguishing between committed and consensual religion by obvious and readily available indices of religiosity such as church attendance.

Lutheran theology knows that the law-oriented life is not distinguishable by measures such as church attendance, financial support of a church, working in the church, or a favorable attitude toward the church. In fact, the easiest way to get those kinds of behaviors is to club people with the law, induce guilt, reward good behavior with bronze plaques or 20-year Sunday school pins, and build a strong institution that law-oriented persons are proud of. As Luther experienced to his severe disappointment, it is much more difficult to live under gospel and know the freedom of a forgiven man in Christ than to build a church with high attendance rates, strong finances, and members who behave themselves.

Our results show that at least for Lutherans, the only population we can generalize to, the two types of religion identified by social science can be distinguished more cleanly by a law–gospel orientation than by the more obvious measures of religiosity. We recommend further theoretical refinement of this theological construct, making it applicable within the framework of other Christian traditions.

In the relationship between consensual religion and prejudice our data support the concept of law orientation as the third variable, together with level of education and doctrinal conservatism, which accounts for the correlation. We have briefly demonstrated above the identity between what Lutheran theologians since the sixteenth century have described as law orientation and our law-orientation factor. Our data show that attitudes of prejudice are a part of that orientation.

Previous researchers have concluded that it is the way religion is held that is correlated with prejudice. Lutheran theology's construct of law orientation identifies both the type of religion and the way in which it is held. The church now has an empirical base for identification of social science research results in its own theoretical language and framework. The past history and experience of the church in dealing with life under law are now clearly available for addressing the basic spiritual needs of men and the practical needs of society.

The connection of law orientation and personality theory predicts that certain doctrines and practices of the church are going to be held and emphasized by the prejudiced, law-oriented personalities in a different fashion than by the gospel-oriented unprejudiced personality. This difference is not easily discovered. For example, law-oriented persons might very readily agree to the same statements regarding the divinity of Jesus as the gospel-oriented. The theologian would predict, however, that for the law-oriented a divine Jesus is a judge, a second Moses, a lawgiver who expects obedience to divine directions. To the gospel-oriented a divine Jesus is first Savior, friend, and grace of God in human flesh who forgives, frees, and calls to newness of life. The theologian can provide the kinds of distinctions expected. The social scientist can operationalize and test those distinctions. Such a joint effort can result in further progress and greater clarity and explanatory power. Out of that can come greater ability to respond to human need both for the church and for social science.

SELF-SEEKING QUALITIES OF A LAW ORIENTATION

The dimension next on the factor of law orientation is named Self-Oriented Utilitarianism (Scale 67). The strongest item (526) shows a self-orientation and privatism. In the pursuit of one's own private interests, religion (Items 472, 474, and 476) is used for a band-aid, for security, and for personal advancement. That's what it's for, and clergymen had better supply it (Item 559).

This use of religion corresponds to the "fleshy motives" and "outward peace" referred to by early Lutheran theologians. A goal in life is security and certainty (Item 325), and society, too, can be used for that purpose (Items 345, 358, and 381). A rather cavalier attitude toward the laws of society is shown in these items. This is what Marty has called "anomie" or "normlessness." When "anomie" is extended into religion, it is peculiarly difficult to cope with. "Anomie is a form of refusing to recognize the power of the law of God or of judgment in human value-systems." [12] Any attempt at judgment or proclamation of the law simply meets dead ears. In the meantime the form of religious practices is used to reinforce the conviction that this is the right way to live. Religion has the function of legitimizing and supporting the anomic life.

Mild agreement with all items brings a score of 57, mild disagreement a score of 28. The weight of Lutherans is slightly closer to disagreement ($\overline{X} = 40.8$) than agreement. Pastors as a group ($\overline{X} = 35.2$) are closer to disagreement with all items. Four out of five Lutherans agree that security is an important goal (Item 325); they are evenly split on the question of immediate gratification of desires (Item 358). Four out of five agree that religion and prayer serve a self-oriented purpose (Items 472 and 476). However, two out of five "tend to agree" and two out of five "definitely agree." Those who "definitely agree" are those who also tend to agree with other items. Those who "tend to agree" are those who disagree with other items on the dimension. [13]

Four out of five disagree with the expression of lawlessness and privatism, that is, ignoring other people's needs (Items 345, 381, and 526). Seven out of ten do not agree that clergymen should "stick to religion" and not get involved in social problems (Item 559). Those persons who agree with all items are those with the highest law orientation as theologically described.

Multivariate Analysis. When self-oriented utilitarianism is compared with 39 characteristics, persons highest on this dimension are those with a moderate to high need for unchanging structure, a moderate to high belief in salvation by works, and with high feelings of pessimism (Scale 35). These characteristics account for 25% of the total variability of scores on self-oriented utilitarianism.

When age is compared to this dimension there is a slow decline from age 15 to the low point of ages 27-28. Then it slowly rises to age 65. Older Lutherans generally tend to slightly higher levels than younger Lutherans while middle-aged Lutherans are the lowest.

The impression made by inclusion of self-oriented utilitarianism on the factor of law orientation is that reliance upon external structures to give shape and meaning to life is inherently self-defeating and frustrating. It simply isn't effective. The angry rejection of external judgment or control that "anomie" embodies flows from frustration. The trap is that external structures remain the object of pursuit of happiness and simultaneously the object of revenge and resistance. The ambivalent nature of reality, both physical and social, is reflected in the mirror image of man's ambivalent response: love and hate. Social reality—that is, patterns of behavior, social systems, other persons and groups—is much more subject to perceptual distortion than physical reality—rocks, roads, steel, and plastic. When that happens—perceptual distortion of social reality—the whole world is out of joint. The personality type holding consensual religion, prejudice, and depending upon external structure is bound to be frustrated. Life under law is inherently anguishing.

A SOCIAL SYSTEM OF MUTUAL SUPPORT

Another dimension contributing to the factor of law orientation is named Mutual Support Among Church, Society, and Individuals (Scale 26). This dimension assumes a social system of mutual support. The church supports society and me, and I support it. As long as everyone cooperates and stays within the system, things will hum along merrily.

The items (688, 679, 696, 698, and 704) that contribute most to this dimension show a sense of satisfaction with the guidance the church gives. The individual says he has a sense of belonging, a sense of fitting in well in his congregation. His church is the moral conscience of society. He wants it to maintain the faith and the Christian "Way of Life" in its institutions (Items 679 and 680). When the church does the same things as other institutions in society, it does a better job (Items 684 and 685). Why? Because it's the church, the moral conscience of the world, the possessor of truth and spiritual insight. Since it's all that, supporting it financially is a delight and a joy (Items 692 and 694). Payment is given for services rendered.

The appearance of financial support items on this dimension suggests that for many giving money to the church is on a *quid pro quo* basis. You do this and I will do that. It is not surprising that one of the first things some people do when they become dissatisfied with the church is to stop giving it money.

A score of 79 means agreement with all items. Disagreement with all items results in a score of 26. On the average, laymen tend more toward agreement than disagreement ($\overline{X} = 60.16$). Clergymen have a higher average ($\overline{X} = 63.58$). Pastors appear to have a greater investment in the supporting structures of the church than do laymen. It's understandable. They are the chief providers and beneficiaries of the mutual support system.

The appearance of this dimension on the factor of law orientation highlights the difficulty of using obvious measures of religiosity or favorable attitudes toward the church to assess religion. People support the church for a variety of reasons. For the law-oriented, as long as the church does what they want it to—supports and legitimizes their lives—it is natural to feel good about it and support it.

Multivariate Analysis. An analysis that accounts for 30% of the total variability across all scores identified characteristics that powerfully contribute to high endorsement of the mutual support system. They are a moderate to high level of emotional certainty of faith (Scale 66), a high belief in Christian Utopianism (Scale 36), and being married. Those who express doubts about faith in God and Jesus, do not feel good about religious practices (Scale 66), and are unhappy with the church, reject the mutual support system. A person may be quite certain about his faith and not have much interest in a Christian Utopia. But if he is quite unhappy with his church, he is likely to have below average interest in mutual support. If he is relatively happy, even a bit disgruntled with his church, he will remain about at the average.

The one consistent significant effect is age. Scores of two-year age groups on this scale show a decline from age 15 to the low point at ages 19-20. There is a sharp rise to ages 35-36 when the curve flattens out, rising more slowly to age 65. Here again, the common pattern of increase with increase in age is evident.

Additional Dimensions of Law Orientation

Two dimensions appear on both of the two major factors: gospel orientation and law orientation. They are the dimensions of the Exclusive Truth Claim of Christianity Exaggerated (Scale 16) and Christian Utopianism (Scale 36). In each case the contribution they make to each factor is about equal in strength (see factor loadings in Tables 5.1 and 6.1). What does that mean?

The strongest dimensions forming each factor are those with the highest loadings. In gospel orientation it is Transcendental Meaning in Life together with a number of dimensions of belief, measures both of cognitive dogma and of emotional content. On the law orientation of Lutherans, the strongest dimensions show a consistent emphasis upon external structures over spirit and internal life.

We assume that these two groups of strong dimensions represent higher positions in the hierarchical structure of beliefs, values, and attitudes of two distinct groups of persons. We have two types of hierarchical ordering of the total belief, value, and attitudinal system, each represented in one of the factors.

Each distinct type of hierarchical ordering shapes the meaning of the dimensions of belief, value, or attitude beneath the higher levels. By this model the two dimensions that are on both factors have a different sense or meaning depending upon the effects of dimensions higher or more central in the hierarchy. Consequently, the two dimensions in question do not have the same significance or meaning on both factors. They gain additional or surplus meaning from the context in which they are set. They have properties derived from the configuration of each type of hierarchical ordering.

On the factor of law orientation the two dimensions are appropriated and serve that hierarchy. The exclusive truth claim of Christianity is warped into service and exaggerated. It serves to legitimize the exaltation of structures. The church is the form of truth. Indeed, it is truth set in concrete. All else is error and evil, rightly despised and degraded. The same process affects the relationship between church and society. This results in the expansion of the relationship of church and society into the concept of a Christian Utopia and the establishment of the necessary mutual support system to bring about the Utopia.

On the factor of gospel orientation, these two dimensions take on a different significance. The exclusive truth claim of Christianity is maintained but not exaggerated into identification of the structure of the church with truth. The relationship between church and society is real and inevitable. Both are in the same world. Yet a tension is kept alive. One is not the other.

Another way of understanding the appearance of these two dimensions on both factors is through personality theory. If the two factors reflect two distinct personality types, each will differentially perceive and hold to the content of the beliefs, values, or attitudes reflected in the dimensions. In either case, the dimensions are not identical in form or function when set within the context of the factor.

The dimension of Exclusive Truth Claim Exaggerated contains items previous researchers claimed formed a causal link between orthodoxy of belief and prejudice. Our results suggest that the link is not to orthodoxy of belief but rather to the false religion of law orientation. Theoretically the antidote to law orientation is the gospel. The corrective for prejudice then becomes orthodox proclamation of the gospel rather than abandonment of orthodox belief.

A belief that theoretically may mediate the difference between the contextual meaning of the dimensions is discussed next.

SALVATION BY WORKS

This dimension, Scale 15, is a crass statement of "religion-in-general," the belief that doing right things, being sincere, and following the rules is what makes God think you're all right and opens the gates of heaven (Items 17, 31, 43, 44, 45, 54). It includes a syncretistic attitude: all religions are basically the same (Items 18 and 28), that is, they are systems of merit. This is the practical atheism of Lutheran theology. Merit is won by following the rules of achievement orientation set by the society (Items 26, 42, and 53). Society sets the standards, both of sin and merit (Item 30). A hard core, naive secularism is evident in the confidence that science will know everything (Item 51).

Agreement with all items gives a score of 97. Disagreement with all gives a score of 31. The average for laymen ($\overline{X} = 65.67$) places Lutherans in the middle between agreement and disagreement. Clergymen are widely divergent from laymen. Their average is 38.99. Belief in salvation by works is resoundingly rejected by pastors but not by laymen.

Seven out of ten Lutherans agree that all religions lead to the same God while four out of ten agree that all religions are equally important to God. About five in ten agree that hard work is directly beneficial. About four in ten agree with direct statements of salvation by works. One in ten gives society and science ultimate power.

Salvation by works appears on both law orientation and gospel orientation. However, it is negative on gospel orientation and positive on law orientation. This is the only dimension with strong opposed associations on the two factors. This suggests that the sharpest discrimination between the two factors lies along the dimension of belief in salvation by works.

Multivariate Analysis. Seven analyses simultaneously comparing up to 39 characteristics with this dimension have been done. Three of these analyses will be reported here. The first compared nine external characteristics. Members of the ALC and LCA with less education than high school scored higher on salvation by works. Members of the LC-MS with more than an eighth-grade education and up to the level of a post-graduate degree scored lower. These characteristics account for 11% of the total variability across all scores.

The fourth analysis included characteristics from previous steps and characteristics of beliefs and values. Persons with low commitment to Transcendental Meaning in Life (Scale 28) but with a high Need for Religious Absolutism (Scale 43) are highly committed to salvation by works. Those who have a high commitment to transcendental meaning, low need for unchanging structures (Scale 37), and are highly involved in personal practices of piety (Scale 41) are less inclined to believe in salvation by works. This analysis accounts for 20% of the variance across all scores.

The seventh analysis included a different mix of belief and value characteristics. Persons scoring moderate to high in self-oriented utilitarianism (Scale 67) who are members of the ALC or LCA score high in salvation by works. This analysis accounts for 22.4% of the variability.

AGE AND CHURCH BODY AND SALVATION BY WORKS

Age is consistently significant. The relationship is basically curvilinear, that is, in this case, U-shaped. Younger and older Lutherans are more likely to have a belief in salvation by works than those in middle age.

Church body affiliation is also consistently significant. Members of the LC-MS on the average consistently are lowest, with LCA highest in some comparisons and ALC highest in others.

The dimension of salvation by works is negatively related to the gospel orientation but is positively related to law orientation. This suggests that the sharpest and most obvious distinction between the two factors is on salvation by works. However, we do not wish to overlook the possibility that more subtle and less obvious forms of law orientation are equally prevalent. Law orientation stresses external structure over spirit and grace. It includes a component of harsh and critical judgment of other persons and groups. It contains a claim of superiority, of exploitation, of achievement orientation. It shows an ambivalent attitude toward society and its institutions. A clever and sophisticated pharisee is not going to get caught by the broad mesh net of the items on Scale 15. Nevertheless, we may expect that these basic elements of law orientation will still be present in less obvious form.

Boasting about one's own opinions and beliefs and condemning those of others is a universal human habit. Ability to criticize others occurs most readily where belief in achievement (in religion: belief in salvation by works) plays a potent role. Theoretically, where a sense of grace, forgiveness, and humility tempers the belief that achievement brings merit, glib and knee-jerk responses critical or judgmental of others are not as likely to occur. Prejudice, rejection, and need for static, rigid structure are not found on the heart of Lutheran piety where rejection of salvation by works suggests a sense of grace for some.

The remaining dimensions on the factor of law orientation cannot be fully treated here. Three dimensions support the understanding that the factors shows a basic elevation of external structure over spirit and grace and reliance upon achievement to measure the value of a man.

Horatio Alger Orientation (Scale 69 in Appendix C) developed from a group of items based on previous research.[14] It shows belief that human activity must accomplish things that can be measured by external standards. The person who agrees with that basic idea also is pessimistic about human nature and feels men need to be firmly controlled by external sanctions. His time orientation is toward the past.

Acceptance of Middle-Class Norms (Scale 50 in Appendix C) measures willingness to accept conventional societal norms, including some hypocritical norms. Together with Self-Oriented Utilitarianism this dimension highlights the ambivalent relationship to society that runs through the whole factor. Society and its structures must not change (Scale 37). They are standards by which everything, including self, is judged (Scales 34, 56, 57, and 15). Yet a person needs to bend or break the conventions of society to make any kind of life for himself (Scale 67).

Desire for a Dependable World (Scale 52) was discussed in Chapter 4. On law orientation it shows the consistency of resistance to change and a desire for stable structures in society.

Feelings of Pessimism (Scale 35) accentuates the contribution that alienation makes to law orientation. Together with Self-Oriented Utilitarianism (Scale 67) feelings of pessimism shows that some persons likely to typify law orientation are alienated persons. They are like spectators of life, involved but yet not involved. They are going through the motions of life in a haze of resignation, provoked to passion only when the rhythm of the motion is interrupted.

NEGATIVE DIMENSIONS OF LAW ORIENTATION

The human nature of Jesus is not acceptable to the law orientation of Lutherans. Law orientation among Lutherans is docetic, denying the true humanity of Jesus. There is no relationship between law orientation and the divinity of Jesus.[15] This shows that law orientation has no systematic relationship with the divinity of Jesus, either positive or negative. The law-orientated person may or may not accept the divinity of Jesus. But there is a systematic relationship with the human nature of Jesus. The law-oriented person tends to reject it.[16]

This dimension of belief in the human nature of Jesus (Scale 5) contains items describing Jesus in very human terms. Items such as "strong physically" (2) or "told jokes" (8) are included with stronger and more controversial statements like "felt sexual attraction" (13) and "struggled to discover who he really was" (15). Only one item, "strong physically," gained agreement from a majority of Lutherans (54%). Two out of five Lutherans agree that Jesus was "not necessarily attractive physically" (Item 6). One out of five agrees with the remainder of the items. This suggests that most Lutherans have a limited view of Jesus as a human being. They may be ready to accept purely physically limiting statements about Jesus' body but are not able to fathom the personality of Jesus as a truly human personality. The humanity of Jesus is a hollow, empty humanity for most Lutherans.

Agreement with all items brings a score of 42. Denying all items gives a score of 6. The average for all laymen (13.38) is close to rejection of all items. The average for pastors (26.03) is closer to agreement with all. Pastors are much more willing to describe Jesus in human terms than laymen are.

Multivariate Analysis. Analysis shows that characteristics most likely to describe persons accepting Jesus as a human being are rejection of a need for unchanging structures (Scale 37) and rejection of a need for religious absolutism. Ability to accept the humanity of Jesus is antithetical to two of the most potent forces in law orientation among Lutherans.

Belief in the humanity of Jesus can mean either that the person accepts both natures of Jesus, or that he accepts his humanity but rejects his claim of divinity. We combined the dimensions of the divinity and the humanity of Jesus to get information about persons likely to accept or reject both natures. When this combination was analyzed, those likely to accept or reject both natures of Jesus are best characterized by high commitment to transcendental meaning (Scale 28), are under 39 years old, and are willing to serve the church and community (Scale 47). Persons most likely to believe Jesus was only a man show a low commitment to transcendental meaning (Scale 28) and are generally liberal in doctrinal beliefs (Scale 44).

These findings suggest that efforts by the church to present the humanity of Jesus as a real and full humanity, not an empty humanity devoid of feeling, might be a potent force in resisting the inhibiting effects of law orientation.

There is also an indication that acceptance of the humanity of Jesus is associated with willingness to accept change and to be involved in service. This point will be made more clear in the discussion of mission and ministry in Chapter 7.

In this connection looking at belief in the humanity of Jesus by age is hopeful. Scores on the Humanity of Jesus scale are plotted by age on Figure 6.1. The curve is the opposite of that on all other dimensions of belief and misbelief except belief in God as Immanent Trinity (Scale 58). The highest level on both dimensions is in the youngest ages with a steady decline to age 65. This again suggests that a fundamental shift in the view of God may be happening as described in Chapter 5. If a new view of God does emerge, everything in the church will be affected.

Other dimensions negatively associated with law orientation form a

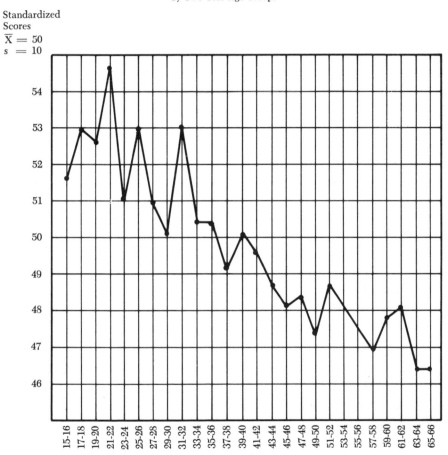

Figure 6.1 Average Scores on Humanity of Jesus (Scale 5) by Two-Year Age Groups

Standardized
Scores
$\overline{\text{X}} = 50$
$s = 10$

Two-Year Age Groups   15-66

separate factor that will be treated in Chapter 7. This negative association shows that law orientation resists any change in the concept of mission and ministry. Consequently, any changes in traditional models of mission and ministry are going to run head on into Lutherans whose type of religion is law orientation.

FAMILY LEVEL OF EDUCATION AND LAW ORIENTATION

Family level of education is negatively associated with law orientation. The negative association with the other dimensions of the factor means that persons most likely typifying law orientation are persons with a lower level of education in their family and personal lives. This is the same finding reported in many studies.

This does not mean necessarily that lack of intellectual ability characterizes law orientation. Persons most likely enmeshed in the inherently frustrating system of law orientation are those closest to the bottom of society, most weighed down by the structures. The pathos of this position has been evident throughout the factor. In the search for a home after the Garden, men turn to society, its forms and structures. These are elevated into the status of encompassing all reality, into being home in the universe. They are inadequate to meet that need. So what do you do? You try harder. You resist any change in structure. You judge all of life, self, and others by structures. It doesn't work. Frustration, resentment, and resignation follow. Home is nowhere.

Summary

Lutheran theology asserts there is only one false religion: living under the law without knowledge of the gospel. It has defined the form this false religion takes within the church. It has described the beliefs, attitudes, and behaviors connected with law orientation. Our findings support the validity of that theological theory.

Approximately 40% of the Lutheran population will manifest varying but significant degrees of law orientation. For those whose religion is primarily law orientation, external structures, including patterns of behavior, social system, and social stratification, assume ultimate importance. Rigidity, resistance to change, exploitation of religion and society for satisfaction of personal needs, absolutism, external conformity to consensual morality, and attitudes of prejudice toward other persons characterize such persons. There is also a tendency for law-oriented persons to reject a full-orbed humanity of Jesus. Belief in salvation by works tends to distinguish a law orientation from a gospel orientation at the most obvious level.

These results agree with major conclusions based upon previous research. There are two types of religion. One, law orientation, is highly associated with prejudice; while the other, gospel orientation, is not. Our results suggest that whereas law orientation is highly associated with lower levels of education, gospel orientation is not associated with education. Thus for those not able to grasp abstract concepts requiring a high level of intellectual ability, a growth in gospel understanding is still possible. This appears to have positive consequences for the individual in relationship with God and in relationship with society.

Notes

1. Preus, R., 1970.
2. Elert, W., 1962, p. 29.
3. Elert, W., 1962, pp. 405-414.
4. Plotting the relationship between Factor 1 and Factor 2 shows them to be clearly orthogonal, clustered around axes at a 90° angle. Their eigenvalues are the largest for any factors, 6.2 and 5.4 respectively.
5. Moore, W. E., 1969.
6. Two-way analysis of variance, all possible permutations of the six variables across 78 scales. The criteria selected for statistical and practical significance are given in Appendix A, pp. 353-354.
7. Two-way analysis of variance, see above Note 6.
8. Dittes, J., 1969.
9. Dittes, J., 1969, p. 634.
10. Factor loading of Scale 55, Family Level of Education, on Factor 1 is −.22.
11. Factor loading of dimensions reflecting prejudiced attitudes on Factor 1 are: Scale 34, .01, essentially unrelated; Scale 56, .09, essentially unrelated; Scale 57, .14, essentially unrelated though possible suggestion of very slight positive relationship.
12. Marty, M., 1964, p. 104.
13. The reciprocal averaging weights show that this is the case.
14. Kluckhohn, F. R. and Strodtbeck, F. L., 1961.
15. Factor loading for Scale 6 on Factor 2 is .04.
16. Chemnitz, M., 1971.

But one demand universally emerges from the situation everywhere, that is, back to the recapturing of the vision of what God in Christ meant the Christian community to be—a fellowship of believers, rooted in God and His divine redemptive order, and therefore committed to the service and salvation of the world; going to the bottom in its criticism of and opposition to the evil of the world, but at the same time going to the bottom in its identification with the sufferings and needs of the world.

—Hendrik Kraemer, *The Christian Message in a Non-Christian World*

7. Mission and Ministry

Three questions are answered by Lutherans in this chapter: Should the church become involved in social issues? What is the place of conscience in ministry and mission? How do Lutherans evaluate the present ministry of their own congregations?

Each answer is based on the information supplied by a factor consisting of six, seven, or eight dimensions.

One factor describes social involvement. Of the eight dimensions in this factor, seven reflect a concern for others and a desire to become involved on behalf of the less fortunate. This kind of activity is resisted, even opposed, by the misbelieving or law-oriented Lutheran. However, the majority of Lutherans opt for a new style of ministry in which social action is made an integral and necessary part of gospel proclamation.

The second question, regarding the place of conscience in mission and ministry, is answered by the eight dimensions of another factor. The data show that a majority of Lutherans carry a hopeful concern for the welfare of the less fortunate and feel responsible for what is happening in the community, nation, and world. Though they feel responsible, they want a freedom of conscience to live the ministry to which they feel called. They want to be freed from being pushed around, reprimanded, or scolded for not being involved in the top social or political priority of a zealous leader.

How do Lutherans evaluate the present ministry of their own congregations? The majority of Lutherans, especially those over age 24, positively evaluate the work of their congregation. The negative attitudes that do surface are more a reflection of the person and his own personal crises than they are a reflection of what each congregation is not doing or doing badly. Three dimensions in this factor show that negative attitudes toward one's family and congregation are associated with a non-identification with one's parents, a strong orientation to one's own age group, and, in some cases, involvement in the youth counter culture.

Luther wrote, "Now if someone is happy, we should not have the sour look the hypocrites have. They want to be something special, and in their unseemingly earnestness they pretend that they alone are wise and holy. All those who are happy and do not have the sour look they have they call fools and sinners. No, the joy of happy people should please us if it is not against God." [1]

The "joy of happy people" interests Lutherans. They want to be happy themselves and they want others to be happy. The question of what is the mission and ministry of the church has to do with the basic relationship of the church and the world. [2] The key to understanding concepts of mission and ministry lies in recognizing that religious belief is not merely "religious," that is, limited exclusively to God or a mystical experience of God. The classical "proofs" for the existence of God demonstrate that there is an essential equivalence between believing in *a certain* God and believing certain things about the world.

Religious belief is an interpretive activity. It is not limited to interpreting only a narrowly defined slice of experience. Rather, if it is truly religious, it interprets all that there is. Every event in the life of the believer points to and expresses the nature and reality of God. Religious belief is also the fundamental rule and governs the believer's response to all events. Insofar as concepts of mission and ministry are the response of the believer to the world, they reflect the type of religious belief he holds.

The Third Assembly of the Lutheran World Federation (Minneapolis, 1957) showed a continued interest in the "joy of happy people." "We are called to translate love and compassion into the structures of justice. In matters of civil liberties and racial integration, of concern for the uprooted and for people in areas of rapid social change, and of care for the mentally and physically disabled, our love fails if it does not materialize in recognition of human rights." [3]

Styles of caring about happy people change from age to age. That is a cultural problem. In an age of scarcity that officially endorsed a highly ascetic vision of the good life, Lutherans emphasized a shockingly positive view of drinking, dancing, music, sex, food, and science. In our affluent age that is preoccupied with oppression of men by other men, equally shocking views of men's rights may express the same religious belief. The one essential is that creation stays God's creation, and that man knows he belongs directly to God's creation. Therein lies the source of "the joy of happy people" for many Lutherans.

The current concern of Lutherans for happy people in God's good world is expressed in several groups of dimensions that combined in the factor analysis. The first of these factors is given in Table 7.1.

Table 7.1　Factor 3: Acceptance of Responsibility for Church and Christian Activity to Further Social Justice, Lay People Only (Parent Scales)

Load	Scale	Dimension Title
Positive		
.69	78	Openness to Change Within the Church
.66	65	Church Involvement in Social Issues
.61	12	The Church, Me, and Social Justice
.60	42	The Role of Pastors in Social Action
.59	64	Power Orientation to Social Issues
Negative		
−.30	56	Social Distance—Radical Life Styles
−.32	34	Generalized Prejudice

Should the Church Become Involved in Social Issues?

On the whole Lutherans as a group are quite positive toward social justice. This attitude tends to be stronger among younger Lutherans though surely is not limited to those under 30. The tendency is stronger in the direction of individual responsibility, but most will also accept church involvement while limiting the pastor's role a bit more than pastors themselves do. By and large there is no evidence of strong or massive resistance to the church being moderately active in social issues. There is, rather, a desire for the church to instruct and guide. Both clergy and laity, especially those in leadership positions or those who are willing to serve, tend to a greater acceptance of mission and ministry in social issues.

The sharpest resistance to this thrust comes from persons whose personal needs tend to be strongly tied to form and structure, who are more peripheral in their membership, and who show many of the characteristics of misbelief as outlined in Chapter 6.[4]

At the end of the chapter on law orientation of Lutherans we reported a number of negative loadings on dimensions of social justice. Each of these dimensions is part of the factor of mission and ministry to people.

Persons strongly typifying law orientation are opposed to the kind of mission and ministry represented in these dimensions.

We know where the most vehement resistance to caring about happy people in the cultural style of today will be found—in law orientation. This does not say that there is no possibility of questioning or resisting concern with social issues other than out of law orientation. There surely are valid substantive questions about the church's role in social issues. Rather it says that the violent, irrational, reflexive rejection of church involvement in social issues is likely rooted in the kind of misbelief detailed in Chapter 6.

Those who have honest and searching concern about the church getting sold down river by "the social gospel," or losing its theology in social involvement, should examine where some of the support for resistance to today's style of caring for people comes from. Conversely, those who fervidly embrace social involvement for the church in good conscience, caring about happy people, must care too about those who don't agree. Some are not stupid, nor are they cruel or heartless. They are hurting. They have no home either, but live in an alien, demanding, oppressing world of law.

OPENNESS TO CHANGE WITHIN THE CHURCH

A dimension of openness to change within the church (Scale 78) has a broad range of items that show concern with a diversity of social issues. The key item (536) shows that the person who would agree with all items feels that his church's doctrines encourage and support the attitudes shown in the other items. By his understanding he is faithful to his beliefs in holding the other attitudes.

He desires variety in worship services (Item 547). He is oriented to change in schools (Items 689 and 691) but wants continued support of church colleges (Item 682). He wants the church to speak out on social issues (Item 707), declaring the absolute truths he believes men can know (Item 48). He supports broader roles for women in the church (Items 708 and 709) and shares ecological concerns (Item 701). He speaks of revelation of God apart from Scripture (Item 47) and makes a distinction between law and gospel (Item 505). As a whole the scale reflects a loyal churchman rather highly oriented to the development of an open and responsible stance toward various contemporary questions having to do with happy people. (See Scale 78 in Appendix C, Section IV.)

The major thrust of Lutherans on this dimension is in the direction of agreement. The average (56.2) is closer to agreement (score = 76) than disagreement (score = 33) with all items. Pastors are more in agreement than laymen. The average for pastors is 63.3. Greatest disagreement, three out of five, is on the two items dealing with changes in school and the statement that only the gospel can change a man's life. Half agree and half disagree that couples should have only two children and that Lutheran doctrine encourages social reform. Three out of five favor continued support for colleges, a broader role for women in the church, and variety in the order of worship.

Multivariate Analysis. Persons more likely to accept these attitudes are under 26 years old and are students. Disagreement with these attitudes is more likely found among persons over 26 years old with an educational level up to college graduation who are members of the LC-MS and married. Married persons not highly oriented to social justice are likely to reject these attitudes also.

Age is related to this dimension. It is younger Lutherans who are most willing to express desire for more openness in the church. A higher educational level tends to be associated with higher interest in openness within the church, but mildly so. Among those over 26 years old with more than a college degree, clergymen show higher interest than do the others. Members of the ALC and LCA over 26 years old with up to a college degree are slightly more inclined to the openness reflected in this scale than comparable members of the LC-MS.

These findings suggest that pastors, who generally wish more openness within the church than laymen, will find their support coming from younger persons, most likely unmarried or students. Resistance is likely to be highest among middle-aged, married persons. Pastors of the LC-MS are likely to face somewhat more resistance than their brethren in the ALC and LCA.

Not all young persons are highly committed to issues of social justice, however. Among those ages 15-22 who don't show much interest in social issues, there is a division. Those who don't show much need for structure in their life also want more openness in the church than those who want some structure in their lives. This says that persons who more readily tolerate openness in their own personal lives, even if they aren't very highly oriented to social issues, can accept more openness in the church.

Among older persons (ages 23-65), those who emphasize the humanity of Jesus or recognize *both* his humanity and divinity, are more open to change within the church than persons who have a more limited view of both natures of Jesus or who emphasize only his divinity.

The pattern of the characteristics that tend to raise scores suggest two correlates to acceptance of greater openness in the church. One is closer identification with change in the culture, with a weakening or rejection of religious elements in life. The other is through a clearer understanding of the fullness of the two natures of Jesus and an emphasis upon spiritual growth that is not closely identified with cultural factors. Under either circumstance one is likely to find a greater acceptance of openness in the church.

CHURCH INVOLVEMENT IN SOCIAL ISSUES

A dimension of church involvement in social issues (Scale 65 in Appendix C) is next on the factor, Acceptance of Responsibility for Church and Christian Activity to Further Social Justice. The strongest items on the scale (256, 257, and 348) show the range of attitudes people have about the church's involvement in social issues. Is it the appropriate ministry of the church, or is ministry done apart from social issues?

On the questions specifically relating to the role of the church, Lutherans are almost equally divided. Half favor involvement and half resist (Items 256 and 257). On all of the other items of this scale except one (310) about four out of five Lutherans are in agreement. They agree that racial discrimination should end and that the church should help. They agree that people can be trusted. Fifty-two percent agree that all war is morally wrong, a surprising finding in a church body which has traditionally held that there is a possibility of just warfare. Nine in ten agree that a disease model explains deviant behavior. Eight in ten want ecumenical mission work. However, three in five are not willing to abolish the death penalty.

Lutherans don't differ much on attitudes toward social issues themselves, but do differ more on whether the church should get involved. In spite of being conservative politically and theologically, most Lutherans share a rather liberal stance toward these kinds of social issues. There may well be more inflammatory social issues, such as open tolerance of homosexuality, on which Lutherans might differ more sharply. On the relatively safe kinds of social issues represented in this scale, they are consistently liberal. Also pastors are more strongly inclined to agreement than laymen.[5] This says that Lutherans on the whole have a commitment to a just and liberalized society. If they are going to fight, it will be about whether the church institution itself should be an active participant or whether it should leave its members free to participate as individual citizens.

Multivariate Analysis. What kinds of people tend to favor church involvement in social issues? One group of persons committed more highly to church involvement in social issues is made up of those who show little need for unchanging structure and are from 15-26 years old plus several scattered two-year groups above age 26. (The relationship of age is not clean-cut here. A person can be middle-aged and have little need for structure and be quite open to church involvement in social issues.) A second group of persons who will readily accept church involvement in social issues is made up of those with a low level of generalized prejudice and a low level of need for unchanging structure. What appears to count most in getting to rather high levels of acceptance of church involvement in social issues is rejection of putting oneself or others into rigid boxes or categories.

What kinds of people resist the church's involvement in social issues? One group is made up of people of a scattering of middle ages from 33 to 65 who are quite pessimistic about life and show considerable need for unchanging structures in life. (Here, too, age is not consistently related. Some middle-aged persons may be more resistant to this characteristic than others.) The other low group is composed of persons who score moderate to high on generalized prejudice, low on belief in salvation by works, and high on need for unchanging structures.

Where is the battle for mission and ministry being fought? Law orientation among Lutherans, the choice of structure over spirit, emerges as one polarity around which the battle is being fought. For some people (law-oriented), identity and meaning are borrowed from stable structures external to the individual. When those structures change or get a little slippery, it is for them not just the structure. It is the very substance of life itself that is being drained off. Is it any wonder that intense, even violent, emotion frequently follows?

The church is caught in a cleft stick here. On a human level, the love it wants to show requires concern with the social issues of today. As the contemporary situation has shaped up, when the church does go ahead, it is perceived as a loveless and rejecting church by many for whom structure is the substance of life.

THE CHURCH, ME, AND SOCIAL JUSTICE

If the church is to engage in mission and ministry to people today, what is the role of the individual Christian? The next dimension (Scale 12) shows that Lutherans on the whole accept responsibility for their individual participation in building a just society. Seven out of ten want their church to help them by instruction and by giving opportunity for service. However, actions like cutting off financial support of church institutions to force integration are not attractive to six out of ten. Seven in ten agree that a business should not discriminate against blacks, but 52% reject working to let Negroes buy houses wherever they wish. Six out of ten reject the judgment that their congregations have failed in civil rights issues.

Clergymen score considerably higher than laymen on this dimension (clergy $\overline{X} = 65.03$, lay $\overline{X} = 52.97$). The weight of both groups is closer to theoretical agreement (score = 73) than disagreement (score = 19) with all items. Once again the concept of active involvement in social issues is not rejected by Lutherans.

Multivariate Analysis. By comparing large numbers of characteristics simultaneously with this dimension, we find that persons who are committed to church involvement in social issues and who are also highly committed to personal leadership in their congregations score highest on this scale. Apparently the persons the church either has in leadership or who are willing to be leaders are most highly committed to individual responsibility in social justice. Conversely, those who reject leadership or service roles in the church are least likely to express agreement with this dimension of individual responsibility for social concerns. This means that both clergy and lay leaders in the church are accepting responsibility for social justice. Younger pastors (under age 50) are the highest scoring group. People likely to score lowest on this scale are laymen of mixed ages who report never going to Sunday school during the period of their church membership.

If we assume that the commitment of pastors and lay leaders is going to have an effect on the church, we can look for increased involvement in the social issues that define today's style of mission and ministry to people.

THE ROLE OF PASTORS IN SOCIAL ACTION

What is the attitude prevalent among Lutherans about pastors' activity in social issues? The forty-second dimension tells us. Seven out of ten Lutherans accept their pastor as a citizen. They do not want to make him a political eunuch. He can support candidates and take stands. However, if he tries this from the pulpit, he is in trouble with seven out of ten Lutherans. Apparently the pulpit has special meaning for most Lutherans. It is not viewed as a political or social rostrum for preachers.

Seven in ten Lutherans are also ready for their pastor to lead and instruct them on social issues via study groups. But that's where they draw the line. Beyond that there is increasing resistance to forms of social activism by pastors. Nine in ten Lutherans don't want their pastors engaged in civil disobedience.

The average for laymen (39.19) places the weight on the side of disagreement with all items, thus tending to restrict the pastor's range of activity. The clergy average (46.93) is closer to agreement with all items expressing a broader range of activity. There is some tension between the idea laymen have of the role of pastors and that which pastors have. However, it is not a sharp and savage cleavage.[6]

Multivariate Analysis. Persons most likely to be farthest from the pastors in their idea of the pastor's role are those who reject church involvement in social issues and who deny having pessimistic feelings. Other persons likely to restrict the role of pastors show a high need for structure, have been married more than six years, and also deny feelings of pessimism.

Persons closer to the pastor's own idea of what their role should be are those highly committed to social involvement of the church and free of a need for structures in their lives. A second analysis found persons denying need for structures who also tended to be peer-oriented—that is, those who pay more attention to people of their own age and status—to be more favorable toward an activist pastor.

POWER ORIENTATION TO SOCIAL ISSUES

This dimension (Scale 64) is most interesting.[7] Two groups of persons are responding to the items out of differing perspectives. We know this from the markedly different pattern of correlation this dimension has (Scale 64) when compared to the dimension of church involvement in social issues (Scale 65).[8] There is essentially no systematic relationship between this dimension (Scale 64) and the measures of prejudice. There is a strong negative relationship between prejudice and the dimension of church involvement in social issues (Scale 65). There is a positive relationship between this dimension (Scale 64) and salvation by works, pessimism, peer orientation, and self-oriented utilitarianism. There is either a negative relationship or no relationship between church involvement in social issues (Scale 65) and salvation by works, pessimism, peer orientation, and self-oriented utilitarianism.

On the face of it the items on power orientation look like liberal social reform attitudes. But they do not really work that way. We find that persons high on this dimension include *both* those who most reject unchanging structures and those who need unchanging structures. Those showing higher power orientation to social issues believe in salvation by works, are highly pessimistic, and *either* reject or need structure in their lives.[9]

On this scale we are getting both the pessimistic left *and* the pessimistic right, the frustrated reformers and the frustrated preservers. They agree that social issues are most important, one group out of desire for change and the other out of desire to squash the revolutionaries. They agree that reform is crucial, but for one reform is change and for the other reform is return. The frightening thing is that they also agree that "in the last analysis it's having the power that makes the difference" (Item 436). There are the makings of civil war.

Multivariate Analysis. Those persons who reject the belief of salvation by works, yet who are moderately committed to church involvement in social issues, are those who are likely to reject the view that the power struggle is what is ultimately significant in settling social issues.

On the other hand, those persons who *do* believe in salvation by works, and are highly committed to church involvement in social issues, and are generally not very pessimistic in their view of human nature will tend to agree that "It's having the power that makes the difference." Persons of all ages, from the youngest to the oldest, hold this view, so the factor of age here appears to be insignificant.

A third subgroup does show a consistent age pattern. They are moderate to high in belief in salvation by works, not very pessimistic, and *not* very interested in church involvement in social issues. They are moderately or highly committed to need for unchanging structure in their lives. This group has both the youngest (ages 17-26) and the oldest (ages 55-65) expressing a power orientation toward social issues.

For both clergy and laity the average for the group is midway between the theoretical points of agreement and disagreement with all items. Expression of concern with social issues and desire for change in the church and society are not rejected by Lutherans as a whole.

These findings suggest that viewing the current situation in society as a conflict which will be settled by possession of power by one group or the other is most characteristic of those who are are on the extremes of a number of dimensions. It is significant that those dimensions are the ones that are heavily involved in prejudice: belief in salvation by works, pessimism, and need for structure. What happens in persons who measure themselves by external standards, are pessimistic, but who resist or embrace structure while engaging in a power struggle? Win or lose, structure is then crucial. Here are the seeds of the tyranny and bigotry of left and right.

NEGATIVE ASSOCIATION

The dimensions making up this factor are negatively associated with generalized prejudice (see Table 7.1 above). This is consistent with the thrust of the factor: acceptance of responsibility for church and Christian to actively further social justice. Removal of segregation and elimination of prejudice are a part of that thrust.

What Is the Place of Conscience in Mission and Ministry?

In May 1652 John Milton addressed a famous sonnet to Oliver Cromwell, Lord Protector of England, asking:

> Help us to save free conscience from the paw
> Of hireling wolves, whose Gospel is their maw.

The factor next reflecting one attitude of Lutherans toward mission and ministry to people is a contemporary echo of that plea. In the pressure of accepting today's style of mission and ministry through active involvement in social issues, please leave room for the man of free conscience to exercise his compassion as his conscience guides him.

The factor has five dimensions that are unique to it. Two are positive and three negative:

FACTOR 4
Lay People Only (Parent Scales)

Load	Scale	Dimension Title
Positive		
.64	60	Individual Christian Responsibility
.56	59	Social Utility of Christianity
Negative		
−.52	62	Service Without Proclamation
−.63	35	Pessimism
−.67	61	Image of Lutherans as Different

The five dimensions are assessing the same factor but getting opposite poles. In understanding the factor and its meaning for mission and ministry the context of both positive and negative poles must be kept in mind.

For persons strongly committed to the heart of Lutheran piety, a sense of mission and ministry comes naturally. For these people, conscience does not exclude involvement in social issues, but it may affect the shape or pattern of involvement. There is a relationship between the heart of Lutheran piety and individual Christian responsibility.[10]

INDIVIDUAL CHRISTIAN RESPONSIBILITY

Persons who feel quite earnest about their individual Christian responsibility and sincerely look to their church to help them be compassionate, caring persons feel they have a responsibility to their society. They are not just trying to assure pie-in-the-sky by their religion. They may not be very responsive to big promotions or noble causes. Their sense of responsibility tends more toward individualized activity growing out of their personal conscience.

The strongest positive expression is given in Scale 60 named Individual Christian Responsibility. The key item is a statement recalling much of the preaching about the doctrine of the royal priesthood (340). Every Christian is a witness. Strong agreement with all of the other items reflects a man of firm conscience. He is strongly committed to loyalty to Scripture and the family (Items 296 and 357). He respects the consciences of others (Item 298). He follows his own conscience and thinks one should protest when he observes wrong (Item 362). He knows that doubts may assail him (Item 349) yet is willing to abandon Christianity if he becomes convinced that resurrection is false. His conscience would not allow him to continue (Item 309). This is the only item on the scale which most Lutherans reject. From 73% to 94% agree with all other items, but only 29% agree that they would leave the faith if the resurrection were myth. Most, however, will only *agree* with the items, not *strongly agree*.

Pastors agree more strongly than do laymen. The pastors' average is 60.05 while the average for laity is 56.22. Agreement with all items gives a score of 54. Strong agreement gives a score of 71. On the whole, therefore, Lutherans tend to agree with the items of this scale.

Multivariate Analysis. Persons who are more committed to individual Christian responsibility are not pessimistic and are conservative in their doctrinal beliefs. If a person is mildly to highly pessmistic the way to a sense of individual responsibility is through a high commitment to personal piety, to transcendental meaning in life, and to church involvement in social issues. However, if a person is inclined toward pessimism, does not engage in personal piety, and rejects transcendental meaning in life, he will likely place less emphasis on individual Christian responsibility.

Social Utility of Christianity

The dimension named Social Utility of Christianity (Scale 59) shows a strong emphasis upon positive emotions. A majority of Lutherans agree that the church helps develop and maintain compassionate concern for other people. They also think that kind of compassion is beneficial both to individuals (Items 546 and 544) and to the society (Items 538 and 541).

The average score for all laymen is 19.93 which is very near the theoretical midpoint of 19 for agreement with all items. Pastors average at 21.84, slightly closer to strong agreement. However, the persons of most interest would be those who consistently strongly agree or disagree. It is hard to say No to any of the items. It would be almost like saying No to motherhood and apple pie. Those who did say No or those who say Yes most emphatically tell us the most about this dimension.

Multivariate Analysis. Strong agreement with the four items of this dimension (Scale 59) characterizes about 15% of Lutherans while an additional 58-69% agree. The connection between strong agreement with these items and concern with society and individuals is clear when we find out who is likely to score high. Persons highly committed to establishment of a Christian Utopia and moderately to highly committed to church involvement in social issues will be more inclined to strong agreement with the compassionate concern expressed in this scale. Further, those who are only moderately committed to the idea of a Christian Utopia, who show moderate to high interest in the church being actively involved in social issues, and who deny pessimism are likely to express greater compassionate concern. The same is true of persons who scored in the top half of the dimension assessing church involvement in social issues. Also, many who may feel that the church should not be actively involved but do agree with liberal social attitudes may show up here strongly endorsing individual compassion.

Persons who reject the idea of a Christian Utopia and who express doubts about the faith and religious practices tend to disagree with the idea of the church helping them develop compassion.

Service Without Proclamation

This dimension (Scale 62) reflects a rejection of the idea of proclaiming an exclusive Christian message. According to the items of this dimension, the church has no business trying to change other people's religion (Item 320). Meeting the physical needs of persons is more important than preaching either law or gospel (Items 531 and 534). Aesthetic needs determine the meaning of worship (Item 539) rather than any specific content. The idea behind agreement with these four items is that it is all right to respond to people's needs but inappropriate to present a claim that Christianity is better or more truthful than the religion they now have. This unsophisticated understanding of the theological position known as "social gospel" is the negative side of ministry and mission.

Most Lutherans do not agree with this view. The average for all laymen (23.22) is at the point of disagreement with all items. Pastors tend more toward disagreement. However, 40% of all respondents agree with the statement that we shouldn't try to change other people's religion (Item 320). This gives some insight into the weakness of support for mission work done in the nineteenth-century manner of sending missionaries to foreign heathen lands. One in five agrees with the other three items.

Multivariate Analysis. Persons likely to agree with this view of Christianity tend to be pessimistic, believe in salvation by works, and reject a transcendental world view. Those who strongly reject this view of Christianity as social gospel are not pessimistic and are conservative in their doctrinal beliefs.

The two other dimensions that are negatively associated with this factor show that persons who perceive their individual Christian responsibility in terms of compassionate caring for others also reject essentially negative or critical views of Lutherans, and are not pessimistic but are rather hopeful.

SUMMARY

The loyal churchman deeply concerned with his own conscience and the conscience of others has been the center of our discussion here. He sees the church training and equipping him for compassionate caring by helping him to develop and maintain a sympathetic emotional stance toward other people. He may or may not want the church as an institution to be actively involved in social issues. He may be rather indifferent to such matters unless it appears to him that the proclamation of the gospel is threatened by that kind of involvement. He sees his kind of mission and ministry—centered around individuals—as an expression and outgrowth of his own faith commitment. He believes if he lives this out in his life, it will have an effect upon the society in which he lives.

At the opposite pole is the person who is basically negative toward the church. He rejects its mission and ministry except as it may meet a limited range of needs. He tends to be pessimistic about his own life and to show prejudiced attitudes. He does not expect the church to change anything.

How Do Lutherans Evaluate the Present Effectiveness of Their Church's Ministry?

Mission and Ministry and Me

Now we come to a personal evaluation of the church's mission and ministry. How does it feel to *me?* Is the church doing anything for *me?* The factor is bi-polar. There are two positive dimensions and two that are negatively associated with the factor. It tells us about the persons who feel best about the church and those who feel alienated from it:

FACTOR 8
Evaluation of the Present Effectiveness of the Church's Ministry

Load	Scale	Dimension Title
Positive		
.59	18	Identification with Parents
.56	13	Family and Congregational Caring Life
Negative		
−.52	63	Peer Orientation
−.55	27	Disappointment with the Church

Family and Congregational Caring Life

For Lutherans there is little psychological separation between their family life and their congregational life (Scale 13). Both are of one piece. The mission and ministry of the church is intimately experienced within the family group (Items 589, 593, 596, 597, 601). Caring for others is seen as integral to both family and congregational life (Items 588, 592, 593, 594, 598, 603, 605, 606, 607). Caring for others includes both direct personal service (Items 593, 605, 606, 607) and commitment to broader social issues (Items 588, 592, 594, 603). There is a sense of belonging to the congregation (Items 590 and 601) and confidence that the purpose of mission and ministry is understood by the members (Item 599).

Most Lutherans tend to agree with this view of the church's impact upon their lives. The average for laymen (X = 96.22) is closer to theoretical agreement with all items (score = 127) than disagreement (score = 39). Clergymen are slightly more favorable (X = 101.68). About three out of five agree with all items except for two (588 and 597). Three out of five do not feel that their congregations are active in social issues. Half do not believe their congregation is trying to bridge the "generation gap."

The person saying No to all items is essentially rejecting any effort at ministry by the church, feeling it is either nonexistent or meaningless and futile. He is also showing a rather severe judgment of his family life. One-fifth of Lutherans tend toward a pretty dismal view of their congregational and family life. Five percent quite emphatically reject a positive understanding of church and family.

Multivariate Analysis. Persons who are likely to have a positive view of church and family are those who say they are quite or very happy with the church and have family devotions at least occasionally to daily; they may have some dislikes of their family life, but by and large they are happy with their family. They tend to engage in personal practices of piety (Scale 41) and generally feel a sense of purpose and meaning in their lives (Scale 68). Those who tend to a jaundiced view of church and family generally say they are unhappy with the church and are from 15-32 years old.

A second analysis shows two ways to find persons with a positive view of church and family. They both start out with people who say they are happy with the church. Then those highly active in personal witnessing who are married and have children show up highly positive about church and family. For those not active in personal witnessing activities but who are quite certain about their faith, middle-aged (approximately ages 30-52), and very happy with their church, a positive view of church and family as shown in the items of this dimension is quite possible. On the other hand, persons who say they are unhappy with the church and are either quite young or quite old are more likely to reject many of these items.

The general impression is that persons can be happy with church and family in a number of ways, but if you're unhappy, there's only one way. It just isn't meeting my needs. It is more characteristic of younger and older Lutherans to feel that way.[11] It may be that this dimension shows why. If congregational and family life are of one piece and mission and ministry are viewed from that perspective, we would expect most things that happen to reflect that unity. Church programs are built with the unconscious assumption that family units are the church. In family life the church and faith are frequently used to buttress up roles and systems of behavior. Persons without a family of their own—the young adult and the older person whose family is gone—are going to have the strongest sense that their needs aren't even recognized, much less met.

SUPPORTING THE CHURCH

For those perceiving church and family as a unitary dimension and feeling quite positive about it, the dimension of Mutual Support Among Church, Society, and Individuals (Scale 26 loads almost as heavily on this factor, .41, as on Factor 2, .47) shows the other half of the relationship: what I give to the church. It has meaning in my life. I appreciate its guidance and programs. I support that. (This dimension is more fully discussed in Chapter 6 because it is more closely related to law orientation.) Its appearance here as well as on the heart of Lutheran piety and law orientation of Lutherans tells us that the whole question of support given to the church is a very complex matter. This dimension has significant positive loadings on three factors out of the sixteen generated in the second-order factor analysis. In each case the factor loading is positive and of somewhat the same magnitude. Only one other dimension (Scale 36, Christian Utopianism) appears with significant positive loadings on more than two factors. This means that people come at the question of the support they give the church and what they expect out of the church from at least three different approaches. (There may be more, but we have found three for lay people.) One is closely connected with beliefs, largely cognitive and doctrinal, forming the gospel orientation. A second is tied in with law orientation and expectation of positive return to the individual. The third shows a sense of more individual gain from mission and ministry in family life and caring for others and a readiness to support out of that framework. That makes quite a few taskmasters for the church to serve.

IDENTIFICATION WITH PARENTS

On what issues do I see myself as like my parents or different from them? The dimension (Scale 18) is named Identification with Parents. Nine out of ten Lutherans like and respect the adults they know (Item 384). Two out of three Lutherans feel that they are the same as their parents when it comes to being respectful of authority (Item 409), believing in democracy (Item 412), being honest with themselves (Item 414), and concerned with the situation in the country (Item 418). A sizable proportion, about one-third, see themselves more likely to compromise (Item 408), more open to other persons and the world (Items 413 and 415), and more optimistic than their parents (Item 416). If Lutherans see themselves changing along attitudes like these, here is the direction: toward greater flexibility and openness.

The highest scores are attached to the perception of being quite similar to parents. We discover that along with a positive evaluation of church and family life and a commitment to support the church goes a positive identification with parents.

DISAPPOINTMENT WITH THE CHURCH

The opposite pole of the factor is a negative evaluation of the church. The dimension (Scale 27) is called Disappointment with the Church. The key item (697) is a flat statement that the teachings of the Lutheran church have nothing to do with real life. There is readiness to abandon church colleges and agencies (Items 686 and 703). The church is blind or ineffective (Item 687). The church is money-grubbing (Item 693) and cold and heartless (Item 695). Finally, the school is in the same condition—basically ineffective (Item 690). Somewhat less than one-fifth of Lutherans are likely to agree with all or most of these statements. An additional 5-11% are undecided but tend more toward agree-ment than disagreement. Approximately one quarter of all Lutherans are quite disappointed with the church.

The issue that generates the greatest expression of negative feeling is money. Almost one-half feel there is too great a stress upon money. One-third feel that nobody in their congregation would know or care if they dropped out. One-third feel that the church is blind or ineffec-tive in addressing "today's problems." We don't know if this is a higher or lower level of discontent compared to previous years or generations. This is the way it was in the summer of 1970. However, none of the three principal areas of complaint—money, lack of warmth, and irrele-vance—is exactly new to the church's consciousness. Those complaints have been around for a long time.

It is significant that this negative feeling relates to a larger dimension: positive or negative evaluation of the church. Specific complaints are not separate, isolated problems that can be solved one by one to reach the millenium. Our results show that a given person has either a basic posi-tive or negative evaluative stance toward the church. If it is negative, there won't be one complaint. There will be many. If one complaint is fixed up, nothing is going to change anyway. Another grievance will replace the one taken away. The problem is not issues, questions, or programs. It is people.

Multivariate Analysis. What do we know about persons likely to show a high level of disappointment with the church? In each case a high level of dis-content is found in persons who experience lack of emotional certainty of faith, or doubt. When doubt is added on to a high level of responsiveness to one's own peer group, high disappointment results. This tends to indicate that the greatest reservoir of discontent linked to doubt may be among youth, but one can also find persons other than youth largely shaped by the influence of their peer group.

A second subgroup of persons who are not highly peer-oriented but who are highly pessimistic and who deny a transcendental world view also show disappointment with the church. This can be at any age—young, middle-aged, or older. For both groups a dimension of belief or value is the most powerful influence. This confirms the point that the problem is not in programs or techniques, important though they may be. The problem of disappointment with the church is basically the problem of belief—unbelief.

Persons least likely to score in such a way as to show disappointment are the ones who *say* they are happy with the church. If they deny pessimism, reject salvation by works, and had a father who was religious and active in church, they will not likely be disappointed. Another group of contented churchmen may or may not be peer-oriented to a moderate degree. If they deny pessimism and reject a view of Christianity as social gospel, they tend to show a low level of disappointment. Contentment with the church is most associated with beliefs, not with specific issues or questions.

Peer Orientation

A negative feeling about the church is also related to Peer Orientation (Scale 63). Peer orientation constitutes rejection of older persons and the family unit as a significant source of influence. It includes a negative evaluation of church as well.

Mission of the Church

We included items in the survey giving respondents a chance to express their views of a traditional model of mission: proclaiming the gospel to *all* the world. But the items did not form a cohesive group. Some appeared on dimensions other than a clear-cut mission–evangelism. Those with specific reference to an evangelistic missionary task did not form a single dimension. This tells us that attitudes regarding mission work are not simple and clear-cut but rather form a complex, many-sided network. Further research is required to understand more about this difficult question.

However, we can present a simple table of response frequencies to the specific mission–evangelism items and the items which are connected with a theological basis for world-wide missionary work. Be cautious in interpreting these figures inasmuch as they do not describe a singular, clean dimension (see Table 7.2).

A general impression from the percentages is that most Lutherans endorse a traditional view of the missionary task with a strong feeling for joint mission work with other Christians. There is a desire that mission activities seek to meet physical problems as well as spiritual needs. However, 40% agreed that other people should be left alone and that we should not try to change their religion. This indicates why the items would not form a scale. There is more going on in the minds of Lutherans than a simple question, "Should we or should we not send missionaries to preach the gospel?"

The basis for many mission sermons has been, "Men must believe in Jesus to be saved. If they don't know Jesus, they go to hell! Therefore give generously so missionaries can save them from hell." Do Lutherans think so? Again the items to be reported did not form a scale. Hence all that can be done is to report the percentages of the individual items (see Table 7.3).

The percentages illustrate the reason for failing to get clear-cut dimensions. Three out of four Lutherans say all religions lead to the same God, yet three out of four Lutherans, and some of them must be the same people, say belief in Jesus Christ is absolutely necessary for salvation. Half of the respondents reject the statement that all religions are equally important before God, but only 13% agree that being ignorant of Jesus prevents salvation. Something very curious is going on.

Table 7.2   Response to Missionary Task Ideas

Item Number	Item	Strongly Agree	Agree	Disagree	Strongly Disagree
525.	The primary task of the Church is to proclaim the Gospel so that people believe in Jesus Christ as their Saviour.	34%	53%	8%	1%
528.	To present Christianity as one religion, missionaries should plan evangelism together with other missionaries representing various denominations.	11	63	19	2
542.	It is equally important to preach the Gospel and to work to improve the material well-being of people so that these two aims are kept in balance.	11	60	22	2
537.	Missionaries must teach people to give of their time and treasure in response to Christ's love for them regardless of their poverty.	9	58	25	3
320.	Christians should leave other people alone and not try to change their religion.	5	35	46	11
531.	Missionaries should not proclaim God's Law too often to people suffering from poverty and sickness.	3	20	59	15
534.	The Church's task to help eliminate physical sufferings of people is more important than proclaiming the Gospel by preaching and teaching.	2	17	60	16
540.	Our missionaries should not cooperate in joint evangelism with missionaries of other denominations, as such actions hinder the spread of the pure Gospel.	2	10	62	22

Table 7.3 Response to Items Concerning Salvation Only Through Jesus Christ

Item Number	Item	No Response	Yes	No	?
18.	Although there are many religions in the world, most of them lead to the same God.	2%	72%	23%	3%
28.	Being tolerant means that one accepts all religions—including Christianity—as equally important before God.	3%	41%	44%	12%
		No Response	1	2	3
420.	Do you think that belief in Jesus Christ as Saviour,	5%	74%	18%	4%
	1. Is absolutely necessary for salvation				
	2. Would probably help for salvation				
	3. Probably has no influence for salvation				
422.	Do you think people being completely ignorant of Jesus, as might be the case for people living in other countries,	6%	13%	39%	42%
	1. Will definitely prevent salvation				
	2. May possibly prevent salvation				
	3. Probably has no influence on salvation				

The most we can say is that most Lutherans appear to say belief in Jesus is necessary *for me* and the Christian faith is right and true *for me*. They appear to reject statements implying the same for the other person. What this means for the traditional model of mission is not clear. It seems to imply that the mission sermon appealing for support for the salvation of the heathen is politely turned off by most Lutherans. When we look at these individual items in relation to age, it becomes evident that this latter attitude is likely to be most characteristic of younger Lutherans.

Summary

Three factors, each composed of a number of dimensions, reveal different ideas about what the mission and ministry of the church in today's world is. Lutherans are still concerned with happy people in God's good world. They seek meaningful ways to oppose "the evil of the world" and identify "with the sufferings and needs of the world."

There is widespread acceptance among Lutherans of the vision of a just and humane society. There is little evidence of commitment to a classic laissez faire social system. But there is disagreement among Lutherans as to what role the church and pastors have in moving toward that vision. We know that some of the resistance to active church involvement in social issues derives from misbelief.

A second avenue to expression of Christian compassion to society is through individual Christian responsibility. Men who stress a free conscience see their individual responsibility in clear and unequivocal terms: to serve other men. There is no indication that this idea excludes active church involvement, but rather this approach appears to exist side by side with an active church role.

A third idea about mission and ministry covers what a man feels about the direct impact of the Christian faith and the church on his religious and family life. Men evaluate mission and ministry as a whole either positively or negatively. A negative evaluation is most closely linked to a crisis in belief rather than to specific issues.

A major component of the understanding of mission and ministry in the past has been the concept of conversion of the heathen throughout the world. Lutherans today are confused about this issue. It appears that many have compartmentalized their faith, on the one hand claiming the necessity of the Christian faith for them, but on the other hand accepting the validity of other religions for other people. This may be called relativism or synergism. Whatever it is called, Lutherans are not likely to respond enthusiastically to the rallying cry, "Evangelize the world!"

Notes

1. Elert, W., 1962, p. 458.
2. Elert, W., 1962, p. 454.
3. Lutheran World Federation, Messages of the Third Assembly, 1957, p. 114.
4. Specific data supporting these summary statements will be supplied in the detailed discussion of this factor as the chapter proceeds.
5. Pastors' average is 69.04. Range was 44 through 97.
6. Both averages, clergy and lay, are within one standard deviation on the distribution of scores.
7. Though the scale is technically the weakest of all 78 scales, Rxx = .45, it is very interpretable and adds a meaningful dimension to this factor.
8.

Scale	Scale Name	Correlation with Scale 64 Power Orientation to Social Issues	Correlation with Scale 65 Church Involvement in Social Issues
12	The Church, Me, and Social Justice	.15	.41
15	Salvation by Works	.30	−.05
34	Generalized Prejudice	.05	−.56
35	Pessimism	.22	−.22
37	Need for Unchanging Structure	.04	−.40
56	Social Distance—Radical Life Styles	−.09	−.46
57	Social Distance—Racial and Religious Groups	.02	−.35
63	Peer Orientation	.32	.15
67	Self-Oriented Utilitarianism	.21	−.20

9. These statements are based on AID analysis. This is the only AID analysis on which we found Q_1 and Q_4 on a dimension used as a predictor variable forming a separate subgroup together.
10. The dimension that has the highest factor loading (.64) on this factor also has a fair sized factor loading (.34) on the first factor, the Heart of Lutheran Piety. This suggests that the style of mission and ministry reflected in this factor is related to the first factor, the Heart of Lutheran Piety.
11. In AID analysis, younger and older age groups were lowest in averages for two-year age groups. The middle age groups were the higher in averages.

Why should a coral snake need two glands of neurotoxic poison to survive while a King snake, *so similarly marked,* needs none. Where is the Darwinian logic there . . . ?

—Joan Didion, *Play It as It Lays*

8. Lutheran Life Styles

The fascination of this chapter is found in its treatment of some very practical aspects of congregational life: attendance, congregational activity, personal piety, involvement in community issues, personal evangelism, neighborliness, supporting others in times of crises, moral behaviors, and drug usage. Most pastors will find the information both instructive and encouraging.

Three patterns of behavior are singled out for view: religious life styles, sharing and servicing activities, and questionable moral behavior. These emerge from the study as distinctive life styles that characterize sizeable portions of the Lutheran family. Information about each life style gives answers to the questions that head each section:

What are the religious life styles of Lutherans?

How involved are Lutherans in interpersonal helping activities?

What are the moral behaviors of Lutherans?

The answer to the first question makes it abundantly clear that the religious life style of most Lutherans goes beyond a to-be-expected devotion to matters of church and personal piety. It includes also an involvement in community activities and for a minority, public issues. Significantly, the dimensions of congregational activity and personal piety show up as important indicators of profound faith.

The answer to the second question shows that Lutherans who are involved in personal evangelism are the first to show neighborliness or

174

give help to others in times of crises. Furthermore it shows that a third of the "sleeping giant" declare a willingness to become involved if asked. There is, apparently, a potential for greater helping and sharing activities than is presently expressed by the one in four.

Striking evidence appears in the last section of the chapter of how biblical ignorance and a preoccupation with one's own self-development are highly related to questionable moral activities. An involvement in commonly condemned activities is an expression of a deeper need.

The chapter concludes with a look at the very small number of Lutherans (2%) who become involved in drug use. Significantly though, a higher percentage hold attitudes that make them highly susceptible to pressure to use drugs. These are essentially youth who find authority hard to accept.

Individual Christians express their association with the life of the church and with other community organizations in a variety of behavior patterns. A vast range of personal and private activities, as well as participation in public affairs, gives shape to their lives. Previous chapters have described Lutheran values, beliefs, and concept of mission; this chapter focuses on behavior. Is there a strong connection between what Lutherans profess and what they practice? Is there a close association between the "hearer" of the Word and the "doer?"

Three kinds of life styles emerge from the data, each with its distinctive behavioral measures. The life styles of Lutherans to be discussed here include their religious life styles, their self-reports of sharing and service activities, and their contrasting patterns of moral behavior.

What Are the Religious Life Styles of Lutherans?

The dimensions which give shape and understanding to Factor 6[1] are:

Load	Scale	Dimension Title
.69	40	Congregational Activity
.63	45	Organizational Memberships
.61	47	Personal Involvement in Church and Community
.43	41	Personal Piety
.30	21	Personal Evangelism
.29	74	Personal Initiative on Church and Public Issues

All of the above dimensions reflect some facet of a religious life style. Before describing their special emphases, a rather obvious starting point will be used in describing religious life styles because it has been so widely used as the one and only measure of a religiously oriented life, namely, worship attendance.

WORSHIP ATTENDANCE

One of the most visible and hence most popular measures of the extent to which religion touches the lives of persons is the frequency with which they attend worship services. This tends to be particularly true in the Western world where religious bodies are usually formally organized around a center of worship—be it a temple, synagogue, church, or mosque. Frequency of worship and frequency of other church-related activities of an educational, social, recreational, or service nature vary considerably among Lutheran respondents. It is thus an open question whether the paramount motive for worship attendance is worship, social, or private utility. Only as we are able to understand the larger context in which specific behaviors take place, can we reliably interpret them. It should be obvious that personal motivations for church attendance are complex and can vary greatly. For example, a family of regular church attenders could involve contrasting patterns of activity. A sixteen-year-old youth could attend regularly primarily to strengthen ties to a girl friend; his twin sister attends because of a deep commitment to Christ as her Savior; the father attends regularly to please his wife and enhance his business visibility; whereas the mother may attend for mixed reasons and fluctuating motivations such as exchanging gossip, allaying personal isolation and insecurity, and keeping an eye on her husband.

As reported in Chapter 2, Gallup (1971) found that persons expressing a Lutheran preference were more likely to attend weekly worship than those preferring other major Christian bodies, 43% versus an average of 38%. Among Lutheran church *members* in this study, 56% reported attending worship about once a week or more, "if not prevented by unavoidable circumstances." (As any pastor knows, the list of "unavoidable circumstances" varies among parishioners.) An additional 23% attend worship two or three times a month, with the remainder of 21% attending less than once a month.

CONGREGATIONAL ACTIVITY

A dimension (Scale 40) of congregational activity provides a straightforward measure of the active churchman. The highest possible score of 59 is obtained by persons who report they are *very active* in their congregation; they *regularly* spend evenings at church; they *regularly* receive Communion; they keep well informed about their congregation; they find congregational participation a major source of life satisfaction; and they have held three or more church jobs or committee assignments during the past year. (See Scale 40, Appendix C, Section IV.)

It is understandable that the average clergy score of 56 is only three points below the maximum. The scores of lay people average 34, the midpoint between the lowest possible score of nine and the maximum possible score of 59. Low scoring laity live on the fringes of congregational life; they are inactive, poorly informed, and practically devoid of joy or satisfaction in congregational participation.

Although 56% of Lutherans attend worship regularly, a broad pattern of participation characterizes other congregational activities. Diverse styles of congregational activity are indicated by the fact that Lutherans do not cluster at any given point of activity level. Nearly the same number of Lutherans score at all points, from the inactive to the very active.

As indicated in Chapter 2, no more than one-half of Lutherans participate in an organized community activity (Scale 45). This means that for the other half the congregation is their only contact with organized group life.

Which Lutherans are the most involved in congregational activity? We find that the best indicators of active Lutherans are:

1. High worship attendance
2. Older age, with college age youth least active
3. Strong value orientation to a transcendental meaning in life
4. Close friends among congregational members
5. Frequent family devotions
6. High Sunday school attendance, particularly church school teachers
7. High church and community involvement and willingness to serve
8. Self-descriptions of being as religious as, or more religious than, parents.

An interesting typology of Lutheran congregational involvement was revealed by an analysis which distinguished six groups of Lutherans, particularly four subgroups of Lutherans who regularly attend worship. Least involved, as most would suspect, was a group of 942 persons (21%) who attend church less than once monthly. Their average score on Congregational Activity was 20.4, which is one standard deviation below the total lay average. Somewhat higher in church activity was the 23% (1,015) who reported attending worship two or three times a month. The most interesting distinctions are the differences among the 56% of Lutherans who are regular churchgoers. As indicated in Table 8.1, half of the regular church worshipers fell in the middle range of a dimension measuring Personal Involvement in Church and Community (Scale 47), a dimension to be discussed next. A smaller group of 424 had very little personal involvement and had an average score slightly below the total average. This left two groups of the Lutherans most active in their congregations. Both groups were regular worshipers and had high scores on the dimension measuring personal involvement. The most active had the additional advantage of reporting that two or more of their best friends were also members of their congregation.

PERSONAL PIETY

A dimension related to congregational activity is the one that describes personal practices of piety (Scale 41). Although these two dimensions

Table 8.1 High and Low Scoring Groups on Congregational Activity (Scale 40)

Group Description	Average Score	Number of People
Weekly attendance, high personal involvement, with two or more close friends in congregation	50.9	507
Weekly attendance, high personal involvement, with none or one close friend in congregation	45.2	326
Weekly attendance, moderate personal involvement	39.2	1,230
Weekly attendance, low personal involvement	31.2	424
Worship attendance two or three times monthly	29.4	1,015
Worship attendance less than once monthly	20.4	942
Total	34.0	4,444

Lay Average Score = 34.0
Standard Deviation = 14.0

(Congregational Activity and Personal Piety) are closely related, they form two separate dimensions.[2] The Congregational Activity scale focuses on the public dimension of a religious life style, whereas the Personal Piety scale focuses on the private dimension.

In the Personal Piety scale, five of the items identify frequency of specific behaviors: Bible reading, discussing faith with family, giving a percentage of income to church work, reading about the faith, and taking time for private meditation. These behaviors are personal and private types of activity. Other items show personal identification with the congregation, such as cooperating with pastor, fitting in with congregation, having congregational influence, choosing church activities over other kinds of activity, and preferring Bible study to social fellowship. These are not highly visible, yet public, actions. There are also items showing the strength of religious values and experiences in shaping priorities, such as generosity of giving, carryover of religion into daily life, awareness of the presence of God, and faith winning over science when the two appear to be in conflict.

All in all, persons scoring high on the Personal Piety scale attach great importance to the Christian life, to private devotions, and to congregational involvement. Their motivations, however, are not known. For some, personal piety is a natural fruition of a deep and profound faith commitment. For others a naive or self-serving religiosity may be the strongest force. Lutherans with high scores could include both latter-day pharisees and humble publicans.

Most laymen are concentrated near the average score of 77.8, but a few persons do have scores extending out to the extreme low and high scores of 31 and 117. By contrast, clergy scores vary from a low of 77 to a high of 117, which is a much narrower range of scores. In effect, clergy scores *begin* at the average lay score for both Personal Piety and Congregational Activity. The diversity of lay scores on these two dimensions should dispel any simple stereotype that equates church membership or weekly attendance automatically with personal piety or congregational activity. It is also possible that some Lutherans are highly active in their congregations but are not highly active in personal piety, or vice versa. The most common pattern, however, would be similarity in both dimensions.

When we look for characteristics of Lutherans with a high level of personal piety, we discover that one of them is church attendance. The other prime characteristics that point toward personal piety are Emotional Certainty of Faith (Scale 66) and Personal Evangelism (Scale 21). Lutherans who are certain of their faith and regular in church attendance show higher levels of personal piety than do Lutherans who are uncertain of their faith and low in church attendance as shown in Table 8.2.

Table 8.2 High and Low Scoring Groups in Terms of Personal Piety (Scale 41)

Group Description		Average Score	Number of Persons
A. High faith-certainty, high church attendance		90.3	1,335
B. High faith-certainty, attendance less than weekly		79.0	507
C. Moderate or low faith-certainty, high attendance	Mod. or high evangelism	80.1	868
D. Moderate or low faith-certainty, low attendance		70.7	902
E. Moderate or low faith-certainty, low evangelism, moderate or low attendance		66.8	529
F. Moderate or low faith-certainty, low evangelism, very low attendance		55.0	303

Average Lay Score = 77.8
Standard Deviation = 15.6

Age is related to practices of personal piety, also. Persons age 35 and over have higher scores. College-graduate women have the highest scores, and noncollege-graduate males have the lowest scores.

In regard to values, a sharp difference again occurs between highly active Lutherans and those greatly concerned with practices of piety. A high value on Transcendental Meaning in Life (Scale 28) is related to practices of personal piety. Another related dimension is one's sense of Individual Christian Responsibility for his own faith and witnessing to others (Scale 60).

A practical and helpful result of the kinds of analyses our research team made is that we can now have a greater understanding of the relationship of personal piety not only to other dimensions of belief and values, but also to matters of behavior. Based on the analyses, we can illustrate that practices of personal piety (such as personal and private activities of Bible reading or meditation, identification with the congregation, and tying one's faith in with everyday life) serve as a bridge to other kinds of behavior. We feel this is significant, inasmuch as concerned pastors and lay leaders often raise questions about the importance of specific practices of piety—whether they exist alone or are related to any other aspects of a person's life.

We can illustrate their importance in the following diagram in which we can see that personal piety is a bridge between values and beliefs and various kinds of behavior (Figure 8.1).

Figure 8.1 Personal Piety (Scale 41) as a Link between Factor 1 (Beliefs and Values) and Factor 6 (Religious Life Styles)

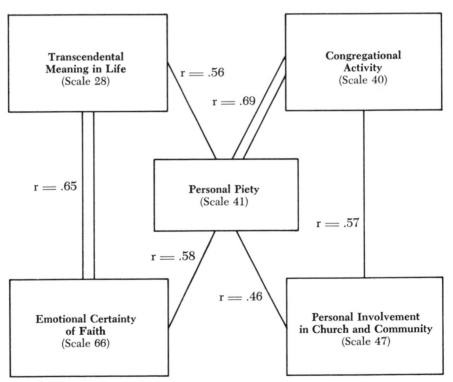

PERSONAL INVOLVEMENT IN CHURCH AND COMMUNITY

One question which nags most pastors is, "How many are willing to become involved in a serving activity?" Is the congregation ready to move if given direction, or are the majority content to let others do the work?

Some important information is available about Lutherans in their response to items that describe a range of service activities necessary to church and community. Items composing this scale (Scale 47) represent a blending of both past behavior and projected future behavior. The response choices were as follows:

HR — Have been asked to do this but *have refused.*

WR — Have never been asked, but I *would refuse* if asked.

HT — Have done this but really didn't want to. Felt I *had to* do it.

WD — Have not been asked, but if I were I *would do* this.

HD — Have been asked, and I *have done* this willingly.

A willingness to serve *(if asked)* was reported by 36%. The ways they would serve include: teach Sunday school, serve on a committee to improve conditions in the neighborhood, help in repair tasks, attend a political party caucus, help plan fellowship events in the congregation, work for youth, serve on a citizens review board, participate as a campaign worker, serve on congregational committees concerned with social issues, etc. Another segment (24%) said they *have* participated in these ways and have done so willingly. The total of these two (60%) tells us that there is a large reservoir of willingness to be tapped for meaningful activity. Less than a third indicate distaste for most of the activities mentioned.

Who are the Lutherans most willing to become involved? They cannot be identified by sex, church body, or census region. However, age, education, and size of congregation are important indicators. Middle-aged persons are generally the most active. When it comes to leadership roles in both church and community, persons with the most education tend to be the most active. Members of congregations with less than 250 members are the most involved, or willing to be. This finding suggests that more demands and opportunities for leadership occur in smaller congregations than in larger ones. Where this is the situation, one is likely to find a greater willingness to be involved.

PERSONAL INITIATIVE ON CHURCH AND PUBLIC ISSUES

Another dimension also picks up the theme of involvement in church and community affairs. Its focus, however, is on more personalized and less structured types of participation or leadership. It highlights the degree to which an individual makes his personal views known to official decision makers, whether in church or society, using direct and indirect means of communication (e.g., writing letters, taking a public stand, making personal contacts, or running for office).

Except for signing a petition or speaking personally to a pastor, less than 20% of Lutherans take any personal initiative on these matters. This pattern of response appears to be rather uniform across the entire age range of Lutheran laymen. This evidence suggests a supine posture for most Lutherans and appears to confirm the beliefs of many youth; namely, that church members do not put forth much effort to influence *either* church or public policy. It appears that apathy or noninvolvement describes the typical pattern for most laymen.

What characterizes those Lutherans who *are* active on issues? The most actively involved are clergymen. Their average score on this scale is 44.3, as against an average of 23.7 for laymen. (Total possible scores range from 18 to 98.) Though the age pattern is somewhat irregular for the sample of clergy, the oldest and youngest clergy are likely to have lower scores, while clergy in the age range of 41-55 have the highest scores.[3]

The laymen who compare most favorably with clergy on this scale are educated males. Conversely, Lutheran laymen with a high school education or less tend to show no initiative on controversial church or public issues. Their involvement in church and community affairs is also limited. In other words, level of education among the laity is associated with lay initiative in both church and public affairs.[4]

How Involved Are Lutherans in Interpersonal Helping Activities?

Another theme in the data directs attention to day-to-day sharing and serving activities on a direct one-to-one basis. The dimensions of Factor 5 are:

Load	Scale	Dimension Title
.86	22	Neighborliness
.78	20	Supporting Others in Crises
.66	21	Personal Evangelism
.28	74	Personal Initiative on Church and Public Issues

Personal Evangelism had minor loading on Factor 6, Religious Life Styles, and also is closely associated with Scale 41, Personal Piety. It thus serves as an appropriate tie to interpersonal behavior.[5]

PERSONAL EVANGELISM

This dimension focuses on what a Christian who has received the good news of the gospel is doing to bring it to others. The items in Scale 21 ask the respondent to indicate the frequency, during the past year, with which he loaned religious books, invited others to church, shared the gospel through home visitation, witnessed for Jesus in several ways, distributed Christian tracts, made declarations of faith to others, participated in evangelistic rallies, conducted Bible study in homes, or encouraged fellow Christians to be better witnesses. Each item could be answered "frequently," "occasionally," or "never."

There is a rather startling contrast between laymen and clergy on personal witnessing, as dramatically illustrated in the line drawing of Figure 8.2. Lutheran laymen pile up at the low end. A large proportion of Lutherans seldom share their faith in the specific ways that our items measure. The average score for laymen is 31.9. The clergy average is 66.5, that is, twice as high as for lay people. If a layman were to answer "occasionally" to each of the 13 items, he would receive a score of 46. A score this high was exceeded by only 11% of Lutheran lay people, while 44% reported *no* personal witness during the past year. To summarize, almost half of our people do not witness in these ways and only one-tenth acknowledge considerable witnessing.

What do we know about the people who *do* engage in evangelistic activities? What differentiates persons who show little interest in personal evangelism from those who are active in sharing their faith with others? Analysis has revealed that the degree of Personal Piety (Scale 41) is the single most important element, followed by the dimension to be discussed next, Neighborliness (Scale 22). Persons with lowest scores on Personal Evangelism had low scores on both of these dimensions, with an average score of 23.2, and numbered 1,190, over one-fourth of all laity. Conversely, persons with high scores on both dimensions had an average score of 49.3, but their numbers included only 369 persons. Other groups had scores converging on the lay average of 31.9. Neighborliness and evangelism go together, so it is to that dimension we turn next.

NEIGHBORLINESS

The dimension of Neighborliness (Scale 22) deals with activities of a helping-hand nature, not crisis events. The good neighbor is one who "frequently" does all or more of the following: helps a friend or neighbor on a work project; takes care of a friend's or a neighbor's children or home during his absence; helps others by giving money or labor to help someone complete a task; gives help to persons in difficulty (law, auto breakdown, unavailable transportation, etc.); or invites a new neighbor or friend into his home.

Laymen have an average of 39.4 and clergy average 44.6. A person responding "occasionally" to each item would receive a score of 42. Very few persons reported not doing any of these activities. On the other hand, few said they were "frequently" engaged in *all* or most of these acts. Clearly, most Lutherans consider themselves to be good neighbors.

Figure 8.2 Distribution of Personal Evangelism Scores (Scale 21) Among Lay People and Clergy

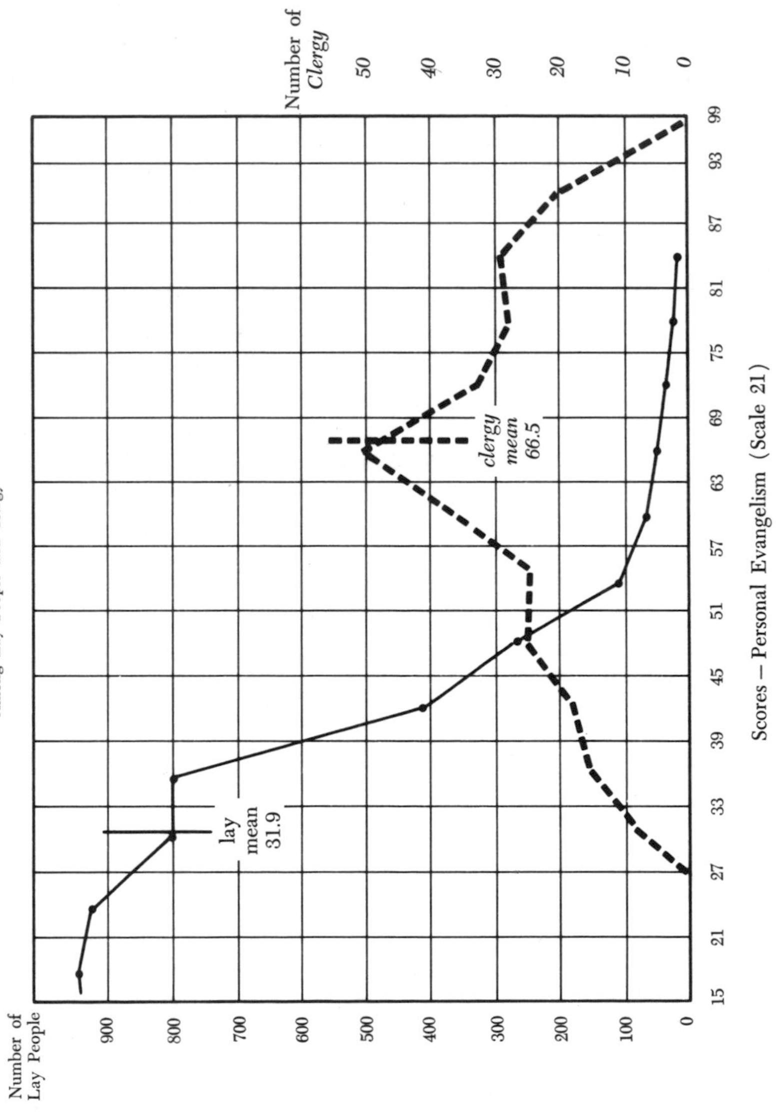

SUPPORTING OTHERS IN CRISES

Giving aid or comfort to people in crisis situations (Scale 20) includes activities like visiting a friend in the hospital, attending a funeral, contributing to a special fund for a friend or neighbor, or running errands for someone disabled. Four out of five Lutherans have had some experience in rendering this type of service during the course of a year. A small group (about one in four) has "frequently" served in this way. A person answering "occasionally" to each item would receive a score of 19. The average for Lutheran laymen is above this point, namely 26.4. Clergy, who frequently comfort the sick, bereaved, and troubled in their pastoral duties, show an average of 37.9.

SUMMARY

The dimensions which form Factor 5 all are closely related and pertain to the level of interpersonal helping or serving activities. How are they related to other dimensions and factors described in the study? The close relationships within Factor 5 are revealed by Figure 8.3. Personal Evangelism is also closely linked with Factor 6 through Scale 40, Congregational Activity. Personal Piety (Scale 41) is the prime linkage from Factor 1 to both of these life style dimensions. It is clear that a faith buttressed by emotional certainty (Scale 66) and personal involvement on both a group and personal basis is also nurtured by strong personal worship and spiritual growth.

What Are the Moral Behaviors of Lutherans?

Two behavioral dimensions bear on this question (Scale 23, Questionable Personal Activities, and Scale 73, Drug Culture Orientation), with each dimension related to the other but with its primary factor loading on a separate minor factor. The first of these, Factor 11, has a strong flavor of youth and is identified by the following scales:

Load	Scale	Dimension Title
.54	9	Biblical Ignorance
.42	23	Questionable Personal Activities
.36	29	Values of Self-Development
.33	15	Salvation by Works

The loadings on this factor are not as high as others discussed, but combine a variety of dimensions involving beliefs, misbelief, values, knowledge, and personal activities. It is this last dimension which is helpful in identifying this factor.

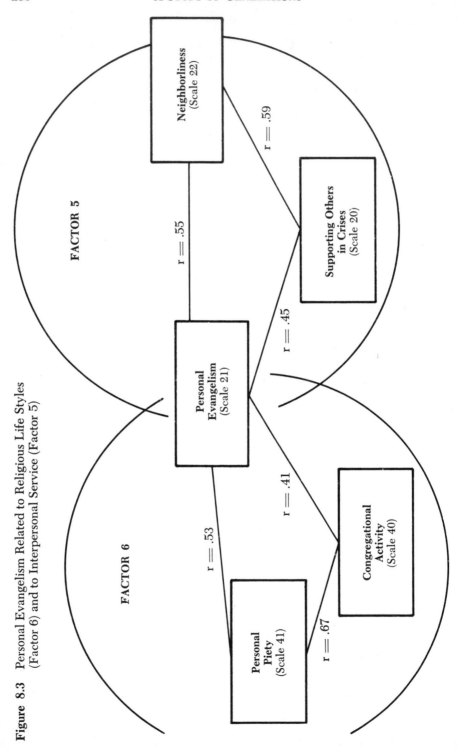

QUESTIONABLE PERSONAL ACTIVITIES

A broad range of behaviors were described in the questionnaire in order to gain information on the private life styles of Lutherans (see Scale 23, Appendix C). Some of these behaviors are strongly disapproved of or are condemned by most members of society; others, such as lying or swearing, are common to most people. Some are activities over which there are conflicting judgments as to their acceptability (e.g., drinking, gambling, and attending X-rated movies). Respondents were asked to indicate in which activity they participate and how frequently.

A person reporting none of the behaviors listed in Scale 23 would receive a score of 21. (They attended no movies, never swore, told no lies, etc.) Reporting "occasionally" for each item would give a score of 59; "frequently" would give a maximum score of 101. Actual scores ranged from 21-95 for laymen and 23-71 for clergy, with nearly identical averages of 42.0 and 42.1 respectively.

The most common score was 35, which would be received by persons who report "occasionally" attending movies, telling lies, drinking, swearing, gambling, and reading pornographic literature, and "never" engaging in the other activities, during the past year. Persons with average scores would engage in one or more of these activities "frequently," and/or "occasionally" would do one or more of the other listed activities.

About one-half of the Lutheran population participates in these activities to some degree. About one in 10 participates "frequently." If these items give some assessment of moral behavior, then one can conclude that a moral breakdown is hardly rampant among Lutherans.

The single most important variable that separates persons scoring high and low on questionable personal behaviors is that males on the average score higher. The second most important variable is age. The overall pattern shows that male scores are much higher than female averages during ages in the twenties, with this difference gradually decreasing as age increases to the sixties. Highest scores for females occur at ages 17-20 and for males at ages 19-22.

What other characteristics are associated with high or low involvement in these questionable personal practices? Our analysis, illustrated in Figure 8.4, reveals that the higher a person's scores on Personal Piety and Emotional Certainty of Faith, the lower are his scores on Questionable Personal Activities (Scale 23).[6] Also note that the highest scores on Personal Piety are heavily concentrated among females, with lesser numbers among males ages 31-65, and just a handful among males ages 15-30. The same pattern exists for Emotional Certainty of Faith.

Just the opposite relationship holds for the other scales plotted on Figure 8.4. This means that persons heavily engaged in Questionable Personal Activities are likely to embrace the values ranking uppermost in Self-Development, such as adventure, pleasure, personal power, and physical attractiveness.

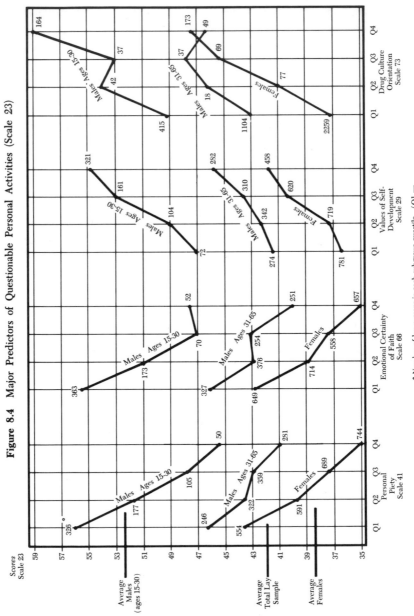

Figure 8.4 Major Predictors of Questionable Personal Activities (Scale 23)

* Number of lay persons in each subgroup quartile (Q1 = lowest scoring 25% of the persons)

We can comment also on the place of Bible knowledge or the lack of it. Our data reveal that Lutherans with high scores on Questionable Personal Activities and high scores on Values of Self-Development are likely to be ignorant or misinformed about the Bible. That is, they will have very little knowledge of basic biblical facts.

DRUG CULTURE ORIENTATION

The final behavioral dimension to be described is one with negative loading on another minor theme of the data. This Factor 12 has acceptance of authority or conventionality as its positive pole and emphasis on individualism as its negative. The dimensions of it are:

Load	Scale	Dimension Title
.53	51	Acceptance of Authority
.49	72	Orientation to "Doing" Influenced by the Church
−.31	29	Values of Self-Development
−.35	73	Drug Culture Orientation

Today we see another kind of culture being formed that rejects or is disenchanted with the "straight society." This culture, often identified as a drug culture, is found also among Lutherans. Their life style is reflected in the dimension entitled Drug Culture Orientation.

The content of Drug Culture Orientation needs careful description (Scale 73). The major weight and content of the scale relate to drug usage, shown in Table 8.3. Respondents were asked:

"With which of the following have you experimented (tried once or twice)?"

"Which of the following do you use occasionally?"

"Which of the following do you use regularly?"

In each case, the questionnaire allowed four choices: *(a)* alcoholic beverages; *(b)* marijuana (pot), hashish, peyote, or psilocybin, etc.; *(c)* LSD (acid) and/or other strong psychedelics; and *(d)* heroin and/or "speed,"

Table 8.3 Percent of Lutherans Reporting Use of Alcohol and Other Drugs (Lay People and Clergy Combined)

	Regular Use	Occasional Use	Tried Once or Twice
Alcohol [7]	25%	76%	84%
Marijuana	1	2	5
LSD (acid)	< 1	1	1
Heroin, "speed," amphetamines, barbituates	1	1	1

amphetamines, or barbituates. (In forming the scale by the empirical procedures of cluster and factor analysis, responses related to alcohol usage dropped out of the scale. Reasons for this are not hard to find. Alcohol has fairly common usage among Lutherans; other drug use is rare.)

In addition to report of drug use, three other items, widely separate in form, content, and location in the survey, are on the dimension. One asked respondents to choose what they would consider most important in choosing a church if they were to move. The first five possible choices involved Lutheran churches, the sixth mentioned Protestant churches, and the seventh said, "Considerations other than these." This last choice (given by 5% of the respondents) was drawn in as part of this scale, indicating a general non-Protestant or nonestablishment orientation toward religious structures. This would allow room for Eastern religions, mysticism, or cultic expressions of many varieties.

Another item asked persons to identify themselves politically, allowing 12 choices to the invitation: "I think of myself as . . . " Three choices each ("liberal," "moderate," or "conservative") related to Democrats and Republicans. Other choices included: American Independent Party, Independent, Socialist, Communist, Other, and "Not interested in politics." The *single* choice which became part of this Drug Culture Orientation scale ·was the 1% of respondents who said, "Other." One can speculate what *other* choices are left, given the wide response choices offered. Plausibly, various nonstructured anarchistic or tribal patterns were envisaged. Other militant or radically-oriented movements could also have been included under "Other," as could various peace or nonviolent models.

The last item related to respondents' views on "frequent family worship in the home." One choice given by 4% of respondents was " . . . family worship . . . is undesirable because it is often hypocritical or just dull routine." Here is another rejection of a traditional religious expression.

The lowest possible score, rejecting each item, is a score of 12; the highest is 72. Actual scores ranged from 12-68 for laymen and 12-27 for clergy. In both groups, however, the average scores were extremely low; 13.0 for laity and 12.3 for clergy, which means a nearly total rejection of these items.

It is important to recognize the significance of these scores. Describing family worship as hypocritical or dull, and rejecting other statements, would produce a score of 13; considering a non-Protestant church in addition, would produce a score of 15. If in addition the person rejected the listed political labels, his score would be 18. In other words, a person could receive a score as high as 18 and have no experience with the drugs listed. By the same logic, a person could not receive a score higher than 18 without checking usage of one or more drugs.

We can follow a sequence from low to high scores. Clergy are lowest with 12.3. The average score of Lutherans over age 22 is 12.4 which is near the bottom point of 12 on this scale. All Lutheran youth in the study ages 15-22 have an average score of 15.2. Of these youth, those who are much involved in Questionable Personal Activities receive an average score of 17.1. Of these, the youth who are strongly peer-oriented average 18.5. These strongly peer-oriented Lutheran youth who engage in questionable activities are less exposed to drug use in smaller communities than in metropolitan areas. Our data do not allow projecting of trends, but if we accept the growing body of research data indicating a diffusion of drug use from metropolitan centers, then we can expect rising exposure for youth in smaller communities.

Persons who are highly involved in questionable personal activities are also likely to be involved with drugs. As would be expected, a mind-set toward drugs is largely a youth phenomenon.[8]

It is essential to remember, however, that only about 2% of Lutheran youth are included in this Drug Culture Orientation. The vast majority are typical American youth, though they are affected by trends in our society.

Summary

The religious life styles of Lutherans include the traditional behaviors of congregational activity, private practices of piety, and personal evangelism. Approximately one-half of the Lutherans have a style of life that includes all three kinds of behavior. People of strong personal piety hold to traditional biblical doctrines and value a relationship to God and man that transcends natural interests.

The 40% who are involved in personal evangelism contrast with non-witnessing Lutherans in their helping activities on a one-to-one basis. They are more likely to support a friend in a crisis situation or show kindness to a neighbor in a time of need. Both types of activity involve a majority of Lutherans.

The helping behavior of Lutherans is expressed in several ways. It is shown (1) in personal acts of kindness to individuals in a community; (2) in an involvement in institutional activities that minister to the welfare of man; and (3) in personally initiated activities that are designed to bring about institutional changes.

Three out of five Lutherans are willing to share in assuming responsibility in church and community activities if asked to do specific tasks. At present about one in four participates actively and is glad to do so. It is a smaller percentage who take the initiative to correct wrongs or make changes wherever church or public issues are involved.

The moral behavior of Lutherans is strongly influenced by what they value, believe, and know. Questionable behavior characterizes those who are preoccupied with self-development goals, who are not certain of their faith, and whose neglect of personal piety is shown in an ignorance of biblical facts. Closely related, too, is an orientation to the drug culture and its style of life.

Notes

1. Both religious life styles and dimensions measuring sharing and service activities formed separate factors (6 and 5), whereas the two dimensions measuring contrasting patterns of moral behavior became part of two related factors (11 and 12), each containing a mixture of dimensions.

   Scale 45, Organizational Memberships, was a measure of the membership in a variety of organized community groups, fraternal, political, occupational, cultural, etc. Scores were highly skewed, giving the scale little discriminating power for the study. It thus receives only brief mention. Scale 41, Personal Piety, involves both value preferences and reports of behavior. Its primary loading for laity was on Factor 1 (.55), yet its strongest correlation was with Scale 40 (Congregational Activity) ($r = .69$). It is discussed here because it provides a bridge among Factors 1, 5, and 6. Dimension 21, Personal Evangelism, loaded most heavily on Factor 5 and only secondarily here on Factor 6. It would be appropriate to discuss it here as a dimension of religious life styles or under Factor 5 as a dimension of interpersonal helping. It is discussed in the latter position as a bridge to Factor 5.

2. Although Scale 41 (Personal Piety) was most highly correlated ($r = .69$) with Scale 40 (Congregational Activity) and the relationship between these two scale dimensions was stronger than that between any other pair of belief or behavioral dimensions, their highest loadings on the second order factor analysis were in separate factors for the lay sample. Scale 40 had predominant loading (.69) on a behavioral factor (6), whereas Scale 41 (Personal Piety) involved both the belief factor (1) with the seventh highest factor loading of .55 and a behavioral component, Factor 6, with a minor loading of .43. On a similar factor analysis involving *both* laity and clergy, the factor loadings shifted appreciably in an interesting fashion. A comparison of factor loadings of major scale dimensions for the two samples on basic belief and behavior factors show:

Belief Factor			Behavior Factor		
Scale Number	Lay Only	Clergy & Lay	Scale Number	Lay Only	Clergy & Lay
	Factor One	Factor One		Factor Six	Factor Three
28	.80	.78	40	.69	.66
14	.74	.72	47	.61	.59
66	.73	.71	41	.43	.57
44	.72	.70	74	.29	.48
41	.55	.51	21	.30	.53

When clergy and lay were combined, it is clear that the more intense activities of clergy as reflected in Scales 41 (Personal Piety), 74 (Personal Initiative on Church and Public Issues), and 21 (Personal Witnessing) gave these scales stronger loading on factors identifying religious behavior. When only lay were involved, the close relationship between belief and practice was diminished, as reflected in the shift of primary loading for Scale 41 (Personal Piety) from the behavior factor (.43) to beliefs (.55), whereas the respective loadings were .57 and .51 when clergy were included. We can conclude that laity are more likely to profess a faith without a commensurate response in their behavior or that clergy have more opportunity to reflect their basic beliefs in their behavior than the laity do.

3. Although scale scores are heavily weighted in favor of initiatives more likely exhibited by clergy, there is a marked contrast in clergy and lay life styles in this regard. In one analysis including both clergy and lay, clergy-lay score differences accounted for 25.4% of total variance on this scale even though clergy were only 6% of the total sample. (Within the lay sample the best predictor, Scale 47, Personal Involvement in Church and Community, accounted for 8.5% of total variance.)

4. Inspection of the total frequency distribution for laity found 2,524 persons (57%) reporting no initiative on church and public issues (scores 20-21). Other scores and numbers of persons ranked as follows:

Score	N	Score	N
22-25	895	42-45	27
26-29	532	46-49	14
30-33	242	50-53	10
34-37	105	54 & Over	25
38-41	71		

5. Intercorrelations among the first three dimensions of Factor 5 were:

	Dimension 20	Dimension 21
Dimension 21	.45	
Dimension 22	.59	.55

Dimension 21 also correlated .53 with Personal Piety (Dimension 41) and .41 with Congregational Activity (Dimension 40), which suggests a bridging role for Personal Evangelism (Dimension 21) between Factors 6 and 5. See also Chapter Note 1.

6. Figure 8.4 shows major multivariate effects on Scale 23, Questionable Personal Activities, using AID analysis. The major splits were made for sex, followed by age for males. The diagram reveals the persistent effects of the four leading scale dimensions on Scale 23, after controlling for sex and age.

7. From the response pattern, it is clear that persons did not view "regular use," "occasional use," and "tried once or twice," as mutually exclusive choices, since 185% checked the three choices for alcohol use. If the same cumulative logic was used for drug item responses, then total usage is best reflected by the "tried once or twice" response. In either case, the total reported users of marijuana was between 5-8%; and 1-3% for the other drugs.

8. It is possible, of course, that persons could have falsified their self-reports, either disclaiming their drug use or by giving us a put-on falsely claiming or exaggerating their drug usage to tweak the nose of an "up-tight" establishment. A careful case-by-case analysis could provide evidence suggesting gross error in some self-reports.

To me, under my hand, in the Dark Room
Laid in a bath of chemicals, your ghost
Emerged gelatinously from that tomb;
Looking-glass, soot-faced, values all reversed
The shadows brilliant and the lights one gloom.
Reverse of that reverse, your photograph
Now positively scans me with
Your quizzical, ironic framed half-laugh.
Your gaze, oblique under sun-sculptured lids.
Endlessly asks me: "Is this all we have?"

—Stephen Spender, "On the Photograph of a Friend Dead"

9. How Lutherans Feel About Themselves and Others

This chapter completes the in-depth portrait of Lutherans by answering the questions: How do Lutherans feel about themselves? How do they view others? Where is prejudice found?

It is significant that most Lutherans hold positive attitudes toward themselves and others. Unfortunately, however, a large minority cannot accept people whose life styles, values, and beliefs stand in greatest contrast to their own. This issue of prejudice and social distance is given special attention in the final section of the chapter. The evidence here shows that the soil of prejudice is not Christian beliefs, but rather the heresies of the church; or more specifically, the law orientation to life that causes people to exalt form over spirit.

In the Preface we said that a portrait of Lutherans would give more than a profile of their values, beliefs, opinions, and behavioral patterns. We promised that it would reflect also the underlying structure of these qualities of life and show how Lutherans vary on each dimension. With this chapter, the in-depth portrait is relatively complete. It may be well, therefore, to summarize how this portrait evolved.

Chapter 4 uses background colors in sketching the stance Lutherans take toward life; it describes how they view the "good life." The two chapters which follow make these values more concrete by identifying the beliefs and misbeliefs that typify the Lutheran church. Chapter 7 shows how these values and beliefs are expressed in a sense of ministry and mission, and Chapter 8 describes how they are reflected in behavioral life styles.

The final touches on our portrait of Lutherans come in this chapter with the addition of the highly personal feeling dimensions—how Lutherans feel about themselves and others.

The happiness (or unhappiness) of Lutherans is reflected in their sense of purpose in life, in their feelings of isolation and pressure, and in their anxiety over matters of faith.

Their openness, or lack of it, is seen in how pessimistic they feel about other people, how different they feel Lutherans are from other people, and how strongly they are oriented to their own peer group.

Their relationships to others are shown in the amount of social distance they want to maintain between themselves and others.

These ways of feeling about oneself and looking at others will be reported in this chapter.

How Do Lutherans Feel About Themselves?

Three dimensions formed a factor giving an assessment of what Lutherans feel about themselves. The dimensions of Factor 7 are:

Load	Scale	Dimension Title
.70	68	Life Purpose
−.68	17	Feelings of Isolation and Pressure
−.70	49	Anxiety over My Faith

An additional dimension indicating Acceptance of Middle-Class Norms (Scale 50) had a light load of .30. The three basic measures of self-assessment provide a coherent and mutually supportive picture of how Lutherans see themselves.

SENSE OF PURPOSE

Respondents were asked to make choices on nine items in the survey, each item allowing seven responses. A middle response indicated neutrality, and three responses on either side each indicated degrees of acceptance of either a positive or negative evaluation of life as they experienced it. The items in Scale 68 and the percentages of Lutherans who chose a negative, neutral, or positive response to each item is provided in Appendix C, Section IV. These data indicate that Lutherans overwhelmingly report their lives are filled with meaning and purpose, with only a small minority reflecting despair and meaninglessness in their lives.[1]

One out of two Lutherans (50%) feel a strong sense of purpose, and for them life is meaningful. If they could choose, these people would prefer nine more lives like the one they know (Item 244). They see a reason for being on this earth (Item 248); they have a satisfying life purpose (Item 255); they face their daily tasks as a source of pleasure and satisfaction (Item 254); and they describe their life as "running over with exciting good things" (Item 246).

Fewer feel that their life goals are being achieved (26%) (Item 245) and that the world fits meaningfully into their lives (27%) (Item 249).

A large percentage of Lutherans (59%) feel their life has been very worthwhile even if they should die today (Item 247). The largest percentage (62%) see themselves as very responsible people (Item 250).

These data strongly support the conclusion that the overwhelming majority of Lutherans find meaning in their lives. However gratifying this response, we also observe a segment of respondents for whom this is not true. They are troubled, or "hurting." Their cup of life is filled with bitter gall and meaninglessness. Their numbers are not large in terms of the total sample of Lutherans, but 6% of the sample choose the two bottom ranks to declare that they see life as purposeless, meaningless, and filled only with despair. This is not a deep clinical assessment of personality but simply a general self-appraisal of how meaningful, rich, confusing, or frustrating people find life.

The Lutherans most likely to score low regarding life having meaning are youth. Their scores on life purpose rise until age 29 after which they level off on a plateau. After reaching maturity, persons with a higher education affirm a greater sense of life purpose than those of the same age with lesser education. Highest scores on life purpose come from clergy and laity with graduate school training.

There is an additive relationship between age and education after formal education is normally completed that favors higher levels of a sense of meaning and purpose for older persons, especially those fortunate enough to have received higher education. Conversely, the lowest levels of a sense of meaning and purpose are concentrated among youth. They also are more likely to express unhappiness with their family, church, school, or work role. In general, persons with high scores on Life Purpose (Scale 68) are:

1. Quite free from feelings of isolation and pressure (Scale 17), pessimism (Scale 35), and anxiety over their faith (Scale 49).

2. Not estranged from other age groups (Scale 63), and accepting of middle-class norms (Scale 50).

3. Express happiness or satisfaction with family (Item 280), work (Item 282), and church life (Item 278).

4. Age 23 and over, married, not students, and likely to be college graduates.
5. Certain about their faith (Scale 66), believe in a personal, caring God (Scale 14), and face life and death with serenity (Scale 71).
6. High in their personal practices of piety (Scale 41) and actively involved in church and community (Scale 47).
7. Positive in evaluation of church and family (Scale 13) and less likely to express keen disappointment with the church (Scale 27).

Frequency of church attendance (Item 481) was found to have little positive effect on one's sense of purpose. Apparently there is no magical association between simply attending church and finding peace of mind or purpose in life. Something more than a mechanical or coerced appearance within the sanctuary is needed: the message of hope, love, and forgiveness must be heard, understood, and accepted.

Perhaps of even greater interest is the lack of any strong relationship between the dimension of life purpose and dimensions of Factor 3 relating to social involvement of the church. Lutherans with strong life purpose may see the church as an instrument of challenge and change, as a source of comfort, or both.

The other scale dimensions provide enrichment of our understanding of self-assessment among Lutherans: Feelings of Isolation and Pressure and Anxiety over My Faith. They give added information about how Lutherans feel about themselves.

FEELINGS OF ISOLATION AND PRESSURE

Both theory and life itself testify that we, as human beings, differ in the strength of our feelings of estrangement from other people and about the whirl of events around us. In our most euphoric moments our elation makes us dance with joy. At other moments we may feel bitterly alone, isolated, pressured, misunderstood—much as Job in the midst of his desolation. About one-fourth of Lutherans have some salient feelings of isolation and pressure (Scale 17). Those troubled most by these feelings are the 1% who think of committing suicide (Item 663) or the 8% who sometimes feel hated by God (Item 388).

A substantial minority (34%) feel left out of things that go on around them (Item 397), and 35% often have the feeling that their ideas are out of date (Item 403). The loneliness theme is picked up by two items (405 and 401): "people around here are not too friendly" (26%), and "I feel all alone in the world fairly often" (19%). The pressure of contemporary life is picked up by the two items most heavily endorsed by Lutherans. It may be indicative of today's pace that 65% of Lutherans often feel that "it would be good to get away from it all" (Item 383);

48% say that they are conscious of so many problems that they are ready to just "blow up" (Item 385).

It is evident that pathos and torment typify those who score high on this dimension; a person who is lonely and feels cheated by life contemplates desperate moves. Fortunately, most Lutherans bunch up at the nonisolated end of the scale, as reflected by low clergy and lay average scores of 28.3 and 31.5, respectively. The higher scores, which diminish to a maximum isolation score of 61, describe only a few persons. Lutherans having high scores on this dimension are apt to be concentrated among youth under 24 years of age and among those having less than a high school education. They also lacked a sense of Life Purpose (Scale 68) and expressed considerable anxiety about their faith, which is the third dimension that forms a basis for self-assessment.

ANXIETY OVER MY FAITH

A dimension live with poignancy is the concern of Lutherans over their faith (Scale 49). About one in four Lutherans (23%) is anxious ("very much" or "quite a bit") about his faith. Some (13%) are afraid of losing their faith (Item 366) and anxious (15%) because God does not seem to hear them when they pray (Item 371). About the same number (17%) wonder if they will go to heaven when they die (Item 363) and are bothered (17%) because they feel unable to give a reason for their faith (Item 364).

The most pronounced of these concerns over faith center in a feeling of distance from God and an inability rightly to live the faith; 40% do not feel close enough to Christ (Item 365); 33% wish they had a deep faith in God (Item 372); 35% are bothered because they are not living up to their Christian convictions (Item 369); and 25% do not like it that they cannot share their faith in a natural way (Item 370).

Significantly, 13% of the population say they once were anxious about these matters but are anxious "no longer." An average of 27% declare that such matters have "never" made them anxious.

What, then, typifies the respondents who are bothered about their faith and how they relate to God?

Persons who are most anxious about their faith feel isolated from others, lack a sense of purpose, are strongly peer-oriented, are unhappy with their church and with their family life, and voice uncertainty about their faith. They have not reached a position of peace in their faith that allows a healthy tension between certainty and uncertainty, between feeling guilty and at the same time forgiven *(simul justus et peccator)*.

A clear pattern of anxiety over one's faith is associated with age. People are less anxious with increasing age; it is youth who are most perplexed and insecure in their faith.

SUMMARY CONCERNING SELF-ASSESSMENT

We have described three interlocking dimensions and reported on how Lutherans feel about themselves and their relationship to life in general. A feeling of being isolated is tied to an anxiety over one's faith; both have a negative relationship to having a sense of purpose in life. It is likely that there is a reciprocal relationship between these three dimensions with the result that a change in the feelings concerning one is accompanied by a change in the feelings concerning the other two.

One can conclude that a purposeful life is closely related to: (1) being involved in instead of isolated from life; (2) knowing a certainty of faith rather than being anxious about it; (3) being buttressed by practices of personal piety; and (4) enjoying satisfying experiences with family, work, and church.

How Do Lutherans View Others?

Is it characteristic of Lutherans to be suspicious of outsiders, critical of strangers, or distrustful of other age groups? One wonders if membership in a confessional church encourages in any way the attitudes associated with an ingroup-outgroup mentality. Do Lutherans see themselves as different from other Christians? Do the characteristics of an ethnocentric group tend to be found among Lutherans? Some answers are available in the data that tap these dimensions of Lutheran life.

Each dimension that is now about to be discussed involves a judgment on the part of Lutherans as to the persons or groups with whom they are or are not willing to identify themselves. One of these dimensions, Peer Orientation (Scale 63), is included in Factor 8 which has a central theme of identification with church and family life as well as positive–negative evaluations of their performances. The dimensions and their loadings are:

Factor 8

Load	Scale	Dimension Title
.59	18	Identification with Parents
.56	13	Family and Congregational Caring Life
−.52	63	Peer Orientation
−.55	27	Disappointment with the Church

PEER ORIENTATION

Most Lutherans are able to relate to people of ages other than their own. Only one in five shows by his answers that his orientation is primarily or exclusively to his own age group.

An intriguing and elaborate dimension (Scale 63) is composed of a clustering of 18 items drawn from four separate parts of the questionnaire. Fifteen of these items refer specifically to youth or to alleged relations between generations. Another item passes judgment on the wisdom of the past. The remaining two refer to church work as "busy work" and that what the congregation asks them to do "just doesn't seem meaningful." The rich range of items involved and the variety of response possibilities available allow persons to respond along a continuum from a very low distinction between generations at one extreme, to the other extreme at which a vast gulf is perceived between their age group and others.

Score patterns on Peer Orientation are graphically displayed in Figure 9.1. Although lay and clergy averages were nearly identical, 36.4 and 36.6 respectively, there were vast differences when age and education were considered.

Who are most prone to be peer-oriented? Figure 9.1 shows that the age of the person responding is important for both laity and clergy. The youngest age groups of both feel closest to peers and/or alienated from older persons. Education has a relatively minor, but definite, effect together with age.[2]

The overall impression given by our data is that most Lutheran youth, by and large, have a broad orientation to all ages of people. Lutheran youth in general do not have a narrow or exclusive loyalty to their own age as their predominant reference group. Their lives appear to involve more harmonious relations with older persons and more favorable assessments of them.[3]

Two other dimensions provide clues to the group orientations of Lutherans. One measures a general acceptance or rejection of human beings and the world in general leading toward cynicism or pessimism (Scale 35). The other measures the extent to which Lutherans are perceived as a distinctive group, including both flattering and critical stereotypes (Image of Lutherans as Different, Scale 61). Both loaded negatively on Factor 4, introduced in Chapter 7.

Factor 4

Load	Scale	Dimension Title
.64	60	Individual Christian Responsibility
.56	59	Social Utility of Christianity
−.52	62	Service Without Proclamation
−.63	35	Pessimism
−.67	61	Image of Lutherans as Different

Both dimensions (Scales 35 and 61) reflect some degree of gullibility and proneness to stereotyping, whereas the dimensions which have positive loadings reflect more discriminating judgments and discernments. Unlike Factor 8, which has a consistent pattern with age, the

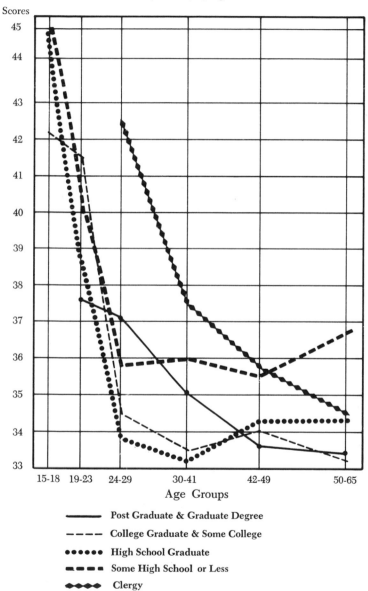

Figure 9.1 Comparison of Scores for Lay People and Clergy on Peer Orientation (Scale 63) by Age and Education

dimensions of Factor 4 have varied patterns. Both young and old have highest scores on pessimism (Scale 35), whereas no age differences appear on how different Lutherans are viewed (Scale 61).

PESSIMISM

Some Lutherans reflect a sour and pessimistic, if not a cynical attitude toward man. For these people the world is like a jungle where self-centered opportunism is a necessity. How prevalent are these attitudes?

It is possible to say that a pessimistic stance does not typify most Lutherans. No more than one in five (18%) agrees with the pessimistic outlook reflected in the items of this dimension (Scale 35). Twenty-six percent agree that a person must look out for himself since there is no one else to depend on for help (Item 286); 22% feel that an experienced person knows that most people cannot be trusted (Item 328); and 19% are convinced that there is little chance to get ahead on a job unless a man gets a break (Item 306).

Counterbalancing the above is a group of almost equal size (17%) that "strongly disagree" with these statements of pessimism. They are joined by a larger body of Lutherans (65%) who "disagree" with these items, establishing that most Lutherans respond on the positive side of the ledger.

Persons giving highly pessimistic responses tend to be under age 24 or over age 56 and tend to be relatively isolated from others. The age pattern is significant. Here is one of the few dimensions where young and old have similar scores. Both report more pessimism than is found among adults of the intermediate age groups. Lowest pessimism scores occur for Lutherans around 30 years of age.

Why should this be so? One possible explanation relates to level of education which increases each year until the middle or late twenties. After age 30, however, there is a declining percentage who have had an opportunity for higher education, which means that persons most deficient in educational background are high school youth and older persons. If pessimism is identified with a limited education, then it is understandable that it is strongest for the younger and the older persons and least for those age 30.

Another plausible explanation focuses on the stability and social acceptability of social roles. Young persons do not yet have adult identities in work and family life; older persons are losing theirs. This could be related to their feelings of pessimism. Conversely, if pessimism is lowest around age 30, it could reflect a satisfaction with marriage, parenthood, and work roles which have become stabilized and meaningful channels for personal expression.

The dimension of Pessimism (Scale 35) is also associated with hostility and negative evaluations of others which will be discussed later in this chapter. It is positively associated with major dimensions of Factor 2, Law Orientation (Misbelief), and Factor 11, Self-Development Values, and negatively associated with Factor 1, the Heart of Lutheran Piety, and the other two factors mentioned in this chapter, Factor 7, Positive Self-Assessment, and Factor 8, Identification with and Evaluation of Church and Family. It is also very revealing to note that the highly pessimistic person is more apt to accept a power orientation to social issues (Scale 64) than to want the church to take an active role (Scale 65), both of which are dimensions of Factor 3.[4]

IMAGE OF LUTHERANS AS DIFFERENT

How vivid or blurred is the image Lutherans have of themselves? Do they see Lutherans as different in any way? Six items about Lutherans form a separate dimension, Scale 61, and none of these items receives much support, although they refer to a variety of matters: religious practices and beliefs, Lutheran personalities, life styles, and ethnic heritage (Items 319, 322, 332, 344, 359, 361). The flavor of the items and their minimal endorsement can be gleaned by examining them in Table 5.3 of Chapter 5. The large majority of Lutherans view themselves positively and identify themselves with the main body of Christians.

Attempts to separate groups who score high or low on the scale, Image of Lutherans as Different, using background characteristics, were unsuccessful. Neither were clear differences found for this scale on the basis of age, sex, education, and the like. A positive relationship was found, however, with two related dimensions, Pessimism (Scale 35) and Generalized Prejudice (Scale 34).

It appears that a substantial majority of Lutherans strongly reject any stereotyping or labeling of Lutherans as different, irrespective of whether the alleged differences are critical or flattering. The minority of Lutherans who do accept the idea of a distinctive Lutheran image do so with perhaps two different perspectives in mind. One is a critical evaluation of Lutheran traits, as typified by Items 319, 344, and 322. The other three items (361, 332, and 359) suggest an ethnocentric, if not chauvinistic, attitude.

Where Is Prejudice Found?

Two additional approaches were used in getting a picture of how Lutherans view others. One approach elicited attitudes in response to statements indicating how distant or how intimate Lutherans feel toward twenty categories of persons that they could consider to be similar or different from themselves. Two measures of social distance emerged from this approach (Scales 56 and 57). The other measure of attitudes toward others was based on agreement or disagreement to fifteen statements; seven involved negative evaluations of Jews and eight made negative judgments of blacks and poor persons. These statements all formed one dimension entitled Generalized Prejudice (Scale 34).

All three of these measures loaded highly on Factor 2, Law Orientation. Major dimensions on Factor 2 are:

Load	Scale	Dimension Title
.76	37	Need for Unchanging Structure
.70	43	Need for Religious Absolutism
.69	34	Generalized Prejudice
.69	56	Social Distance—Radical Life Styles
.65	57	Social Distance—Racial and Religious Groups
.53	67	Self-Oriented Utilitarianism

SOCIAL DISTANCE

Measuring social distance between racial and religious groups began with Emory Bogardus over 40 years ago, when he developed tools to check how close people prefer their relationships with others. His list of categories was used in this study. Lutherans were asked to indicate the degree of intimacy they would prefer to have with other persons identified only by labels into which the respondents might read their own meaning. Seven degrees of social distance were provided as choices, ranging from being willing to marry into the group (no social distance) to the wish that persons in the group would be debarred from this country. Intermediate responses included, "have as close friends," "have as next door neighbors," "work in same office," "speaking acquaintances only," and "not want in community."

An extremely interesting finding emerged that has significance transcending the scope of this study. Two distinct dimensions were formed on the basis of how close Lutherans feel toward people of 20 different groups. One consisted of persons toward whom Lutherans feel *more* socially distant. A second consisted of persons toward whom they feel *less* distant. Figure 9.2 shows that highest intolerance is shown for communists who on the average would be permitted to be only speaking acquaintances if Lutherans had their choices. Starting, then, at the top of Figure 9.2 and moving down, notice not only that the average desired social distance narrows but that the *range* of permissible contact, once it is allowed, widens as one moves from communists to whites.

The types of persons who are least welcome to Lutherans are communists, homosexuals, drug addicts, hippies, and Students for a Democratic Society (S.D.S.). In descending order, the social distance is gradu-

Figure 9.2 Social Distance Ranges (Averages for Lutherans—Clergy and Lay People Combined)

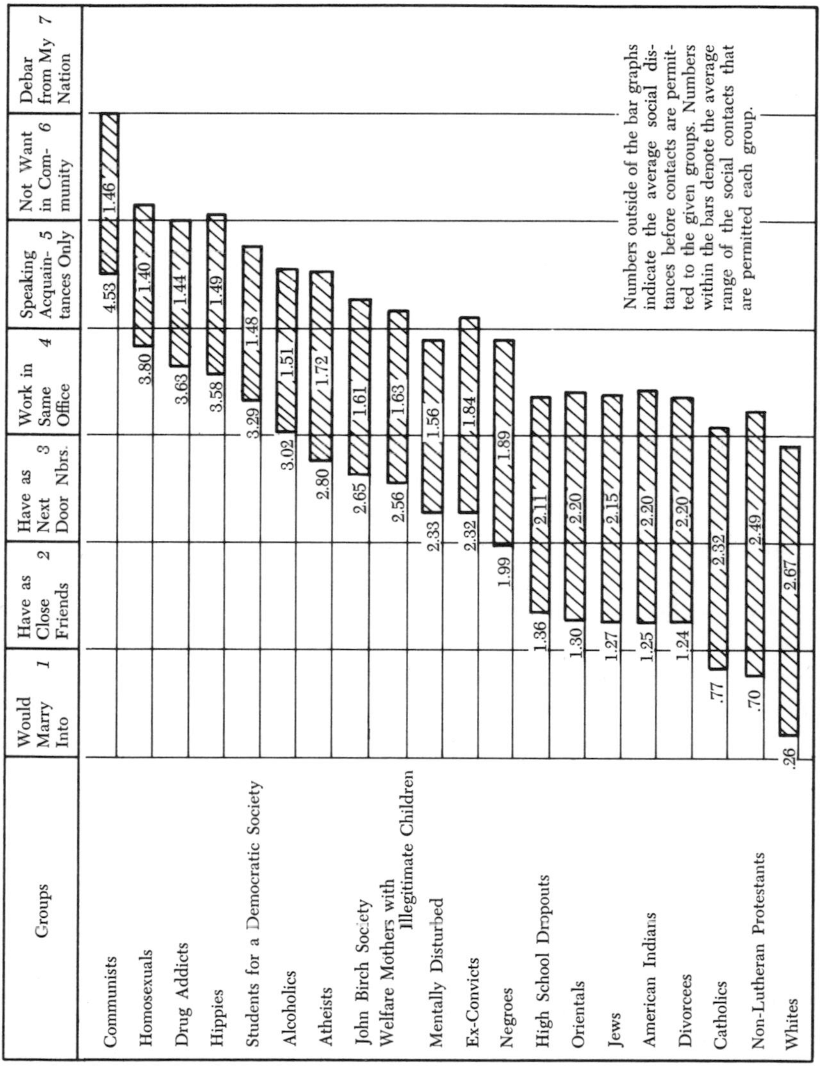

Groups	Would Marry Into 1	Have as Close Friends 2	Have as Next Door Nbrs. 3	Work in Same Office 4	Speaking Acquain-tances Only 5	Not Want in Com-munity 6	Debar from My Nation 7
Communists					4.53	1.46	
Homosexuals				3.80	1.40		
Drug Addicts				3.63	1.44		
Hippies				3.58	1.49		
Students for a Democratic Society				3.29	1.48		
Alcoholics			3.02	1.51			
Atheists			2.80	1.72			
John Birch Society			2.65	1.61			
Welfare Mothers with Illegitimate Children			2.56	1.63			
Mentally Disturbed		2.33	1.56				
Ex-Convicts		2.32	1.84				
Negroes		1.99	1.89				
High School Dropouts	1.36	2.11					
Orientals	1.30	2.20					
Jews	1.27	2.15					
American Indians	1.25	2.20					
Divorcees	1.24	2.20					
Catholics	.77	2.32					
Non-Lutheran Protestants	.70	2.49					
Whites	.26	2.67					

Numbers outside of the bar graphs indicate the average social distances before contacts are permitted to the given groups. Numbers within the bars denote the average range of the social contacts that are permitted each group.

ally less for alcoholics, atheists, members of the John Birch Society, welfare mothers with illegitimate children, the mentally disturbed, ex-convicts, and Negroes. These 12 categories formed one dimension (Scale 56) to indicate the people whose life styles are seen as most contrasting.

The companion dimension (Scale 57) consists of eight categories of persons. In descending order of desired social distance they were: high school dropouts, Orientals, Jews, American Indians, divorcees, Catholics, non-Lutheran Protestants, whites.

When the 20 groups were divided into four subgroups on the basis of racial, religious, political, and social differences, some interesting contrasts appeared. Those found to be most threatening to Lutherans were groups identified as political and social, whose members have contrasting life styles and values. Those found to be less threatening were racial and religious groups for whom Lutherans set more personal limits. This may be an indication of awareness of more compatible life styles and values.

The shape of the score distributions for the social distance scales is quite instructive (Figure 9.3). Note how most lay people locate at the high end of the Major Social Distance scale (Scale 56), that is, reject those of radical and contrasting life styles. Also, note how the majority locate at the low end of the Lesser Social Distance scale (Scale 57) to show general acceptance of high school dropouts, Orientals, Jews, etc. In a pattern nearly identical to that of Generalized Prejudice, these scales are closely related to both education and age. Youth and the better educated adults are far more accepting of people who are different.

Clergy means on both scales are decidedly lower than laymen's, particularly on the Major Social Distance scale. This may mean that the clergy are more willing than laity to meet people where they are, in whatever their social condition, and relate to them in some significant way. Or, it may mean that they are more out of touch with these cultural groups and hence are not as conscious of the problems that generate feelings between the groups.

Lutherans, both clergy and laity, are diversified in their viewpoints on social distance, as shown in Figure 9.3. Standard deviations on Scale 56 were 15.0 for laity and 16.9 for clergy; for Scale 57 the clergy were slightly more homogeneous with a standard deviation of 7.8 versus 10.0 for laity.

About two in five Lutherans (40%) tend to prejudge people of minority groups or people generally criticized as measured by Scale 34, Generalized Prejudice. A review of the items tells what kind of people Lutherans are likely to reject (see Appendix C, Section IV).

The group drawing least disfavor is the Jews. The percentage of Lutherans who agree to prejudicial statements about Jews ranges from 15%,

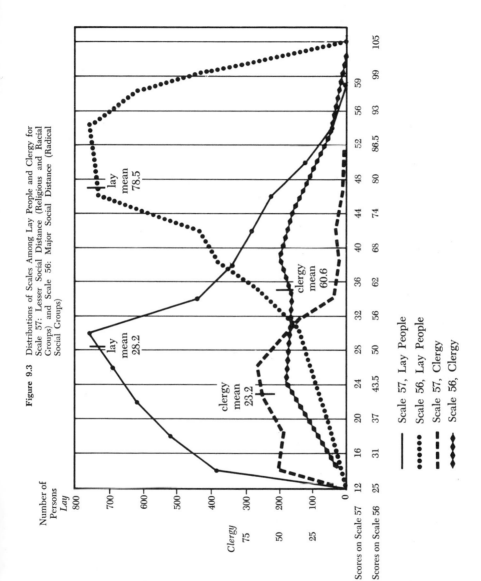

Figure 9.3 Distributions of Scales Among Lay People and Clergy for Scale 57: Lesser Social Distance (Religious and Racial Groups) and Scale 56: Major Social Distance (Radical Social Groups)

"Jews don't care what happens to anyone but their own kind" (Item 330), to 28%, "Jews have a lot of irritating faults" (Item 313). Fewer Lutherans (21%) also are willing to treat conscientious objectors as traitors to their country (Item 303). A somewhat larger number (33%) agree to segregation of blacks from whites (Item 295). Thirty percent concur that people have a right to keep others out of their community (Item 347).

The greatest rejection is reflected in items that speak of punitive and unsympathetic attitudes: 56% believe there is no punishment too severe for those guilty of a sex killing (Item 284); 59% think Negroes could solve many of their problems if they would not be so irresponsible and carefree about life (Item 342); 64% believe that most people who live in poverty could do something about it if they really wanted to (Item 327); 69% object to Negroes and whites dating each other (Item 307); and 77% agree that poor people would be better off if they took better advantage of their opportunities (Item 339).

In general, however, it can be said that most Lutherans answer in a nonprejudiced direction. The typical Lutheran layman agrees with five prejudiced statements and disagrees with ten. The clergy are less likely to indicate anti-Semitic or racially prejudiced attitudes. The fact does remain, however, that a substantial minority of Lutherans agree or strongly agree with a number of items.

Clergy have the lowest scale scores, even though their average age is much higher than laity. Women who are college graduates have responses most similar to clergy. Males without college degrees are most likely to affirm prejudiced statements. The influence of age and education is seen in the average scale scores found in Figure 9.4. Here a strong age influence can be seen for clergy and for four educational categories of laymen.[5] As would be expected, youth are least prejudiced. Graduate-trained adults do not score higher with age until they reach age 50.

Although age and educational status have marked influence on attitudes of prejudice, a stronger influence can be credited to misbeliefs and psychological states that are also dimensions of Factor 2, Law Orientation. Dimensions more identified with prejudice and social distance follow a uniform pattern.[6] A Need for Unchanging Structure (Scale 37) is the dimension most closely associated, followed by a Need for Religious Absolutism (Scale 43). Persons threatened by change feel the need for a stable and secure world; absolutizing religious life is but one manifestation. An instrumental view toward religion (Scale 67) is also strongly related to prejudice, having an influence similar to that associated with age.

In other research it has been argued by Glock and Stark (1966) that Christian religious beliefs are a cause of prejudice.[7] Their evidence is

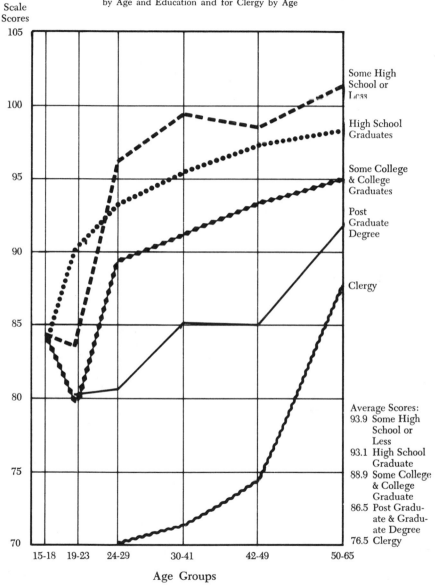

Figure 9.4 Generalized Prejudice (Scale 34): Average Scores for Laity by Age and Education and for Clergy by Age

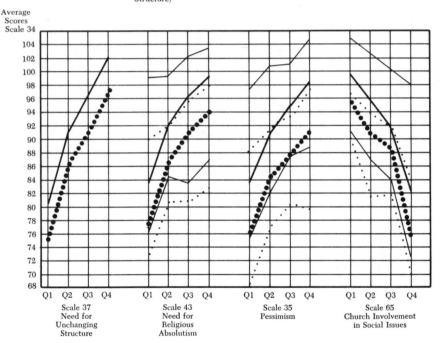

Figure 9.5a Generalized Prejudice Scores (Scale 34) for Major Predictor Variables for Total Laity and for Youth (Ages 15-28) with Subgroups Controlled for Scale 37 (Need for Unchanging Structure)

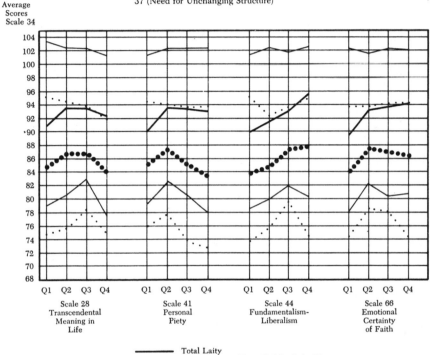

Figure 9.5b Generalized Prejudice Scores (Scale 34) for Major Dimensions of the Heart of Lutheran Piety for Total Laity and for Youth (Ages 15-28) with Subgroups Controlled for Scale 37 (Need for Unchanging Structure)

drawn from a cross-sectional survey similar to *A Study of Generations*. Our data have been submitted to a more elaborate analysis and fail to support their thesis. We do find bigotry and prejudice within Lutheranism, as our understanding of man, even Christian man, would suggest; however, we fail to find that prejudice is related to the belief system most central to Lutherans, namely, the Heart of Lutheran Piety (Factor 1).

Rather we find prejudice strongly connected with generalized rigidity of personality, and to a lesser extent with misbeliefs and heresies, many of which are not unique to Christianity. Law-oriented persons, threatened by change, are prone to attitudes of prejudice; prejudiced persons are apt to cling to a law orientation.

An example of many analyses performed to check this thesis is portrayed in Figures 9.5a and 9.5b on pages 210-211. The figures show the results of AID analyses for the total lay sample (heavy line) and for youth ages 15-28 (heavy dots).

In addition to the obvious major effect of Need for Unchanging Structure (Scale 37), there is a systematic and consistent increase in prejudice associated with the dimension of Pessimism (Scale 35) which reflects an exploitative ideology towards others. Need for Religious Absolutism (Scale 43) also shows a strong independent influence, even when controlled for Need for Unchanging Structure (Scale 37), as indicated by dotted lines.[8] An expected negative relationship exists between Generalized Prejudice and Scale 65, Church Involvement in Social Issues.

By contrast, there is no relationship between prejudice and the four major dimensions which represent the Heart of Lutheran Piety (Chapter 5). Even when controlled by Scale 37 (Need for Unchanging Structure), there is no relationship with prejudice other than a very slight indication of a possibly *negative* one. In fact, the data suggest that if further controls were introduced for age and education, the actual relationship might well be definitely negative. For neither the total sample nor for youth is a positive relationship found between prejudice and the major belief dimensions of the Heart of Lutheran Piety.

Prejudice may find its roots in many different places. Therefore, to unravel the cause–effect relationships would require a complex analysis. As noted in our theoretical framework, we have not assumed a simple uni-directional model of influence but rather an open model that acknowledges the possibility of an elaborate set of interacting and reciprocal elements. Cross-sectional research can identify which variables have a relationship with prejudice, but it cannot arbitrate a particular causal process.

Summary

The major findings of *A Study of Generations* regarding Lutheran attitudes toward self and others are numerous, but the highlights would include the following:

1. Most Lutherans are a happy people. If they could choose, these people would prefer nine more lives like the one they know now. It is not surprising, therefore, that only a fourth feel as though they were on the outside of the festival of life or are anxious about their faith. It is the young who are most troubled with feelings of purposelessness, isolation, and estrangement from God. Those who hold a positive attitude toward themselves usually report positive experiences with family, work, and church life, and also strong religious beliefs and practices.

2. It can also be said that most Lutherans are open in their attitudes toward others. No more than one in five takes a pessimistic stance toward life, sees himself as odd and different, or relates only to his peer group. Significantly, most Lutheran youth trust adults and are able to relate to them as well as to other youth. Those who do tend toward pessimism and a stereotyped image of Lutherans show less sense of Christian responsibility and concern for those about them.

3. Though a happy and relatively open people, Lutherans do not relate equally well to all people. Those whom they are most ready to reject are people whose life styles, values, and beliefs stand in greatest contrast to theirs. Racial differences are less of a barrier.

4. Therefore, for example, fewer are prejudiced toward Jews, whereas more are prejudiced toward blacks and poor people.

5. The major dimensions that are strongly related to prejudice and social distance are, in order of significance: Need for Unchanging Structure (Scale 37) and Need for Religious Absolutism (Scale 43). These are followed by lesser relationships with Self-Oriented Utilitarianism (Scale 67), Mutual Support Among Church, Society, and Individuals (Scale 26), The Exclusive Truth Claim of Christianity Exaggerated (Scale 16), and Pessimism (Scale 35).

6. The dimensions that are most strongly related *inversely* (negatively) to attitudes of prejudice are those concerning the church's involvement in social issues and people's openness to change in the church and society, as exemplified by Scale 65: Church Involvement in Social Issues; Scale 42: The Role of Pastors in Social Action; and Scale 12: The Church, Me, and Social Justice.

7. The most important finding is that prejudice and desire for social distance are *not* positively related to the basic value and belief system of Lutherans, referred to in this book as the Heart of Lutheran Piety.

Notes

1. The highest possible score on Life Purpose (Scale 68) was 76; whereas the lowest possible score, 14, would be the nadir of absence of life-meaning and utter despair. An average around the neutral response to each question would provide a person with a score of 30. Standard deviations were 11.7 for laity and 7.6 for clergy. The average score of 51.9 for laity and 58.6 for clergy indicates high personal assessment of life purpose and meaning. A small minority of about 4% have scores less than an average neutral reponse of 30, indicating they are troubled, or "hurting."

2. Results of two-way analyses of variance concerning Peer Orientation (Scale 63):

   N = 4,444 lay people

Test	Probability
Additivity (Interaction)	p = .000070°
Age	p = .000008
Education	p = .001400

   N = 301 clergy

Test	Probability
Additivity (Interaction)	p = .641000
Age	p = .000008
Church Body	p = .86+

   ° Interaction present

3. An examination of correlations of Peer Orientation to other dimensions shows the direction and strengths of relationships. As already noted, the closest relationship is with Scale 27, Disappointment with the Church (r = .42); the surprise comes in noting that the polar contrast is with Emotional Certainty of Faith, Scale 66. Listed below are the zero order intercorrelations for lay people in descending order for largest positive correlations, followed by ascending strength for largest negative correlations.

Scale	Correlation with Peer Orientation (Scale 63)	
		Positive
27	Disappointment with the Church	.42
17	Feelings of Isolation and Pressure	.37
64	Power Orientation to Social Issues	.32
73	Drug Culture Orientation	.30°
29	Value of Self-Development	.29
23	Questionable Personal Activities	.26
35	Pessimism	.25
		Negative
50	Acceptance of Middle-Class Norms	−.25
68	Life Purpose	−.28
13	Family and Congregational Caring Life	−.30
26	Mutual Support Among Church, Society, and Individuals	−.33
66	Emotional Certainty of Faith	−.36

   ° This correlation is the highest positive correlation with Scale 73, Drug Culture Orientation, which has a positively skewed J-curve distribution. It could hardly be much higher correlation given the high proportion of respondents who received minimum scores on the scale. The reverse is true for Scale 66, Emotional Certainty of Faith, which is highly skewed in the reverse direction.
   The listing reveals rather starkly the characteristics which identify the strongly peer-oriented youth and the majority of youth who have a broader orientation to the adult world.

4. Correlations of Pessimism (Scale 35) with representative dimensions of major factors are as follows:

Factor	Scale Number and Name	Correlation (r)
1	28 — Transcendental Meaning in Life	−.23
2	34 — Generalized Prejudice	.38
	67 — Self-Oriented Utilitarianism	.35
	37 — Need for Unchanging Structure	.28
	15 — Salvation by Works	.24
3	64 — Power Orientation to Social Issues	.23
	65 — Church Involvement in Social Issues	−.21
4	61 — Image of Lutherans as Different	.44
(Includes Scale 35)		
	62 — Service Without Proclamation	.34
	60 — Individual Christian Responsibility	−.36
7	68 — Life Purpose	−.24
8	27 — Disappointment with the Church	.28
	63 — Peer Orientation	.25

5. Results of two two-way analyses of variance (Scale 34):

N = 4,444 lay people

Test	Probability
Additivity (Interaction)	p = .000062*
Age	p = .000019
Education	p = .000029

N = 301 clergy

Test	Probability
Additivity (Interaction)	p = .393000
Age	p = .000005
Church Body	p = .14+

* Interaction present

6. Rank order of misbelief scales among all scales positively correlating with prejudice and social distance.

Scale Number	Title	GENERALIZED PREJUDICE Scale 34		SOCIAL DISTANCE Scale 56 Life Style		Scale 57 Race & Religion		Average
		r	Rank	r	Rank	r	Rank	Rank
37 —	Need for Unchanging Structure	.59	1	.57	1	.46	1	1.0
43 —	Need for Religious Absolutism	.41	2	.41	2	.38	2	2.0
67 —	Self-Oriented Utilitarianism	.40	3	.28	4	.30	4	3.7
26 —	Church, Society, and Individuals	.31	5	.33	3	.27	5	4.3
16 —	The Exclusive Truth Claim of Christianity Exaggerated	.30	6	.28	5	.37	3	4.7
35 —	Pessimism	.38	4	.16	14	.20	9	9.0
52 —	Desire for a Dependable World	.22	10	.20	10	.21	8	9.3
69 —	Horatio Alger Orientation	.19	11	.23	8	.19	10	9.7
15 —	Salvation by Works	.25	8	.17	12	.17	12	10.7
36 —	Christian Utopianism	.17	13	.17	13	.22	7	11.0

The rank order for Scale 37, Need for Unchanging Structure, is first for each measure of prejudice and social distance; it is also the dimension with highest loading on Factor 2, Orientation to Law, or Misbelief. Consistently, Scale 43, Need for Religious Absolutism, has second ranking on each measure and on factor loadings for Factor 2. The next three dimensions (Scales 67, 26, 16) are very similar in correlations and also in factor loadings, suggesting fairly close similarity in strength of relationships. The other five dimensions carry substantially lesser order of consistency, as well as strength of relationship.

Scale 37 is by far the most potent variable, having about 35% variance in common with both Scales 34 and 36 and about 22% for Scale 57. Scale 43 is consistent in having 14-17% in common with each prejudice and social distance scale. The next three scales (67, 26, 16) each tend to have about 9-10% variance in common with the three prejudice measures. The other five Factor 2 dimensions have between 2-6% variance in common with prejudice, averaging about 4% in common. The single exception to this was the 14% common variance of Scale 35, Pessimism, with Scale 34, Generalized Prejudice. Part of this relationship being stronger is possibly related to response-set, as the items for both Scales 34 and 35 come from the same portion of the schedule along with Scale 36.

The consistency of these results is reinforced by identifying these variables with their primary and secondary factor loadings, as well as showing their relative predictive power in relation to Generalized Prejudice (Scale 34), as revealed by AID Analysis. (See chart on p. 217.)

7. Specifically Glock and Stark identify what they call "orthodox Christian belief" as the first link in a long, complex chain that leads to anti-Semitism, not attitudes of prejudice in general. Inherent in this claim is the claim that attitudes of prejudice are group-specific; i.e., anti-Semitism is independent of other prejudices, and thus there really is no such thing as generalized prejudice (G-factor). Our data contradict this claim of Glock and Stark. The most discriminating seven of the ten Selznick and Steinberg (1969) anti-Semitism items that were reported by Glock and Stark (1966) were included in *A Study of Generations*. They scaled empirically as a separate set of seven with reliability of .84. However, they also scaled empirically, *with exactly the same weights* as when they scaled alone, together with eight other items having to do with Negroes (also referred to as blacks), poor people, conscientious objectors, and persons guilty of sex killings, with an overall reliability for the 15 items of .86 (see Scale 34, Appendix C, Section IV). Among Lutherans, at least, anti-Semitism is *not* a separate entity but is just one facet of generalized prejudice. (The other eight items, by the way, also scaled separately empirically, with exactly the same weights as when grouped with anti-Semitic items, with a reliability of .79. See Scale 34 of Table IV.7, Appendix A, Section IV.)

Their primary claim, of course, was that orthodoxy leads through a labyrinthine route to anti-Semitism. In Chapter 4 we argued that what they call "orthodoxy" is not. In fact, it is not even uniquely Christian. In Factor 1, the Heart of Lutheran Piety, we believe we have identified that which comes close to the heart of Lutheran belief today. The first dimension of Factor 1 includes the three "orthodoxy" items together with several other items. Scale 34, Generalized Prejudice, includes anti-Semitism as a nonseparate facet of a subgroup of items. Scale 37, Need for Unchanging Structure, is the first dimension of Factor 2, Law Orientation. We are now about to show that when they are controlled for Need for Unchanging Structure, the primary dimensions of Factor 1 are clearly not positively related but show signs of a negative relationship to Generalized Prejudice. In fact, the dimensions of the Heart of Lutheran Piety, Factor 1, are not correlated with measures of prejudice even when not controlled for Need for Unchanging Structure which is *highly* correlated with measures of attitudes of prejudice.

8. Scale 37, Need for Unchanging Structure, was most related to prejudice and

Summary of the Major Predictors of Generalized Prejudice (Scale 34)

Scale Number	Correlations with Scale 34		Means		Percent Variance			Laity Loading on Second-Order Factors				
	Lay	Clergy	Lay	Clergy	Laity Total	Laity Youth 15-28	Clergy	1	2	3	4	Others
37	.59	.71	100.8	91.1	23.4	21.3	N.A.		.76			
56	.57	.55	78.5	60.6	22.7	N.A.	N.A.		.69	-.30		
65	-.53	-.66	63.8	69.0	-17.2	-21.1	N.A.		-.35	.66	.31	
57	.46	.46	28.2	23.2	15.3	N.A.	N.A.		.65			
43	.41	.32	70.3	67.3	12.7	13.7	5.7		.70			
67	.40	.45	40.8	35.2	10.2	9.2	10.5		.53			
35	.38	.52	35.9	32.7	9.9	10.0	21.0		.32			11 = .35
42	-.36	-.61	39.2	46.9	N.A.*	-8.4	N.A.		-.34	.60	-.63	
26	.31	.34	60.2	63.5	6.5	6.1	6.6	.36	.47			8 = .41
16	.30	.47	63.5	65.5	6.4	5.0	15.4	.48	.49			
12	-.29	-.42	53.0	65.0	N.A.	-7.6	N.A.			.61		
61	.27	.33	37.0	38.5	3.4	2.8	10.2	-.29	.38		-.67	
15	.25	.23	65.7	39.0	4.2	2.8	4.3		.44			
36	.17	.28	40.8	41.1	N.A.	N.A.	N.A.	.44				11 = .33
Age					10.4	2.9	14.0					
Employment					9.5	...	...					
Family					6.3	...	7.8					
Education					4.5	2.3	...					

* N.A. means "Not Available" because the variable was not used in this analysis since it was already known to have only an effect carried by other predictors.

made the first split for both the total lay sample and the youth sample of Lutherans ages 15-28. Other predictors most associated with prejudice are indicated in the upper diagram (Scales 43 and 35 positively, and Scale 65 negatively). Self-Oriented Utilitarianism, Scale 67, had about the same predictive
power as Scale 35, Pessimism, and correlated r = .35 with Scale 35. Scale 35
is portrayed because it has more independent predictive power, when controlled
for either Scale 37 or 43. The top detail-line for total laity (——————————)
shows subgroup means for persons in the top quartile (Q4) on Scale 37; and
the bottom detail-line for total laity (———————) for persons in the lowest quartile (Q1) on Scale 37. Subscores on the two middle quartiles are not
shown, in order to simplify the diagrams, but were nearly identical with lines for
total laity.

The low subgroup for youth ages 15-28 (..........................) were youth
who were in the lowest quartile (Q1) of the total lay sample on Scale 37. The
second AID split for the youth sample was on Scale 65, Church Involvement in
Social Issues; therefore, the high subgroup of youth (.......................) were
youth in the top three quartiles (Q2, Q3, Q4) of total sample on Scale 37 and
also in the lower three quartiles (Q1, Q2, Q3) of Scale 65. Notice that the
high youth group has subgroup means nearly identical with the *total lay* sample.

As indicated in the lower diagram, there is a negligible negative relationship
between prejudice and scales measuring the Heart of Lutheran Piety (Scales 28,
41, 44, 66) for both the total sample and for youth who presumably have more
recently been instructed in the basic doctrines of the faith. Middle subgroups
have not been plotted to simplify the diagrams; however, differences were slight
and negative in direction:

	Total Laity					Youth			
	28	*41*	*44*	*66*		*28*	*41*	*44*	*66*
Q1	94.6	94.0	94.6	93.6		86.6	85.8	84.9	84.6
Q2	94.4	94.5	93.5	94.0		84.2	83.8	82.7	81.0
Q3	93.4	94.0	93.5	94.6		82.8	81.1	83.0	86.6
Q4	93.2	93.1	94.2	93.6		80.3	83.4	84.3	82.8

[The young] have exalted notions because they have not yet been humbled by life or learnt its necessary limitations . . . [Men in their prime] neither trust everybody nor distrust everybody, but judge people correctly . . . [Elderly men] are moved not by feeling but by love of gain . . .

—Aristotle, *Rhetoric*

Section III

10. Generations in Tension

Little has been said about generations since they were identified in Chapter 1. The contents of Chapters 2 through 9 focused quite exclusively on identifying dimensions and using them to give a general portrait of Lutherans. What has been shared so far might best be entitled "A Study of the Lutheran Family."

The purpose of this chapter is to show that four generations are represented in the family portrait and that each generation has its distinctive features. In some areas the differences are great enough to create tensions and even conflict.

This chapter gives answers to such pertinent questions as these: How might one understand generational differences? What characterizes the generations? Is there a generation gap? Where is tension greatest between youth and adults?

Tension between generations has been with us since the beginning of time. Ancient masters like Plato and Aristotle spoke of this tension or conflict as a necessary ingredient for change. They believed that without the struggle between generations where sons opposed their fathers, change in the political life of a nation, general forms, and patterns would go unchallenged and unchanged.

219

Generations in tension is not only a fact of history but a reality of life which congregational leaders must recognize. There are differences between generations which can cause divisions but which also can lead to creative changes that are blessings of God.

We can hardly overstate the concern that was expressed by church leaders (whom we consulted in the fall of 1969 and the summer of 1971) over the future of all institutions and specifically the church. Student riots; the rise of counter cultures (hippie, commune, drug, etc.); the advent of books by Reich, Roszak, and Mead; and the tragic events of Kent State had sown their seeds of doubt. Intelligent people were wondering if today's youth were indeed a new breed, and if so, whether or not they could support and maintain the church as an institution. College presidents were convinced of a profound chasm between generations and feared that this chasm was widening.

In response to these widespread expressions of concern, a special effort was made to measure the degree to which a generation gap does exist. For instance, in our survey, we incorporated items from Margaret Mead's book of 1970 (Culture and Commitment) in order to test her thesis that a radical break has occurred between youth and adults.

Due to space limitations, we cannot report all that we found that is germane to the question raised regarding the youth population. We can treat here only the issue of generational tension and relegate the additional information on youth to a later publication.

How might one best describe generational tension, a phenomenon of life that has been with us since the beginning of history? To what extent is there a generation gap in our present society? What are the areas of greatest tension between youth and adults?

A Rationale for Understanding Generational Tension

An important procedure in research is to formulate a theoretical framework for understanding an important issue and then to test its validity with research data. When the theoretical formulation or rationale is supported by the data from the research, then we can use the rationale to determine how to deal with the problem.

In March 1970 our research team developed a specific rationale for understanding generational tension. Using the procedure mentioned above, we tested the rationale through research. You will discover that the rationale was quite adequate. Where the research evidence said the rationale was inadequate, we have modified it. We now have a basis for drawing conclusions about generational tension. Following is our original rationale.

Our point of view is that there has always been tension between youth and adults, and that in our day this tension is accentuated by a period of unprecedented social upheaval. The issues of the day are more intense; the despair of some individuals is extreme. A cleavage has begun as youth have openly challenged some of the value assumptions that our society holds. This cleavage does not necessarily mean, however, that there is a radical break between youth and adults. Rather, it presents the tension between youth and adults on emphases or polarities that are essential to life. In times of social upheaval and change such as ours the tension is intensified.

It is assumed that the generations under study will vary in the importance they give to the two emphases or polarities to which we alluded in the above paragraph and now list below:

Structure	**Newness**
Tradition, regimentation, standards, organization, conformity	Creativity, new forms, new styles of life, new expressions of change and (even) revolution

Inasmuch as adults are more oriented to tradition and structure, and youth are more oriented toward action and change, it is assumed that a model of mutual tension is needed to account for the conflict in emphases that characterize younger and older generations. The expected differences are shown below (A = Youth; B = Middle Age; C = Older Adults; the sign < means "is less than"; the sign > means "is greater than").

Conflicts Between Generations

Conformity to structure and tradition	A < B < C	Least for youth (A) and greatest for adults (C, 50-65)
Commitment to change and new forms	A > B > C	Greatest for youth (A) and least for adults (C, 50-65)

The model of mutual tension assumes that the greatest tension will occur between generations A (ages 15-29) and C (ages 50-65) as illustrated below.

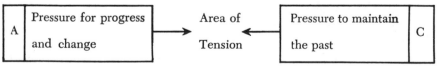

In light of this basic model one would expect differences between generations in their response on each of the following major descriptive categories which are a part of *A Study of Generations:*

Beliefs
Values
Mission and Ministry of the Church
Institutional Loyalty
Perception of Self and Others
Life Styles

A comparison of scores for each age grouping will show where differences are the least and where they are the greatest.

One point should be clear. We assume that a significant number of adults will join the youth who take a liberal stance, prefer variety and newness, opt for recovery of personal dignity, and react against the law-and-order theme. And it is also assumed that there are young people whose stance toward life will support the most conservative and traditional positions.

Historical–Cultural Effects

Generational differences result, of course, from other factors than those which have been traditionally observed. There are the pervasive influences of historical events (e.g., world wars, depressions) and cultural pressures (e.g., national feeling tones or moods) that are felt more keenly during times of social upheaval.

Three national trends or developments which have special significance for this study are feelings of alienation, "now" orientation, and disenchantment with the institutional church. Although these feeling tones, like clouds, affect people of all ages, it is assumed that their greatest effect is upon youth—those people who are most subject to change.

Therefore, if Lutherans are classified as youth (A) and adults (B and C), one can expect the evidences of cultural and historical constraints to appear most strikingly in the youth population. To illustrate:

Alienation	A > BC	Greater for youth than adults
"Now" orientation	A > BC	More characteristic of youth than adults
Disenchantment	A > BC	More widespread among youth than adults

These assumptions will be tested by comparing scores on scales appropriate to each attitude or stance toward life.

Two Kinds of Youth

It may be that the observed differences in the above comparisons are not great. Greater differences will likely appear if the youth are divided into those who relate only to their peer group (peer-oriented) and those who relate to people of all ages (broadly-oriented).

A division of the youth into A_1 (peer-oriented only) and A_2 (broadly-oriented) can be accomplished by using appropriate items to which all youth have responded.

If grouped as follows:

A_1 Peer-oriented only
A_2 Broadly-oriented

one can expect more of those classified as A_1 to show the effects of the three cultural trends. Hence:

Alienation	$A_1 > A_2$	Greater for peer-oriented youth
"Now" orientation	$A_1 > A_2$	than for broadly-oriented youth
Disenchantment	$A_1 > A_2$	

Furthermore, one can expect A_1 youth to differ in related qualities that are important to this study.

Mistrust of adults	$A_1 > A_2$	
Inability to delay gratification	$A_1 > A_2$	Greater for peer-oriented youth
Disenchantment with the institutional church	$A_1 > A_2$	than for broadly-oriented youth

It is expected that A_2 youth—who by definition are willing to relate to adults and accept their guidance—will share similarities with adults in their value orientation.

With respect to a generation gap, it is assumed that differences between youth and adults on all major categories of comparison are greater for A_1 youth. Hence the differences between peer-oriented youth and adults are expected to be greater than differences between broadly-oriented youth and adults.

Furthermore, it is expected that A_2 youth feel:

—accepted by adults
—understood by adults
—appreciated by adults

With respect to Lutheran youth (A_1 and A_2), all will be especially sensitive to two important elements in church life:

—an accepting community characterized by mutuality and warm interaction
—meaningful activities that minister to people's needs

It is assumed that these needs are ones about which youth are especially conscious. And it is further assumed that youth will be more
critical than adults about the lack of mutuality and mission in their
congregation. (See Chapter Note 1 for a discussion of additional factors.)

SUMMARY

The suggested model consists of two polarities held in tension, both
of which are essential to life—structure and spontaneity (or newness).
The emphasis of adults in contrast to an opposing emphasis of youth
creates the conflict of mutually recognized tension. This tension is accentuated during revolutionary times of social upheaval. It is further
increased by such factors as cultural moods, an orientation to one's peer
group only, socio-economic pressures, and a committed or consensual
relation to the Christian faith.

Traditional source. In our conceptual model we imply that there are
two basic sources of conflict between generations—the one traditional
to man through the centuries, and the other specific to the social upheaval
of today. The psychodynamics of youth and adults are well known.
Young people have always been associated with revolution, and older
adults with the status quo. Lutherans especially know this because the
Reformation did involve a conflict of generations. Most of Luther's
followers were under 30 years of age, and most of his opponents were
over 50. At times Luther was unable to control his student following.
In their zeal for advancing the cause of the Reformation, they often
resorted to violence, intimidation, and rioting.

Social revolution. It is commonly assumed that the emotion-laden
events of the 1960s and the social changes of our day have intensified
the tension that traditionally has existed between generations. Though
Reich's book, *The Greening of America* (1970), focuses upon a very
limited subculture of American youth and makes statements that are
untenable, it does make two contributions that are of value to our
understanding of the social revolution. The first contribution is found
in the implied thesis that generational tension has its source in conflicting world views. The second contribution is a description of three world
views which find their origin in the periods of history that roughly approximate this study. These descriptions are valuable because they picture how people tended to look at life during the periods before and
after the two world wars. As clearly defined world views, they can serve
as a conceptual framework for understanding the cultural setting of
different generations. (See Chapter Note 2 for a brief review of these
three world views.)

TESTING THE RATIONALE

A Study of Generations provides ample evidence for testing the rationale given above. A total of 52 scales supply relatively precise information on how Lutherans differ by generations in what they value, believe, misbelieve, hold as mission, feel, and do. A series of quite unprecedented comparisons makes it possible to draw conclusions that have a solid empirical base. An important gross summary of comparisons by generation using the 52 dimensions is given in Table 10.1. It will serve as a basic reference for this chapter.

Conclusions About Generations

Did the survey data support the rationale of the research team? Did we find a radical disjuncture between youth and adults, namely, a serious generation gap such as many have feared?

We did find general support for the rationale presented earlier. There were, significant exceptions in specifics which demanded that we modify our rationale, but the major premises stand.

First of all, Table 10.1 shows that significant differences among generations exist along 45 of the 52 dimensions relevant to the rationale. Measurements on these 45 dimensions, as expected, show tension across broad areas not only of belief but also of value, attitude, opinion, and life style. However, the differences are in no case terribly large, such that they might properly be called chasms or immense gaps. The model of definite tension fits, but not radical separation beyond bridging with communication or beyond the possibility of mutual understanding.

Second, by examining the number of underlinings in each age-group column in Table 10.1, it appears that tension between generations is, again as expected, greatest between youth (ages 15-29, and especially ages 19-22) and the oldest adults (ages 50-65). Scores for these two age groups show the greatest contrast on nearly three-fourths of the dimensions where differences of statistical significance do exist. But the hypothesis that generally the greater the difference in age, the greater the tension (A > B > C) was not upheld throughout. Modification of the rationale was required on this matter.

Third, the two emphases on polarities of structure and newness (spontaneity) are definitely exhibited by older adults and youth respectively. (Note scales 26, 56, 52, 78, 37, 43, 57, 16, 44, 50, 65, 64, and 69 of Table 10.1.)

Fourth, we also found that more youth than adults have feelings of alienation, that fewer youth are willing or able to delay gratification, and that more youth are disappointed with their church. (Note especially Scales 23, 78, 17, 49, and 27 of Table 10.1.)

Table 10.1 Comparisons of Average Standardized Scores ($\bar{X}$ = 50.0, s = 10.0) for Three Subgenerations of Youth and Three Generations of Adults on 52 Dimensions Ranked by High-Low Score Differences

(Highest scores underlined twice; lowest underlined once)

Scale	Title	Youth 15-18	19-23	24-29	30-41	Adults 42-49	50-65	Difference in Highest and Lowest Scores	Probability
63	Peer Orientation	59.7	54.2	48.3	47.0	48.0	48.2	12.8	< .0001
41	Personal Piety	45.1	43.8	47.6	50.3	52.3	54.3	10.5	< .0001
23	Questionable Personal Activities	54.5	56.9	51.9	48.8	47.4	46.8	10.1	< .0001
26	Mutual Support Among Church, Society, and Individuals	44.8	43.9	48.0	50.9	52.2	53.8	9.8	< .0001
20	Supporting Others in Crises	45.0	46.2	46.9	49.4	52.0	54.7	9.8	< .0001
56	Social Distance—Radical Life Styles	44.8	43.9	48.3	50.9	52.4	53.5	9.6	< .0001
52	Desire for a Dependable World	45.6	45.9	46.5	49.1	51.8	55.2	9.6	< .0001
34	Generalized Prejudice	44.5	44.4	48.6	50.5	52.4	53.7	9.3	< .0001
66	Emotional Certainty of Faith	44.4	44.8	49.2	51.2	52.2	52.7	8.3	< .0001
78	Openness to Change Within the Church	55.4	55.6	50.8	47.6	47.4	48.6	8.2	< .0001
37	Need for Unchanging Structure	48.4	45.6	47.1	49.3	51.2	53.8	8.2	< .0001
43	Need for Religious Absolutism	47.6	45.8	48.0	49.3	51.0	54.0	8.2	< .0001
17	Feelings of Isolation and Pressure	56.3	52.3	49.3	48.3	48.9	48.5	8.0	< .0001
57	Social Distance—Racial and Religious Groups	47.3	45.8	47.5	49.5	51.5	53.8	8.0	< .0001

Table 10.1 (continued)

68	Life Purpose	44.1	47.1	50.4	51.4	51.4	51.8	7.7	< .0001
73	Drug Culture Orientation	55.5	55.1	49.3	48.2	48.1	48.4	7.4	< .0001
16	The Exclusive Truth Claim of Christianity Exaggerated	48.6	46.0	47.7	49.2	51.3	53.4	7.4	< .0001
44	Fundamentalism-Liberalism	47.2	45.7	48.5	50.4	51.3	52.6	7.0	< .0001
50	Acceptance of Middle-Class Norms	45.4	45.4	49.2	51.1	51.8	52.3	7.0	< .0001
21	Personal Evangelism	48.9	46.9	46.9	48.8	51.0	53.8	6.9	< .0001
40	Congregational Activity	49.8	44.7	48.2	50.6	51.3	51.7	6.9	< .0001
29	Values of Self-Development	55.3	52.1	49.1	48.8	48.4	49.1	6.9	< .0001
65	Church Involvement in Social Issues	53.3	54.3	51.7	49.1	47.6	48.3	6.6	< .0001
14	A Personal, Caring God	46.0	45.6	49.3	50.9	51.8	52.1	6.5	< .0001
42	The Role of Pastors in Social Action	53.8	54.3	51.8	48.7	47.8	48.2	6.5	< .0001
64	Power Orientation to Social Issues	54.0	53.3	49.5	47.7	47.8	50.6	6.3	< .0001
71	Attitudes Toward Life and Death	45.8	45.8	49.8	51.1	51.5	52.0	6.2	< .0001
28	Transcendental Meaning in Life	46.1	46.1	49.8	50.4	51.6	52.3	6.2	< .0001
13	Family and Congregational Caring Life	45.8	45.9	49.2	51.3	51.6	52.0	6.2	< .0001
49	Anxiety over My Faith	53.6	52.6	51.0	49.9	48.9	47.4	6.2	< .0001
69	Horatio Alger Orientation	47.2	47.0	48.1	50.1	51.3	52.6	5.6	< .0001
36	Christian Utopianism	49.5	47.5	48.0	49.1	50.4	52.9	5.4	< .0001
5	Humanity of Jesus	52.3	53.0	51.6	50.4	48.2	47.7	5.3	< .0001

Table 10.1 (continued)

9	Biblical Ignorance	53.7	51.9	51.0	49.0	48.9	48.6	5.1	< .0001
54	Desire for Detachment from the World	53.3	50.6	48.2	48.3	48.7	51.5	5.1	< .0001
19	Religious Experience	50.4	47.4	48.4	48.9	50.6	52.3	4.9	< .0001
67	Self-Oriented Utilitarianism	51.8	49.8	47.7	48.1	49.4	52.4	4.7	< .0001
27	Disappointment with the Church	52.5	51.9	49.4	48.5	49.8	49.7	4.0	.0001
35	Pessimism	51.9	50.7	48.8	48.4	49.7	51.0	3.5	.0001
58	Awareness of the Immanent Trinity	51.0	49.7	50.9	51.2	50.0	48.0	3.2	< .0001
59	Social Utility of Christianity	48.5	48.6	49.8	49.5	49.9	52.0	3.5	.0001
51	Acceptance of Authority	50.1	49.8	51.1	51.4	49.9	48.2	3.2	.0001
15	Salvation by Works	51.5	50.8	48.9	48.5	49.2	51.4	3.0	.0001
47	Personal Involvement in Church and Community	48.9	48.1	49.8	50.7	50.9	50.2	2.8	n.s.
60	Individual Christian Responsibility	48.1	48.5	50.8	50.2	50.4	50.9	2.8	.0001
62	Service Without Proclamation	49.2	49.8	48.6	49.7	50.2	51.3	2.7	n.s.
12	The Church, Me, and Social Justice	51.6	51.1	51.0	49.9	49.1	49.1	2.5	n.s.
8	Biblical Knowledge	49.1	49.2	48.8	50.0	50.0	51.3	2.5	n.s.
53	Desire for a Controllable World	49.9	50.1	49.7	49.1	49.5	51.4	2.3	.0001
18	Identification with Parents	49.0	50.1	50.5	51.1	50.3	49.0	2.1	n.s.
6	Divinity of Jesus	50.6	48.7	50.0	50.1	50.3	50.0	1.9	n.s.
61	Image of Lutherans as Different	50.2	49.5	49.7	49.8	50.0	50.4	.9	n.s.

Fifth, we found that Lutheran youth divide into two quite contrasting groups: the peer-oriented youth and the broadly-oriented youth. Youth who are broadly-oriented take their signals from people of all ages—adults as well as contemporaries. Peer-oriented youth feel more alienated and more critical of their church and show less ability to delay gratification. They resemble most the stereotype commonly held of youth. About 20% of Lutherans ages 15-28 are peer-oriented.

In general, the research data do support the rationale, except for the modifications given below.

Modifications of the Rationale

Some qualifications are needed to account for the exceptions that are strikingly in evidence and to make allowances for the discriminations that can be made when the youth population is divided into subgroups. As mentioned above, on some dimensions, such as Scale 20 in Table 10.1, average scores rather smoothly rise from younger to older generations. But this is not the case throughout. Furthermore, careful study of Table 10.1 raises the question of how big the difference in scores must be before two age groups are really different. For example, scores of 44.5 and 44.4 for ages 15-18 and 19-23 on Scale 34 surely are not evidence of real difference in the whole population of Lutherans of those ages. But what about the scores of 59.7 and 54.2 for those same subgenerations on Scale 63? Generally speaking, a difference of approximately 3.0 standardized score points between the averages of two sample generations is required before one can be reasonably certain ($p = .0001$) that those two generations of all Lutherans are significantly different on a given dimension. This means that, for example, in the matter of peer orientation (Scale 63 in Table 10.1) youth of ages 15-18 are significantly more peer-oriented than youth of ages 19-23 who again are significantly more peer-oriented than all of the four generations between the ages of 24-65, which are essentially identical in level of peer orientation. To clarify distinctions such as these throughout the rest of the tables in this chapter, heavy vertical lines between columns separate generations whose average scores on a given scale are significantly different at a probability of one in ten thousand ($p = .0001$). Where there are no heavy vertical lines between columns the generations involved are *not* significantly different or in tension though their average scores vary slightly.

Seven patterns of generational tension, each with variations, were identified from a detailed statistical analysis of all of the possible generational contrasts in Table 10.1 (see Chapter Note 3). The seven basic patterns are:

a. Ages 15-18 vs. 19-23 vs. 24-65
b. Ages 19-23 vs. 15-18 *and* 24-41 vs. 42-49 vs. 50-65

    c. Ages 15-23 *and* 50-65 vs. 24-49
    d. Ages 15-23 vs. 24-65
    e. Ages 15-29 vs. 30-65
    f. Ages 15-41 vs. 42-65
    g. Ages 15-49 vs. 50-65

Just what generations are in agreement or contrast depends, among other factors, upon the dimension or issue under consideration. There definitely is no uniform predictable pattern of tension across generations. This in itself is one of the strongest arguments against the idea of a simple "generation gap." Rather, name the generations and there are some issues where there is general agreement and some matters over which there is tension. Generational tension is a matter of which generations, concerning which issue.

High school youth. There are only a few dimensions upon which youth ages 15-18 by themselves tend to differ from all other generations. Nevertheless they will likely provoke considerable concern as well as interest, as summarized in Table 10.2. High school youth as a subgeneration differ significantly from college age youth who also differ significantly from the oldest subgeneration of youth (ages 24-29) together with all three adult generations. They differ on a remarkably interrelated set of dimensions where proportionately more youth ages 15-18 are peer-oriented, feeling isolated and under pressure, placing high priority on self-development, and participating extensively in questionable personal activities (exceeded only by college age youth in this respect.) Consistent with this, proportionately fewer of them have a strong sense of definite purpose and meaning in life. These biases of teenage youth reflect the poignantly painful struggle of adolescence.

In keeping with these distinguishing characteristics of the high school subgeneration, one might expect them to be less active in congregational life. Yet congregational activity (Scale 40 in Table 10.2) of high school youth on the average is at exactly the same level as that of all three adult generations (ages 30-65) and contrasts sharply with the much lesser participation by college age youth. This suggests that possibly if high school youth were as independent from their parents and other adults as are college age youth, more of them might be considerably less active in congregational life.

Transitional youth. It is evident from the preceding paragraphs and information given in Chapter 2 that youth, ages 23-28, are in a transitional period. Though their self-reports classify them as part of the youth generation, yet in some ways they already contrast with the younger ages as an adult contrasts with youth. The most dramatic illus-

Table 10.2 Average Standardized Scores by Generation Where High School Youth Contrast with All Others

(Heavy vertical lines separate generations in tension where average scores are significantly different at p = .0001)

Scale	Title	Scores: 15-18	19-23	24-29	30-41	42-49	50-65	Difference in Highest and Lowest Scores
		Highest	**Higher**	**Lower**				
63	Peer Orientation	59.7	54.2	48.3	47.0	48.0	48.2	12.8
23	Questionable Personal Activities	54.5°	56.9	51.9	48.8	47.4	46.8	10.1
17	Feelings of Isolation and Pressure	56.3	52.3	49.3	48.3	48.9	48.5	8.0
29	Values of Self-Development	55.3	52.1	49.1	48.8	48.4	49.1	6.9
68	Life Purpose	**Lowest** 44.1	**Lower** 47.1	**Higher** 50.4	51.4	51.4	51.8	7.7
40	Congregational Activity	**Higher** 49.8	**Lowest** 44.7	**Lower** 48.2	**Higher** 50.6	51.3	51.7	6.9

° High school youth on the average contrast with all other generational groups on Scale 23, but in this case vary from the pattern and show next to the highest rather than the highest average.

trations of this appear in their dramatic drop in scores on Peer Orientation (Scale 63), Feelings of Isolation (Scale 17), and, as will be shown later, Desire for Detachment from the World (Scale 54).

College age youth. There are four other dimensions upon which high school and college age youth differ significantly, with college age scoring lowest of all generations on the average. These are the only unique biases of college age youth alone, other than their lowest levels of congregational activity and highest levels of participation in questionable personal activities, as mentioned above. And again on these four dimensions, as shown in Table 10.3, high school youth and two older subgenerations (ages 24-29 and 30-41) are in agreement while in considerable tension with older generations. The tension over structure, absolutism, exclusivism, and prejudice is relatively strong and is greatest between the oldest generations and college age youth who least desire rigid and unchanging social structures, absolutistic religious stances or claims of having "the truth," as well as keeping socially distant from persons who are different religiously and racially.

Youngest and oldest in tension with middle generations. Contrary to the expectations of our rationale, high school and college age youth as well as the oldest generation (ages 50-65) are equally inclined to live a life more detached from the world, to be more pessimistic about things as a whole and especially people, and to believe more commonly in salvation by works. And more high schoolers *and* oldsters see religion as a way to advance their own interests. (See Table 10.4.) The younger and older may demonstrate these same relatively negative characteristics for different reasons: the young out of their fear and insecurity of not measuring up or not finding a worthy place in the world; the old out of disappointment or fear of no longer having a place where they are needed, or of not having been all that they hoped. Both especially need to experience the gospel.

Joint characteristics of high school and college age youth. If there is any one pattern of generational tension that predominates, it is clearly the two youngest subgenerations of youth (ages 15-23) versus the subgeneration of youth in transition (ages 24-29) together with all three adult generations (ages 30-65) as shown in Table 10.5. These contrasts outline specific dimensions of the antithetical structure–newness emphasis of age and youth in the church as: non-change versus change in the church and society, norms and exclusiveness versus variety and acceptance of great diversity, certainty of clearly stated belief versus the anxiety of doubt and questioning, power versus lack of opportunity or ability to affect decisions, and finally individual responsibility versus

Table 10.3 Average Standardized Scores by Generation Where College Age Youth Are Lowest in Contrast with All Others
(Heavy vertical lines separate generations in tension where average scores are significantly different at $p = .0001$)

Scale	Title	Scores: Ages:	Lower 15-18	Lowest 19-23	Lower 24-29	Lower 30-41	Higher 42-49	Highest 50-65	Difference in Highest and Lowest Scores
37	Need for Unchanging Structure		48.4	45.6	47.1	49.3	51.2	53.8	8.2
43	Need for Religious Absolutism		47.6	45.8	48.0	49.3	51.0	54.0	8.2
57	Social Distance—Racial and Religious Groups		47.3	45.8	47.5	49.5	51.5	53.8	8.0
16	The Exclusive Truth Claim of Christianity Exaggerated		48.6	46.0	47.7	49.2	51.3	53.4	7.4

Same

Table 10.4 Average Standardized Scores by Generation Where Youngest and Oldest Contrast with Middle Generations
(Heavy vertical lines separate generations in tension where average scores are significantly different at $p = .0001$)

Scale	Title	Scores: Higher		Lower			Higher	Difference in Highest and Lowest Scores
	Ages:	15-18	19-23	24-29	30-41	42-49	50-65	
54	Detachment from the World	53.3	50.6	48.2	48.3	48.7	51.5	5.1
35	Pessimism	51.9	50.7	48.8	48.4	49.7	51.0	3.5
15	Salvation by Works	51.5	50.8	48.9	48.5	49.2	51.4	3.0
67	Self-Oriented Utilitarianism	51.8	49.8	47.7	48.1	49.4	52.4	4.7

Same

Table 10.5 Average Standardized Scores by Generation Where Youth Ages 15-23 Contrast with All Others

(Heavy vertical lines separate generations in tension.)

Scale	Title	Lower 15-18	Lower 19-23	24-29	30-41	42-49	50-65	Difference in Highest and Lowest Scores
41	Personal Piety	45.1	43.8	47.6	50.3	52.3	54.3	10.5
26	Mutual Support Among Church, Society and Individuals	44.8	43.9	48.0	50.9	52.2	53.8	9.8
56	Social Distance—Radical Life Styles	44.8	43.9	48.3	50.9	52.4	53.5	9.6
34	Generalized Prejudice	44.5	44.4	48.6	50.5	52.4	53.7	9.3
66	Emotional Certainty of Faith	44.4	44.8	49.2	51.2	52.2	52.7	8.3
50	Acceptance of Middle-Class Norms	45.4	45.4	49.2	51.1	51.8	52.3	7.0
14	A Personal Caring God	46.0	45.6	49.3	50.9	51.8	52.1	6.5
13	Family and Congregational Caring Life	45.8	45.9	49.2	51.3	51.6	52.0	6.2
28	Transcendental Meaning in Life	46.1	46.1	49.8	50.4	51.6	52.3	6.2
71	Attitudes Toward Life and Death	45.8	45.8	49.8	51.1	51.5	52.0	6.2
60	Individual Christian Responsibility	48.1	48.5	50.8	50.2	50.4	50.9	2.8
78	Openness to Change Within the Church	55.4	55.6	50.8	47.6	47.4	48.6	8.2
73	Drug Culture Orientation	55.5	55.1	49.3	48.2	48.1	48.4	7.4
64 *	Power Orientation to Social Issues	54.0	53.3	49.5	47.7	47.8	50.6	6.3
49	Anxiety over My Faith	53.6	52.6	51.0	49.9	48.9	47.4	6.2
27	Disappointment with the Church	52.5	51.9	49.4	48.5	49.8	49.7	4.0

* Significantly different generational groups on Scale 64 from highest to lowest scores are: a) 15-23, b) 24-29 and 50-65, and c) 30-49.

corporate responsibility. Again there is remarkable consistency among the several dimensions even to the extent that youth are anxious over their faith and less youth are emotionally certain of their faith, as well as more youth disappointed with the church and less youth seeing their own families and congregations as truly caring about and for people in all their needs (Scales 49, 66, 27, and 13 in Table 10.5).

That the tension for some may grow out of basically different world views or consciousness, as suggested by Reich and mentioned earlier, is not without support. (See contrasts on Scales 14, 28, 71, 73, and again 66 and 49 in Table 10.5.) Basic beliefs, values, and the certainty of one's convictions are a considerable source of tension.

The rather great contrast in scores on personal piety may indicate difference in quantity of practice of personal piety, or it may indicate tension over the appropriateness of traditional expressions of piety, or both.

Youth in tension with adults. The same polarity between structure and spontaneity shows up in dimensions 52, 44, and 69 as shown in Table 10.6. However, equally a strong theme here is the tension over Christian expression in terms of personal *agape* service (Scale 20) rather than in terms of broader social action or attempts at manipulation of the structures of society (Scales 65 and 42).

Older adult generations. Tables 10.7 and 10.8 show dimensions where oldest Lutherans tend to differ significantly from those ages 15-41 or 49. If one wants a complete picture of matters in which the oldest generation contrasts with other generations, one must also carefully reexamine Tables 10.3, 10.5, and 10.6 to see the following: proportionately more persons of ages 50-65 have a need for unchanging structures especially in family and church, a need for dogmatic stance in religious matters, a desire to keep socially distant, a tendency to exaggerate the importance of their particular church body, a need to be able to depend on church and societal organization, and very consistent habits of personal piety as well as personal evangelism.

AREAS OF NO TENSION

A Study of Generations (Table 10.1) gives dramatic evidence that in some areas there is neither tension nor chasm between youth and adults. About two-fifths of the areas under study show no significant score difference between one subgroup of youth (ages 15-29) and any one of the adult generations (ages 30-65). In addition to those places of no contrast shown in the last three tables, there are no contrasts between youth and adults in their desire for a controllable world, their belief in the divinity of Christ, their knowledge of the Bible, and their views of

Table 10.6 Average Standardized Scores by Generations Where Youth Subgenerations Contrast with Adult Generations (Heavy vertical lines separate generations in tension where average scores are significantly different at p = .0001)

Scale	Title	Scores: Ages: 15-18	19-23	24-29	30-41	42-49	50-65	Difference in Highest and Lowest Scores
			Lower			Higher		
20	Supporting Others in Crises	45.0	46.2	46.9	49.4	52.0	54.7	9.8
52	Desire for a Dependable World	45.6	45.9	46.5	49.1	51.8	55.2	9.6
44	Fundamentalism-Liberalism	47.2	45.7	48.5	50.4	51.3	52.6	7.0
69	Horatio Alger Orientation	47.2	47.0	48.1	50.1	51.3	52.6	5.6
			Higher			Lower		
65	Church Involvement in Social Issues	53.3	54.3	51.7	49.1	47.6	48.3	6.6
42	The Role of Pastors in Social Action	53.8	54.3	51.8	48.7	47.8	48.2	6.5
9	Biblical Ignorance	53.7	51.9	51.0	49.0	48.9	48.6	5.1

Table 10.7 Average Standardized Scores by Generations Where Ages 42-65 Contrast with Others

(Heavy vertical lines separate generations in tension where average scores are significantly different at p = .0001)

Scale	Title	Ages: 15-18	19-23	24-29	30-41	42-49	50-65	Difference in Highest and Lowest Scores
21	Personal Evangelism	48.9	46.9	46.9	48.8	51.0	53.8	6.9
5	Humanity of Jesus	52.3	53.0	51.6	50.4	48.2	47.7	5.3

Table 10.8 Average Standardized Scores by Generations Where Generations Across Ages 15-49 Demonstrate No Tension

(Heavy vertical lines separate generations in tension where average scores are significantly different at p = .0001)

Scale	Title	Ages: 15-18	19-23	24-29	30-41	42-49	50-65	Difference in Highest and Lowest Scores
36	Christian Utopianism	49.5	47.5	48.0	49.1	50.4	52.9	5.4
59	Social Utility of Christianity	48.5	48.6	49.8	49.5	49.9	52.0	3.5
58	Awareness of the Immanent Trinity	51.0	49.7	50.9	51.2	50.0	48.0	3.2

Lutherans as possibly different. They are similar, also, in the extent to which they see Christianity as social gospel (Scale 62), and also in the numbers willing to become personally involved in issues of church, community, and especially social justice.

Most striking of all is the lack of contrast between youth and adults in the way they identify with their parents. Essentially the same proportion of Lutherans of all generations see their parents as similar to themselves (Scale 18 in Table 10.1).

If there is a generation gap between youth and parents today, it is the same gap which older Lutherans have known. If there is a radical disjuncture between Lutherans born before World War II and those born after World War II (as claimed by Margaret Mead), there is no evidence of this break on two-fifths of the dimensions under measurement.

If one is to speak about a generation gap, one must identify the generation and the area that is involved. The extreme variation in areas of tension makes it quite evident that tension (or an open break) is pertinent only to certain dimensions. To speak about a general gap between Lutheran youth and adults as a fact of life is a myth.

Areas of Greatest Tension

No dramatic chasm exists between most youth and adults. It cannot be said that Lutheran youth are a new breed with radically different values, beliefs, and attitudes. On the contrary, our research has shown that various youth and adults view life similarly on a broad variety of the dimensions under study. Rather than speak of a generation gap, it is more accurate to speak of a tension between youth and adults—a tension which is neither static nor constant. Tension between the youth and adult generations varies from a great deal to practically none, depending on the area we study. Furthermore, this tension (when it exists) is not necessarily a negative force. Though it may erupt into conflict and open rift, it can be a stimulus to innovation and needed change.

Inasmuch as the areas of greatest *difference* between youth and adults are potentially the areas of greatest tension, we will examine them in some detail. In order of greatest intensity they include:

—distrust of adults
—priorities given to personal piety
—unwillingness to delay gratification
—feeling for people
—discrepancy between rhetoric and action
—openness to change in congregational life and ministry
—feelings of alienation

DISTRUST OF ADULTS

The area of greatest tension centers in the distrust many youth have of adults. This attitude of distrust is a serious one because youth generally see the local congregation as run by adults. We found that whenever youth's attitude is anti-adult, it is also likely to be anti-church. A dramatic illustration of this is shown when Lutherans are divided on the basis of age and attitude toward church. Figure 10.1 illustrates this. Group A is the 45% who are older youth (ages 21-28). They are less distrustful of adults than Group B, the 55% (ages 15-20) who are the most distrustful. The contrast in anti-adult feelings is greatest between Group C, the 21% who are older and least disappointed in their church, and Group F, the 19% who are younger and the most disappointed in their church. If the scores are translated into percentages, the percentage score for Group C would be 15% (little distrust) as compared with 85% (much distrust) for Group F.

How else might youth who distrust adults be characterized? Here are characteristics commonly found among youth who distrust adults: They are unhappy with their family; liberal in theology; least likely to see their congregation as a reconciling community; least able to affirm a faith; most troubled with feelings of isolation and pressure; more separated from their parents; more given to personal gratification; most convinced the church should be involved in politics; most attracted to a life of detachment; most given to an instrumental view of Christianity; most ardent advocates of social reform; least committed to faith; and least convinced of a Christian hope.

PRIORITIES GIVEN TO PERSONAL PIETY

A second source of tension between youth and adults is found in the area of the priority they give to their faith. In the summer of 1970 fewer youth than adults saw Christianity as "big" in their lives. This is seen in the fact that no more than one in five (21%) youth (ages 15-23) saw Christian beliefs as underlying his whole approach to life. This contrasts with one out of two (51%) adults (ages 50-65).

Though there were marked differences in frequency of Bible reading, the practice was hardly in vogue with either youth or adults. Thirty-two percent of the adults (ages 50-65) reported daily or weekly Bible reading, and no more than 12% of the youth (ages 15-23) reported reading the Bible this often. This contrasts with the 1950s, for instance, when approximately three times as many youth of high school age read the Bible than do now. In surveys taken in 1959 and 1962, 43% of ALC and LC-MS youth reported that "during the past six months I have read the Bible" daily, several times a week, or about once a week.

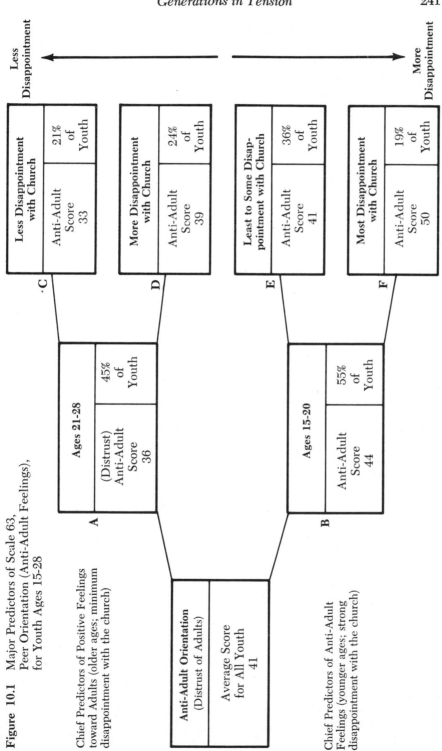

Figure 10.1 Major Predictors of Scale 63, Peer Orientation (Anti-Adult Feelings), for Youth Ages 15-28

Less Disappointment

More Disappointment

Less Disappointment with Church	
Anti-Adult Score 33	21% of Youth

C

More Disappointment with Church	
Anti-Adult Score 39	24% of Youth

D

Least to Some Disappointment with Church	
Anti-Adult Score 41	36% of Youth

E

Most Disappointment with Church	
Anti-Adult Score 50	19% of Youth

F

Ages 21-28	
(Distrust) Anti-Adult Score 36	45% of Youth

A

Ages 15-20	
Anti-Adult Score 44	55% of Youth

B

Chief Predictors of Positive Feelings toward Adults (older ages; minimum disappointment with the church)

Anti-Adult Orientation (Distrust of Adults)	
Average Score for All Youth 41	

Chief Predictors of Anti-Adult Feelings (younger ages; strong disappointment with the church)

Some other expressions of personal piety, however, show less contrast between youth and adults. Percentage differences are not as great with respect to: cooperation with the pastor, being keenly aware of the presence of God, reading literature about one's faith, and using periods of time for religious thought and meditation.

Predicting personal piety. If one were to predict the youth who are most involved in practices of personal piety, one would be accurate if he used as his indicators: high involvement in the congregation, emotional certainty of faith, and frequent Bible reading. In our analyses these three variables outranked 36 others in predictive power.

To characterize the youth least involved in religious practices, we found that the best indicators are these: doubts or does not believe in a personal, caring God; has had vague or no religious experiences; has strongly negative feelings toward his church; rejects or gives low value to transcendental presuppositions; rejects Christian dogma in favor of liberalized attitudes toward truth claims; gives little importance to the sacraments, prayer, or faith; has strong dislike for an orderly, stable world; rejects the stable church as being a positive force in society; prefers service to mankind without proclamation; has strong anti-adult feelings; has doubts or negative feelings about a faith; has little or no sense of purpose; and holds a pessimistic view of life and death.

UNWILLINGNESS TO DELAY GRATIFICATION

The traditional emphasis in the Christian community has been upon restraint and control. The faithful have been told to put off or hold down the immediate expression of many feelings, especially those of sexual desire and aggression. They are told to live in self-discipline with the confidence that the happiest life comes as a result of controlling their desires.

The unwillingness of many youth to practice restraint and control creates a third area of tension. This is shown in the percentage of youth (ages 19-22) as compared with adults (ages 50-65) who participated occasionally or frequently "during the past year" in one of the following activities:

—being drunk (58% youth versus 25% adults)
—swearing (89% versus 70%)
—having sexual intercourse outside of marriage (37% versus 18%)
—attending X-rated movies (72% versus 24%)
—reading pornographic literature (64% versus 37%)

The extent of difference between these percentages may well have been the same 50 years ago. After all, impulsiveness has always been associated with youth and greater restraint with age. Hence this area of tension can be expected.

Much has been said about a shift in time orientation, that youth today are more oriented to the present than to the future. We did find this true for more Lutheran youth than adults, but the differences between the two were not great. Some indication of the number of youth who admit to a "now" orientation is given by two items in the survey.

Thirty-five percent of all youth (ages 15-29) admit they "have no moral reason for delaying an experience that will give them pleasure" (Item 395). Fifty-five percent agree that in times like these a person ought to "enjoy what he can now and not wait" (Item 358). Though these two items are but a tenuous indication, they do give some estimate of how many Lutheran youth are not inclined to postpone gratification.

Interestingly, however, the two items quoted above show little contrast with the percentages of the oldest age group (ages 50-65). About the same percentage of older adults as of youth are conscious that a lack of resoluteness in ethical matters leads them to compromise. The problem of delaying gratification, like the mood of alienation, is apparently a pervasive cultural pressure that is felt by all ages, though more sharply by youth.

What variables best indicate the person who is unable or unwilling to delay gratification? The most powerful predictor of the 39 variables used is youth's attitude toward premarital sexual intercourse. The 48% who believe that premarital sex relations should be declared "not permissible" show the most restraint (Group A in Figure 10.2). In contrast to them are the 52% (Group B) who accept varying degrees of permissibility (e.g., those who believe sex relations are: entirely permissible; permissible if partners care for each other; or permissible if partners plan to marry eventually).

Apparently youth's view toward premarital sex is a powerful predictor of the direction a young person will take with respect to delay of gratification. Group C is the 41% of Lutheran youth who reject both premarital sex and an orientation toward drug use. Their restraint is reflected also in lesser participation in questionable activities (see Chapter Note 4). Underlying this evidence of restraint is an apparent willingness and ability to delay gratification.

However, youth who say "no" to premarital sex but "yes" to the life style of a drug culture (Group D), are much more involved in questionable personal activities. (Their score on this scale jumps from 41 to 50, an increase of nine points.) Such an increase shows how strongly the acceptance of a drug culture style of life is associated with less restraint.

The seriousness of this area of tension focuses on Group F, the 18% of Lutheran youth who would permit premarital sex and would become involved with the life style of the drug culture. Their high involvement in questionable personal activities shows an unwillingness or inability to delay gratification.

Figure 10.2   Two Predictors of Restraint in Personal Gratification (attitude on premarital sex, and noninvolvement in drug culture)

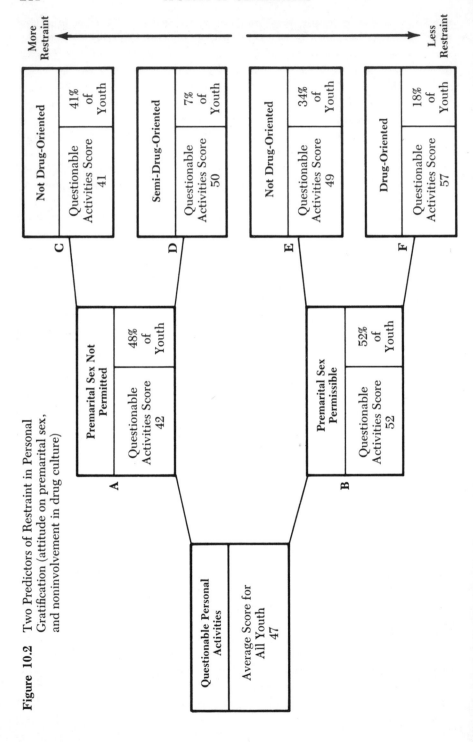

Drug culture orientation. Related to "gratification now" and "anti-adult" feelings is a way of life popularly known as the counter culture. This culture, which gained national prominence in the late 1960s embodies a set of values, beliefs, and practices that oppose those of adult society. A sampling of this way of life is found in a group of items that identify Lutherans who are oriented toward drugs and hold attitudes of rebellion toward commonly accepted norms.

The two strong indicators of youth who identify with the drug culture are lack of restraint in matters of personal gratification and a strong orientation to one's own age group (a dimension that also reflects a distrust of adults). By virtue of their peer orientation, these youth are more subject to the social pressures of their age group. If drugs are pushed, they are the more likely to succumb.

Which youth will most likely resist social pressures to use drugs? Our analyses show that these youth will likely display the following characteristics: intent to delay gratification, openness to adult influence, residence in a small-sized community, a conviction of Christ's divinity, and having a mother whose religiousness is attractive.

FEELING FOR PEOPLE

Youth's sensitivity to the needs of people is a recurring motif in the rise of student groups that has occurred everywhere and at various times in history. Students have served as a conscience of society when in protest they have risen to declare that adults, too occupied with maintaining their institutions, have failed to meet human needs. Their protests usually have been followed by service activities among the poor and the oppressed. The history of these well-meaning efforts is that they usually have been short-lived.

In *A Study of Generations* data, strong feeling for a maligned people emerges in items specific to people commonly condemned, shunned, or oppressed. An illustration appears in youth's response to five items dealing with blacks (Table 10.9). Youth (ages 15-18 and 19-23) feel strongly against excluding blacks or any other racial group from church activities (46% and 48% respectively). Of these age groups, 55% strongly disagree with the statement that black people are by nature inferior to whites. A similar bristling reaction (55%) is given to the statement which blames the social problems of blacks on bad character without reference to environmental factors. Fewer (34% and 26%) use the "strongly disagree" response to the idea that whites or blacks have the right to keep others out of their neighborhoods. When the "disagree" responses are added to the "strongly disagree" ones, the result is a strong contingent of youth (percentages are in the 60s) who are impatient with the racial prejudice of adults. Table 10.9 shows how responses of "strongly disagree" taper

Table 10.9   Feelings for Black People

Study of Generations	Age Groupings					
Items	15-18	19-23	24-29	30-41	42-49	50-65
	Percent Who "*Strongly* Disagree"					
291. Excluding blacks (or other racial groups) from church activities would be justified in some communities.	46%	48%	43%	30%	23%	16%
295. Although there is no essential difference between blacks and whites, it is preferable for them not to mingle socially.	41	38	23	15	10	7
300. Colored people are by nature inferior to white people.	55	55	44	36	28	21
347. People (white or black) have a right to keep others out of their neighborhood if they want to, and this right should be respected.	34	26	15	13	10	8
	Percent Who "Disagree"					
342. Negroes could solve many of their own problems if they would not be so irresponsible and carefree about life.	55	54	44	37	28	19

off as people advance in years. The percentages for the oldest Lutherans (ages 50-65) are only a fraction of the percentages for youth.

Youth's strong feeling for oppressed people is manifest also in the way youth answered the social distance items. When asked whom they would accept as close friends or next-door neighbors, they declared an openness and acceptance that stands in sharp contrast with adults. Over half (55%) of the youth ages 15-23 would be willing to have welfare mothers (with illegitimate children) as friends or close neighbors. This contrasts with 33% of the adults. An even larger percentage of youth (62%) declare the same openness toward Negroes, as compared with 47% of the adults. Most reluctant to welcome controversial persons are Lutherans of ages 50-65. Interestingly, they are the ones who presumably have heard the most sermons.

The open-arms attitude of youth drops off sharply, however, toward people who embody a threatening ideology. No more than one in three (33%) youth (ages 15-23) would offer friendship or neighborliness to hippies or members of the S.D.S. (Students for a Democratic Society). A few more would take their chances with an atheist (42%) or with a John Bircher (48%). The averages for adults are: hippies (14%), S.D.S.

members (20%), atheists (32%), and John Birchers (54%). Note that John Birchers are less of a threat to adult Lutherans than they are to youth.

Another indication of youth's feeling for people comes in their response to anti-Semitic items. Though the majority of all Lutherans disagree with these prejudiced statements, a solid front of opposition comes from four out of five (80%) youth (ages 15-29); they clearly answer as a generation. Actually, the break in percentages is not between youth and adults but between Lutherans ages 15-41 and 42-65. It is among adults age 42 and older that we are most likely to find Lutherans who will agree to anti-Semitic statements.

DISCREPANCY BETWEEN RHETORIC AND ACTION

It is not surprising that adults do more than young people to help people during times of personal crises. Matters such as death, serious illness, and severe financial hardship relate more to the adult years and to the adult world; hence, one can expect more activity in this area from adults. This explanation, however, does not sufficiently explain the sensitivity between generations on matters of helping others.

It appears that for all of youth's rhetoric about their feelings for people, they do less than adults in actually performing specific acts of kindness. It seems that they cannot be depended upon to follow through on projects that involve helping others.

Evidence of the noninvolvement of many youth is given by seven interconnecting items that form a Neighborliness dimension. The items include these possibilities: cared for a friend's children while the parents were sick; contributed to a special fund for a person for whom a tragic event occurred; helped a friend meet normal responsibilities at a time he could not; gave help to a total stranger who was in trouble. A count made of the age groupings which drew the highest percentage of "never" for each act of kindness gives this result. All but one of the seven items drew its highest percentage of "never" from one of the youth age groupings: three for the 15-19 year-olds; four for the 20-23 year-olds; and one for the 24-29 year-olds. Apparently many of the youth have not learned, as yet, to extend their concern to others in expressions of service.

A somewhat different story appears when the percentages are examined for those who "frequently" help others in the ways defined by the items. In general, the differences are quite minimal. One cannot say that any one age group frequently extends itself more than another.

From what has been said about youth's identification with the needs of people, one would have expected that more youth than adults would be involved in acts of kindness. Even more surprising is the fact that fewer youth than adults aspire to a life of being used to help others grow. This is seen in the percentages of Lutherans who aspire to a life of "being used by others." Following is one item from a list of "Ways of Life" items used in the study. Respondents were asked to indicate how much they liked or disliked this "way":

> *Way 13.* A person should let himself be used. Used by other persons in their growth, used by the great objective purposes in the universe which silently and irresistibly achieve their goal. For persons and the world's purposes are dependable at heart, and can be trusted. One should be humble, constant, faithful, uninsistent. Grateful for the affection and protection which one needs, but undemanding. Close to persons and to nature, and secure because close. Nourishing the good by devotion and sustained by the good because of devotion. One should be a serene, confident, quiet vessel and instrument of the great dependable powers which move to their fulfillment.

Percentages by age groups of those who responded affirmatively toward this way of life are as follows:

Age Groups	Percent Choosing This Way of Life
15-18	14%
19-23	15
24-29	15
30-41	19
42-49	29
50-65	32

A similar range of percentages results from an item that is one of a list of desired qualities within a person's life. Each respondent was asked to rank the qualities in terms of their importance to him. The percentage who said that "service (devotion to the interests of others)" was "extremely important" to them is as follows:

Age Groups	Percent Choosing The Quality of Service
15-18	15%
19-23	15
24-29	10
30-41	15
42-49	23
50-65	24

An interpretation of such information seems necessary inasmuch as the data stand in contradiction to the thesis that a new concern for people is becoming evident among today's youth.

Three observations can be made. First, the data given here are not peculiar to Lutheran youth; rather they document what has been widely noted among student populations. Thousands will assemble for a mass protest, but only a few will give themselves to long-range tasks that are designed to meet social needs. There is more rhetoric than action, and this is an undeniable source of tension between youth and adults.

Second, people such as Reich *(The Greening of America)* overgeneralize about all youth on the basis of the idealism of a few. The undeniable willingness of some to devote their lives to meeting human needs is matched by others who couldn't care less. When total percentages are compared with adult percentages only, the expected idealism of youth fails to become evident.

Third, many adults have been unrealistic in expecting youth to match talk with action. As noted earlier, self-development values are an important part of a maturing period during which youth learn to look beyond themselves to put their concerns into the action of life. What they need to learn is the sense of responsibility that counterbalances their desire to seek absolute ends for themselves only.

OPENNESS TO CHANGE IN CONGREGATIONAL LIFE AND MINISTRY

Inasmuch as this study relates uniquely to the parish ministry, it is important that we speak about the areas of tension between generations over a congregation's life and ministry. We still see how these areas of tension affect one's views of mission, clergy, and worship.

Significantly, disappointment with the church does not emerge as an area of sharp contrast between generations. In fact, the evaluations of adults (ages 30-65) resemble the evaluations of older youth (ages 24-28). Evidently, critical feelings toward the church, though strongest for youth (ages 15-23) are not peculiar to the youthful years.

Mission of the church. There are conflicting opinions on the mission of the church. Some favor an exclusive preoccupation with preaching the gospel and others insist that social reform must come first (Item 256). The preaching accent finds its greater adherents among older Lutherans, and the social action emphasis draws its highest percentages from the youngest (those most recently confirmed!). They seem divided evenly: about half the youth would emphasize social issues and about half the adults would have the gospel preached exclusively.

We can note the impatience of youth and their strong feelings regarding the present involvement of their church in social issues (Item 257). It is their conviction that far too little has been done in this area. This opinion is held by the majority (57%) of youth ages 15-23. A smaller group of youth and adults think that "too much" has been done in the area of social concerns. Their proportions range from one in five youth

(20%) to a few more than one in three adults (36%). What do other types of items tell us about their opinions on mission?

About 89% of the adults affirm that the primary task of the church is to preach the gospel, and 81% of the youth are in agreement with this essential purpose (Item 525). In contrast, about one in four of all youth (28%) says he prefers that the primary accent be the elimination of suffering or working for some kind of social reform (Item 534).

A majority of youth (63%) are convinced that the church is an antidote for the malady of selfishness and that it is absolutely needed in today's world (Item 541). More of the adults ages 30-65 (74%) view the church in this hopeful way. Both groups, however, show general agreement (70%) that it is equally important to preach the gospel and to work toward improving the material well-being of people (Item 542). The problem for more of the youth is that they simply feel these two emphases are out of balance. They, more than the older generations, reflect a greater sensitivity to the welfare of people, a concern for social change, and a conviction that structures must not stand in the way of responding to human need.

Role of today's clergy. Sharper contrasts become apparent when the role of the clergy is defined. The youth of today (ages 15-23) are far more in favor of restyling the traditional expectation of the clergyman than are older Lutherans, as seen in Table 10.10. In their opinion (61%), controversial topics should be treated openly in the Sunday morning sermon. This approach is preferred by twice as many youth as adults ages 50-65. The great majority of youth (79%) approve an active role for the pastor in organizing study groups to discuss public issues.

Youth's approval for an activist role, however, diminishes for those activities where the pastor's involvement shifts from marching in civil rights demonstrations to that of risking arrest. Though four in five would applaud their pastor's leadership in organizing study groups, less than one in five (19%) would approve his risking arrest in a demonstration that involves civil disobedience.

These two issues—the role of today's clergy and the mission of the church—create tension between the youth and the older adults. They can be the cause of a schism within a congregation's life. But since the older adults tend to control congregational decisions, many youth, disappointed over what is not done, may choose rather not to be involved.

Worship practices. The church also assembles as a worshiping community to sustain faith. However, the attitudes of members toward the worship service and liturgy are another source of tension. Most youth react negatively to the controlled, formal, and unchanging liturgical service. Most youth want free and spontaneous prayers in the service and

Table 10.10 Role of Today's Clergy

Study of Generations Items	Age Groupings					
	15-18	19-23	24-29	30-41	42-49	50-65
Please indicate for each of the following how much you approve or disapprove of clergymen who take that action.						
			Percent Who "Approve" and "Strongly Approve"			
515. Deliver a sermon on a controversial political or social topic.	60%	62%	61%	46%	35%	30%
517. Organize study groups within their congregations to discuss public affairs.	79	80	75	64	58	51
518. Organize social action groups within their congregations to accomplish directly some political or social goal.	53	58	47	32	27	26
519. Participate in civil rights protest marches.	37	40	26	14	12	8
520. Participate in anti-war protest marches.	33	37	23	10	9	6
521. Participate in civil rights civil disobedience (risk arrest).	21	18	11	6	6	3

greater opportunity for a variety of experiences. Some indication of this is seen in the first two items of Table 10.11. Three in four (74%) of youth ages 15-23 feel that free and spontaneous prayers are more conducive to worship than those which are written and read. The same high percentage (74%) prefer variety in the morning service as against having the same liturgical service Sunday after Sunday. Interestingly, about one out of two adults agrees with the youth on both points.

The more formal aspects of a worship service are not important for most Lutherans. Less than a fourth (22%) of either the youngest or the oldest require beauty for a service to be meaningful. Interestingly, the percentage drops to 14% for people between ages 19 and 49. Also, no more than one in three older adults (33%) feels that a more formal and liturgical service is better. For youth ages 15-23 the average is 20%.

In spite of youth's negative attitude toward a formal liturgical service, well over half (56%) like to think that a similar liturgy is employed by Lutheran churches throughout the world. The other half, of course, disagree. Though a sense of world-wide community is attractive, what is most important about a worship service is variety, spontaneity, and personal involvement. When these elements are lacking, the youth express their displeasure over what many adults accept with reluctance.

Table 10.11 Worship Practices

Study of Generations Items	Age Groupings					
	15-18	19-23	24-29	30-41	42-49	50-65
	Percent Who "Agree" and "Strongly Agree"					
545. Prayers in church services are better if they are free and spontaneous rather than read from a service or prayer book.	76%	72%	66%	56%	52%	51%
547. I like variety in the order of service rather than the same order every week.	75	72	62	52	48	45
539. A worship service must be beautiful to be readily meaningful to me.	22	14	12	14	16	22
543. The more a worship service is formal and liturgical, the more it has meaning for me.	21	19	24	28	29	36
533. I like to think that Christians all over the world are going through nearly the same liturgical service in their public worship.	59	53	58	58	62	67

What has been said, however, fails to explain why tension is so easily awakened by attempts to alter the liturgy. Some members of a congregation are incensed when changes are made in the order of service. They want the order of service to remain as it is, and they say so with strong feeling. Obviously something deeper is involved.

Two additional dimensions are involved whenever youth press for change in their worship service. One is the need for religious absolutism (discussed in Chapter 5), a need which generally increases with age. It causes older members to become rigid about liturgy and anxious that every detail be executed well and remain unchanged. When alterations are introduced in the service, people with a strong need for religious absolutism become highly uncomfortable.

A second and related dimension is openness to change (discussed in Chapter 7). Those least receptive to change within a congregation are adults between the ages of 30 and 65. They can be expected to resist most vehemently the proposals of members most open to change, namely youth between the ages of 19 and 23. This issue of change/no change is a serious one because it involves changing (or leaving unchanged) something that is closely linked to what each individual believes.

Lest the general emphasis on feeling for people and wanting changes in the church be associated only with youth, it is well to point out that a substantial minority of Lutheran adults respond in the same way the youth do.

FEELINGS OF ALIENATION

The term "alienation" is one which is being used increasingly with reference to youth and students, though it is not a twentieth-century phenomenon. On the contrary it is the theme of history, beginning with the estrangement of Adam and Eve from God. From that time and on, in all centuries, this theme has appeared in myth, history, literature, and life. It has been seen as a quality of life that touches every man. Religions speak of man's alienation from a divine order and consider it their central function to heal this estrangement.

The preceding chapters have already noted how the youthful generations of Lutherans are more troubled with feelings of alienation. They, more than the older generations, are anxious about their faith, alienated from their church, and separated from the festival of life. An estimate follows of the extent to which these feelings of alienation trouble Lutheran youth.

Alienation from God. A pastor's hope for his youth is that they might know a relationship with God that is free of uncertainty and fear. The hope is for a certainty or sense of identity about one's place in the family of God that can be held in the midst of uncertainty. What we learn from the study is that a troubled awareness of one's distance from God is linked with a feeling of distance from people. Of 39 predictors used, the most powerful predictor of an uncertain relationship with God is a feeling of isolation. In other words, a sense of distance from God often includes a sense of distance from man. What is especially pertinent to a parish pastor is the fact that nearly two in three (63%) Lutheran youth are conscious of a sense of aloneness—of being separated from both God and man (Group B in Figure 10.3).

There are, however, counterbalancing elements within Lutheran youth. One major element that offsets feelings of isolation is knowing a sense of purpose. Youth who are conscious of a life purpose (Group E) are less anxious about their faith even though they are conscious of feeling isolated and under pressure. Their life purpose apparently lessens the effect of feeling alienated from others. This effect applies to one in three Lutheran youth.

It is the remaining 30% (Group F) who are most troubled over their faith. Gripped with a feeling of purposelessness and lacking a personal faith, they are conscious, like the prodigal son, of being a long way off from the "waiting father." They are anxious over their lack of a confident relationship with God.

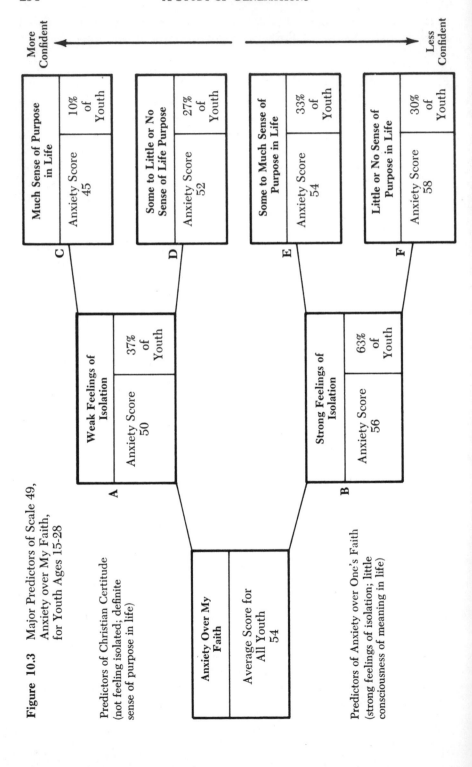

Figure 10.3 Major Predictors of Scale 49, Anxiety over My Faith, for Youth Ages 15-28

Aside from the two predictors mentioned here (Feelings of Isolation and Life Purpose or Meaning) no other variables used in this study are strongly related to a sense of being alienated from God (see Chapter Note 5). One should not overemphasize their importance, however, because they account only for a small part of the feelings of anxiety. But one can use them as clues in determining directions. A close family and congregational fellowship, and a responsive awareness among members to the needs of others, could lower anxiety. These two qualities of life (an experience of mutuality and a sense of mission) relate directly to certainty of one's Christian faith (Scale 66).

Alienation from the church. Two questions frequently asked are these: Will youth in the future support the church? and, Do Lutheran youth have negative feelings toward their church?

For most youth there is a sense of being on the outside of their congregation's interest and life. Over half the youth (ages 15-23) feel that older people in the congregation are suspicious of them. They also feel that they have no influence on the decisions being made by the congregation. In other words, the institutional life of the congregation has evolved in such a way that leadership and influence is in the hands of people over 30. Up to one-half of the youth agree that "hardly anyone in the congregation would miss me if I stopped going."

Apparently the normal pattern of congregational life tends to isolate youth from the center of concern and decision-making. About half of the youth do not feel involved or a part of the life of their congregation. But the other half agree that "the church is doing a pretty good job of involving youth and teaching them about the Christian life."

A related reason for disengagement from the life of the church may be both a cause and a reason for being on the outside of their congregation's life. It relates to how many of youth's close friends are members of their congregation. To the survey item which asks how many of their five closest friends are members of the congregation they attend, 51% of the 20-29-year-old youth say, "None." This means that the social glue of normal friendships does not draw these youth into their congregation's activity. This is an important loss. In an earlier study of Lutheran youth, the one major contribution that could be credited to the youth organizations was that they provided the occasion for informal friendship groups to be formed within the congregational fellowship. This helped maintain the fellowship of the congregation during the week and provided support in the sharing of common beliefs and values. Though no doubt this kind of supportive fellowship still continues to occur for many Lutheran youth, it is quite lacking for half of our youth.

What are the chief sources of youth's disappointment in the church? Thirty-nine variables were used to locate the best predictors of disappointment with the church. The outcomes underscore the importance of being made to feel welcome and a part of a congregation. We found that the strongest predictor of youth's attitude toward his church is how well he fits in with groups in his congregation. The acceptance that he feels is the best indicator of how he will evaluate his congregation. If he feels that he fits in poorly and if he also is uninspired by the Sunday morning service, the probability is strong that he will have a critical attitude toward his church. On the contrary, if he feels that he fits in well and is relatively free of general pessimism, he will take a positive view. That, in brief, is the story of Figure 10.4.

We see that 57% of the youth (Group A) feel that they fit well into some group in their congregation and 43% (Group B) do not. This is sobering because most of the youth were raised and confirmed in their congregations. Yet close to half do not feel a part of their church family. Some of these, however, do feel positive about their Sunday morning services.

A healthy proportion (43%) hold positive feelings toward their church (Group C). Their low score (21) on Disappointment with the Church classifies them among the positive evaluators. Note, however, that the most important variable on how one feels about his congregation is the awareness of how well he fits into his congregation.

Critical attitudes mount for the 14% (Group D) who, though very much a part of their congregation, are plagued with strong feelings of pessimism. Their score on Disappointment with the Church advances from 21 to 26, a sharp increase in critical feelings.

Of the ones who feel they fit poorly with groups in their congregation, close to three in ten (29%) are at times inspired by the Sunday morning service (Group E). Their evaluation of their church is no more critical than the pessimistic-type youth who are part of the "in group" at church. The two groups (D and E) score alike and include 43% of the sample.

Serious anti-church feelings are expressed by the 14% who neither fit in with nor are ever inspired by the worship service (Group F). Their average score of 32 is a sharp increase. The strongly negative feelings of this group dramatizes the importance of two elements in the life of a congregation: relationships and inspiration.

Alienation from life. There are three dimensions of alienation—pessimism, isolation, purposelessness—that affect Lutheran youth between the ages of 15 and 28. Each of these chilling winds makes a different impact, and the presence of each is predicted by quite different variables. Following is a brief summary of what we found.

Feelings of pessimism are tied in strongly with youth's belief and value orientations. When values center in the person (and not in others and in God), and when beliefs about Christianity are self-serving, the

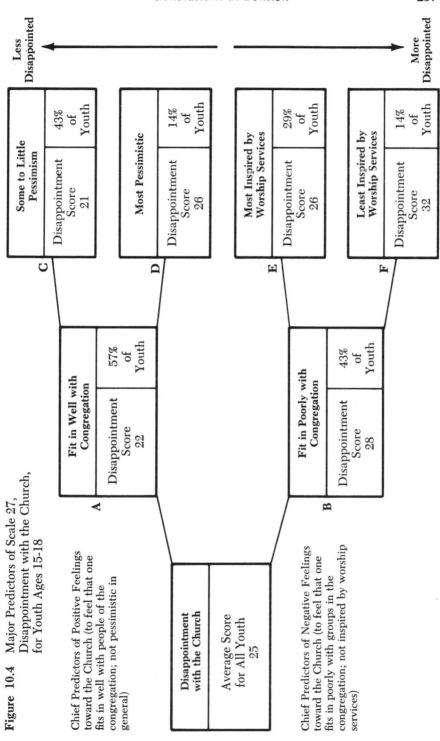

Figure 10.4 Major Predictors of Scale 27, Disappointment with the Church, for Youth Ages 15-18

Chief Predictors of Positive Feelings toward the Church (to feel that one fits in well with people of the congregation; not pessimistic in general)

Chief Predictors of Negative Feelings toward the Church (to feel that one fits in poorly with groups in the congregation; not inspired by worship services)

Less Disappointed

More Disappointed

Disappointment with the Church

Average Score for All Youth 25

A Fit in Well with Congregation

Disappointment Score 22 | 57% of Youth

B Fit in Poorly with Congregation

Disappointment Score 28 | 43% of Youth

C Some to Little Pessimism

Disappointment Score 21 | 43% of Youth

D Most Pessimistic

Disappointment Score 26 | 14% of Youth

E Most Inspired by Worship Services

Disappointment Score 26 | 29% of Youth

F Least Inspired by Worship Services

Disappointment Score 32 | 14% of Youth

likelihood is a pessimistic view of life. Such youth are distrustful of adults, critical of their church, resistant to change, and convinced that salvation is something one earns. The pessimistic Lutheran is, in effect, alienated from Christian hope and the truth of the Christian gospel. To be turned about and become optimistic would be like a conversion. Of Lutheran youth, 17% classify as optimistic and 18% as pessimistic. The bulk of younger Lutherans are in between.

Feelings of pressure and isolation come about in quite different ways. Such feelings are strongly associated with an unhappy family, with younger ages (15-20), and with a concern over one's relationship to God. A young person who feels pressured often feels as though he were outside the family of God and outside a family that really cares about him. His feelings of aloneness relate to a distance from people and from God.

Purposelessness, the third dimension of alienation, is seemingly a culmination of the two feelings that are described above. The Lutheran youth who combine strong feelings of isolation and strong feelings of pessimism are the ones most likely to lack a sense of mission or purpose. About 28% of Lutheran youth are found in this group.

What about youth who are caught in a sense of life purpose? Theirs is generally the good fortune of not feeling isolated, of being certain of their faith, and of having many friends.

Summary

When all data are examined simultaneously, four generations of Lutherans emerge: ages 15-29, 30-39, 40-49, and 50-65—give or take one or two years at each of the boundaries. The youngest generation also forms empirically into three subgenerations: ages 15-18, 19-23, and 24-29.

The claim of a pervasive generation gap among Lutherans, in the sense of a chasm or radical and consistent break, is a myth. Nevertheless, there are distinct tensions across the generations that center primarily in differences of belief and value. The tension focuses on two emphases or polarities about which youth and adults respectively tend to gather: newness, creativity, spontaneity, change, variety, and even revolution—versus structure, tradition, regimentation, standards, organization, and conformity. This polarity includes beliefs, values, attitudes, opinions, and styles of life.

Though much of the tension is between the youngest (especially ages 15-23) and the oldest (ages 50-65), a tension which often increases with difference in age, there are nevertheless exceptions where young and old agree. Other than the two emphases mentioned above, there is no uniform pattern of generational tension. Which generations are greatest in tension and which are in agreement varies from issue to issue such that there are seven clearly discernible patterns of tension, each with its different set of issues.

On 40% of the 52 dimensions studied there were no differences between one of the youth and one of the adult age groups. Still, significantly more youth were found to have feelings of alienation, to be disappointed with the church, and to be unwilling or unable to delay gratification.

About 20% of youth ages 15-28 are peer-oriented. Rather than take their signals from people of all ages, like the rest of Lutheran youth, they relate almost entirely to their own age group, are even more alienated, critical of their church, and less able to delay gratification.

High school youth differ significantly from all other generations by being more peer-oriented, participating more in questionable personal activities than any except college age youth, expressing more feelings of isolation and pressure, placing more priority on self-development values, and seeing less purpose in life.

College age youth show just six distinguishing characteristics, and they are *lowest* scoring in five of them: congregational activity, need for unchanging structures, need for religious absolutism, desire to keep socially distant from persons of different race and religion, and tendency to exaggerate the truth claim of the church by identifying the truth with only their denomination. They report the highest incidence of participation in questionable activities.

Youngest and oldest (ages 15-23 and 50-65) are significantly different from other generations in desire for detachment, inclination to be pessimistic, belief in salvation by works, and tendency to use religion for their own purposes.

High school and college age youth together on the average contrast with all other ages who are similar in a series of emphases:

Emphases of Ages 15-23	*Emphases of Ages 24-65*
more change	less change
variety	norms
acceptance of diversity	exclusiveness
anxiety and questioning	certainty of belief
little affect on decision making	power
corporate responsibility	individual responsibility

Youth (ages 15-29) also differ with adults (ages 30-65) in that there are less youth helping others in times of crises, desirous of a dependable world, fundamentalist, and convinced that hard work will always pay off; while more youth are biblically misinformed, favor the church's involvement in social issues, and encourage pastors toward more extreme participation in social action.

Fewer Lutherans ages 50-65 are aware of the close presence of the triune God in their lives, while more proportionately who are 50-65 years old need unchanging structures in family and church, are inclined toward religious absolutism, desire to keep socially distant, tend to exaggerate the importance of their church body, need to be able to depend on church and societal organization, and practice consistent traditional forms of personal piety and personal evangelism.

All in all, the areas of greatest difference between youth and adults include: priorities given to different expressions of piety; trust of adults; willingness or ability to delay gratification, including drug culture orientation; feeling for people; discrepancy between rhetoric and action; openness to change in congregational life and ministry with emphasis on understanding of mission, the role of clergy, and appropriateness of worship practices; and finally, alienation from God, church, and life in terms of pessimism, feelings of isolation and pressure, and purposelessness.

Tension is not necessarily a negative force. It may explode into apparently irreconcilable conflict; it can be a stimulus to helpful innovation and needed change.

Notes

1. There are several additional factors which need to be controlled when showing generational differences. They are: socio-economic level, parental church activity, parents' education, and financial pressures.

   Possibly the most important factor to be controlled relates to *how* (instead of *what*) one believes. An assessment on this continuum of religious response will divide the population into committed and consensual religionists.

   It is assumed that when the sample of Lutherans (L) is divided by this assessment, (committed, consensual) differences will appear in at least three of the major areas (irrespective of generation):

Values:	L Committed ⪌	L Consensual
Mission:	L Committed ⪌	L Consensual
Self and Others:	L Committed ⪌	L Consensual

   It is expected that the most committed youth and the most consensually oriented adults will show especially marked generational differences in these areas:

Mission:	A Committed ⪌	BC Consensual
Values:	A Committed ⪌	BC Consensual
Self and Others:	A Committed ⪌	BC Consensual

2. *Consciousness I:* Reich describes Consciousness I as the world view that characterized the American farmer, the small businessman, or the worker of pre–World War I days. His goal was success in the competition of life where hard work, self-denial, character, and morality were the winning ingredients. In this world view, competition is seen as the law of man and of nature; life is basically the harsh pursuit of self-interest; production, invention, and achievement are the symbols of progress.

   Reich believes that this point of view evolved out of the period of history when communities were regulated by customs or religion, when government was administered by local people, and when the principal activity and form of self-expression was work.

   Underlying Consciousness I is a conviction that any social problems can be traceable to bad character. For instance, urban crime is attributed to moral breakdown. A lower crime rate, therefore, can be brought about by more stringent law enforcement, rather than better attention to environmental factors.

A Consciousness I man contends that the least government is the best government; he favors lower taxes and insists that welfare recipients be required to work. In general, his way of curtailing subversive activity is to employ stern measures and to work for a moral reawakening. For the most part, this world view holds that an organization should not dominate the individual, but that the individual should be free to pursue his road to happiness and material success. The assumption of this pursuit is that business gain and self-interest automatically benefit all people.

Consciousness II: It is Reich's thesis that because the world view of Consciousness I was unable to cope with the power of industrial giants, it became necessary for the government to intervene. During the 1930s and 1940s, under the initial leadership of Franklin Delano Roosevelt, a public state was created. The basic thesis was that man—an aggressive, competitive, and power-seeking being—can be contained only by law. Hence, the focus needs to be upon domination by government where reasonableness is the theme in contrast to the unreasonableness of the early buccaneers. The central motif, then, is control and the rejection of unfettered diversity and unresolved conflict. The assumption, too, is that society is best if it is planned, organized, rationalized, and administered.

As described by Reich, Consciousness II differs from Consciousness I only in the means and the terms involved in the competitive struggle for success. Just as the accent in Consciousness I is on sacrifice for an individual's good, the focus here is on sacrifice for the common good. It is assumed that economic progress and quantitative advance can be nothing but good. What is needed is a rational hierarchy of authority and responsibility, and a system of education which equips workers for goals which are beyond themselves.

In this characterization the heavy focus is upon scheduling and organizing people. As a result of the strong emphasis on standards, there emerges a meritocracy of ability and accomplishment. The heavy accent on excellence resulted in people being rated in terms of ability or status.

According to Consciousness II, life goals should center in the power, success, status, acceptance, popularity, achievement, rewards, and excellence that are achieved by being part of an organization. One should shun mystery, failure, helplessness, and faith because these are not logical and rational.

Consciousness III: Consciousness II lost sight of the individual; Consciousness III seeks his recovery. According to Reich, this latter world view began as the result of a betrayal. Those who felt they had been betrayed—namely, the alienated youth of the counter culture—are credited with originating Consciousness III. These are youth who have seen the emptiness of their parents' lives and the contrasts between realities and their parents' ideals. In looking at their government, youth of the counter culture are convinced that this is not the land of the free.

In its idealized form, Consciousness III seeks freedom from the automatic acceptance of what society imposes, freedom to build one's own life style. It rejects the concept of excellence and merit. For the people of Consciousness III, the highest value in life is a genuine relationship with others. Hence, a deep personal commitment to the welfare of your fellow citizens means that you must respond with yourself. This encourages an openness to all people and an ideal of a community where everyone feels a togetherness without destroying the uniqueness of each individual.

The people who share in this world view do not like the authority and status distinction that have become associated with work. Neither do they wish to participate in work that does not help liberate the person or contribute something worthwhile to mankind.

In reacting against what is rational, planned, linear, disciplined, and controlled, youth of Consciousness III (and adults who join them) place a high value on what is spontaneous, disconnected, and non-linear. They welcome experiences that might help to restore a dulled spirit. Many have placed a strong emphasis on finding this lift to one's spirits in the world of nature.

Entry into Consciousness III is seen as tantamount to a conversion experience because it involves changing one's life goals and putting oneself outside the existing system. The key factor in effecting this conversion is to pattern oneself after people who have already made this break from what they call the machine-like system of Consciousness II.

It is assumed that once there is freedom from imposed standards, rules, and regulations, one can draw new energies from life; the ideal is liberation from all restraints that thwart and inhibit expression.

Consciousness III adherents feel that their primary task is to help others to a recovery of self.

3. A one-way analysis of variance by six generational age groups was followed by use of Scheffé's method of making post hoc comparisons for all mean contrasts ($a = .0001$) where the overall F test showed significance ($a = .0001$). See Winer (1962) pp. 88 ff. or Hays (1963) pp. 483-87.

4. A more exact probing of the issue of personal restraint is possible through items that ask respondents to report whether they have been involved (occasionally or frequently) in one or more of 13 questionable activities (e.g., lying, premarital or extramarital sexual intercourse, swearing, being drunk, etc.). High scores indicate little restraint, whereas low scores reflect either restraint or nonexposure.

5. The predictor variables used were: educational level, religiousness of parents, region, age, socio-economic class, size of community and congregation, happiness of family, evaluation of one's church, use of Bible, family devotions, number of friends, theology, church body, beliefs (Scales 15, 16, and 19), attitudes toward congregation (Scales 13 and 27), service to others (Scales 20, 21, and 22), involvement in questionable activities (Scales 23, 24, and 25), values (Scales 29, 30, and 31), attitudes toward others (Scales 32, 33, and 34), distance from parents, religious experience, and feelings of pessimism. As other studies over the past ten years have shown, this dimension is a submerged concern that is quite unrelated to other variables.

Our political life is conducted on the basis of liberty, and in our day-to-day relations with one another, we are not suspicious of the behavior of our neighbor, nor are we angry with him if he lives in a way which suits himself, nor do we show toward him the kind of annoyance which, while it does no actual harm, is unpleasant for the man who observes it.

—Thucydides

11. Slices of Diversity

This should be a most welcome chapter. It summarizes an enormous number of statistical data to give some long-awaited answers to the questions: How extensive are the differences associated with region, sex, church body, education, size of congregation, age, and clergy–lay status? How do these differences compare in size?

The chapter gives clear evidence that differences related to size of congregation, region, sex, church body, and even education are not very important! Too much is made of variation among Lutherans on the basis of these variables.

What emerges as highly significant are differences associated with age and clergy–lay status. Contrasts between youth and older adults on all dimensions are paralleled by similar contrasts in response between youngest and oldest clergy. Even more marked are the differences in outlook between clergy and the laity they serve.

Though this chapter deals with slices of diversity based on these variables, it should be underscored that the greatest differences among Lutherans are related to what they believe and value.

Diversity is one of God's gifts to the church. It is a diversity of gifts of the Spirit, ability, expressions of faith and life, of persons and personalities, not of truth. One of the strongest impressions coming out of the months of working with *A Study of Generations* data for all members of the research team is the richness of God's gift of diversity to the Lutheran church. In two sentences Will Rogers both honored and illuminated the creative diversity present in the Democratic party of the 1930s, often brawling, struggling, and intense, but alive, vibrant, and active: "I am not a member of any organized political party. I am a Democrat." A Lutheran in the 1970s can say, "I am not a member of any staid, dull, encrusted religious body. I am a Lutheran."

Tolerance and acceptance of diversity is an old problem for men. Thucydides saw acceptance of diversity as the principal difference between Athens and the other Greek city-states. Immediately after drawing the distinction between believer and unbeliever, Paul affirms diversity:

> There are varieties of gifts, but the same Spirit. There are varieties
> of service, but the same Lord. There are many forms of work, but all
> of them, in all men, are the work of the same God. In each of us the
> Spirit is manifested in one particular way, for some useful purpose.
> (1 Cor. 12:4-7, NEB)

Paul is saying that being a believer, knowing the gospel, encourages acceptance of diversity. The law is the enemy of diversity. It tries to solidify and imprison God's rich alphabet stew of gifts into a single letter, forgetting that unity comes from the single pot, not from the letters in the pot.

In society and church, from Thucydides and Paul to the present day, the balancing of unity and diversity has been a difficult juggling act for men. Most of the time we seem to be dropping the balls rather consistently. We expect everybody else to be like us. We are puzzled, hurt, or angry when we find out that other people are not carbon copies of us, that they feel, think, and do things differently than we do. It may be that a clearer understanding of the diversity God gives will permit both more ready acceptance and more accurate perception as to when diversity becomes disunity.

In this chapter we shall examine some of the ways we can slice into the diversity of God's people. There are many ways to cut into the diversity God has given to Lutherans. We have selected the characteristics of sex, education, size of congregation, region of country, clergy–lay distinction, and church body membership, not because they are necessarily the best ways of understanding the diversity in the church, but because rather lively debates have formed around some of these characteristics. (Because of the high level of interest, most diversity connected with age is handled in a separate chapter.)

Are pastors and people so different, so far from each other that there is no way to avoid serious conflict? Is the Lutheran church bound to experience a new wave of anti-clericalism?

Is it true that religion and the church are for kids and little old ladies, while the real man goes about doing other things that really count? Is it true that the smarter a person is and the more education he gets the farther away he gets from the "simple gospel"? Is education an enemy of faith?

Are the three major Lutheran bodies so far apart that fellowship or unity of any sort is impossible? Is the Missouri Synod the citadel of truth or the paragon of rigid sectarianism, while the LCA is the hotbed of liberalism or the embodiment of Christian love and compassion? Is the ALC floating somewhere in the middle, like the Victorian bride, not knowing exactly what is going to happen to her but quite sure it is likely to be rather nasty?

Anybody who is strongly committed to one particular answer to any of the above stereotypes is not likely to change his mind after reading this chapter. The questions presuppose answers that remove any diversity from consideration. We are not going to attempt to prove or disprove any one answer from any of them. Rather, we will attempt to illuminate the form that the diversity of the Lutheran church takes when we look at a limited set of characteristics and the differences, if any, associated with them.

Before reporting on these characteristics, one point needs to be established. As noted in previous chapters, none of the characteristics reported in this chapter are as powerful or significant in telling us about diversity as are characteristics of beliefs, values, and attitudes. This is clearly established by the procedures of analysis we used. When we simultaneously compared large numbers of characteristics with a single dimension, it was seldom that characteristics like sex, education, or region of country proved to be as good predictors as other characteristics (See Appendix A, p. 354). Nevertheless, though small, the persistent and meaningful differences associated with these characteristics help to clarify the diversity of the Lutheran church.[1]

Where are the greatest differences among these seven characteristics? The distinction between lay people and clergy is the most clear-cut expression of diversity among the seven characteristics. Age is next in rank of magnitude of diversity expressed. Then follow education, church body affiliation, sex, and region of country. Size of congregation is last. All differences associated with these last five characteristics are slight, but the above rank order gives a rough idea of their relative significance.[2] Table 11.1 gives an estimate of the size of the differences associated with these seven characteristics. They will be discussed in sequence from lowest to highest degrees of variation.

First, one further point regarding diversity itself needs to be made. The gift of diversity which God gives the church is a diversity in unity. The

Table 11.1   Average Standard Score Differences Across the Dimensions of
              Factors 1 through 9 According to Standardized Scores Based
              on Maximum Differences Between Subgroups

Comparisons		Average Differences
Clergy–Lay, total		8.0
ALC Clergy–Lay		8.0
LC-MS Clergy–Lay		7.6
LCA Clergy–Lay		8.2
Age		
Age within Clergy		5.6
Age within Laity		6.0
Education, total		4.0
Education within Men		2.4
Education within Women		1.9
Church Body		
LC-MS/LCA	Clergy	2.0
	Laity	1.9
LC-MS/ALC	Clergy	1.6
	Laity	1.4
ALC/LCA	Clergy	.6
	Laity	.2
Sex		
Women vs. Men		1.3
College Graduate Women and Men		1.6
Non-college Graduate Women and Men		1.0
Region		1.2
Size of Congregation		.7

unity of the church centers in Christ. Varying theological opinions as to
what constitutes unity in Christ have been advanced in the history of
the church. At the present time this is a subject of vigorous debate in
the Lutheran church. In reporting the diversity evident in the data we
do not wish to imply that all diversity is either good or bad. Whether
or not the diversity to be reported affects the question of unity, and
whether such possible effect is positive or negative, must be left to the
reader's theological judgment.

Lesser Kinds of Diversity

DIVERSITY AND CONGREGATIONAL SIZE

The size of the congregation a Lutheran belongs to is associated with
only one major area of diversity: practice of the faith. Persons in congregations with under 250 communicant members report more expression
of personal piety, congregational involvement, and personal witnessing.[3]

There are several possible explanations for this. Smaller congregations simply may require more involvement from the limited number of persons available. It is harder to hide. It may be that smaller congregations also enforce greater intimacy and warmth in personal relations within the congregation. Our data also show that persons who feel they are at home in their congregations and have a number of personal friends there also tend to be more active. Then again, smaller congregations may tend to be more involved in trying to build up or maintain their existence. The struggle for survival may result in higher levels of activity.

REGIONS AND DIVERSITY AMONG LUTHERANS

Of the five regional groups, Lutherans living in the East (see Chapter 2, Figure 2.4) are consistently the lowest scoring on the dimensions reflecting the heart of Lutheran piety (Chapter 5), while Lutherans living in the Western region tend to be the highest scoring group on all but two dimensions. Lutherans in the East North Central region are the most conservative doctrinally (Scale 44), while Lutherans in the West North Central region are highest scoring on belief in the Divinity of Jesus (Scale 6).[4] Lutherans in the East are also consistently the lowest scoring group on dimensions of religious practice (Chapter 8).[5] However, on dimensions reflecting a concern for social justice and favoring church involvement in social issues (Chapter 7), Lutherans in the East are consistently the highest group.[6] No consistent regional pattern emerged on dimensions of misbelief. Lutherans in the South and East have the highest and those in the West the lowest levels of Generalized Prejudice (Scale 34).[7] Lutherans in the West North Central were highest in the Need for Religious Absolutism (Scale 43), Self-Oriented Utilitarianism (Scale 67), and desire for Social Distance—Racial and Religious Groups (Scale 57).[8] More Lutherans in the East believe in Salvation by Works (Scale 15),[9] while those in the West are the most highly committed to the concept of a Christian Utopia (Scale 36).[10] These regional differences, however, tend to closely parallel church body lines. It may be that a more useful explanatory variable here is church body rather than region. In any event, it appears that Lutherans in the East tend toward closer identification with the surrounding culture and have a greater interest in social activism. Lutherans in the Midwest and West may tend to get the feeling that there is also an ecclesiastical "Eastern Establishment" when their greater conservatism and absolutism meet the expression of faith of the brethren in the East.

HOW DO MEN AND WOMEN SHOW DIVERSITY?

On all dimensions reflecting beliefs, values, attitudes, and behavior that may be regarded as positive, Lutheran women consistently show slightly higher scores than do Lutheran men. The men consistently show slightly higher scores than women do on dimensions reflecting misbelief or a law orientation, questionable behavior, and pessimism. The differences between men and women are most pronounced on the dimensions involving basic beliefs and questionable behaviors.[11] In the area of religious practices women are more active in personal practice of piety and personal witnessing. They also have slightly more biblical knowledge.[12] Men show a greater tendency actively to express their personal views on controversial issues to authorities in both church and society.[13] As a whole, women make a stronger showing on measures both of belief and of expression of faith. Yet men tend to communicate their concerns more actively than women. This may mean that the church is hearing the most from the group less highly identified with its faith and life.

Women indeed do tend to be more religious than men. Women are more likely to look like Christians are thought to look. This means pastors are going to find women to be the ones appearing most responsive to their preaching and teaching. It would be easy to suppose that while women are in the church praying earnestly, the men are out in the world sinning boldly. However, it may only be that men more honestly report their ideas and behavior. It may also point to a serious problem for the church: ministry to men. Men also tend to report more pessimism and greater confusion about the faith. They are more prone to be victims of the accusing, demanding force of the law. They may be hurting more.

DIVERSITY OF THE CHURCH BODIES

The diversity among the lay members of the ALC, LCA, and LC-MS is not as significant nor as large in degree as the diversity related to age, education, and clergy–lay status. In other words, there is greater diversity between young and old, between those highly educated and those with little education, and between pastors and laymen, than there is on the average among the laymen of the three church bodies. Sex, region, and size of congregation show less diversity than church body affiliation.

Most of the differences among lay members of the three church bodies are found on the dimensions that make up the four major factors described in Chapters 5, 6, 7, and 8. There are fewer significant differences among clergymen in the three bodies than among the lay members.[14] Differences among clergymen by church body are smaller than the differences among laymen by church body on the heart of Lutheran piety, but they are larger than among laymen by church body on misbelief and matters of mission and ministry.[15] Clergymen contrast most sharply over beliefs (Chapter 5) and the church's stand about social justice (Chapter 7). Among laymen diversity by church body is most evident in the area of beliefs (Chapter 5). For both clergy and laymen the differences among church bodies are systematic and regular.

Heart of Lutheran piety. Lay members of the LC-MS as a group consistently have the highest average scores on all dimensions of the heart of Lutheran piety. Lay members of the LCA consistently have the lowest averages, while members of the ALC are in between, generally closer to the LCA than to the LC-MS (see Table 11.2).

The sharpest lay differences among the church bodies are found on the dimension of fundamentalism–liberalism (Scale 44). On all items more members of the LC-MS are willing to set clearly the limits of the Christian faith. The diversity between LC-MS laymen and ALC and LCA laymen is greatest on the items dealing with (1) authority of Scripture (Item 76); (2) the Office of the Keys (Item 87); (3) the vicarious atonement of Christ (Item 81); (4) the Eucharist (Item 85); and (5) the nature of man (Item 88).[16] It is clear that more lay members of the LC-MS tend toward a stronger conservative or even fundamentalist stance than do laymen of the ALC and LCA.

Other sharp differences on individual items among lay members of the three church bodies are on the dimensions of The Exclusive Truth Claim of Christianity Exaggerated (Scale 16) and Transcendental Meaning in Life (Scale 28). Larger proportions of members in LC-MS (83%) state that belief in Jesus Christ is absolutely necessary for salvation, than do those in ALC (71%) or LCA (63%) (Item 420). Twenty percent of LC-MS members assert that if people in other countries are completely ignorant of Jesus, this definitely prevents their salvation (Item 422). This compares with 10% of ALC and 8% of LCA members who assert the same. Half of the LC-MS members agree that "Jews can never be forgiven for what they did to Jesus until they accept Him as the true Saviour" (Item 41). One-third of ALC and one-fourth of LCA members agree. Two-thirds of the LC-MS members believe the devil actually exists (Item 91) as compared with one-half of the ALC and one-third of the LCA members. Eighty-two percent of the LC-MS members believe miracles actually happened as the Bible says they did (Item 89) compared to 69% for ALC and 61% for LCA.[17]

Of all items on the dimensions forming the heart of Lutheran piety there are two where the sharpest contrast among laymen is between the LC-MS and ALC rather than the LCA. More members (one-third) of the ALC state that loving your neighbor (Item 618) and doing good for others (Item 619) are absolutely necessary for salvation than do members of the LC-MS or LCA. On the other hand, more members (one-fifth) of LC-MS definitely reject these statements than do members of ALC or LCA.[18] If the ALC brings unique emphases into American Lutheranism, this suggests that one such unique emphasis might be

Table 11.2 Comparisons Among Lay Members of the LC-MS, ALC, and LCA on the Dimensions of the Heart of Lutheran Piety
(Factor 1)
Standardized Scores

Scale Number	Name	LC-MS (N = 1565)	ALC (N = 1355)	LCA (N = 1524)	P
28	Transcendental Meaning in Life	52.1	48.7	45.3	.000003
14	A Personal, Caring God	51.6	48.6	46.5	.000020
66	Emotional Certainty of Faith	50.5	48.6	47.2	.000030
44	Fundamentalism–Liberalism	53.5	47.9	45.6	.000006
46	Importance of Christian Practices in My Life	50.5	49.3	48.5	.000040
71	Attitudes Toward Life and Death	51.2	48.9	46.6	.000030
41	Personal Piety	49.4	47.5	46.5	.000040
19	Religious Experience	51.2	48.7	47.4	.000020
58	Awareness of the Immanent Trinity	51.4	49.5	48.0	.000040
6	Divinity of Jesus	52.8	49.1	47.0	.000010
16	The Exclusive Truth Claim of Christianity Exaggerated	52.6	48.4	46.2	.000001
36	Christian Utopianism	51.7	49.0	47.5	.000020
8	Biblical Knowledge	50.3	48.4	48.0	.000050

what previous researchers have termed "ethicalism," that is, ethical activity based upon humanistic values rather than supernaturalism.[19]

Chapter 5 showed that most Lutherans think that they are not different from other Christians and are generally positive toward unity among Lutherans. When we examine the individual items given in Table 5.3 by church body affiliation, we find that more in the LC-MS than in the ALC or LCA *do* see Lutherans as being different, more strict in beliefs, and more strongly committed to salvation by faith alone. There are also fewer members of the LC-MS who are interested in unity with the other church bodies and more who are convinced that complete doctrinal agreement is required for unity.[20] Pastors and laymen of LC-MS differ here in that more laymen than pastors resist unity.[21] Nevertheless, a majority (62%) of the members of LC-MS tend to endorse the desirability of unity among Lutherans. About two-thirds of the members of LC-MS also tend to agree that Lutherans are not really different from other Christians.

Other than these two points where the ALC stands out on one and the LC-MS on the other, the general rule for almost all individual items of the dimensions of Factor 1 discussed in Chapter 5 is that larger proportions of lay members of LC-MS endorse them, while the smallest proportions endorsing them are consistently found in the LCA.

However, of the 13 dimensions related positively to Factor 1, The Heart of Lutheran Piety, on only four do clergy contrast significantly by church body (in order from largest to smallest contrast): The Exclusive Truth Claim of Christianity Exaggerated (Scale 16), Fundamentalism–Liberalism (Scale 44), Divinity of Jesus (Scale 6), and Transcendental Meaning in Life (Scale 28). LC-MS pastors in all cases score highest on the average, while LCA pastors on the average score lowest.

Misbelief. There is a mixed pattern of differences among the laity of the three church bodies on the dimensions forming the factor called law orientation (Chapter 6). There are no significant differences on the dimensions of Need for Unchanging Structure (Scale 37), Need for Religious Absolutism (Scale 43), Generalized Prejudice (Scale 34), Self-Oriented Utilitarianism (Scale 67), Social Distance–Radical Life Styles (Scale 56), Social Distance–Racial and Religious Groups (Scale 57), Mutual Support Among Church, Society, and Individuals (Scale 26), Pessimism (Scale 35), and Horatio Alger Orientation (Scale 69).[22] Differences are found on three dimensions: The Exclusive Truth Claim of Christianity Exaggerated (Scale 16), Salvation by Works (Scale 15), and Christian Utopianism (Scale 36). More members of the LC-MS, about two out of five, are likely to take a very firm stand on the truth claim of the Christian faith, with some tendency to identify the truth claim with the visible Lutheran church. The LCA has the smallest proportion of members, about one out of five, willing to take that position. About three out of five members of the LC-MS agree with the idea of a Christian Utopia as compared to about two out of five members of the LCA. On the other hand, the LCA has more members, about three out of five, who agree with rather obvious statements of a belief in salvation by works. The smallest proportion, about two out of five, is found in the LC-MS.

Clergymen of the three church bodies show diversity in the same directions. Pastors of the LC-MS are the lowest scoring group on Salvation by Works (Scale 15) and the highest scoring group on The Exclusive Truth Claim of Christianity Exaggerated (Scale 16). The differences among clergymen of the three church bodies on The Exclusive Truth Claim of Christianity Exaggerated (Scale 16) are the largest we found on all dimensions.[23] Significantly more clergymen of the LCA believe in salvation by works, but here the differences by church body are smaller among clergy than among laymen.

Mission and ministry. When one examines attitudes concerning mission and ministry, the diversity among church bodies reverses direction. Proportionately more laymen and clergy of the LCA consistently indicate their own openness to change in church and their desire for their church's and pastor's involvement in social issues. The smallest proportion of laymen and clergy with like propensities are from the LC-MS.[24] There are no significant differences among church bodies in the willingness of either laymen or clergy to serve in ways likely to build a more just society (Scale 12). Here, again, both the clergy and laity of the ALC are amazingly consistent by being in the middle. However, members of the ALC are generally much closer to the LCA than to the LC-MS on questions of church involvement in social issues and openness to change.

Differences in response to individual items are consistent with this pattern with a single exception. About two out of five members of the ALC agree that the "death penalty is barbaric and should be abolished" (Item 310).[25] This is a significantly larger proportion than in either the LCA or the LC-MS.

The sharpest conflict of opinion centers on the question of the role of women in the church.[26] In the LCA 75% agree that women should be ordained (Item 709). This compares to 66% in the ALC and 45% in the LC-MS. While 90% of the members of the ALC and LCA feel women should be able to hold office and vote in congregations (Item 708), only 70% of the members of LC-MS agree.

On the dimension stressing individual conscience and responsibility

(Scale 60) lay members of the LC-MS on the average score highest, while lay members of the LCA more frequently support a concept of mission and service without proclamation (Scale 62). Two-thirds of the members of LC-MS agree that if they were convinced the resurrection of Jesus had not occurred they could not be a Christian (Item 309). One-half of the ALC and one-third of the LCA members agree.[27] On the other hand, 26% of the LCA members say that eliminating physical suffering is more important than preaching the gospel (Item 534). This compares to 20% of the ALC and 12% of the LC-MS members.[28]

Diversity in life styles. Of the factors and dimensions discussed in Chapter 8 dealing with religious behaviors, there are only three dimensions with significant differences among the three church bodies. They are Personal Piety (Scale 41), Personal Evangelism (Scale 21), and Disappointment with the Church (Scale 27). For the first two, members of the LC-MS score the highest and members of the LCA score the lowest. However, members of the LCA express most disappointment with the church, while members of LC-MS express least disappointment.

More members of LC-MS, about two out of five, report giving above 6% of their income to the church (Item 467) than do members of the ALC and LCA, where it is one in four. About one-half of the members of LC-MS say they have been keenly aware of God's presence (Item 475) compared to about one-third in ALC and LCA. About the same proportions in the three church bodies claim that their Christian beliefs lie behind their whole approach to life (Item 477). Three-fourths of the members of LC-MS say they accept faith over science (Item 507) as compared to slightly less than one-half in the ALC and LCA.

While members of LC-MS generally report slightly more personal witnessing than do members of the other two church bodies, there is one more single item on which the ALC is the extreme group. More members of the ALC (25%) report having Bible study groups in their homes (Item 668) than do members of the LCA (17%) or the LC-MS (22%).[29]

Summary of diversity among church bodies. More members of the LCA and ALC tend to be committed to a concept of mission and ministry that emphasizes church involvement in social issues. A greater proportion of the members of the LC-MS take a conservative theological stance, emphasize the importance of individual conscience, and practice traditional forms of piety. The clearest diversity lies in the tendency of more members of the LC-MS definitely and firmly to assert the truth claim of the Christian faith and to exaggerate it by identifying the truth with a single denomination, while more members of the LCA show a willingness to say they believe in salvation by works.

Diversity and Education

Education reflects diversity among Lutherans most conspicuously in the area of misbelief. Those with the least education are consistently more law-oriented than those with higher levels of education.[30] College trained Lutherans are the highest scoring group on dimensions assessing religious practices and concern for social justice. College experience is related to greater religious discernment for women than for men. Women college graduates consistently score higher than male college graduates on dimensions reflecting the heart of Lutheran piety (Chapter 5), religious practices (Chapter 8), and concern for social justice (Chapter 7). On the major dimensions of misbelief (Chapter 6) college trained males tend to score higher than college trained women. However, this may reflect the persistent relationship of sex to belief throughout the educational experience rather than any unique quality of the kind of education women and men get.

Education is not connected with rejection of the faith. Rather, it appears to be a factor in more discriminating evaluation of misbeliefs. Those more highly educated persons who remain in the church tend toward a more rich expression of their faith in personal practices and in their concern for a just and compassionate society.

Diversity Between Clergy and Laity

Is there a broad and widening gap between Lutheran pastors and the people they are called to serve and to shepherd? This is a vital and absorbing issue. For almost all Lutherans the relationship between pastor and people within a parish setting is one of the most fundamental spiritual realities experienced in their lives. We shall therefore report fully on the matter of clergy–lay differences using the major factors and dimensions discussed in Chapters 5 through 9 to organize this information.

Heart of Lutheran Piety

Most Lutheran clergy and laymen share a basic understanding of their faith. This is indicated on numerous belief dimensions. Clergy, as leaders of a flock, can be expected to show higher commitment and pro-religiosity on dimensions that are unambiguous in their interpretation. Thus, as shown in Table 11.3, on the dimensions of Transcendental Meaning in Life (Scale 28), Certainty of Faith (Scale 66), and Belief in a Personal, Caring God (Scale 14) there are significant differences, but they do not indicate that pastor and people are on opposite sides. Pastors are just naturally more likely to agree with statements that show a generally positive view of the faith. The clergy–lay differences are greatest be-

Table 11.3 Comparisons between Laity (N = 4,444) and Clergy (N = 301) on the Major Dimensions of the Heart of Lutheran Piety (Factor 1) Standardized Scores

Scale Number	Name	Clergy	Laity	Probability
28	Transcendental Meaning in Life	55.5	49.6	< .0001
14	A Personal, Caring God	54.2	49.6	< .0001
44	Fundamentalism–Liberalism	51.8	49.9	n.s.
66	Emotional Certainty of Faith	54.7	49.7	< .0001
19	Religious Experience	56.6	49.7	< .0001
58	Awareness of the Immanent Trinity	57.4	49.5	< .0001
5 °	Humanity of Jesus	64.0	49.0	< .0001
6	Divinity of Jesus	53.4	49.7	< .0001
16	The Exclusive Truth Claim of Christianity Exaggerated	52.2	49.9	n.s.
36	Christian Utopianism	50.3	50.0	n.s.

° Scale 5 is not in the first factor but is included here because of its logical relationship to Scale 6.

tween clergy and male college graduates; they are substantially less between clergy and college graduate women. There is, of course, much wider latitude in religious commitment among the laity than among the clergy. Nevertheless, the differences between clergy and laity are generally not great in magnitude and do not support the idea of inevitable conflict due to sharply divergent beliefs or attitudes.[31] In fact, along the three dimensions that may come closest to allowing an expression of the distinctive content of the Christian faith (Scales 44, 16, and 36) there are no significant differences at all between clergy and laity.

On basic understanding of religious doctrines (Scale 44, Fundamentalism–Liberalism) the overwhelming majority of both clergy and laity reject the fundamentalistic response (Choice A) and the liberal responses (Choices D and E). Generally between 80-90% of both clergy and laity endorse intermediate choices. This is independently confirmed by the choice of theological label (See Table 5.2 in Chapter 5) to describe one's own position. A fundamentalist label was chosen by 7% of the clergy; 8% of the college graduate males; 11% of the college graduate women; 14% of the non-college women; and 17% of the non-college males.

There are two doctrines where there appears to be some difference of belief between clergy and laity (Items 87 and 88, Scale 44), namely, the nature of man and the Office of the Keys: "Pastors have the right and the power to forgive sins and to excommunicate the unrepentant sinner" (Item 87). Educated laity, both men and women, rejected this idea decisively. One out of five Lutherans with a college degree went to the extreme of rejecting this aspect of the Office of the Keys as either unwarranted interference or magical superstition. Laymen as a group tend to modify and weaken the statement, while pastors tend to accept it. There is some disparity between clergy and laity on the doctrine of the nature of man. Three percent of the clergy expressed a belief that man is either inherently good or neutral, while 30% of the laity believe man is good or neutral. Pastors tend much more to the view that man is evil than do their lay people.

While there may not be a basic disagreement between clergy and laity about what the faith is, there does seem to be a significant tension about the office and authority of the pastor. Lutheran laymen tend not to think in terms of any sort of "spiritual discipline." Particularly they tend not to see the pastor as a person with spiritual power. Many have the view that man is by nature good. It may then follow for them that the pastor's function becomes to help a good man in his struggle to live. If the pastor sees himself as attempting to control the base passions of evil men, there is going to be misunderstanding and confusion between them.

A very significant difference between clergy and laity is in their understanding of Jesus. Clergy uniformly recognize both the divinity and the humanity of Jesus (Scales 5 and 6). This indicates that pastors accept the unity of the two natures of Jesus. By contrast, the overwhelming majority of Lutheran laity readily accept the divinity of Jesus, but they have more difficulty endorsing his humanity. Most Lutheran lay people may accept the formal statement of the doctrine that Jesus was both God and man, but they have difficulty describing *how* Jesus was a real man. To be sure, there are some who say Jesus was only a real man and not true God, but their numbers are relatively few. It is more common to overemphasize the divinity of Christ, so that his humanity is rejected or becomes relatively hollow or unreal. Clearly this calls for more attention by all who are engaged in a preaching and teaching ministry.

Misbelief. On all major dimensions of law orientation, as shown in Table 11.4, with one exception, the laity score higher than do pastors. The sharpest differences are on the dimension of Salvation by Works (Scale 15). Laymen as a group tend more toward acceptance of this dimension while clergy resoundingly reject it.[32] This clergy–lay disparity indicates that Pelagianism is part of the natural state of man and that the marvelous gift of salvation by grace through faith in Jesus Christ must continually be proclaimed and reflected by the lives of the people of God.

Significant clergy–lay differences were noted in Need for Unchanging Structure (Scale 37), Self-Oriented Utilitarianism (Scale 67), and in three dimensions reflecting views of others: Generalized Prejudice (Scale 34) and Social Distance (Scales 56 and 57). On each of these measures laymen score much higher than pastors.[33] Clergy–lay differences on Need

Table 11.4 Comparisons Between Laity (N = 4,444) and Clergy (N = 301)
on the Major Dimensions of Misbelief (Factor 2)

Standardized Scores

Scale Number	Name	Clergy	Laity	Probability
37	Need for Unchanging Structure	42.7	50.5	< .0001
43	Need for Religious Absolutism	46.6	50.1	< .0001
34	Generalized Prejudice	40.5	50.6	< .0001
56	Social Distance— Radical Life Styles	39.4	50.8	< .0001
57	Social Distance— Racial and Religious Groups	45.3	50.3	< .0001
67	Self-Oriented Utilitarianism	42.2	50.4	< .0001
26	Mutual Support Among Church, Society, and Individuals	52.8	49.8	< .0001
15	Salvation by Works	34.5	51.1	< .0001
69	Horatio Alger Orientation	46.4	50.2	< .0001
35	Pessimism	46.3	50.3	< .0001

for Religious Absolutism (Scale 43) and Pessimism (Scale 35) are smaller but still highly significant. Again laymen tend to score somewhat higher. Each of these dimensions indicates a persistent temptation to idolatry of form over substance, of attempting to encapsulate the gospel into a single container satisfying to ourselves or meeting our own personal needs. The intrinsic frustration that results from living under the law is reflected in the higher level of pessimism. These temptations are more likely to ensnare laity than clergy, although the evidence suggests that all fall short and can be victims of one or more of the heresies present in the church from its inception.

The only dimension endorsed more frequently by clergy than by laity is The Exclusive Truth Claim of Christianity Exaggerated (Scale 16). Those clergy who score highest on this dimension tend to be older in age, to lean toward fundamentalism (Scale 44), and to emphasize the divinity of Jesus, weakening the unity of his human and divine natures (Scales 5 and 6). They also tend to be fearful and resistant to change. While this pattern typifies a few clergy and laity, the majority of both clergy and laity reject it. Persistent effort by educational agencies can help articulate the solid substance of Lutheran piety and overcome the human tendencies reflected by these misbeliefs.

Practices of the faith. Table 11.5 includes a set of behavioral dimensions composed of what Lutherans say they do about the practice of their faith in their personal piety (Scale 41), congregational activity (Scale 40), and church and community involvement (Scale 47). There are sharp clergy–lay differences in the practice of the faith. This is

Table 11.5   Comparisons Between Laity (N = 4,444) and Clergy (N = 301) on the Major Dimensions of Religious Practices (Factor 6)

Standardized Scores

Scale Number	Name	Clergy	Laity	Probability
41	Personal Piety	65.8	48.9	< .0001
40	Congregational Activity	64.1	49.0	< .0001
47	Personal Involvement in Church and Community	65.1	49.0	< .0001
21	Personal Evangelism	71.3	48.6	< .0001
74	Personal Initiative on Church and Public Issues	71.9	48.5	< .0001
27	Disappointment with the Church	42.7	50.5	< .0001

particularly evident in personal witnessing (Scale 21) and involvement in personal activities expressing one's opinions to persons in authority (Scale 74). Part of this is entirely natural and expected, as the clergy are employed full-time to give direction and leadership to a body of believers. This does not explain away, however, a low level of involvement and activity by substantial numbers of laymen.[34] These differences are by far the largest that exist between pastors and people.

Actions for social justice. Social justice is a key concept in another factor. The dimensions of this factor are: Openness to Change Within the Church (Scale 78), Church Involvement in Social Issues (Scale 65), Power Orientation to Social Issues (Scale 64), and The Church, Me, and Social Justice (Scale 12). The results are consistent in showing that clergy uniformly show higher commitment to personal and church involvement in social issues than laity do. Clergy and laity are alike in that younger persons, either clergy or lay, are most eager to press for church involvement in the struggle for needed social reforms. LCA clergy appear slightly more activistic in this regard. Laity with higher education, unless they happen to be older professional men, are also more likely to share the attitudes of the clergy. It appears that clergy are exerting leadership roles in these matters. Younger college trained laity share their goals. It is the older laity who are less willing or resist a more active posture by the local congregation aimed at alleviating social distress. There is an area of tension here. The tension is not about the idea of a just society. Rather, it centers about the appropriate role of the pastor and the church. Some seem to be saying, "Help me and train *me* to do the job," while about an equal number of others are saying that the church as institution must be working for change and reform in society.

Church loyalty. The degree to which clergy and laity show loyalty to the church (Chapter 7) is a significant question. One dimension represents a positive evaluation of the church (Scale 13). The other provides a critical assessment of the church (Scale 27). Clergy generally said more complimentary things about church and family than did the laity.[35] However, there is a sharp disparity in response between older and younger clergy. The youngest group of clergy (ages 24-29) did *not* share the optimistic assessment given by older clergy groups. On Scale 13 their average was 23.3 points lower than pastors over age 50. The next age group of clergy, ages 30-41, had an average 9.5 points less than clergy over age 50. A similar pattern exists for laity, but it is not as definite as for the clergy. Younger pastors tend to have a more critical view of the church, as do the younger lay people. This is not rejection of the church, however.

These and other data extensively presented in the preceding chapters identify a solid core of Lutherans, both clergy and lay people, highly committed and loyal to their God and to their church. But Lutherans are divided in their attitudes about how well their church is going about doing their Master's business. It is clear that some pastors and some lay people find no fault with their church. Others find little worthwhile in it, at least for themselves. The majority are somewhere in between.

Other diversity between pastors and people. The life styles of clergy and laity can be compared across a variety of single items. There are many items in which clergy patterns did not differ substantially from life style patterns of comparable laymen. Several rather sharp differences do stand out, however.

Lutherans were asked to indicate how active or inactive in church their parents were during the respondent's youth. The model that parents present to children has long been felt to be important. Most clergy tend to come from homes where one or both parents were very active in their church. Modeling piety does appear to be significant. Laity report much greater diversity in parental levels of church activity.[36]

Another clergy–lay contrast is reflected in employment. Lutherans were asked how many hours they worked each week for pay. It appeared most appropriate to compare clergy with male college graduates although clergy training is at a postgraduate degree level. The comparable lengths of their work weeks are reported in Table 11.6. The disparity is striking. Eight out of ten pastors work over 50 hours per week as compared with two out of ten of the laymen who are college graduates. Two out of ten pastors report working over 70 hours a week. Despite this long work week, there is a sharp diversity between clergy and laity in their comparable family incomes. Total annual household income for clergy and

Table 11.6   Average Length of Work Week for Clergy and Other Male College Graduates

Hours Per Week	Other Male College Graduates	Clergy
Over 70	4%	18%
61-70	6	27
51-60	12	35
41-50	39	14
31-40	27	1
21-30	1	0
11-20	1	1
1-10	3	1
None	4	3
No Response	3	4
Total	100%	100%

male college graduates is reported in Table 11.7. One-half of Lutheran clergymen report *total* annual household incomes under $9,000. Two-thirds of Lutheran men who are college graduates earn over $12,000 each year. This is a powerful message to the pastor that what he is and what he does are not valued as highly as what other men of comparable ability and training are and do. The additional touch of irony is that some of the most poorly paid pastors may also be among those frantically working over 70 hours per week.

Table 11.7   Average Annual Household Income for Clergy and Other Male College Graduates

Annual Household Income	Other Male College Graduates	Clergy
$24,000 or more	13%	1%
$21,000-$23,999	5	1
$18,000-$20,999	12	3
$15,000-$17,999	14	6
$12,000-$14,999	25	15
$ 9,000-$11,999	16	35
$ 6,000-$ 8,999	10	32
$ 3,000-$ 5,999	3	3
Under $3,000	1	3
No Response	1	3
Total	100%	100%

There are significant differences between pastor and people within the Lutheran church, but none of them are surprising. Neither do they indicate that sharp conflict is inevitable. Surely it is normal and expected that pastors would reflect the highest level of belief commitment, religious practices, and a more full grasp of some doctrinal positions such as the unity of the two natures of Jesus. Also it is hardly new to find the level of misbelief higher among laity. All that this says is that pastors continue to have work to do. Considering the history of the prophets, it is not disconcerting to find pastors showing higher levels of concern with social justice. Though there are differences between pastor and people about how far the church goes in social concern and how it best expresses concern, the differences are not so large as to portend doom. Indeed, one may say that the most encouraging element is the level of support laity give to their pastors to be teachers and guides regarding social issues.

Summary

These and other data presented in the preceding chapters have identified a solid core of Lutherans highly committed and loyal to their God and to their church. But Lutherans are divided over how well their church is going about doing their Master's business. It is clear that some Lutherans find no fault with their church; others find little worthwhile in it, at least for themselves. The vast majority are somewhere in between.

The differences that do exist have been demonstrated in preceding chapters to be mainly concerning the nature and depth of belief and the values undergirding the life style of the person, including his attitudes toward himself and others. Such matters are generally much more pervasive and far-reaching in their effects than the issues around which this chapter has been organized such as difference of region, church body, or clergy–lay status. We do not mean to imply that some of these latter differences are not important or do not exist. But what is unmistakable is that there is vastly more that *unites* Lutherans by region, church body, or clergy–lay role than divides them. Differences in age, educational background, strength of faith, or value orientations, are much more crucial in identifying life styles, world views, and attitudes toward self, others, and loyalty to church than are regional or church body differences.

Differences *within* church bodies and regions are vastly greater than differences among them. The hope and dream of a united witness is shared by most Christians. These data give mighty reassurance and support to those who believe Lutherans share a common understanding of their faith. At the same time they clearly illuminate the differences and highlight the tensions that still divide Lutherans.

These data also give indications of ferment. There are widely pluralistic patterns of thought about what the church is or ought to be at this time in history and in the United States. Voices both within and without the church are clamoring for change; other equally strident voices are attempting to limit the gifts of the Holy Spirit to particular structures and vessels. If the church has a treasure in an earthen vessel and attempts to fulfill its divinely appointed mission, then a cloud of witnesses, with different gifts yet one in loyalty to the gospel, can find room for growth in truth and grace within the Lutheran churches of the United States.

Notes

1. Two other points need to be made regarding the characteristics reported in this chapter. We need to be clear on the practical significance of finding diversity associated with such characteristics. Say that we find a persistent difference associated with gender: males tend to show more quality x than females. What do we do about it? If quality x is undesirable, we can hardly go about trying to change the gender of all males in the Lutheran church. The most we can do is to try to understand how males happen to have quality x, and then ask if we can find realistic and acceptable ways to reduce quality x and increase quality y, the more desirable quality.

   Finding diversity associated with age, sex, region, size of congregation, education, and church body membership does not explain *why* such diversity exists. When dealing with a social–psychological–spiritual system of beliefs, values, and attitudes we have the influence of an incredibly complex, interactive, mutual feedback causal system. The forces affecting the relationships we uncover are both known and unknown. They range from the effect of a single mutated gene that makes some persons mentally retarded, to the model of discipline presented by one's parents, to the action of the Holy Spirit in Baptism. This brings us to the third point.

   When we find diversity associated with such a set of demographic variables most people seem to assume that they are causes of the diversity. Thus, if males show x, there is something about being male that causes x. However, clearly, unless we are prepared to deal with the assertion that x is directly caused by genetic inheritance, maleness is not a cause in and of itself. Rather, maleness is a shorthand way of speaking of all other influences affecting an individual subsequent to the matching of xy chromosomes at the time of conception. The same caution applies to all of the demographic variables dealt with in this chapter. They are best not thought of as directly causing the effects to be described.

2. The rank ordering of these seven characteristics is based upon an averaging of all standard score differences associated with each of the seven characteristics across all dimensions of the first nine factors. This gives a rough estimate of the relative magnitude of the differences.

3. Two-way analysis of variance, laity only, Scales 40, 41, and 21, $p = < .00001$, Scale 47 $p = < .0001$.

4. Two-way analysis of variance, laity only, shows Region 1 (East) lowest and Region 5 (West) highest on Scales 28, 14, 71, 19, 16, and 26 at $p = < .00001$ and Scales 66, 46, and 58 at $p = < .0001$. Region 2 (East North Central) averages highest on Scale 44, $p = < .00001$.

5. Two-way analysis of variance, laity only, shows Region 1 (East) consistently lowest, $p = < .00001$ on Scales 40, 41, and 47.

6. Two-way analysis of variance, laity only, shows Region 1 (East) consistently

highest on Scales 65, 64, and 42 at p $=$ $<$ .00001 and on Scales 78 and 12 at p $=$ $<$ .0001.

7. Two-way analysis of variance, laity only, p $=$ $<$ .00001.

8. Two-way analysis of variance, laity only, p $=$ $<$ .0001 on Scales 43, 67, and 57.

9. Two-way analysis of variance, laity only, p $=$ $<$ .000001.

10. Two-way analysis of variance, laity only, p $=$ $<$ .00001.

11. Two-way analysis of variance, laity only, shows females scoring higher on Scales 28, 14, 66, 46, 71, 6, and 19 at p $=$ $<$ .0001 and at p $=$ $<$ .001 on Scales 58 and 6. Men score higher on Scale 23, questionable behaviors, at p $=$ $<$ .00001 and on Scales 34, 29, 35, 61, 63, 67, 69, 73, and 74 at p $=$ $<$ .0001.

12. Two-way analysis of variance, laity only, shows females scoring higher on Scales 41, 21, and 8 at p $=$ $<$ .0001.

13. Two-way analysis of variance, laity only, shows men scoring higher than women on Scale 74 at p $=$ $<$ .0001.

14. Clergymen of the three church bodies differ significantly (p $=$ $<$ .001) on 10 dimensions. Laymen differ significantly (p $=$ $<$ .0001) on 25 dimensions. A larger criterion of probability was allowed for significant differences among clergy because of the smaller number in the clergy sample (N $=$ 301).

15. Average difference between clergymen of LC-MS and LCA is .29 standard deviations (one standard deviation $=$ 10.0 standardized score points). Between laymen, average difference is .46 standard deviations. Corresponding average difference between the LC-MS and ALC is .20 standard deviations for clergymen and .28 for laymen. On dimensions of misbelief average difference between clergymen of LC-MS and LCA is .34 standard deviations, while between laymen it is .24. Average difference between clergymen of ALC and LC-MS is .28 and for laymen .16. On dimensions of social involvement of the church, average difference between clergy of LCA and LC-MS is .65 standard deviations; ALC and LC-MS .48. For laymen it is .20 and .17 respectively.

16. When the frequency of response is tested, X^2 figures for these five items range from 395 to 295. The lowest X^2 figure on the 13 items of Scale 44 is 47.73, Item 79.

17. For the items discussed in this paragraph X^2 figures range from 367 to 185.

18. For these two items X^2 figures are 46 and 44, p $=$ $<$ .000001.

19. Stark, R. and Glock, C., 1968, pp. 69-76.

20.   Lay People Only

Item No.	LC-MS		LCA		ALC		X^2	p
	Agree	Dis-agree	Agree	Dis-agree	Agree	Dis-agree		
308	39%	57%	19%	80%	21%	75%	215.91	.00000
317	64	29	72	21	67	24	36.54	.00000
319	26	69	18	80	20	75	45.70	.00000
329	74	22	82	16	79	16	33.52	.00001
332	29	66	19	78	21	74	51.09	.00000
336	51	43	37	60	38	56	103.67	.00000
510°	62	33	70	27	70	24	37.36	.00000
40°°	40	47	33	52	32	52	30.10	.00000

° A merger of all Lutheran groups in the United States into one organization is desirable.

°° Unity among Christians can come only after complete doctrinal agreement.

21.   Clergy Only

Item No.	LC-MS		LCA		ALC		X^2	p
	Agree	Dis-agree	Agree	Dis-agree	Agree	Dis-agree		
308	71%	29%	58%	41%	61%	38%	4.4	.5000
317	48	52	87	22	81	17	40.2	< .0001
319	53	47	29	70	30	69	16.9	.0010
329	56	44	53	46	62	35	9.0	> .0500
332	51	49	46	53	33	64	6.6	> .2500
336	57	43	60	39	46	52	4.8	.5000
510°	58	42	79	20	62	37	20.6	.0005
40°°	30	67	10	87	10	85	18.9	.0010

° A merger of all Lutheran groups in the United States into one organization is desirable.

°° Unity among Christians can come only after complete doctrinal agreement.

22. These findings speak directly to the claim that "orthodox" Christian beliefs cause anti-Semitism. The causal chain was asserted to run from "orthodox" beliefs to religious hostility to Jews to particularism to anti-Semitism. We have already demonstrated that lay and clergy members of the LC-MS are the most conservative and the most "orthodox" as measured by the same items used in previous research. They are also the most "particularistic" and exclusivistic. Again this includes the same items used earlier. If the claim that orthodox belief causes anti-Semitism is correct, it would predict that lay and clergy members of the LC-MS should show higher levels of anti-Semitism than those less orthodox. They do not.

23. Average standardized scores ($\overline{X}$ = 50.0, s = 10.0) for clergy by church body are:

Scale Number	Name	LC-MS (N = 95)	ALC (N = 102)	LCA (N = 104)	p
15	Salvation by Works	47.7	49.8	53.3	.000843
16	Exclusive Truth Claim of Christianity Exaggerated	56.7	48.3	43.6	.000000

24. Average standardized scores for clergy by church body are:

Scale Number	Name	LC-MS (N = 95)	ALC (N = 102)	LCA (N = 104)	p
78	Openness to Change in the Church	46.4	52.8	52.8	.000004
65	Church Involvement in Social Issues	46.2	52.0	54.4	.000002
64	Power Orientation to Social Issues	47.2	51.0	54.3	.000002
62	Service Without Proclamation	46.4	51.5	53.8	.000011

25. On this item X^2 = 36.10, p = < .000001.

26. On this single item, 709, X^2 figure is 302. On other items where there are significant differences between church bodies, the X^2 figures range from 128 to 20.

27. On this item X^2 = 211.

28. On this item X^2 = 178.

29. On this item X^2 = 29.9, p = < .000001.

30. The results reported throughout this section are based upon two-way analysis of

variance. Unless it is part of a consistent pattern, no anova results are reported where the probability level of the F ratio is higher than $p = < .0001$. Data similar to those in the above notes are available upon request for every dimension and all permutations of the six variables of sex, age, education, region, size of congregation, and church body affiliation.

31. With the few exceptions to be noted, all differences are well within one standard deviation on each scale. Most are also within the standard error of measurement for each scale.

32. Lay average on Scale 15 is 65.7 while clergy average is 39. Agreement with all items brings a score of 97 while disagreement with all items results in a score of 31.

33. Lay averages are between .5 and 1.2 standard deviation units above clergy averages.

34. This perennial problem of low levels of Christian piety among many members of the church is described more fully in Chapter 8.

35. Clergymen as a group had a higher average on Scale 13 and a lower average on Scale 27. $p = < .00001$ in both cases.

36. Clergy-lay contrasts in reported church activity of parents during respondent's youth.

	Lay		Clergy	
	N	%	N	%
During (my) youth MOTHER was:				
Very active in church	1063	24	156	52
Moderately active in church	1706	38	95	32
Hardly active at all in church	1023	23	38	13
Had nothing to do with church	652	15	12	5
		100%		100%
During (my) youth FATHER was:				
Very active in church	809	18	145	48
Moderately active in church	1155	26	74	25
Hardly active at all in church	1294	29	47	16
Had nothing to do with church	1186	27	35	12
		100%		100%

12. Summary of Findings

You best can understand what Lutherans will think and do if you first know what they value and believe.

You best can determine which Lutherans are open to a ministry of renewal and change if you know which are oriented to the gospel.

You can assume that for members of a congregation today, a constant requirement is to accept diversity and to use times of tension as times of opportunity.

You can assume that differences among Lutherans due to region, sex, and church body are relatively small compared with clergy–lay differences and those based on age and education.

These are some of the conclusions drawn from a 1970 study of Lutherans in the United States between the ages of 15 and 65. The purpose of this survey, called *A Study of Generations,* was to derive a descriptive profile of the beliefs, values, attitudes, opinions, and religious life styles of Lutherans. A representative sample of 4,745 Lutherans gave approximately 7,000,000 bits of information from which a relatively detailed and reliable portrait could be drawn.

The task of assembling the information could be compared with the task of fitting together 7,000,000 pieces of a massive jigsaw puzzle with the box cover picture missing. To minimize the subjective influence of the research team in assembling the data, empirical methods were used which would allow the data to organize themselves.

Every major step in assembling the data was accomplished by procedures which, if replicated, would give essentially the same information as reported here. Most of the 7,000,000 answers organized around one of 78 descriptive dimensions, and these dimensions formed 14 factors. Interpretations as to what these dimensions and factors signified were made from a study of the response patterns of all respondents.

The conclusions given above provide the perspective for the following summary profile which is based on the findings reported earlier in this book. They are presented in this form in order to be comprehensive and faithful to the documentation which supports these findings.

Summary Profile

THE VALUES AND BELIEFS OF LUTHERANS ARE THE BEST INDICATORS OF WHAT THEY WILL THINK AND DO

A common assumption is that the best predictors of a person's attitude and behavior are such factors as his age, occupation, level of education, sex, or financial status. It is true that these factors do account for some of the variation in beliefs, attitudes, and behavior among Lutherans. However, there is nothing as powerful in predicting a Lutheran's attitudes or his behavior as knowing what he values and believes.

Most Lutherans accept a transcendental view of life as their basic value orientation. Either the mind of Western man has not been completely or significantly secularized or members of Lutheran churches in 1970 are not representative samples of Western man. At any rate, most Lutherans reject a secularist view which maintains that the meaning of the world lies within itself alone. They value such qualities as love, salvation, forgiveness, service to others, an ethically responsible life, and family happiness.

In general, most Lutherans choose a God-directed life over the self-directed life, the supernatural over the natural, dualism over monism. In contrast to the value dimension that accepts a transcendental meaning in life is the value dimension of self-development. Persons preoccupied with values of self-development place a high priority upon pleasure, personal freedom, physical appearance, achievement, and recognition, preferring the natural over the supernatural. They adopt a world view and life style that can become inimical to the purposes of the church. About one out of four rejects transcendental values in favor of the values of self-development.

For most Lutherans faith in Jesus Christ is at the heart of what they value and believe. For them Christianity is to believe and know Christ; in that sense they believe and know the gospel. This life orientation emerges as one of the most distinctive characteristics of a Lutheran. The evidence indicates that about three in five Lutherans live in this orientation to the gospel.

Most Lutherans classify themselves as conservative in their theological stance and are convinced of the historic expressions of the Christian faith. They think in terms of a biblical world view and in frames of reference that resemble the classical Lutheran theology of the sixteenth century. The doctrines to which they hold most firmly are the biblical accounts of the birth of Christ, his death, and his resurrection. They believe in the Bible as God's word and in the law of God as a guide and judge of men's lives. They believe in Christ's death as an atonement for sin. They believe in the gifts of the Spirit, Baptism, the real presence of Christ in Communion, the return of Christ, and God's response to intercessory prayer. In short, Lutherans maintain the historic quality of the faith, basing it upon the reality of Christ's birth, death, and resurrection; and they believe that he is the way of salvation.

Some doctrines which are neglected by contemporary theology are some of those most potent in the piety of Lutherans. These are the doctrines of eternal life, providence, and sanctification. Some Lutherans classify themselves as fundamentalists, and of this group a disproportionate number hold exaggerated truth claims of the Christian faith. Others classify themselves as liberals, and this is reflected in their tendency to question these Christian doctrines. Such Lutherans view death as an unknown and noble reality, or as simply the end of it all. The self-labeled conservatives, by contrast, view death as the beginning of a new life.

There is an experiential emotional element in Lutheran piety that is related to a sense of faith, devotion, and practice of piety. The contribution that it makes to personal piety, however, is not through intense special experiences, but rather through feeling God's presence and assurance of salvation. About one out of two Lutherans report having had some type of religious experience. A small group of 6% say they are sure they have had an experience of speaking in tongues; 12% think they have.

Though Lutherans hold to a particular faith that makes exclusive truth claims, most are not exclusivistic in their attitudes towards other Christians. For instance, most Lutherans accept other Lutherans as fellow Christians; two out of three say they are ready for a merger into one Lutheran church. Though this proportion varies by church body, a majority in each group (ALC—70%, LC-MS—62%, LCA—71%) favor such action. It is fair to say that most Lutherans yearn for a valid expression of the catholicity of the church. There is a sense of its unity and wholeness and a search for ways to know and feel that unity. Most Lutherans do not see themselves as different from other Christians and are willing to allow for divergence and variety within the larger framework of faith.

Lutherans in 1970 tended to separate the two natures of Jesus and to overemphasize the divinity of Jesus. Those who most emphatically de-emphasized the humanity of Jesus were the ones most resistant to change, more authoritarian, and more prejudiced in their attitudes towards others. For such people a divine Jesus is a new lawgiver, a second Moses, who legitimizes their present stance.

Those who recognize Christ's humanity, or view his two natures in balance, are generally more ready to take the initiative on church and public issues and to be more forgiving in their relationships with others. Acceptance of the humanity of Jesus is associated with a willingness to accept change and to be involved in service.

Youth accept the humanity of Christ more readily than do adults and differ also in their view of God. More of the young people see God as immanent and transcendent. Older Lutherans tend to focus more exclusively upon his transcendence.

What Lutherans value and believe reflects an orientation to either the law or the gospel. These two, law and gospel, were found to be more than theological constructs. They emerged in the data as realities in the individual lives of God's saints and sinners. About three in five reflect an awareness of a personal God who cares for them in Jesus Christ, a certainty of faith, a positive attitude toward life and death, and a sense of ministry and mission. Conversely, about two in five show the effect of experiencing life as demand, exalting form over spirit. The result is a warped religiosity that inhibits, limits, and misdirects the concept of mission and ministry.

About two out of five Lutherans believe in salvation by works. Of these, the greater percentage is found in the youngest and the oldest age brackets. Lutherans most likely to reject salvation by works are those in the middle age group (30-49).

Contrary to what some theologians are saying about the contemporary irrelevance of a distinction between the law and the gospel, the data strongly indicate the importance of viewing the task of ministry and mission in terms of the difference between *(a)* living in, believing, experiencing, and accepting the gospel of grace, faith, hope, relationship, and forgiveness; and *(b)* living under the law in the sense of structure, achievement, authority, right and wrong, and justice.

An Orientation to the Gospel Is the Best Indicator of Lutherans Who Are Open to Renewal and Change in the Ministry of the Church

Seven out of ten Lutherans hold that the mission of the church is to preach the gospel and to work toward improving the well-being of people. It is the conviction of the overwhelming majority of Lutherans that of these two emphases, the primary task of the church is to preach the gospel. The current awareness of many Lutherans, and especially of youth, is that too little attention has been given to the second emphasis.

Most Lutherans reflect a liberal stance on social issues and express a commitment to a just and liberalized society but are quite evenly divided on the question of church body involvement. When interviewed as to what their ideal church would be like, the hope which Lutherans expressed most frequently was for a congregation that ministers to the range of needs in a community, including needs related to health, finances, and counseling. They showed a strong desire for a church that exemplifies and shows love to all mankind.

Though no more than one out of two Lutherans strongly identifies himself with efforts by the church to bring about social justice, most lay leaders and clergy have accepted this responsibility. If we can assume that the commitment of pastors and lay leaders has an effect on the members, we can look for an increased involvement of the Lutheran church in social action as part of its mission and ministry. At present about one in two participates in some community organization. Only a minority are involved in community and political activities.

Most Lutherans look to their pastors for leadership in the struggle for justice and amelioration of suffering. They resist, however, the idea of their pastor becoming involved in some form of activism. Most Lutherans do not want their pastor engaged in civil disobedience or in using the pulpit as a political or social rostrum. Neither do they want to be told what they must do. Rather, they want the freedom of conscience to respond to situations of need as they see fit.

Within the Lutheran church there are two distinct groups of people who call for a greater involvement in social issues. Those of one group speak out of a sense of mission, love, and conscience. Theirs is a social conscience rooted in Christian commitment. Those in the other group, though using a similar rhetoric, reflect a different orientation. This second group includes both advocates and enemies of social change who see the conflict as a power struggle. Herein are seeds of the tyranny and bigotry of both right and left. Those in this latter group are characterized by attitudes of pessimism, generalized prejudice, and belief in salvation by works.

About one out of four Lutherans views Christianity as a social gospel. They are convinced that the church has no business in trying to change other people's religions, but feel rather that the church should be meeting the physical needs of people. Such persons view Christianity as a religion of good works. They reject a transcendental world view and are pessimistic in their view of life.

The primary resistance to a ministry that is open to significant changes comes from those who are oriented to the law and not to the gospel. The most vehement resistance to caring about people, that is, carrying out a serving mission and ministry, is found among the two out of five Lutherans who misbelieve. Their obstacle is the need for unchanging structures. They tend to distrust others and exploit religion and society for their own advantage.

A sense of conscience, responsibility, and a personal obligation to be involved in the mission of the church characterizes three out of five Lutherans. They feel quite earnest about their individual Christian responsibility and look to their church to help them become compassionate, caring Christians.

Three out of five Lutherans are willing to accept responsibility in church and community activities if asked to do specific tasks. At present only one in four willingly participates in church or community activities. However, an additional one in three says he would serve if asked. This greater willingness is found especially in small congregations.

The loyalty of Lutherans to their church is shown in relatively stable church memberships and in the strong tendency to marry within their own denomination.

Lutherans are least involved in matters which require that they take personal initiative. No more than one out of five reports having acted to deal with some church or political issue of general concern. Of these, the primary group to spearhead action were college-educated males.

About two out of five Lutherans are actively involved in trying to share their personal faith with those around them. Such Lutherans are the most likely to support friends in crisis situations or to show kindness to neighbors in times of need.

Lutherans over the age of 24 give high evaluations of the current program and ministry of their congregation. No more than one in five was sharply critical of the caring life of his congregation. Those who tended to be most negative about their congregation were also negative about their family. About two-thirds of the youth gave positive evaluations of their congregation and reflected a positive stance toward their church.

The greatest reservoir of discontent for the church is linked with a lack of emotional certainty of faith, namely doubt. In other words, a negative evaluation of one's congregation is closely linked to an anxiety over one's faith. Such a crisis of faith is found particularly among the one out of five youth whose primary influence is his peer group.

A limiting factor in the ministry and mission of the Lutheran church centers in the fact that about two in five tend to hold prejudiced attitudes. They reject people who are different from themselves in life styles, values, and beliefs. Of 20 possible groups toward which people tend to hold prejudiced attitudes, Lutherans express greatest rejection of communists, homosexuals, drug addicts, hippies, and members of Students for a Democratic Society. Strong feelings are also expressed toward people who will not work and those who are on welfare. Racial differences are less of a barrier, with anti-Semitic attitudes characterizing about one in five. Significantly, Lutherans in the United States are a racially homogeneous people, native-born Americans, most of whose grandparents claim a Scandinavian or German birthplace. Compared with the overall United States population, they are average in socio-economic status and above average in educational level. They are less likely to have grown up in the farm areas or in large metropolitan centers.

Prejudice is mediated by the misbeliefs of Lutherans. Misbelief is most strongly the need for unchanging structure and the need for religious absolutism, reflecting the theological construct of life under the law. There is no direct relationship between prejudice and the value dimension of a transcendental view of life. Neither is there a direct relationship between prejudice and the belief dimensions which make up the heart of Lutheran piety and which do not appear as part of the misbelief factor. The indirect relationship between prejudice and belief is that misbelief appropriates and shapes the content of orthodox belief for its own purposes of legitimizing hatred and violence.

ACCEPTANCE OF DIVERSITY AND TENSION IS A CONSTANT REQUIREMENT FOR MEMBERS IN A LUTHERAN CONGREGATION

A Lutheran congregation consists of subgroups that contrast on enough dimensions to make tension a normal experience and acceptance of diversity a constant requirement. The single greatest source of tension stems from differences in the values and beliefs of church members. There are wide gaps between members who accept a transcendental world view and those who are preoccupied with the values of self-development, between members who are gospel-oriented and those who are law-oriented. Tension in the area of values and beliefs was identified in the interviews of Lutherans as one of the principal obstacles to the realization of their ideal church.

Another source of difference, and presumably tension, relates to age. There is a generational conflict between youth and adults that is especially significant in certain areas. Level of education ranks next as a source of difference in how Lutherans believe and respond. An additional source of tension is found in clergy–lay differences. (The word "tension" as used here can imply creativity and opportunity as well as strained relationships.)

Lutherans in this study differ enough by age groupings to justify speaking about four Lutheran generations. These generations emerged as distinct age groups: those born before World War I (ages 50-65); those born between World War I and the Depression (ages 40-49); those born after the Depression and before World War II (ages 30-39); and those born after World War II (ages 15-29). Smaller generational units appeared in the fourth age group which classified youth into the age groups of 15-18, 19-23, and 24-29. Lutherans in each age group differ enough in beliefs, values, attitudes, and behavior to be classified this way by empirical methods.

In general, the tension between youth and adults grows with increasing distance of years. However, the tension between youth and adults is not always greatest between youth (ages 15-29) and the oldest adults (ages 50-65). There are seven distinct patterns of generational tension. For example, when it comes to feelings of pessimism, the youngest and the oldest (ages 15-23 and 50-65) contrast with the middle generations (ages 24-49). In participation in congregational activities the contrast is greatest between youth ages 19-23 and adults ages 30-65. In matters of prejudice, social distance, and anxiety over one's faith, the contrast is between ages 15-23 and all other ages. Which generations will agree and which will be in tension depends upon the issue or behavior under consideration. Yet, despite this great variation, the fact remains that the contrast or tension is generally greatest between youth of ages 15-23 and adults of ages 50-65.

Differences between youth and adults are very slight in some areas but strikingly great in others. Dimensions where contrasts are greatest (in descending order) are: peer orientation, personal piety, questionable personal activities, need for mutual support among church and society, social distance from radical life styles, personal assistance in crisis situations, desire for a dependable world, prejudice, certainty of faith, openness to change within the church, need for religious absolutism, need for unchanging structures, feelings of isolation, a sense of life purpose, and drug culture orientation.

Older Lutherans favor a stable and predictable world, whereas younger Lutherans place less value upon orderliness and the preservation of the past. However, there is no difference between generations in their desire for a controllable world—one that is stimulating and enjoyable. Neither is there a marked contrast between young and old in the number of those who prefer a life of detachment—a life that often is identified with the counter culture. The oldest generation, ages 50-65, rivals the youngest in their attraction to this way of life that escapes the demanding and pushing world.

The ages of 21 and 22 mark a time of flux and searching, a time when a large number of young people have suspended judgment in what they believe. With respect to belief scores, beginning at age 15 there is a drop to a low point, ages 21-22. Following these ages there is a sharp increase in acceptance of beliefs to about age 30. Thereafter, the curve rises steadily to age 65. It is evident that fewer youth than adults know the personal aspects of the Christian faith such as certainty of faith, an awareness of a personal, caring God, and a positive attitude toward life and death. Fewer of the youth, in fact less than half, live in a gospel awareness that constitutes the heart of Lutheran piety.

Lutheran youth's lack of certainty about their faith is matched by an inattention to practices of piety which stimulate and awaken faith. It is with respect to personal practices of a faith that the contrast between generations is especially marked. No more than one in five youth sees his Christian beliefs as underlying his whole approach to life. This contrasts with one out of two adults. Also, no more than 12% of the youth read their Bibles daily or even once a week. This percentage of Lutheran young people is less than one-third the percentage (42%) who ten years ago read their Bibles daily or weekly.

Tension is high between youth and adults on matters of social issues. There is an impatience of youth mingled with strong feelings about what many see as their church's present lack of involvement in social issues. It is the conviction of the majority (57%) that far too little has been done. Nevertheless, youth agree with adults that it is equally important to preach the gospel and to work toward improving the well-being of people. The problem for more of the youth is that they feel these two emphases are out of balance.

Most youth would restyle the traditional role of the clergyman. The majority favor treating controversial topics in the Sunday morning sermon. This approach is preferred by twice as many youth as adults. Their sensitivities cry out for actions that match words. They want the church to show it cares about the tragedies of the day. They want their pastor to become more aggressively involved in community and national issues.

Youth serve as the conscience of the church on matters dealing with people who are strongly condemned. Their openness and acceptance of oppressed people stands in sharp contrast with older adults. Only for people who embody a threatening ideology is the "open arms" attitude of youth least in evidence. For instance, no more than one in three would offer friendship or neighborliness to hippies or members of the S.D.S. (Students for a Democratic Society).

In spite of youth's expressed concern over their feelings for people, they do less than adults in performing specific acts of kindness. Apparently many youth have not learned as yet to extend their concern to others in expressions of service. Even more significant is the fact that the majority of youth do not aspire to a life of being used to help others in some way. The values of self-development tend to overshadow the desire to seek meaning in a relationship to God and to others.

The ages 19-22 mark a time when Lutherans are least willing to delay or restrain gratification. In sharp contrast to all other generations, youth of this age are the most involved in questionable personal activities. A majority admit to times when they were drunk, swore, attended X-rated movies, or read pornographic literature. About two in five admitted to sexual intercourse outside of marriage.

A few Lutherans under 22 years of age are oriented to the drug culture. This orientation is characterized by a nonestablishment attitude toward religious structures, a rejection of conventional political identity, and a rejection of the traditional religious expression of family worship. These attitudes, coupled with experimentation and with drugs, characterize a significant group (13%) of Lutheran youth. About 2% report use of drugs beyond experimentation.

The institutional life of the congregation has developed in such a way that youth feel leadership and influence is in the hands of people over age 30. The normal pattern of congregational life tends to isolate youth from the center of concern and decision making. About half do not feel involved or a part of the life of their congregation. Up to one half of the youth say, "Hardly anyone in the congregation would miss me if I stopped going." About half feel that the congregation is not doing a good job of involving youth and teaching them about the Christian life.

The best predictor of which young people will be disappointed in their church is their feeling of how well they fit in with groups in their congregation. The acceptance that youth feel is a strong indicator of how they will evaluate their congregation. Over half the young people feel that they fit in well with the congregation. Those who feel they fit in poorly (43%) may still reflect positive attitudes toward their church if the worship service is an inspiring one. Serious anti-church feelings are expressed by 14% of Lutheran youth ages 15-22.

There is no research evidence of a generation gap between Lutheran youth and adults. The charting of scores on 78 scales by two-year age levels shows no evidence of a radical break or consistent pattern of change between youth and adults. The age differences in scores between youth and adults resemble the differences found between the younger and the older clergy. It should be noted, however, that contrasts between generations are not limited to differences between youth and adults. For instance, the sharpest break in attitudes of prejudice occurs between Lutherans over age 42 and Lutherans below age 42. The sharpest contrast for all age groups in desire for detachment from the world is between youth ages 15-23 and youth ages 24-29. The older youth are less inclined to flee a demanding and pushing world than are Lutherans over age 30.

Misbeliefs are most likely to be found among Lutherans who have the least amount of education. More of the less educated have a need for unchanging structures, a need for religious absolutism, are prejudiced, make exaggerated truth claims, seek a Christian utopianism, and believe in salvation by works. At the same time, more of the less educated Lutherans confess their belief in a personal, caring God, report religious experiences, accept a transcendental world view, and reflect the stance of a conservative or fundamentalist.

College-educated lay men and women are closer to the clergy (than non-college-trained laity) in their rejection of misbeliefs, their attention to religious practices, and their concern for social justice. College graduates, whether clergy or laity, are less likely to be threatened by change, less likely to need rigid structures, and less likely to express hostility toward people different from themselves. On the contrary, both share a common concern to bring healing into the lives and structures of contemporary society.

The widest differences occur between clergy and laity on practices of personal piety and involvement in church and community affairs. The vast majority of lay Lutherans take little or no initiative in making their views known to responsible leaders, and here clergy and laity differ the most. As may be expected, the next greatest difference relates to sharing one's faith and being diligent in the practices of personal piety.

The clergy–lay disparity on salvation by works indicates that Pelagianism is still found in the Lutheran church. Grace through faith in Jesus Christ is yet to be understood by two in five Lutherans.

A provocative difference between clergy and lay beliefs relates to their understanding of Jesus. Clergy accept the dual nature of Jesus. Though the overwhelming majority of Lutheran laity accept the divinity of Jesus, they find it difficult to endorse his humanity.

On dimensions measuring a transcendental reference, certainty of faith, and belief in a personal and caring God, the clergy–lay differences are greatest between clergy and male college graduates, and similarities are greatest between clergy and women college graduates. On basic understanding of religious doctrines, the overwhelming majority of both clergy and laity reject the fundamentalist and the liberal response. Generally, between 80% and 90% of both clergy and laity endorse intermediate choices.

One misbelief that is found more frequently among clergy than laity is exaggeration of the exclusive truth claims of Christianity. Laity may be prone to soft-pedal or deny that Christianity makes a radical truth claim about Jesus as the single source of human salvation. Conversely, some clergy make excessive claims that would narrow the instruments of God's grace to one visible earthly manifestation. Clergy for whom this is true tend to be older in age, prone to fundamentalism, resistant to change, and likely to over-divinize Jesus. Such clergy are, however, a small minority. For both clergy and laity, misbelief is more typical of persons over age 50.

DIFFERENCES AMONG LUTHERANS DUE TO REGION, SEX, AND CHURCH BODY ARE RELATIVELY SMALL

There are differences among Lutherans that seemingly have been exaggerated beyond their true significance. Three commonly observed sources of such differences are region, sex, and church body. Though discernible and measurable differences among Lutherans can be attributed to these sources, it is noteworthy that the differences are relatively small.

Slight differences do exist among Lutherans when divided by region. When an analysis for regional differences controls for the possible effects of church body and congregational size, slight regional effects are noted on beliefs, practices of the faith, and concern for social justice. Lutherans living in the East score slightly lower on major belief dimensions and practices associated with their faith. However, they score slightly higher than those living in other regions on scale dimensions involving concern for social justice.

Size of congregation, by itself, has relatively little overall effect on variations in beliefs, attitudes, and life styles. The one area where size of congregation has unmistakable effects is practice of the faith. There is a direct relationship between congregational size and involvement in church affairs. Persons in congregations of under 250 persons are more likely to report being active than persons in large congregations. A higher proportion of relatively inactive members are found in the larger congregations.

More Lutheran women than Lutheran men reflect a gospel orientation. This difference between men and women is even greater among college-trained Lutherans. A higher proportion of the college-trained women accept a transcendental view of life, know a personal, caring God, reflect an emotional certainty of faith, and consider matters of faith to be "very important."

Lutheran women, whether college-trained or not, are stronger practitioners of their faith. They are more diligent in practices of personal piety and are more willing to share their faith verbally with others. Interestingly, they do not differ from men on levels of congregational activity and church and community involvement.

Contrasts between members of the three Lutheran church bodies is one of degree, not of kind. All three bodies are conservative on the whole, stress the Christocentric nature of the faith, set the limits of the faith, and express loyalty and support for church programs. There are no significant differences between the church bodies in level of prejudice or general orientation to change. Neither are there significant differences in congregational activities, degree of hostility to the church, or involvement in questionable activities.

A higher proportion of LC-MS members consistently show greater willingness to clearly define the limits of the Christian faith, saying in effect that a person must believe thus and so or he is not a Christian. There is a stronger emphasis upon the Christocentric nature of the Christian faith among LC-MS members. More members of the LC-MS are willing to insist upon the truth of the Christian faith to the point of embodying that truth in a particular form of the institutional church. Members of the LC-MS are more strongly insistent upon the verbal inspiration of Scripture, denial of evolutionary theory, acceptance of charismatic gifts, maintenance of the pastoral Office of the Keys and spiritual discipline, and the depravity of man.

Members of the LCA and the ALC are the more highly oriented toward church involvement in social issues, while more members of the LC-MS are inclined to resist involvement. Members of the LCA more frequently value service to others and the ethical life than do members of the other church bodies. Members of the LCA and the ALC are more inclined toward openness to change in practices within the church than are members of the LC-MS. Members of the LC-MS are more highly involved in personal practices of piety and personal evangelism than are those of the LCA or the ALC. Also, members of the LC-MS show a higher degree of biblical knowledge than do members of the LCA or the ALC.

Members of the LCA are more inclined to express belief in salvation by works, while LC-MS members show the least amount of acceptance of this doctrine. Members of the LCA are more inclined to endorse statements reflecting American "religion-in-general" than are members of the LC-MS. The LCA tends to show a slightly higher level of disappointment with the church among its members.

Implications

Our goal in this research project and in this report of the findings has been to use responsibly the knowledge, skills, and techniques of the social sciences in service to the church and its task. In pursuit of that goal we include this final section. Here we draw some of the implications of our findings. These implications are several steps removed from the empirical data. They are the result of the best judgment of individual authors as to the meaning of the findings for the church. As such they are subject to the extent of the limited knowledge and perception of the individual, as well as his biases, known and unknown. Nevertheless they are offered as a stimulus to exploration and development of the applicability of the findings to the life of God's people.

IMPLICATIONS FOR CHRISTIAN EDUCATORS

No single curriculum for all Lutherans can conceivably do the job. Many curricula are needed for a widely heterogeneous population.

Specialization in educational ministry should be in terms of the present beliefs, values, attitudes, and even practices of individuals. The significant characteristics of the wide heterogeneity are quite different from those frequently cited. Specialization in educational ministry will likely be less than significant if it is specialization on the basis of region; congregational size; congregational location (inner city, suburban, urban, open country); church body or synod; occupation; sex; general educational level; or even age. If one can explain 10% of the variations in beliefs, attitudes, or habitual behaviors by knowing such things as age, educational level, sex, and geographical location, one can explain 30% or 40% of the variation knowing other beliefs, values, attitudes, and behaviors. This further implies that curricula need to help legitimize, and assist facing the implications of, individual difference.

There is a remarkable consistency to the systems of belief, value, attitude, opinion, and action exhibited by Lutherans. Therefore, educators would do well to expect that if they change people's beliefs or values in specific ways, then people's attitudes, opinions, and even patterns of behavior are likely to change in specific, relatively predictable ways—and *vice versa.*

This means that educators cannot expect to do just anything and get good results. This also means that it is not unwise, but reasonable, to teach for specific learnings and objectives. This does not mean that educators should expect, with one set of procedures, to reach the same objective with a heterogeneous group of learners. But it does mean that with careful application of sound learning theory *and a precise knowledge of the individual learner,* education for very specific outcomes is not only reasonable but should be possible in practice. *A Study of Generations* data give numerous examples of how relatively slight variations at one point are rather regularly associated with very specific variations at other points in the specific combinations of belief, value, attitude, opinion, and behavior. *A Study of Generations* provides evidence of spiritual and psychological laws rigorous as laws in the physical universe.

As an example of the above, it would be wise for Christian educators to place a stronger emphasis on the humanity of Jesus Christ, or, even better, on the duality of his nature as both God and man. Why? Because Lutherans in the United States in 1970 were commonly separating the two natures of Christ and exhibiting a very strong tendency to over-emphasize the divinity of Jesus almost to the exclusion of his humanity. And those who most emphatically de-emphasized the humanity of Jesus tended to be more generally resistant to change, more authoritarian, and more prejudiced in their attitudes toward others; while those who more clearly recognized our Lord's humanity or kept their view of his two natures in balance, tended generally to be more ready to take the initiative on church and public issues and to be more forgiving in their relationships with others.

Contrary to what some theologians are saying about the contemporary irrelevance of the distinction, it will likely be highly relevant for Christian educators to conceive of their task in terms of the difference between (a) living in, believing, experiencing, and accepting the gospel of grace, faith, hope, relationship, and forgiveness; and (b) living under the law in the sense of structure, achievement, authority, right and wrong, and justice. Or, putting it another way: the difference between (a) a supernatural, grace orientation to life; and (b) a natural, achievement orientation to life.

The two most salient factors or themes running through the configurations of belief, value, attitude, opinion, and behavior contrast these two ways of life as (a) the heart of Lutheran piety, and (b) misbelief in a classic theological sense, or, life under the law in a full theological sense.

It is important and necessary to enable people to gain greater knowledge of the Bible. Teach the facts of the Bible, Bible history, and church history. Two small factors in A Study of Generations data are relevant here. One factor identified biblical ignorance with belief in salvation by works; the other factor identified biblical knowledge with a gospel orientation to life in the sense of greater tendency to approach life situations of relationship with other people with a gospel perspective rather than a democratic, humanistic, or authoritarian emphasis. Furthermore, whereas 10 years ago 43% of Lutheran youth reported regular Bible reading, now 10% so report. Yet the vast majority of youth are concerned about the same religious questions. Still further, a transcendental world view in these data is associated with awareness of the historicity of the faith.

If one conceives of education primarily as planned social change, one can expect about two-thirds of Lutherans to be relatively open to variety and change and about one-third relatively resistant. As regards matters of openness to the church's involvement in issues of social justice and change in social structures, educators need to recognize that most Lutherans are liberal in their social attitudes and favor goals of social justice, but are divided as to *how* such goals should be attained. About 50% are favorable to the church *as body* as an instigator of social change, but about 70% emphasize the importance of respect for individual conscience. Practical evidence of this is found in the fact that most Lutherans want their church and pastor to raise the issues, provide guidance, and be a social conscience to them and the nation. But they want this done in a setting which allows discussion and interaction, not from the pulpit. They want guidance and counsel with final decision left to their own consciences in their own individual situations more commonly than they desire use of the pastoral office or name of the church as a source of power in society.

Assuming it is reasonable to concentrate one's efforts on those who need it most, findings imply that it is time for educators to give special attention to *(a)* the less sophisticated, less well educated, who have less power and position, who tend to be less verbally and ideologically oriented; and *(b)* persons ages 19-22. Special attention to the former is required because of their greater tendency toward the way of life identified above as life under the law; special attention to the latter because they consistently show the least clarity and conviction of what they believe, whether right or wrong.

Educational ministry for both of the above groups should include a strong dose of experience of mutuality, feeling, and caring for one another. To illustrate in terms of youth ages 15-29, 63% are touched by anxiety over their own faith and feelings of isolation, while the best predictor of how the young adult views his church is the degree to which he feels he belongs among, and can identify with, the people he thinks of as the church.

Therefore, one of the two most significant implications for educators (together with the law–gospel distinction) is the importance of keeping two emphases in education in balance: *(a)* learning to *experience* and *express* belonging, mutuality, caring, and relating with people; and *(b)* learning to *know* the Bible, church history, and doctrine—the content of the faith. Overemphasis on *(a)* may lead to a tendency toward belief in salvation by works. Overemphasis on *(b)* may lead to, or be accompanied by, rigidity, authoritarianism, inhumanity, and emphasis on conformity.

There are indications in the data that it would likely be quite important to help youth to deal particularly with the question of authority. A finding showed participation in the drug culture to be associated centrally with resistance to authority. About 2% are involved in the drug culture, and about 10-13% are set up for it should they get into the wrong environment.

Christian educators are on the right track with the new confirmation ministry, with its emphasis on lifelong confirmation education and loose identification of who are the teachers and who are the learners across ages and from the breadth of backgrounds and situations of the whole Christian family. The preponderance of Lutherans of all ages do not believe they and others learn best from peers alone or oldsters alone, but learn best from a wide variety of sources where both young teach old and old teach young.

Sympathetic educators will demonstrate greater awareness of the needs of people who are not in nuclear families, especially young adults and very old people, who have the strongest feelings of pessimism, are the most open to change, and show the highest proportion believing in salvation by works.

IMPLICATIONS FOR LUTHERAN THEOLOGIANS

Law and gospel are not merely theological constructs abstracted from experience. They are basic experienced realities in the individual lives of God's saints and sinners. The proper relationship between law and gospel for men in this time must be carefully worked through by those called by God to be the teachers of the church.

Men within and without the church who live under the law experience life as demand. This results in idolatry of form and letter over spirit and grace. The consequences for individual men encompass all of life in every relationship, bringing about frustration, meaninglessness, and alienation from God, self, other men, and creation. Within the church this produces a warped religiosity that inhibits, limits, and misdirects the church. Leaders and teachers of the church need to develop a sensitivity to the anguish of those living under the law.

Preaching and teaching the gospel has effects. Men are freed from the law to live in grace. While free, the man living in grace confronts the dynamic tension imposed by his finitude. He needs the support and help of the brethren in community. Fundamental to that support is recognition and acceptance of the diversity and richness of God's grace and the uniqueness of each man's gift of grace in his life. Models of life in grace tend to freeze into the rigidity of law. Theologians need to set the limits and the parameters of life in grace but avoid the building of models held to be applicable to all men or even to large groups of men. Life in grace is best defined by exclusion—what it *is not* rather than what it *is*.

Lutherans yearn for a valid expression for today of the catholicity of the church. There is a sense of its unity and wholeness and a search for ways to know and feel that unity. Theologians must continue efforts to find acceptable formulas expressing catholicity while maintaining continuity with past confessions.

In a pluralistic and syncretistic world Lutherans presently are uneasy. The relationship between the church and the world is not clear and at present is uncomfortable. The teachers of the church need to provide impetus toward clarity for the church living in the world.

The office of the ministry is respected by Lutherans but limited in acceptable scope. There is limited acceptance of exercise of the Office of the Keys, either binding or loosing sin. The concept of spiritual discipline is relatively unknown.

If Lutheran theology opts for a contemporary theology that empties the truth claim of the faith, most people presently in the Lutheran church will be driven into fundamentalism. If Lutheran theology opts for fundamentalism, close to half of the people presently in the Lutheran church will be driven into liberalism. Lutheran theologians must find ways to avoid either extreme.

If Lutheran theology goes in the direction of contemporary emphasis upon a "religionless Christianity" based upon the assumption that twentieth-century man is completely secularized, a large majority of those presently Lutheran will be confused, troubled, and will not comprehend what is being taught. The "Christian mind" is still present among Lutherans. Theologians who have compassion for the church will speak to that "mind."

Lutherans do not have a clear conception of the nature or reason for mission work. Appeals to support mission work in order to save the souls of heathen who would otherwise perish in hell are simply not heard by most. Lutherans need from the theologians a clarification of the relationship between the truth claim of the Christian faith and the other religions of men. This may take the form of a contemporary framing of an answer to the "Why some and not others?" question.

The doctrine of the church is subject to severe distortion by a sizeable minority of Lutherans in the identification of a visible church body with the truth. Lutheran theologians need to provide a doctrine of the church that is less susceptible to distortion by human psychological need than the visible–invisible dichotomy.

Lutherans do not understand the doctrine of the union of the two natures of Christ. For most the humanity of Jesus is an empty humanity, devoid of the reality of Jesus as a human being like the rest of us. Theologians must find ways to support and teach the unity of the two natures and an adequate and acceptable definition of the human nature of Jesus.

The divinity of Jesus is most strongly isolated from his humanity by those within the church who are living under the law without knowledge of grace. For such persons a divine Jesus as a new lawgiver, a second Moses, legitimizes their present stance of hostility toward others. Theologians must produce an understanding of the divine nature of Jesus that is more resistant to perception of Jesus as lawgiver.

Scripture is accepted as God's authoritative Word by most, but the strongest support for a doctrine of verbal inspiration comes from those who are highly fundamentalist and committed to the modern charismatic movement. Knowing Christ as Lord and Savior and believing in the historicity of his person and life is not made dependent upon a particular doctrine of Scripture by most Lutherans. Theologians, already embroiled in the task of expressing the authority of Scripture, must be aware of this reality in the mind of the church.

A Study of Generations has demonstrated that social science techniques and procedures can accurately and reliably assess constructs derived from theology and aspects of human belief and behavior that have been thought to be inaccessible to empirical research. Theologians must seek to cooperate with social scientists so that the tools available can be brought into service to the calling of the theologian.

Section IV

Appendix A

How the Study Was Conducted

An important aspect of any research study is the account of how the study was conducted and how the data were analyzed. The validity and reliability of the data are contingent upon the care that is used in carrying out every detail of the study which may affect its findings. Because this study is large, involving a complexity of detail, it will not be possible to include all of the documents that would be of interest to the social scientists concerned about research methodology. Therefore reference will be given to the appropriate documents which are on file at Youth Research Center with the understanding that these can be supplied on request.

The two year research entitled *A Study of Generations* began 1 August 1969 and ended 31 December 1971. Inasmuch as the first 14 months were a time of preparation and collecting data, they will be reported as a developmental phase. The last 15 months were devoted quite exclusively to data analysis and reporting. Because these two phases were quite distinct the report which follows will treat first the developmental phase and then the analytic and reporting phase.

Developmental Phase

The study was not funded until there was assurance from the presidents of the three Lutheran bodies (The American Lutheran Church,

Lutheran Church—Missouri Synod, and Lutheran Church in America) that such a study would meet with their approval. Once this had been granted and the study had been funded, the first step was to secure a Steering Committee of men who were well known in the Lutheran church and who would give the supervision and guidance that would be needed in a study of this magnitude and importance.

The research proposal which became the basis for the grant given by Lutheran Brotherhood outlined five steps that would be taken in the developmental stage:

1. Contact will be made with those responsible for some aspect of the broad spectrum of concern and work within the Lutheran church. These key leaders will be invited to indicate what they consider vital information in their area of responsibility and what they would like to learn from such a survey.
2. Contact will be made with a sampling of church members served by some of the church agencies. These representatives of various sub-cultures or groups within the Lutheran church will be queried as to their attitudes, feelings, values, and beliefs. Their open-ended responses will be used to develop items indicative of the diversity of thought among Lutheran laity.
3. Items or scales will be selected from other national surveys whose normative data can be used for comparative purposes.
4. A Steering Committee of Lutheran representatives and social scientists will be used to screen the survey items. A final screening will be given by those who assemble as an Advisory Council.
5. The survey instrument, once completed, will be used to collect data from approximately 6,000 Lutherans, ages 17-60, using standardized procedures. Data from the survey will be used to establish scales and carry out whatever analyses are essential to establish the information as scientifically reliable and valid.

The steps proposed above resolved themselves into four basic tasks: conceptualizing the study, developing the survey instrument, securing the sample, and collecting the data. The time schedule to complete these four tasks was established as follows:

1. Conceptualization: 1 September 1969—30 January 1970
2. Instrument Development: 1 October 1969—1 May 1970
3. Securing Sample Participation: 1 February 1970—1 August 1970
4. Data Collection: 1 June 1970—30 September 1970

CONCEPTUALIZING THE STUDY

Inasmuch as this was the first time such a study of the membership of the three major Lutheran bodies had been carried out, a special effort was made to involve a wide range of resources in conceptualizing the study. Four distinct sources were probed:

1. Lutheran leaders (theologians, administrators, executives)
2. Rank-and-file Lutherans
3. Research literature
4. Social science consultants

The results of this preliminary search for information culminated in seven documents which were reviewed by a group of 59 Lutheran leaders who assembled for a review conference 30 January 1970. What follows is a brief description of how the research team carried out the task of conceptualization.

Lutheran leaders. A systematic effort was made to hear what key Lutherans want to know about their church. Therefore all men in positions of church body administrative leadership and all who were presidents of colleges and seminaries were informed of the study and invited to present their requests, suggestions, concerns, and hypotheses. Approximately 75 denominational executives and educators responded to this letter of invitation with suggestions that could help shape *A Study of Generations*. Of these, 35 enlarged their views in conference telephone calls with the research team during late September and October 1969. Recommendations from these church leaders concerning the content and limitations of the study organized around four foci:

1. The ministry and mission of the church
2. Institutional loyalty
3. Tolerance of diversity
4. Spiritual experience

Concerns about a few miscellaneous areas of content provided a fifth category. All who were consulted seemed to assume that "of course" beliefs would be assessed. A summary of what they shared is entitled "A Summary of Requests, Suggestions, Concerns and Hypotheses from Church Leaders." * (An asterisk will be used throughout Section IV indicating documents available upon request from Youth Research Center, 122 West Franklin Avenue, Minneapolis, Minnesota 55404.) The procedures used in handling these initial data are listed below.

1. All telephone conversations were recorded and transcribed with the exception of four for which the notes of various participants were collated.
2. Every request, suggestion, concern, hypothesis, and issue was carefully identified in every letter and every telephone transcription or compilation of notes.
3. Each of the above was excerpted in cogent form, but in words as close to the author's as possible.
4. Each excerpt was placed on a single 3 x 5 card.

5. Cards were sorted by one researcher in such a way that excerpts were allowed to group themselves on the basis of common content, similarity of utility, or contingency and interrelationship of concept. No preconceived categories were used. The data were allowed to organize themselves according to apparent internal consistencies.

6. After several re-sortings, mergers, and splittings of categories, the researcher identified seven major categories and 27 subcategories and defined each with a descriptive name.

7. Excerpt cards were numbered on the back, and the first researcher's organization of them was recorded.

8. The other two members of the research team were then given a scrambled deck of excerpt cards and a list of all the categories. They were then asked to sort all of the cards into the 27 subcategories without any previous knowledge of how they had been sorted by the first researcher.

9. Interresearcher agreement on the categorization of each excerpt card was then calculated as an estimate of reliability of the seven major categories and the 27 subcategories. (Perfect agreement equals 1.00.)

> Highest agreement between any two researchers on the seven major categories = .82.
>
> Highest agreement between any two researchers on all 27 subcategories = .65.
>
> Agreement among all three researchers on the seven major categories = .78.
>
> Agreement among all three researchers on all 27 subcategories = .62.

These levels of agreement are within the range of interrater reliability that is generally accepted in research literature.

Rank-and-file Lutherans. Sentence completion surveys were used during the period November 1969 to February 1970 to capture the thinking and feeling tone of a wide variety of Lutheran laity. The data compiled from approximately 750 Lutherans were used not only in conceptualizing the study, but in developing the survey instrument. There were three major sources of this preliminary information: subscribers to *Event* (a magazine published by the ALC Men), LC-MS parochial high school students, and Lutheran church college religion classes. A brief comment will be made about each.

A sentence completion form with an accompanying letter was sent by the editor of *Event* to a randomly selected list of 500 subscribers. Each of these subscribers was informed of the study and was asked to assist in the preliminary step by giving his frank response to a randomly selected set of five of the item stems listed below:

> I am losing confidence in . . .
>
> I am strongly convinced that . . .
>
> A Lutheran is . . .
>
> The world today is . . .

The most pressing problem is . . .
The most important thing in life is . . .
I have changed my beliefs about . . .
Religion is . . .
Pastors . . .
In the church, adults . . .
In the church, youth . . .
The church should be more . . .
A Christian is . . .
The most important belief I have is . . .
As a Christian the most difficult thing for me is . . .

These sentence completion forms were sent also to two Lutheran high schools (LC-MS) in the Minneapolis area and to another (ALC) in Sioux Falls in December. Similarly, questionnaires were sent to the deans of 12 Lutheran colleges who had volunteered to assist in this preliminary step by administering the questionnaire to students. (The colleges are located in New York, Indiana, Wisconsin, Minnesota, South Dakota, Nebraska, Texas, and California.) For both the high schools and the colleges the form was given by teachers of religion classes.

No effort was made to follow nonrespondents or to establish the representativeness of the 750 questionnaires that were received. Such precautions were not deemed necessary inasmuch as the purpose of this preliminary survey was only to explore the range of expression that may characterize rank-and-file Lutherans and to gain some estimate, though limited, of a reaction.

The sentence completion data were compiled by Reverend Gordon Solomonson. His report, which gives a classification of the responses and the number of times each was mentioned (with appropriate illustrations) is entitled "Summary of Preliminary Sentence Completion Data." *

Research literature. An unusual opportunity became available to build on the findings of past research. The principal investigator of the study had served as editor of a handbook which made a critical review of the past four decades of research where religion is variable. The manuscripts for this comprehensive and thorough review of thousands of research studies (published June 1971 under the title *Research on Religious Development: A Comprehensive Handbook*) were available to the research team. Extracts were made from these chapters of research generalizations pertinent to *A Study of Generations*. These summaric statements, based on the 22 chapters in the pending publication, were prepared in a third document entitled "Research Generalizations Pertinent to *A Study of Generations*." *

Inasmuch as the above review of research did not include studies published in 1968 and 1969, a second document was prepared entitled

"A Report on Recent Literature and Recent Dissertations." * Special note was made of major studies to which linkages could be made. Those especially singled out were studies by Quinley, Hadden, Hussel, Backus, Chweh, Metz, Duncombe, Rokeach, Sommerfeld, Kersten, and Glock and Stark. In addition, the five volumes of *Handbook of Social Psychology* (1968) were also reviewed and examined for additional input. In light of the sources available to the research team it is reasonable to assume that the research team took cognizance of previous research that was pertinent to *A Study of Generations.*

A team, not an individual, was doing the research; therefore, basic assumptions with which each researcher was approaching the task needed to be stated and then clarified and shaped by the whole team. Also, the team was convinced that one of the best ways to avoid unknowingly becoming a victim of one's own biases is to state them and make them explicit. Therefore, at this point in the early stages of the study, a document was written entitled "A Statement of the Assumptions and Conceptualization upon Which the Project, *A Study of Generations,* Is to Be Carried Out." * In brief form, the four basic assumptions were:

1. *Wholeness.* There is a wholeness to human life that we cannot ever exhaust; therefore, no description or attempted description, scientific or otherwise, will ever be complete. Any attempt at observation, measurement, or description is dependent upon a particular way of slicing into the wholeness of human existence. In other words, we will have to take a point of view.
2. *Methodological Determinism.* When cutting into the flux of human life to observe and measure in a study such as this, we can expect to find lawful relationships.
3. *Methodological Individualism.* The regularities that we maintain are present in human life can be identified through a focus on individuals, not groups.
4. *Metaphysical Indeterminism.* We elect to adopt a model of man as a conscious searcher after meaning, as an active agent in determining the nature and quality of his life. We see man as an actor, not as a passive, determined organism. Man is free as an interactive or transactive being, but only within very rigid limits.

Translated into terms used in the research literature, the requests and suggestions from church leaders consisted of a desire for information about beliefs, values, attitudes, opinions, life styles, and situational or environmental constraints; therefore, two additional documents were written as more complete statements of assumptions and definitions of terms. The documents were entitled "Further Explication of the Model of Man Which Is to Be the Basis of *A Study of Generations,* and Comments on the Problems of Measurement or Assessment Which Result" * and "Beliefs, Values, Opinions, and Attitudes (Defined and Related to a

Theological Framework)." * The following are simplified summaries of our definitions of basic terms:

1. By *belief* we mean a proposition held by an individual as part of a model, explicated or unexplicated, that has a form of an ontological statement; that is, a statement that deals primarily with the question of existence-nonexistence and probability-improbability. Beliefs have to do with what persons hold to exist or not to exist; what is given and what is possible, or what is impossible.

2. *Values* are beliefs of a special type. People ascribe relationships that sum up to a positive or negative view (evaluation) of an object that is physical, social, or ideal. These evaluations guide selective attention and behavior toward or away from the object. These evaluations also, in effect, ascribe moral quality to the process of interaction with the objects and to the objects themselves. We locate values in the persons doing the valuing. We hold that all values come from one fundamental idea: good and evil. The process of valuing, therefore, places all things and interactions in a hierarchy. This definition acknowledges values to be a special form of beliefs. The distinction, then, between beliefs and values is a distinction between beliefs-in (the existence, the probability, or possibility of any thing) and beliefs-that (any thing is better or worse, more important or less important, etc.).

3. *Opinions* are propositions that are deductions from or rationalizations of beliefs and values. They may or may not be logically consistent with a person's beliefs and values, but they will be psychologically consistent.

4. An *attitude* is a readiness or predisposition to act or to perform specific behaviors when given specific stimuli in a specific environment. It represents the action component of the entire model of beliefs-in, beliefs-about *(values)*, rationalizations *(opinions)*, and inclinations to behavior.

Consultations. During the months of November and December 1969 private consultations were held with the following persons concerning research design, data collection and analysis, sampling, definition of terms, scope of the study, and the appropriateness of conceptualization and assumptions:

Dr. May Brodbeck, University of Minnesota
Dr. James Dittes, Yale Divinity School
Dr. Charles Glock, University of California, Berkeley
Dr. Arthur Johnson, University of Minnesota
Dr. Ronald Johnstone, Central Michigan College
Dr. Kent Knutson, Wartburg Theological Seminary
Dr. E. Clifford Nelson, St. Olaf College
Dr. Richard Sommerfield, Capital University
Dr. Bernard Spilka, University of Denver
Dr. Raymond Willis, University of Minnesota

A consultation was also held with a group of 39 Lutheran executives and educators who came at their own expense to an all-day conference on 30 January 1970. In advance of the conference, each participant received the following study documents:

1. "Research Generalizations Pertinent to *A Study of Generations*" *
2. "A Report on Recent Literature" *
3. "A Summary of Requests, Suggestions, Concerns and Hypotheses from Church Leaders" *
4. "A Statement of the Assumptions and Conceptualization" *
5. "Further Explication of the Model of Man" *
6. "Conceptualization—*Study of Generations*" * (described later)
7. "Proposed Items and Scales" * (described later)

The conference was structured in such a way that those present were informed of what the study would attempt to learn, how it would be carried out, and which items formed the item pool from which the survey instrument would be developed. In order to hear the reactions of the men, both to what they read and what they heard, opportunities were provided not only for discussion, but for written reactions to the initial conceptualization.

Discussion was not recorded, so no transcriptions or content analyses were made of it. Written reactions were grouped and organized according to recommendations for additions, recommendations for deletions, and criticism of the conceptualization of the study and content of the item pool.

The tentative decision to interview a subsample of the persons taking the survey was powerfully reinforced at this meeting. Many participants were concerned that, unknown to the researchers, different generations of respondents might derive drastically different meaning from the same questions or statements in the survey instrument. On the basis of discussion a decision was made to devote approximately half of the interview to people's emotional and ideational reactions to specific terms.

Inasmuch as the response of the participants was generally one of wholehearted support and enthusiasm for what had been developed to that date, steps were taken to begin the next two parallel tasks: developing the survey instrument and securing the sample of persons to be surveyed.

DEVELOPING THE SURVEY INSTRUMENT

Building of the survey instrument really began in October 1969 with an investigation of the relevant literature of previous research. For the meeting with church leaders, 30 January 1970, nearly 1,000 items from 70 different sources had been selected as possibilities for the survey instrument from the hundreds of scales and item sets carefully screened from previous researchers. Validity, reliability, and comparability of groups used for reliability studies were all carefully studied in the selection of items that would best assess the matters recommended for study by church leaders and other consultants. An item pool and a 71-page detailed description of all item sources and histories, including matters of conceptualization, operationalization, reliability, and validity, formed a document entitled "Conceptualization—Study of Generations." *

The task of finalizing the survey instrument occupied the months of February through May 1970. It included:

1. Finalizing the conceptual framework
2. Field testing the item pool
3. Preparing survey books I, II, and III with appropriate answer sheets

Finalizing the conceptual framework. The suggestions and criticisms of the January 30 consultation were reviewed by the research team and used in arriving at a final decision of what should be probed through the survey instrument and what should be collected by means of personal interview. An eighth document was prepared entitled "A Theoretical Context for the Study of Generations" * that could serve as a theoretical statement and conceptual framework for a focus on generations. (A brief review of that theoretical statement is found in Chapter 10.)

By the January 30 meeting the research team was emphasizing a model of man as an interactive or transactive system in whom beliefs and values influence attitudes, opinions, or life styles, and in whose experience situational constraints (environment) and life styles (actions) likewise influence opinions, attitudes, values, and beliefs. Neither a phenomenological nor a behavioristic perspective alone was accepted, but both perspectives were accepted as making a valid contribution to the conceptualization, the decisions to be made about data collection, and the corresponding decisions about data analysis. The research team did not take a singular stance about possibilities of cause and effect (from beliefs to behaviors or from behaviors to beliefs alone), but took, rather, an open stance toward both possibilities and prepared to collect and analyze data accordingly.

This position was not significantly challenged in group discussion or in individual consultations, though the brunt of Lutheran theology and education has implicitly assumed the phenomenological position that beliefs lead to behaviors.

The Steering Committee was consulted and provided significant counsel throughout as the conceptualization evolved and each document was written.

Pretesting items. Several matters about which the church leaders were concerned had apparently not been researched previously. Several sets of new items were developed by the research team as a result of these recommendations since, in most such cases, the literature of previous research did not prove to be a good source. Additions to the item pool after the January 30 consultation concerned law-gospel, other value assumptions, now orientation, church roles, clergy roles, woman roles, youth roles, voluntarism, magic motif, sex attitudes, generational trust, general trust and acceptance, personal witness activities, quietism, personal *agape* service, voting behavior, irreligion, drug use, educational experience, and verbal frankness.

The specific wording of a wide variety of items was modified as a result of general criticism, and a few items were dropped because of apparent irrelevance—all as a result of the group consultation.

A preliminary version of the survey instrument consisting of 932 items was ready in mimeographed form for pretesting beginning the second week in March. Ten congregations in the Southwestern Minnesota District of The American Lutheran Church had agreed to provide persons who would take the pretest survey instrument and group-evaluate the items. This pretest data collection was conducted by Reverend Gordon Solomonson, Southwestern Minnesota District Parish Education Director. He selected congregations representing as wide a range of size, constituency, location, and "theological flavor" as his many years of experience within the District gave him awareness.

Pastors of the participating congregations were each instructed to select 20 to 25 people as follows: "The 25 people should represent varied and different backgrounds, e.g., businessman, farmer, employer, employee, Democrat, Republican, new converts to the Lutheran faith, lifelong Lutherans, young, middle-aged, older members (up to age 65), male and female, radical and conservative." One hundred fifty-five persons from 10 congregations spent three and one-half hours completing the pretest questionnaire and discussing the experience for a half hour following at one of eight group administrations between March 12 and 19. They were told that their responses would help develop the survey instrument but would not be included among the survey data. Details of administrative procedure were evaluated and perfected in the process. The following conclusions were drawn from this field testing:

1. A survey that would take the average person three hours to complete could be used without deleterious effects due to length, since people who were forewarned of the time involved did not hesitate to participate. Secondly, at every administration, after spending three and one-half hours taking the survey, people requested opportunity to stay longer to discuss the issues raised by such an interesting and relevant questionnaire. Thirdly, present data showed a minimum of fatigue effects.

2. A maximum of 750 items should be included in a three-hour survey instrument.
3. Use of a broad variety of lengths, types, and forms of items at random throughout would likely enhance the motivative characteristics of an apparently already interesting survey.

Portions of the preliminary version of the survey instrument were pretested in a variety of communities in Illinois, Indiana, the Dakotas, Colorado, Texas, and Missouri by three ALC Regional Parish Education Directors (Rev. Thomas Smrcka, Rev. Stephen B. Knudsen, and Mr. Leonard Nicoley). Whereas the pretesting in Minnesota was primarily to secure a presample of data and to develop methods of survey administration, this more scattered pretesting was predominantly to secure item evaluation information. In this case all participants were asked to answer only random subsections of the questionnaire and then to evaluate each item by selecting one or more of the following critical comments for each:

1. Item okay
2. Hard to understand, unclear (underline)
3. Cannot be answered "yes" or "no"
4. Can have more than one meaning (underline)
5. Uses words I do not yet understand (underline words)
6. A personal matter that is nobody's business and I would resent being asked about it
7. Other reason (please describe on back of page containing the question)

The persons involved in this evaluation were almost all adults participating in some parish education endeavor. In order to be sure that youth were among the critics of the pretest survey instrument, research assistants administered most of the questionnaire to groups of University of Minnesota and Mankato State University students who also provided evaluative data according to the format described above. A small number of Lutheran clergy from the Twin Cities area, in addition to the members of the Steering Committee, also evaluated the preliminary version of the survey item by item.

Evaluative data from all sources were tabulated and were remarkably consistent. Under the careful scrutiny of the Steering Committee the preliminary version of the instrument underwent two major revisions based on evaluative data and pretest data analysis.

Pretest data from the 155 participants in Southwestern Minnesota were summarized and analyzed by the following techniques:

1. Descriptive item statistics including mean, standard deviation, and frequency and percentage distributions
2. Interitem correlations

    3. Cluster analysis (homogeneous keying according to DuBois, Loevinger, and Gleser, 1953) including calculation of Hoyt Reliability for every emerging cluster

Frequency distributions were studied to identify:

1. Unnecessary, irrelevant, or useless response categories
2. Need for additional or modified response categories
3. Obvious misunderstandings
4. Nondiscriminating items
5. Patterns of response across sets of items, suggesting reordering the sequence of items
6. Items eliciting unusually high percentages of nonresponse
7. Logical inconsistencies among responses

Interitem correlations were studied particularly for evidence of undesirable item overlap.

All items had been carefully identified and organized according to specific constructs they were intended to operationalize. Each was also categorized according to whether it was thought to assess primarily a belief, value, attitude, opinion, behavior, or situational constraint. All constructs and their related item sets within each of those six areas of assessment were arranged in rank order from most to least important to the conceptualization and objectives of the overall study. Items were also cataloged and compared for duplication and omissions according to the subjects and/or issues to which they were related. Finally, items were grouped empirically according to patterns of pretest response by cluster analysis as mentioned above. All empirical clusters were compared with the construct(s) that the clustered items were thought to operationalize and with other items hypothesized to represent that construct but that did not cluster, or that clustered with other items unexpectedly. Clusters were, of course, compared carefully with item sets or scales borrowed from other researches to see if they matched—cluster for scale, cluster for set. The fact of a good match with substantial internal consistency reliability was taken as some empirical evidence of the validity of both the hypothesized underlying construct and the items for use in researching adult Lutherans. There were cases of poor agreement between an empirically derived cluster and a previously reported measure or an item set theoretically representing a specific construct. Sometimes nonclustering items were dropped if found to be uncorrelated and apparently superfluous when standing alone. Other times the researchers gained new insight into concepts or possible interrelationships among hypothetical constructs.

Developing the survey books and answer sheets. Throughout the entire process of item analysis the team tried to select and develop a variety of types of items to assess each major variable. The items that were finally included for measuring a specific characteristic often had different numbers of response possibilities, were of varied lengths, and were framed in two or three "language games." We did not think it possible or wise to try to develop a questionnaire in which any one person would find that every item fit his frame of reference or suited his liking. Rather we aimed at a set of items with such a breadth of vocabulary, style, form, and content that every person taking the survey would find some items on each subject that allowed him to express clearly and accurately his beliefs, values, attitudes, and opinions, or to describe his behavior.

The 740 items finally included were selected on the basis of the following criteria:

1. High reliability and particularly construct validity in previous research on comparable or related populations, or in pretesting
2. Singularity of content
3. Clarity
4. Variety of vocabulary and language game
5. Conceptualization either supported by previous research and/or pretest data, or at least not brought into question by pretest results
6. Relevance to the objectives of the study
7. Replication of important research
8. Variety of form
9. Comprehensibility of content and response possibility

With rare exception, enough items were chosen related to each psychological and theological variable to offer the possibility of forming a scale consisting of 6 to 15 items. Sequence was purposely arranged so that often, though not always, the several items assessing a given matter were scattered throughout not only one but all three of the survey books. In order that system and continuity might nevertheless be apparent, each of the three books was a unit by itself: Book I, *Your Beliefs, Values, and You;* Book II, *How You See Yourself and Others;* and Book III, *Your Attitudes and Way of Life.*

Three joined IBM mark-sense answer sheets, one for each book, allowed respondents to draw a single line for each response. This method was chosen because of the economy and accuracy of machine processing of answer sheets, simplicity of response, and familiarity both to most younger respondents and to the Youth Research Center staff.

Detailed records were kept in such a way that all items in the survey instrument can readily be traced from their original form through each stage of modification, if any, to the form in which they appeared in the survey instrument. The 740 items in the survey can be grouped topically with sources as follows:

Beliefs

101 Basic Orientations (Kluckhohn–Strodtbeck, 1961; Schneiderman, 1963)
102 Other Basic Orientations (new by research team)
103 Fundamentalism–Modernism (Gustafson, 1956)
104 Theological Position (Hadden, 1969)
105 Creedal Assent and Personal Commitment (King, 1967)
106 Orthodoxy (Putney–Middleton, 1961)
107 Orthodoxy (Glock–Stark, 1966)
108 Religious Knowledge (Glock–Stark, 1966)
109 Religious Experience (Glock–Stark, 1966)
** (Missing numbers indicate where sets of items were part of the original item pool but were dropped during questionnaire development.)
111 Christian Concepts (Strommen, 1963)
112 Other Christian Doctrines (new by research team)
113 Additional Catechism Assessment (new by research team)
114 Law–Gospel (new by research team)
115 Religious Hostility Toward Modern Jew (Glock–Stark, 1966)

Values

202 Terminal Personal Values (Youth Research Center, 1969; Rokeach, 1969; Stone–Brandel Center, 1968)
205 Importance of Faith (Youth Research Center, 1969)
206 Ethicalism (Stark–Glock, 1968)
207 Devotionalism (Stark–Glock, 1968)
208 Ways of Life (Morris, 1956)
209 Value Assumptions (Wrenn, 1969)
210 Now Orientation (new by research team)
211 Culture (Mead, 1970; new by research team)

Mission and Ministry of the Church

302 Missionary Task Conceptions (Chweh, 1968)
303 Altruism (Maranell, 1966, 1967)
304 Ritualism (Maranell, 1966, 1967)
305 Extrinsic Religion (Allport–Ross, 1967; Feagin, 1964; Allport, 1954; Robinson–Shaver, 1969)
306 Ethicalism (Stark–Glock, 1968)
307 Individual–Social Perspective—selected (Hadden, 1969)
308 Individual–Social Perspective (Hadden, 1967-1968)
310 Clergy Public Affairs—selected (Quinley, 1968)
312 Quietism (new by research team)
315 Woman Roles (new by research team)
316 Youth Roles (new by research team)

Institutional Loyalty

401 Orientation to Change (Neal, 1965)
402 Institutionalization (Jeeves, 1959; Brown, 1962)
403 Traditional Family Ideology (Levinson–Huffmann, 1955)
405 Free Enterprise—selected (Hadden, 1969; Stark–Glock, 1969)
406 Education and Welfare—selected (Hadden, 1967-1968)

407   Social Issues—selected (Youth Research Center, 1969)
408   Church and Worship—selected (Youth Research Center, 1969)
410   National Problems and Draft Resistance (Yankelovich, 1969)
411   Various Programs (Lutheran Brotherhood staff; new by research team)
412   Voluntarism (new by research team)

Selves and Others

501   Dogmatism (King, 1967)
502   Commitment to Intellectual Search (King, 1967)
503   Humanitarianism (Strommen, 1963)
504   Purpose in Life (Crumbaugh, 1968)
505   Social Issues—selected (Youth Research Center, 1969)
506   Generation Gap (Yankelovich, 1969)
507   Concern for Others (Youth Research Center, 1969)
508   Anti-Semitic Beliefs (Selznick–Steinberg, 1969)
509   Concept of a Lutheran (new by research team)
510   Alienation (Spilka, 1969)
512   Fundamentalism—selected (Dynes, 1957)
513   Self as Personal Witness (new by research team)
514   Particularism (Glock–Stark, 1966)
515   Toughmindedness (Eysenck, 1947, 1954; Ferguson, 1944; Kirkpatrick, 1949)
516   Social Distance (Bogardus, 1925, 1933; Westie, 1953)
517   Jungle Ideology (Feagin, 1964)
518   God Relationship (new by research team)
519   Magic Motif (new by research team)
520   Sex Attitudes (Feucht, 1961)
521   Generational Trust (new by research team)
522   General Trust and Acceptance (new by research team)

Life Styles

601   Participation in Congregational Activities (King, 1967)
602   Personal Ties in the Congregation (King, 1967)
603   Financial Behaviors (King, 1967)
604   Financial Attitude (King, 1967)
605   Talking and Reading About Religion (King, 1967)
606   Ritualism (Faulkner–DeJong, 1966)
607   Congregational Life Style (Youth Research Center, 1969)
608   Family Life Style (Youth Research Center, 1969)
609   Intrinsic Religion (Allport–Ross, 1967)
611   Selected Items (Quinley, 1968)
612   Selected Items (Lutheran Brotherhood staff; new by research team)
613   Personal Witness Activities (new by research team)
614   Quietism: Individual–Social (new by research team)
615   Personal Agape Service (new by research team)
616   Voting Behavior (new by research team)
617   Irreligion (new by research team)
618   Drug Use (new by research team)
619   Educational Experience (new by research team)
620   Verbal Frankness (new by research team)

Situational Constraints
     702   Selected Items (Hadden, 1967-1968)
     703   Selected Items (Youth Research Center, 1969)
     704   Selected Items (Lutheran Brotherhood staff; new by research team)
     706   Age (new by research team)
     707   Overseas Experience (new by research team)

SECURING THE SAMPLE

The months of February through June 1970 were used to contact 378 clergymen and gain their cooperation and help in carrying out a survey in their congregations; the task of drawing the sample began in October 1969. What follows is a description of how and why the sample was stratified and drawn, how sample clergymen were involved, and how the second stage sample of Lutheran laymen was selected.

Sampling procedure. A complete printout of all Lutheran congregations from the three church bodies to be involved was generated from the computer storage of Lutheran Brotherhood (based on the ALC 1969 *Yearbook*, the LC-MS 1968 *Statistical Yearbook*, and the LCA 1969 *Yearbook*). This listing classified congregations according to Lutheran church body, size of congregation, and state. This made it possible to stratify the sample and be assured that the random selection of congregations would adequately reflect the right proportion of Lutherans by region and size of congregation. The sample was drawn in this way:

1. A two-stage proportionate stratified random sampling technique was chosen that would reflect the fact that Lutherans are grouped by congregations, but that would concentrate on persons, not congregations. Lists for a sampling frame of persons would have to be secured from congregations. For this practical reason, and because previous study of Lutheran youth had shown variance within congregations was generally less than variance between, the decision was made to draw a first-stage sample of congregations.

2. Previous studies of Lutheran youth had also shown size of congregation to be a significant variable. Parochial statistics were being organized by census area, and the 1970 census would be taken almost simultaneously with *A Study of Generations*. To allow regional comparisons with census and parochial data and to reduce variance along the lines of a known significant variable, the first stage sample was stratified by the number of confirmed members and the nine census areas. The four size categories allowed comparison with data from the "Lutheran Longitudinal Study of the Religious Development of Children" and previous Youth Research Center studies of Lutheran youth. In addition, stratification by church body was considered but abandoned because of the regionality of the church bodies and because of the cumbersome inflation of the sampling that would occur if even one congregation would be drawn from each of the three bodies in each of the already 36 cells of the sampling frame. As it de-

veloped, sampling church body by chance was very proportionate regionally and by congregation size.

3. Congregations with less than 50 confirmed members were deleted for practical data collection reasons, thus reducing the population of congregations by 5.05% and of people by 0.45%. Sixty-four congregations were of unknown size. The rest were grouped into the 36 cell sampling frame (four sizes x nine areas). Actual numbers of congregations to be selected from each cell were calculated on the basis of the following sampling fractions:

50-249	Confirmed Members = 1/100	Congregations
250-449	Confirmed Members = 1/50	Congregations
500-999	Confirmed Members = 1/25	Congregations
1000 +	Confirmed Members = 1/10	Congregations

Each congregation had a five-digit number on the computerized list. Using the Rand Corporation table entitled *A Million Random Digits with 100,000 Normal Deviates* (1955), congregation numbers were drawn at random until the required sample for all 36 cells had been selected. (After a week of drawing random numbers, the numbers of . the last ten potential congregations were placed in a hat, and three were drawn to complete the sample.)

Sample of clergymen. Following the January 30 consultation, letters of invitation were mailed to each of the 378 clergymen who were selected in the first stage sample. A letter of invitation was accompanied by an endorsement and a description of what a local survey would entail. The invitation recommended that the decision to participate not be made by the pastor alone but rather by the congregation or its official boards. This letter of invitation was also accompanied in the ALC and LC-MS by a letter from the church body president encouraging participation. By April 1, 125 congregations had agreed to be in the study. Follow-up letters at that time were sent to all undecided congregations and to all District Presidents and Synod Presidents of the ALC, LCA, and LC-MS to inform them of the study and to encourage them to nudge undecided congregations.

Invitation follow-up. During the month of May, Ralph Underwager telephoned the pastor or lay leader of every congregation that had not made a decision about participation. He approached to provide clarification, give needed information, assuage fears, and assist wherever unusual hindrances had arisen (such as to allow a congregation to send only a list of numbers from which a sample could be drawn, since its constitution prohibited giving the membership list to anyone). Reasons for nonparticipation were legion and were about as frequently personal preferences of the pastors as they were congregational decisions. Most common were perception of it being too much work for its potentials, lack of confidence in survey research or suspicion of the appropriateness of scientific study of the church, bad aftertaste following previous research involvement in areas like parts of Michigan, and the conviction that "we already know our people." Serious attempts to understand and be helpful coupled with prayer and clearly expressed conviction of the value of the study apparently produced results, since by June 1 more than 80% were enrolled, and 316 or 85% (considering legitimate loss of two congregations that disbanded) participated before the summer was over. Table IV.1 on the following page provides a comparison of the sample as drawn with the numbers actually participating by church body, region, and size of congregation.

Sampling Lutheran laymen. The second stage of the sampling process was based upon confirmed membership lists supplied by the 316 cooperating clergymen. The lists which were received at Youth Research Center were to include all names currently on the membership roster of that congregation exclusive only of those under age 15 and over age 65. Age 15 was chosen as a lower limit for purposes of compatibility with previous Youth Research Center studies of Lutheran youth and other national studies of church and nonchurch youth. Age 65 was chosen as an upper limit because it was known that for practical data collection purposes, at some upper age waning physical and mental capacities would present problems. Secondly, in the United States today, age 65 is the most common time of retirement when style of life changes significantly; beliefs, values, and particular attitudes have been shown in other research to change following retirement. Thirdly, pretest experiences had demonstrated that the few persons above age 65 who participated there had significantly greater difficulty with the length and content of the survey.

Membership lists were numbered, and a selection was made from a table of random numbers according to these proportions:

Congregation Size	Probability Ratio for Each
249 and below	1/6.6
250 to 499	1/13.3
500 to 999	1/26.6
1000 and over	1/66.6

Knowing that first and second stage sampling probabilities are multiplicative, notice that as a result of the sampling procedures used, the probability was one in 667 that any confirmed Lutheran between the ages of 15 and 65 in the three major bodies would be selected for participation in the survey regardless of the size of his congregation, his geographic location, or any other characteristic. All persons on congregation membership lists as submitted by their pastors were potentials for the sample whether active or inactive, geographically proximate to the church building, or then living across the continent or around the world. An overall

Table IV.1 Congregational Participation by Church Body, Region, and Size of Congregation

Size	Church Body	New England S*	New England P**	Middle Atlantic S	Middle Atlantic P	East North Central S	East North Central P	West North Central S	West North Central P	South Atlantic S	South Atlantic P	East South Central S	East South Central P	West South Central S	West South Central P	Mountain S	Mountain P	Pacific S	Pacific P	Total S	Total P	Total %
50–249	ALC			1	1	6	6	12	11							2	2	3	3	24	23	96%
50–249	LC-MS			2	1	8	7	8	7	1		2	2	5	4	1	1	4	3	31	25	81%
50–249	LCA	2	2	8	7	3	2	6	5	6	4					1	1			26	21	81%
250–499	ALC			1	1	4	1	6	5					2	1	1	1	1	1	15	10	67%
250–499	LC-MS	2	2	4	3	13	12	14	9					2	2	2	2	8	7	45	37	82%
250–499	LCA			12	7	8	6	3	3	8	6	1								32	22	69%
500–999	ALC	2	2	3	3	11	10	11	10	5	5	1	1	1	1	2	2	5	5	35	33	94%
500–999	LC-MS			3	3	15	10	9	8					2	1			4	4	34	27	79%
500–999	LCA	2	2	15	10	8	7	6	6	2	2			1		2	2	1	1	40	33	83%
1000+	ALC	1	1			13	13	13	13	2	2			3	3	2	2	4	3	38	36	95%
1000+	LC-MS	1	1	2	2	16	11	6	5											25	19	76%
1000+	LCA	1	1	13	12	8	7	7	7	2	2							2	1	33	30	91%
Total		9	8	64	50	113	92	101	89	26	21	4	3	16	12	13	13	32	28	378	316	84%
%		89%		78%		81%		88%		81%		75%		75%		100%		88%				

Group participation percentages (right margin): 50–249 = 85%; 250–499 = 75%; 500–999 = 85%; 1000+ = 89%.

* S = Sample of congregations drawn
** P = Congregations participating

sample fraction of 1/1000 was intended earlier but was changed to 1/667 in order that the minimum number from any congregation, taking into account the expected loss due to nonparticipation, would be approximately 12, which would allow enough degrees of freedom for comparisons of congregations should that prove interesting on the basis of early stages of data analysis.

The sample clergymen were then given the lists of the members of their congregations who were chosen to be in the study. With each list came a set of instructions as to how the survey procedures would be carried out. Clergymen were asked to examine the list again to make sure that none of the persons drawn into the sample were under 15 or over 65. If errors were discovered, the clergyman was asked to correct the entire membership list again, and an entirely new second stage sample was drawn for that congregation (there were few such instances).

As in the case of the first stage sample congregations, so with the second stage sample persons: no substitutions were allowed regardless of availability of persons or the degree to which clergymen felt the persons from their congregations were a good or poor representation. Convincing some clergymen that in the long run the sample would be representative even though it appeared to be made up entirely of inactives and "dead wood" from any given congregation became a considerable task. But the task was accomplished without arbitrary substitutions, to the best of the research team's knowledge.

Persons selected to take the survey were approached by the local pastor or a layman in a leadership position in the case of a vacant pulpit. Youth Research Center provided a letter of invitation to participate, to which the pastor was encouraged to add his own cover letter or personal visit or telephone call. A date for the survey administration in the basement or educational facility of each congregation was arranged by mutual convenience between pastor and seminarian research assistant.

A subsample of two or three persons already part of the second stage sample was selected at random in each congregation for a one-hour interview by the visiting research assistant to be conducted in the interviewee's home or place of business.

The pastor of each congregation was expected to take the survey and be interviewed by virtue of his office. This group of 301 pastors from the 316 participating congregations comprised a separate sample for comparison purposes.

In general, the details of arrangements were handled by eight research assistants who were on the road during the months of June, July, and August visiting each of the sample congregations and collecting the survey data.

COLLECTING THE DATA

The research team with several consultants considered whether to collect data by mail or by personal administration of the survey to groups or individuals. Experience over the past decade in group administration of the Youth Research Survey demonstrated that maximum control of the data collection environment could be gained by use of a few well-trained administrators. Mail surveys, of course, were known to be notoriously poor in securing a high level of participation without very thorough and costly follow-up procedures. Despite the possible disadvantages of response bias being introduced by the environment, no commonly available natural location for group administration of the survey was found other than the church itself, but not the sanctuary. Opportunities for interviewing, careful instruction in follow-up procedures, and uniformity of administration with the likely higher proportion of attendance, finally tipped the balance toward group administration of the survey in the church building, generally in the evening on a date announced one to three months in advance. Every effort was made to encourage extremely candid response and to make clear that no one "other than the computer" would ever know how any individual responded.

The task of administering the survey instrument under standardized conditions and conducting interviews in each of the 316 sample congregations was carried out by eight seminarians. The considerable detail involved in their training, the instructions they followed in each congregational visit, the procedures they used in carrying out an interview, and the efforts made to secure the cooperation of nonrespondents are summarized below.

Selection and training of research assistants. Research assistants had to be highly responsible, capable of making significant decisions on the spot, able to lead a group and elicit confidence, careful to cooperate congenially with a variety of pastors in 40 different locations, and be competent interviewers under time-pressured circumstances—all in addition to traveling three to five hundred miles a day. Youthful seminarians, if well-trained, would both meet the qualifications and appreciate the unusual introduction to the church afforded by such a summer's work. Despite a desire to reflect all three church bodies among the seminarians, it became a practical necessity that research assistants be nearby for training over several months. Therefore, the research team advertised for seminarians who might become research assistants from Luther and Northwestern Seminaries in the Twin Cities only. Applications for the position were received in December 1969. During January 1970 applicants were screened by means of personal interviews with a clinical psychologist and appropriate psychological measures including the Shipley-Hartford, the Minnesota Multiphasic Personality Inventory, the Veterans Administration form biographical data sheet, and the Allport-Vernon value measures. On the basis of the interviews and the psychometrics, eight young men from Luther and Northwestern Seminaries were selected for the position of Research Assistant.

Beginning 23 January 1970 the training program for these men was as follows:

1. A weekend devoted to 20 hours of training in interpersonal skills, group dynamics, and observation techniques. The trainer was Ralph Underwager, Certified Psychologist.
2. During March a total of 20 hours of training in interview techniques, interview recording, and content analysis of interview data. The trainer was John Ziegler, staff member of Youth Research Center.
3. During April and May further training in research techniques, including randomization, sampling technique, and assignment of individuals to research programs. The trainer was Ralph Underwager.
4. During May 20 hours of training in administration of research instruments, further specification of interview techniques, and interview recording. The trainer was Milo Brekke, also of the A *Study of Generations* research team.

Visiting congregations. Each young man had an area of the country assigned to him, and from June 1 through 31 August 1970 he contacted an average of 40 congregations, interviewed randomly selected individuals, and administered the research questionnaire to a randomly selected sample within that congregation. The men also interviewed the pastor in each of these congregations.

It was the responsibility of each research assistant to be in contact with the clergymen of the 40 congregations he was assigned to visit. This meant that his was the task of reminding the clergyman to make the necessary preparations for the research visit and to secure the cooperation of the members who were chosen as part of the sample. Standardized instructions were used for all these procedures to assure that similar information was being given to all people who were invited to be a part of the study.

The research assistant also had the task of carrying out standardized instructions to assure a comparable administration of the survey in each of the sample congregations. Three documents, entitled "Outline of Research Assistant Program," * "Outline for Briefing of Research Administrators," * and "Changes and Supplementary Information," * summarize the details of survey administration and data collection followed in each congregation.

Though all participants answered the 740 items in Books I, II, and III, they did so in a different order. In each congregation a random selection of one-third began with Book I, a second third with Book II, and the remaining group with Book III. This procedure assured that all items in the study would be attacked with equal vigor.

To assure frankness in response, the respondents were assured that their answers were confidential. It was the responsibility of the research assistant to see that this pledge was carried out.

Following the survey administration a check was made to determine how many on the original list were not present to take part. The non-respondents who lived in the community were given to one person in the congregation who had already taken the survey. Laymen were selected wherever possible for three reasons: (1) to avoid overburdening already busy pastors; (2) subtly to communicate to persons followed-up that their pastors would have no opportunity for seeing their responses at any time; and (3) in hopes of minimizing the possibility of respondents giving so-called "right" answers because their pastor was bringing the questionnaire to them. Nonparticipants living outside the community and therefore called "nomads" became the responsibility of the research team.

Interviewing a subsample. Each research assistant had the responsibility of interviewing a random selection of approximately 100 people who also took the survey. The interviews were structured to the degree that is necessary for focusing discussion on a dozen terms and three sequential topics. A conversational method of interviewing was employed using skills which (1) encourage free expression, (2) clarify thoughts, and (3) summarize what has been said.

Interviews consisted of two parts. The first was for the purpose of getting insight into Lutherans' use and perceived meaning of a variety of terms. Differential use and understanding of terms might give some guidance for more appropriate interpretation of survey data. The interviewer began by presenting one of 12 terms and asking the respondent to give his thinking and feeling about the term. Terms were chosen that reflected strictly theological language, strictly everyday conversational language, and, in some cases, both. They were: work, success, sin, law, love, sermon, justice, worship, honest, pastor, Christian life, and adult. The interviewer took notes in the presence of the interviewee, read back his summary, and only if the respondent considered the summary to be accurate and complete did he move on to the next term. The second half of the interview was for allowing free expression and securing in-depth information on people's concepts of the church in its ideal and extant form. In the least presumptuous sense, the researchers hoped that this latter interviewing might in some measure begin to tap the "mind of the church." The areas probed were: ideal characteristics of the church, barriers to the ideal, and what needs doing in today's church.

Summary notes from both parts of each interview were identified with the survey number of the interviewee. Upon their return from the summer of data collection, each research assistant summarized the data from the first half of his interviews using standard procedures for empirical content analyses maximally retaining the key words of the interviewees. Each interviewer developed a matrix from all of his interviews for each word. Cognitive response categories were row headings, and the affective response categories headed columns. Interviewee numbers were listed in the appropriate cells. Interviewer bias was examined by comparison of the eight resulting matrices for each word.

At this writing, analysis of the data about terms from interviews is still in progress, but it has already demonstrated a minimum of interviewer bias and striking differences between clergy and laymen's cognitive and affective responses to the word sin.

Data for all interviewees from the three issues raised in the second half of the interviews are being empirically content analyzed issue by issue. The resulting response categories are being rank-ordered by number of persons so responding. These data should provide some *tentative clues* about present inclinations and tendencies, and possible future directions the Lutheran churches may take.

The present analysis plan calls for relating interview data to survey data for each respondent, as well as making several intergroup comparisons such as by church body.

Follow-up on nonrespondents. Completed answer sheets were sent by registered mail to Youth Research Center by the research assistants no less frequently than every other day at the beginning of the summer and once a week by the end. Each research assistant completed a standardized "Report Form for Group Administration of the Survey" * in every congregation he visited. This summarized the answer sheet numbers that were assigned; number of people in the sample; number of people in attendance; names, addresses, and availability of absentees to be followed-up; person responsible and materials left for follow-up; names and addresses of nomads present from other congregations; and nomads from this congregation not present but needing further contact.

One person in each congregation who accepted responsibility for follow-up was given detailed instructions on procedures for securing the cooperation of nonrespondents yet living in his community. Several letters were sent to these follow-up persons during the months of July, August, and September urging them to complete this phase of the study. During this time contacts were being made by the research assistants with the harder to locate nonrespondents who, though members of a local congregation, had a permanent residence that was in some other location.

Persons responsible for local follow-up brought survey booklets and answer sheets together with a brief set of written instructions to the home of each absentee who resided locally. Completed answer sheets were sent directly to Youth Research Center by follow-up respondents in the self-addressed envelopes provided. Survey booklets were returned to the local persons responsible for follow-up as an indication of completion of the survey. All follow-ups were encouraged to complete the survey at one sitting.

The only other data collected by mail was solicited from nomads, which included servicemen as far away as Vietnam. Each research assistant was responsible for making personal contact with any nomads from other congregations, living in or near the communities he visited. A few nomads responded to the invitation to attend a group administration near their residences, while by far the largest percentage required an approach by mail. Pastors of all nomads were encouraged to call or write their own nomads requesting their participation in some group administration or at least completion of a survey by mail. No systematic attempt was made to discover how many pastors did, but some reported having done so when they attended later regional conferences. From the 378 nomads, which included 60 servicemen, replies were received from 103, including 12 servicemen. The intended mail follow-up of nomads was not carried out. To date no careful analyses of possible systematic differences in the responses from nomads have been made.

The follow-up efforts were discontinued in October when it became necessary to begin the processing of answer sheet data. Table IV.2 lists the percentages that did participate in the study.

Study of nonrespondents. A later study was made of a sample of nonrespondents in order to gain some estimate of what characterized the 35% who did not participate in the survey and who total 2,385. In this investigation information was secured on 401 nonparticipants with respect to the following matters:

1. Manner of nonparticipation
2. Care used in the follow-up procedure
3. Factors in nonparticipation
4. Sex, church body, and region of nonrespondent
5. Employment status
6. Occupation of principal wage earner for the nonrespondent

Inasmuch as it is important to determine whether or not the absence of this group from the total sample introduces a serious bias, a summary of

Table IV.2 Second Stage Sample (Lay People) with Participation by Church Body, Region, and Size of Congregation

Size	Church Body	New England S	New England P	Middle Atlantic S	Middle Atlantic P	East North Central S	East North Central P	West North Central S	West North Central P	South Atlantic S	South Atlantic P	East South Central S	East South Central P	West South Central S	West South Central P	Mountain S	Mountain P	Pacific S	Pacific P	Total S	Total P	Total %	Group %
50–249	ALC			29	12	121	78	206	136							29	17	86	46	471	289	61%	
	LC-MS			12	9	161	110	160	100			68	52	58	43	12	6	47	40	513	360	70%	66%
	LCA	30	26	149	103	60	27	91	55	101	69					21	16			452	296	66%	
250–499	ALC			21	8	20	13	120	82					20	11	17	12	21	19	219	145	66%	
	LC-MS	50	27	64	43	318	189	207	132					51	28	57	39	173	108	920	566	62%	65%
	LCA			195	128	154	103	83	66	123	89									555	386	70%	
500–999	ALC			56	39	257	172	239	150	35	22			27	9	53	34	103	69	770	495	64%	
	LC-MS			66	33	220	160	187	126			15	13	21	17			84	62	593	411	69%	66%
	LCA	38	22	200	141	163	113	152	100	91	58					58	21	17	14	719	469	65%	
1000+	ALC	23	8			265	159	239	160	29	17			44	30	32	23	47	37	656	426	65%	
	LC-MS	15	12	43	24	197	135	101	61											364	228	63%	64%
	LCA			220	153	165	91	138	88	37	20							17	9	592	373	63%	
Totals		156	95	1055	693	2101	1350	1923	1256	416	275	83	65	221	138	279	168	595	404	6829	4444	65%	
%		61%		66%		64%		65%		66%		78%		62%		60%		68%				65%	

* S = Sample of lay people drawn
** P = Lay people participating

the findings is listed below. It should be understood that random procedures were not used in securing the information given below. Nevertheless, it does represent a good estimate of what is usually unavailable information.

Table IV.4 indicates that the pastors of those who conducted the follow-up campaign generally evaluated the effort as moderate to very vigorous, which is consonant with the observations of the research team. As indicated in Table IV.3, 19% refused to participate and gave no reason, while 23.4% gave reasons for their refusal. The content of Table IV.5 is not limited to reasons given by some who refused to participate. The information in Table IV.5 is from the pastors of nonparticipants and reports the pastor's best judgment of the real factors in the nonparticipation, whether or not stated at the time of refusal.

It is noteworthy that on the basis of Tables IV.3 and IV.5 somewhere between 12% and 16% of nonrespondents just could not be located; an additional 2% died between the time of selection and survey; nearly 4% were identified as mentally retarded or illiterate; nearly another 4% were identified as mentally ill. This means that if one assumes that all of the 9% who found the survey administration to conflict with their working schedules and the 7% whose physical health did not permit their attendance could all have taken the survey in some way or another, still at least approximately 23% to 27% of the nonrespondents were legitimate losses. That is, there was no conceivable way in which they could have

Table IV.3   Manner of Nonparticipation

Manner	Percentage
Outright refusal, no reason	19.0%
Refused, gave reason	23.4
Agreed but didn't respond	28.2
Agreed but didn't finish	16.0
Couldn't find person to ask	12.0
Other	0.7
No response	1.7
	101.0%*

* Multiple responses accumulated

Table IV.4   Care Used in Follow-Up

Follow-Up	Percentage
Very vigorous	14.2%
Moderate	55.6
Weak	22.2
None	4.1
No response	4.1
	100.0%

Table IV.5   Factors in Nonparticipation

Factor	Percentage	
"Too busy"	23.2%	
Didn't feel was important	16.5	
Didn't want to be bothered	18.0	
Irresponsible generally	2.0	
		59.7%
Inactive member	38.7%	
Hostile to church	10.0	
		48.7%
Didn't understand what study was really about	9.5%	
Feared being "put on spot"	10.0	
Felt inadequate	14.7	
Task too formidable	1.0	
		35.2%
Unavailable: unknown address, jail, other church		16.0%
Hostile to research	5.5%	
Believed survey undesirable	3.0	
Repulsed by questions on sex	1.0	
		9.5%
Conflict with job requirements		9.0%
Health, physical		7.0%
Health, mental	3.7%	
Mental retardation	1.0	
Illiteracy	2.7	
		7.4%
Ultra-conservative theological view	2.5%	
Spouse/family belief disharmony	2.2	
		4.7%
Family tragedy at time		3.2%
Death		2.0%
Miscellaneous		9.7%
		214.1%*

* Multiple responses accumulated

been involved in the survey. It is also interesting to note that as high as 4% (16% of the 35% who were nonrespondents) of the people on our church rolls could not be located at a given point in time. Considering the mobility of the American people, this perhaps is not surprising but is still a matter for some concern.

If one reduces the original sample by 27% of the nonrespondents as "legitimate losses," the percentage of participation rises to 73%. Ninety-five percent of the pastors responded to the survey (301 from the 316 participating congregations).

Biases due to nonresponse in terms of the above factors are neither large nor many. From Table IV.5 it is clear that the participant sample is somewhat biased in the direction of active church members, though among the participants 25% identified themselves as inactive compared with 39% of the nonrespondents who were so identified by their pastors. However, if one subtracts the percentage of nonrespondents who were simply of unknown location from those who are identified as inactive members, the percentages of inactive survey participants and inactive nonrespondents are comparable. This suggests that generalizations from *A Study of Generations* apply to the members of Lutheran congregations, both active and inactive, except those of unknown location.

Table IV.6 shows that the participant sample may be *slightly* biased toward persons ages 35 through 44; West North Central United States residents; professionals, technical workers, proprietors, officials and managers, including farm managers; and females. The participant sample may be slightly lacking in representation from the East North Central U.S. and among clerical and sales workers, craftsmen, and foremen.

Since the ALC is most heavily represented in the West North Central area and LC-MS in the East North Central area, the possible slight regional biases may indicate a very slight undersampling of the LC-MS in the area where it is most concentrated. If so, it is *very* slight considering the overall church body sample proportions.

Considering the deviations that can occur by chance even in very careful random sampling, any additional systematic error introduced by nonresponse appears to be minimal.

Analytic and Reporting Phase

October 1970 through December 1971 was occupied with processing answer sheets and interview data, forming scales from the 740 items, consulting with church leaders, carrying out multivariate data analyses, and reporting the study.

PROCESSING SAMPLE DATA

In preparation for statistical analyses, data were processed as follows: An IBM 1231 Optical Page Reader was used to transfer responses of each subject from his answer sheets to a single record on magnetic tape. Responses had to be translated into numbers that would best represent

Table IV.6 Percentage Comparisons of Nonresidents with Sample Participants by Age, Region, Employment Status, Occupation, Sex, and Church Body (Notable differences in bold type)

	Nonrespondent %	Participant %
Age		
Under 14 and unknown	2	0.5
15-24	21	24
25-34	17	17
35-44	17	**22**
45-54	23	20
55-64	17	14
65 and over	3	3
Region		
New England, Mid-Atlantic	21	18
East North Central	38	30
West North Central	19	**28**
South Atlantic, East and West South Central	8	11
Mountain, Pacific	14	13
Employment Status		
Student (employed or not)	12	**16**
Housewife (employed or not)	38	39
Full-time employed, other part-time workers, retired, disabled, and unemployed	50	46
Occupation		
Professional, technical, and similar workers— plus proprietors, managers, and officials	17	**23**
Clerical and related workers plus sales workers	**14**	8
Craftsmen, foremen, and related workers	**17**	9
Operatives and related, plus service workers, except domestic	17	19
Laborers and private household workers	20	16
Farm owners, managers, others	15	**26**
Sex		
Male	**51**	42
Female	49	**58**
Church Body		
ALC	33	31
LC-MS	34	35
LCA	34	34

the level of feeling or affect on the item concerned. For example, the responses "never," "no longer," "very much," "quite a bit," "somewhat," and "very little" on items 21-134 and 281-295 were recorded as 1, 2, 3, 4, 5, and 6 because they occurred on the answer sheet in this order. They were subsequently translated to 1, 2, 6, 5, 4, and 3 to make the data meaningful. These translated responses were used in extracting the scales.

Magnetic tape records were then examined for percentage of nonresponse per person as well as per item. Five percent of the subjects (245) were excluded from the scale derivation analyses because they had skipped more than 240 of the items. In cases where subjects were asked to make a response if they agreed and leave it blank if they disagreed, a special technique was used to separate skipping the item from a disagreement response. Items of this sort appeared in groups (for example, items 1-15, 92-96, 97-103, 105-127, 221-235, 236-242, 552-567, 588-607). If a person omitted the entire group, each item was considered as skipped. But if a person answered as many as one of the items in the group, all items not marked in the group were considered as receiving the disagreement response.

None of the items was skipped to a significantly greater degree than the general level of nonresponse for all items, which varied from 2% to 12%. Therefore, no items were deleted from the scaling analysis.

Twenty-four items requested multiple responses. These were specially treated, and a separate character position was allowed for each response possibility. The response possibilities for 46 items were not linearly related but were categorical and not on a continuum. These items were also specially treated with a separate character position allowed for each response possibility in a second listing of these item responses in the record for each individual. This, in effect, allowed for two approaches to the analyses of these 46 unusual items: (a) treating each item separately as if the response possibilities were on a continuum (e.g., scoring response possibilities 1, 2, 3, 4, etc.), or (b) treating each response possibility as if it were a separate item (scoring each response possibility as either a 0 or a 1). During the derivation of scales, in recognition of the possibility that some heretofore unknown continuum might underlie the apparently unrelated response possibilities for any one of these 46 items, each of these items was analyzed first according to the first approach. Only when these items failed to fall into derived scale sets by use of the first approach was the second approach used. In most cases only then did scale sets form, including any of these 46 unusual items.

MULTIVARIATE ANALYSES USED FOR ESTABLISHING INITIAL SCALES

Even with an IBM Model 360-67 with 200 K, an IBM Model 360-50 with 364 K, and a CDC Model 6600 with 64 K available, all items could not be submitted simultaneously for multivariate analyses that would identify subsets of items for potential scales. No computer facility was available that could efficiently manipulate a matrix larger than 40,000 cells (order 200). Questionnaire items were therefore organized into analytically manageable groups by the number of response possibilities of the items as follows:

Type of Item	Number of Items
two-response	127
three-response	189
four-response	102
second set of four-response	148
five-response	62
six-response	28
seven-response	62

The number of four-response items had to be broken into two groups. Logical relationships of item content were taken into consideration in the formation of those two subgroups.

Formation of scales was easily the most complex aspect of instrument development. Major topics to be considered are multivariate analyses and reciprocal averages.

Three techniques of multivariate analyses were used for establishing the initial survey scales. They were: (1) technique of homogeneous keying; (2) principal component analysis; and (3) principal factor analysis. Each of them is briefly described below, along with some justification for using it. More space is devoted to the first of these because the references which describe the method are not easily available.

Technique of homogeneous keying. The theory underlying this technique is given in Loevinger (1947, 1948). Some theory, most of the working details, and an actual research example can be found in DuBois *et al.* (1952). One could also refer to Loevinger *et al.* (1953) and to Gupta (1968a, 1968b) with advantage.

The technique, as applied here, started with a variance-covariance matrix of the initial pool of items—the items which were to be clustered or classified into subgroups or scales. Its purpose was to produce clusters having two properties: (1) relatively independent or having low correlations with the remaining clusters; (2) maximum homogeneity or internal consistency or KR_{20} reliability (Kuder and Richardson, 1937). The latter is also known to be equivalent to Cronbach's (1951) alpha coefficient and Hoyt's (1941) reliability by analysis of variance.

$$KR_{20} = \frac{n}{n-1} \cdot \frac{2 \, \Sigma \, \Sigma \, C_{ij}}{2 \, \Sigma \, \Sigma \, C_{ij} + \Sigma \, V_i}$$

where n = the number of items in the cluster at a given stage

$\Sigma \, \Sigma \,$ Cij $=$ sum of all the covariances between the n items in a cluster at a given time (n items give n (n − 1)/2 covariances in general)

$\Sigma \,$ Vi $=$ sum of the variances of the n items

From the variance-covariance matrix, the technique identified three items which gave maximum reliability and then added to these three, one item at a time, whatever items that increased the reliability maximally.

The process of adding items in this manner continued as long as the reliability kept improving or did not decrease by more than an arbitrarily established amount of .005. Experimentation with and without this tolerance of .005 occasionally showed significant content drift, even allowing such a slight decrease in reliability. Therefore, in the second-level attempts to derive scales from items left over from the multivariate analyses of items grouped by number of response possibilities, no decrease in reliability was allowed.

After the first cluster was formed, a second, third, and subsequent clusters were extracted similarly from the items available at each stage. As a result of this process, most of the items in the initial pool were included in one cluster or another. Those not included were the ones which could not form a cluster within the initial pool of items.

In this technique of forming clusters, it is possible for an item that should belong in one of the latter clusters to lose this possibility by being included in one of the earlier ones. To remedy this possibility, the point-biserial correlation of each item with each of the clusters was examined, and items were reassigned to the cluster for which each had the highest correlation. If an item had rather high point-biserial correlations with two clusters, it was assigned to that cluster with which it had maximum content similarity.

The unique characteristic of this technique lies in the fact that it furnishes an objective, quantitative criterion in the value of KR$_{20}$ for deciding whether a scale should be allowed to continue growing or be terminated. This criterion was coupled with an examination of the item content to decide when the cluster development should end. This made it possible to avoid content-drift in a cluster and, at the same time, to extract scales with maximum reliability. No other multivariate technique of data analysis affords comparable advantages.

Principal components analysis. The method of principal components analysis was used because it can easily handle a very large correlation matrix and reduce the data to a much smaller number of components or scales. The advantage of this technique is found in the fact that it requires less computer time than principal factor analysis. On the debit side, however, its drawback lies in producing very small specific factors which have no use in extracting scales. Details of the method can be seen in Hotelling (1933), Anderson (1958), and Harman (1967).

Principal factor analysis. Though slower than principal component analysis, this method of factorization has the advantage of giving results that are free from the influences of unreliability and specificity of the items; that is, from uniqueness. These considerations provided justification for its use in the present research. Writers such as Harman (1967) think that with the advent of high speed electronic computers this method has become the most preferred and popular.

The results of principal component and factor analyses were subjected to normal varimax rotation (Kaiser, 1956, 1958) in order to make the results not only parsimonious but also psychologically meaningful.

Since the intent was to extract scales which were sufficiently large to give respectably high reliability, complete factorization was not needed. It was deemed sufficient to extract only the strong factors. For this reason, it was decided to stop factorization when the number of factors for any given set of items equalled approximately 1/15 of the number of items. This provided clusters on the average of no less than 10 nor more than 15 items per cluster.

Since multivariate techniques in general tend to take maximum advantage of sampling and measurement errors and this tendency reflects itself in the results produced by them, certain precautions were taken to keep the outcomes free from such influences. The entire sample ($N = 4,745 - 245 = 4,500$) was divided into two random halves which could be called "validation" and "cross-validation" samples. The three techniques of analysis were applied separately and independently to these half-samples.

Notice that there were eight groups of items (those having two, three, four, five, six, and seven possible responses; plus a second set of four-response items; plus a set of 46 unusual items to be analyzed by each response possibility), three techniques of analysis, and two half-samples upon which all analyses were to be carried out. Thus, there would be as many as 48 computer outputs. After observing that on the analysis of six-, two-, and three-item sets the results of principal components and principal factor analyses were for practical purposes identical, the principal components analysis was discontinued. Homogeneous keying and principal factor analyses were completed for all sets of items on both half-samples producing 32 computer outputs. Each had to be scrutinized carefully to decide upon the composition of the initial scales. Since rigorous, objective, quantitative criteria are not available to guide such decisions, recourse had to be taken to the rules listed below.

Arbitrary though it sounds, the practice is a normal one and produced excellent results, as shown in Table IV.8 (see subsection below entitled

"Independence of Scales"). As far as the factor analyses outputs are concerned, each output was handled as follows:

1. All the normal varimax loadings whose *absolute value* exceeded .350 were underlined.

2. The output was inspected to see whether two conditions were satisfied simultaneously: *(a)* most (if not all) of the rows (variables) had at least one underlined loading; *(b)* not many rows had more than one underlined loading.

3. If *(a)* was satisfied but not *(b)*, the number .350 was adjusted a little upward so that some of the underlines could be erased; if the reverse was the case, it was lowered somewhat so that a few more loadings could be underlined.

4. In each case, after one or two such adjustments, the stage could be easily reached when about two-thirds of the items could be clearly assigned to a single factor, about a fifth of the items to no factor at all, and a very few to more than one factor.

Similar procedures were adopted in processing the computer outputs from cluster analyses (homogeneous keying), the only difference being that point-biserial correlations were underlined instead of factor loadings.

The number of underlined loadings and point-biserial correlations against each of the items in the four outputs was used as a rough and quick guide for assigning an item to a scale. In this way 54 initial scales and 56 subscales were extracted. A few items that were initially assigned to more than one scale were considered very carefully. An item was retained in that scale with which it had maximum similarity as demonstrated by the results of the method of reciprocal averages described below and by subject-matter similarity. Thus, each item occurred in one and only one scale, and the procedures as a whole aimed at factorial purity as well as homogeneity.

The factor and cluster analytic procedures sometimes by one method identified relatively large sets of items (e.g., 18) which formed a scale and made good psychological and/or theological sense, and simultaneously by the other method identified two or three subsets of the same items that also formed scales and made good sense. Such results presented the possibility of organizing data by a parent scale with one or more subscales that might afford later analyses of more detailed relationships among variables. From among the 56 subscales initially derived only 10 subscales were included in the scale pool and used in subsequent data analyses because in only six such incidents of set-subset identification were the following criteria met:

1. The weights developed by the method of reciprocal averages (described below) for the possible responses of an item as that item occurred in the subscale were identical to the weights that so developed for that same item in the parent scale.

2. The internal consistency reliability of the subscale was at least .60.

3. The subscale was of special heuristic value because of the construct (social scientific or theological) that it obviously represented.

Only in these 10 subscales (7, 24, 25, 30, 31, 32, 33, 38, 39, and 48 in the final scale pool) as compared with their six parent scales did any items occur more than once among the empirically derived scale sets of items.

RESPONSE WEIGHTING BY RECIPROCAL AVERAGES METHOD

The items of each initial scale and subscale were subjected to the method of reciprocal averages, using one to nine as the possible range of response weights for each item.

Mosier (1946) recounts the virtues or capabilities of the method of reciprocal averages as follows:

> (1) The reliability of each item and the internal consistency of the weighted inventory are maximized; (2) the correlation between item and total score is maximized, and the product moment correlation coefficient becomes identical with the correlation ratio; (3) the relative variance of the distribution of scores (coefficient of variation) is maximized; (4) the relative variance of item scores within a single case is minimized; (5) the correlation between an item and total score is proportional to the standard deviation of the item weights for that item; (6) questions which bear no relation to the total score variable are automatically weighted so that they exert no effect on the scoring.

The method used the item responses in their linear transformation as arbitrary, a priori, input weights for extracting the initial scales. It calculated Hoyt's (1941) reliability and applied an iterative procedure to the input information, changing the latter in such a way that the final set of weights—called reciprocal averages weights—gave the maximum internal consistency possible for a scale in a given situation.

The computer output listed these weights and the maximum reliability reached for each scale. The nonfunctional or noncontributing items were automatically assigned weights having little or no variance. Such items did appear in certain of the initial scales and were discarded. A very few items originally assigned to more than one scale were automatically assigned weights having about equal variance in both of the scales. Usually they were deleted from both the scales and from subsequent scale derivation attempts. They were then available as predictor variables to be examined in relation to a variety of scales and items in later multivariate analyses of the data. A notable example of these was Item 481 which assesses frequency of church attendance, a variable significant enough in the light of previous research to be examined by itself.

Despite numerous attempts to delete or insert one or two items of questionable relationship to the rest of the items in a given initial scale or subscale, and several attempts to merge related small scales, five scales and 47 subscales were shown to have low reliabilities and were therefore discarded. Ten other scales and two subscales demonstrated very adequate reliabilities, but the weights their items were assigned by the method of reciprocal averages indicated that these scales likely were not unidimensional but multidimensional. They also consistently defied attempts to isolate single subdimensions on the basis of subject matter content, so they, too, were set aside to await secondary attempts at scale derivation.

SECONDARY PROCEDURES OF SCALE DERIVATION

Initial methods led to the use of 377 items in the formation of 39 scales and seven overlapping subscales. You will recall that limitations of the computers placed an important restriction on the number of items that could be analyzed simultaneously for scale derivation. Items analyzed together had arbitrarily been restricted to those having the same number of possible responses. Since in some cases widely divergent types of items theoretically operationalized the same construct, this arbitrary restraint left the haunting suspicion that if items of different numbers of response possibilities had been analyzed together, different factors and clusters and therefore different scales might have formed.

Three procedures were followed, first to avoid that possibility throughout, and second to investigate the degree to which that may have happened up to that point: (1) analysis of the leftover items without regard to number of response possibilities; (2a) second-order factor analyses of all *scales*, and (2b) refactoring and clustering of all the *items* in the nine scales with the highest loadings on the first factor identified by the second-order factoring.

Analysis of leftover items. Since most of the initial item sets that upon reciprocal averaging appeared to be multidimensional were of four-response items, and four-response items had been analyzed in two groups, all leftover four-response items (133) were reanalyzed by the multivariate methods described above—with minimal but positive results. From 61 previously unused items, three subscales and eight scales were finally resolved, four of which had small numbers of items (four-eight) and borderline reliabilities (.49-.65) but extremely interesting content (Scales 59-62).

Three groups were then arbitrarily formed from the 302 items still not in any scales: *(a)* a conglomeration of 152 mainly sociological and demographic type items including other varieties that had already demonstrated some kind of uniqueness, *(b)* 104 psychological and theological type items of two through seven responses, and *(c)* the 46 items with nonlinear response possibilities. Factor and cluster analysis of 45 of the most promising of the group A items identified several meaningful sets of two or three sociological items with potential as indices, but because of the small number of items in each none of them would likely scale with adequate reliability.

With no regard for the number of response possibilities of each item, the group B items were resubmitted to the initial multivariate analyses described above. Between the factor-cluster analyses and use of the method of reciprocal averages, there was considerably more experimentation with deletion, insertion, and substitution of items, together with numerous attempts at merger of small scale sets on the basis of item intercorrelations as well as clinical and pastoral experience. Part of this experimentation included separating out 29 items that were among the total of 45 items that Spilka (1971) had just found to form two scales representing the two poles of a committed-consensual continuum of religiosity. A few of these 29 items had already fallen into previously derived *A Study of Generations* scales, while most were among the leftovers then being analyzed as group B items. These 29 items as a separate set were subjected to the now usual multivariate techniques of scale derivation in hopes that Spilka's work would be replicated and a commitment and a consensuality scale would form. Instead, the factor and cluster analytic results did not follow the boundaries of Spilka's scales, and five seeming subdimensions (two of commitment and three of consensuality) were identified. All in all, out of the reanalyses of the variety of group B items, an additional eight scales, six of which were of mixed numbers of response possibility, formed from 81 more items, bringing the total up to 55 scales and 10 subscales from 519 items.

When the response weights within each of the items in these scales were examined, a few were not in the right sequence. For example, instead of a desired sequence such as 1, 3, 4, 6, 8, 9, the list of weights may have been 1, 4, 3, 6, 8, 9. Usually the discrepancy occurred for item responses where the mean scores were very close. In two of these cases, the weights were put in the right order as a subjective judgment.

At one other point additional subjective judgment was exercised in the formation of these scales. Four of them were assigned weights in the last few iterations of the reciprocal averaging that suggested multidimensionality. However, in each case there was no practical difference between the reliability after the last iteration and after some previous iteration that produced weights, for all items, that were consonant with an assumption of unidimensionality for the scale. In view of this invariance of reliability and the very interesting and meaningful content of the items in each case, weights from the earlier iteration were used for each of the four scales in question.

The 46 nonlinear, categorical items were composed of a total of 193 response possibilities, each of which was treated as a single item that was scored zero or one in the scale-deriving multivariate procedures as used before. Because of the interdependence of these "response items," initial scale sets tended to form in pairs that were approximately negative-positive mirror images of each other. Four of the nine scales derived from these items were formed only when these scale-set pairs were merged. Though these nine additional scales were comprised of 95 responses, only 34 additional items were involved, making a total of 74 empirically derived scales (64 parent scales and 10 subscales) from 553 items. Most of the more subtle and intriguing of the scales are among those derived by secondary procedures.

Inasmuch as zeros were used to represent omitted responses, they were assigned weights equal to the weighted average for all responses to the item.

$$\text{Weighted Average} = \frac{N_1w_1 + N_2w_2 + N_3w_3 + N_4w_4 + \dots}{N_1 + N_2 + N_3 + N_4 + \dots}$$

where w_1 etc. = reciprocal averages weights

N_1 etc. = sample sizes of the subgroups giving responses 1, 2, 3, etc.

When all this had been accomplished, the final weights were used to recalculate the reliability of each scale. The resulting figures are given in Table IV.7 along with the names of the scales, their sizes, reliabilities, theoretical raw score ranges, together with standard errors of measurement for standard scores ($\overline{X} = 50$, $s = 10$), and separately for clergy and lay people: their actual raw score ranges, means, standard deviations, and raw score standard errors of measurement.

Nonempirical derivation of four scales. Items 258-277 were the only survey questions of the type developed by Bogardus (1967 a and b) called social distance measures. When included in the empirical multivariate methods for scale derivation described above, these 20 items formed two scales (56 and 57) with very high reliabilities (.90 and .89), that reflected the upper and lower halves of the rank order into which the items fell on the basis of the average responses given by all Lutherans. However, Bogardus (1967b) and Westie (1967) had outlined special methods of scoring these items that theoretically each form an equal-appearing interval scale: social contact range, social contact distance, social contact quality, summated differences (acknowledged by Westie to be closer to a measure of prejudice), and distance quotients. The latter two were used in the development of four specialized quotients that were eventually included in the scale pool as Scales 1 − 4, bringing

Table IV.7   Scale Numbers, Names, and Characteristics

Scale No. and Name	No. of Items	Hoyt's Reliability	Theoretic Range	Standard Score meas.	Clergy N = 301 Actual Range	Clergy Mean	Clergy S.D.	Clergy Raw Score S meas.	Lay N = 4444 Actual Range	Lay Mean	Lay S.D.	Lay Raw Score S meas.
1 Racial Distance	3											
Quotient Subscale			0- 7		0- 5	1.7	.8		0- 7	2.5	1.2	
2 Religious Distance	4											
Quotient Subscale			0- 7		0- 5	2.1	.7		0- 7	2.5	1.1	
3 Political Distance	3											
Quotient Subscale			0- 7		0- 7	3.8	1.5		0- 7	4.4	1.6	
4 Social Distance	9											
Quotient Subscale			0- 7		0- 5	2.5	.8		0- 6	3.1	1.1	
5 Humanity of Jesus	6	.61	6- 42	6.25	6- 42	26.0	10.3	6.43	6- 42	13.4	7.7	4.81
6 Divinity of Jesus	8	.78	15- 65	4.69	15- 65	50.9	12.9	6.05	6- 42	45.4	14.9	6.99
7 Subscale of Scale 6	8	.60	10- 33	6.32	10- 33	27.1	6.4	4.05	15- 65	22.3	7.5	4.74
8 Biblical Knowledge	4	.66	9- 48	5.83	22- 48	46.6	3.3	1.92	10- 33	33.1	10.8	6.30
9 Biblical Ignorance	6	.60	4- 25	6.32	4- 12	4.3	1.5	.95	9- 48	12.1	7.6	4.81
10 Prior Denominational Membership A. Larger Church Bodies	10	.53	19- 80	6.86	19- 44	20.6	4.2	2.88	4- 25	22.4	5.7	3.91
11 Prior Denominational Membership B. Smaller Church Bodies	14	.75	14- 81	5.00	14- 23	14.1	.7	.35	19- 74	14.3	2.1	1.05
12 The Church, Me, and Social Justice	9	.67	20- 73	5.74	25- 73	65.0	8.5	4.88	14- 81	53.0	12.4	7.12
13 Family and Congregational Caring Life	15	.75	39-127	5.00	50-127	101.7	17.0	8.50	20- 73	96.2	18.7	9.35
14 A Personal Caring God	15	.77	69-135	4.80	118-135	132.0	3.5	1.68	39-127	128.2	8.5	4.08
15 Salvation by Works	13	.79	31- 97	4.58	31- 74	39.0	8.5	3.90	70-135	65.7	15.1	6.92
16 The Exclusive Truth Claim of Christianity Exaggerated	12	.68	45- 94	5.66	45- 94	65.5	9.1	5.18	31- 97	63.5	8.7	4.92
17 Feelings of Isolation and Pressure	9	.68	18- 61	5.66	18- 51	28.3	7.4	4.19	45- 92	31.5	8.7	4.92
18 Identification with Parents	9	.64	19- 78	6.00	25- 78	57.3	12.9	7.74	18- 61	59.8	12.0	7.20
19 Religious Experience	8	.69	24- 66	5.57	32- 63	50.0	5.9	3.28	19- 78	43.9	8.9	4.96
20 Supporting Others in Crises	6	.81	6- 53	4.36	11- 53	37.9	9.6	4.18	24- 66	26.4	11.2	4.88
21 Personal Evangelism	13	.89	15-104	3.32	27-104	66.5	17.0	5.64	6- 53	31.9	12.3	4.08
22 Neighborliness	13	.80	15- 95	4.47	19- 95	44.6	14.3	6.40	15-104	39.4	10.8	4.83
23 Questionable Personal Activities	13	.80	21- 99	4.47	23- 91	42.1	10.1	4.52	15- 95	42.0	11.1	4.96
24 Subscale of Scale 23	10	.71	15- 73	5.39	17- 57	33.8	7.7	4.15	23- 95	32.3	8.0	4.31
25 Subscale of Scale 23	3	.71	6- 26	5.39	6- 22	8.4	3.5	1.88	15- 69	9.7	4.3	2.32

Table IV.7 (continued)

Scale No. and Name	No. of Items	Hoyt's Reliability	Theoretic Range	Standard Score S meas.	Clergy N = 301				Lay N = 4444			
					Actual Range	Mean	S.D.	Raw Score S meas.	Actual Range	Mean	S.D.	Raw Score S meas.
26 Mutual Support Among Church, Society, and Individuals	10	.64	25- 79	6.00	32- 79	63.5	9.2	5.52	26- 79	60.2	10.9	6.54
27 Disappointment with the Church	7	.58	11- 49	6.48	11- 49	16.6	6.1	3.95	11- 49	23.3	8.5	5.51
28 Transcendental Meaning in Life	10	.73	37- 87	5.20	57- 87	80.7	6.0	3.12	41- 87	75.8	8.5	4.42
29 Values of Self-Development	10	.69	10- 65	5.57	10- 62	18.3	6.4	3.56	10- 65	22.3	8.2	4.57
30 Subscale of Scale 28	5	.79	10- 45	4.58	18- 45	41.1	5.4	2.47	11- 45	37.8	7.7	3.53
31 Subscale of Scale 28	6	.77	14- 54	4.80	26- 54	49.1	5.7	2.73	15- 54	45.4	8.1	3.88
32 Subscale of Scale 34 (Disadvantaged)	8	.79	19- 72	4.58	19- 70	44.6	11.2	5.13	19- 72	56.3	9.2	4.22
33 Subscale of Scale 34 (Jews)	7	.84	9- 58	4.00	9- 57	31.9	8.7	3.48	9- 58	36.2	8.5	3.40
34 Generalized Prejudice	15	.86	28-130	3.74	28-127	76.5	17.7	6.62	28-130	92.5	15.1	5.65
35 Pessimism	7	.67	9- 60	5.74	9- 59	32.7	7.4	4.25	9- 59	35.9	8.0	4.60
36 Christian Utopianism	11	.74	20- 84	5.10	23- 79	41.1	9.4	4.79	21- 84	40.8	9.0	4.59
37 Need for Unchanging Structure	18	.78	37-154	4.69	45-129	91.1	13.3	6.24	47-145	100.8	12.1	5.68
38 Subscale of Scale 37	11	.70	26- 93	5.48	34- 81	54.1	7.7	4.22	26- 93	59.7	7.7	4.22
39 Subscale of Scale 37	7	.60	11- 61	6.32	11- 54	37.0	6.7	4.24	14- 61	41.1	6.0	3.79
40 Congregational Activity	7	.90	9- 59	3.16	33- 59	56.1	4.6	1.45	9- 59	34.0	14.0	4.43
41 Personal Piety	15	.89	28-120	3.32	77-117	105.8	6.5	2.16	31-117	77.8	15.6	5.17
42 The Role of Pastors in Social Action	10	.86	15- 74	3.74	20- 74	46.9	11.5	4.30	15- 74	39.2	10.0	3.74
43 Need for Religious Absolutism	12	.70	30-100	5.48	42- 89	67.3	7.7	4.22	31- 98	70.3	8.5	4.66
44 Fundamentalism-Liberalism	13	.86	35-115	3.74	75-113	95.1	6.8	2.54	36-115	93.3	9.6	3.59
45 Organizational Memberships	13	.84	13- 48	4.00	13- 16	13.0	.2	.09	13- 47	13.1	.7	.28
46 Importance of Christian Practices in My Life	4	.83	7- 36	4.12	33- 36	35.9	.4	.14	7- 36	35.5	2.3	.93
47 Personal Involvement in Church and Community	17	.90	39-144	3.16	79-144	127.0	11.5	3.64	35-142	91.1	21.0	6.64
48 Subscale of Scale 47	11	.88	20- 93	6.32	46- 93	85.3	8.6	2.98	20- 93	59.5	15.9	5.51
49 Anxiety over My Faith	9	.82	21- 78	4.24	21- 70	44.4	10.6	4.50	21- 78	50.0	13.0	5.52
50 Acceptance of Middle Class Norms	6	.69	12- 54	5.57	15- 54	34.3	7.5	4.18	12- 54	37.7	8.0	4.45
51 Acceptance of Authority	3	.74	3- 26	5.10	3- 26	23.5	4.1	2.09	3- 26	21.2	6.5	3.31
52 Desire for a Dependable World	4	.53	6- 34	6.86	6- 34	14.2	4.6	3.15	6- 34	14.9	5.4	3.70
53 Desire for a Controllable World	5	.53	8- 43	6.86	13- 38	27.5	5.1	3.50	8- 43	30.4	5.1	3.50
54 Desire for Detachment from the World	4	.52	5- 34	6.93	5- 30	15.6	5.1	3.53	5- 34	18.5	5.2	3.60

Table IV.7 (continued)

Scale No. and Name	No. of Items	Hoyt's Reliability	Theoretic Range	Standard Score S meas.	Clergy N = 301				Lay N = 4444			
					Actual Range	Mean	S.D.	Raw Score S meas.	Actual Range	Mean	S.D.	Raw Score S meas.
55 Family Level of Education	4	.70	7- 34	5.48	13- 34	24.4	5.2	2.85	7- 34	17.3	6.0	'3.29
56 Social Distance—Radical Life Styles	12	.90	24-106	3.16	24-100	60.6	16.9	5.34	25-105	78.5	15.0	4.74
57 Social Distance—Racial and Religious Groups	8	.89	12- 63	3.32	12- 50	23.2	7.8	2.59	12- 59	28.2	10.0	3.32
58 Awareness of the Immanent Trinity	9	.51	32- 78	7.00	35- 75	63.3	7.0	4.90	32- 78	55.8	9.5	6.65
59 Social Utility of Christianity	4	.62	7- 35	6.16	13- 35	21.8	4.7	2.90	7- 35	19.9	4.7	2.90
60 Individual Christian Responsibility	8	.65	37- 71	5.92	50- 71	60.1	4.8	2.84	42- 71	56.2	4.9	2.90
61 Image of Lutherans as Different	6	.65	12- 54	5.92	12- 52	38.5	6.4	3.79	12- 53	37.0	6.2	3.67
62 Service Without Proclamation	4	.49	4- 34	7.14	4- 32	21.4	4.9	3.50	4- 34	23.2	5.5	3.93
63 Peer Orientation	18	.62	23-104	6.16	24- 61	36.6	6.9	4.25	23- 84	36.4	8.6	5.30
64 Power Orientation to Social Issues	6	.45	15- 49	7.42	15- 46	31.6	6.0	4.50	17- 49	33.2	5.2	5.94
65 Church Involvement in Social Issues	12	.65	24- 99	5.92	44- 97	69.0	11.0	6.51	33- 99	63.8	9.5	5.62
66 Emotional Certainty of Faith	6	.71	24- 54	5.39	46- 54	52.6	1.7	.92	25- 54	51.0	3.3	1.78
67 Self-Oriented Utilitarianism	9	.53	18- 67	6.86	19- 55	35.2	7.0	4.80	19- 64	40.8	6.6	4.52
68 Life Purpose	9	.80	14- 76	4.47	34- 76	58.6	7.6	3.40	14- 76	51.9	11.7	5.01
69 Horatio Alger Orientation	12	.64	40-100	6.00	40- 93	65.0	13.8	8.28	40-100	70.3	13.9	8.34
70 Gospel Oriented Life	9	.50	39- 77	7.07	39- 77	62.2	7.8	5.52	39- 77	57.3	7.8	5.52
71 Attitudes Toward Life and Death	13	.63	58-101	6.08	75-101	94.7	4.5	2.74	68-101	90.7	7.2	4.38
72 Orientation to "Doing" Influenced by the Church	9	.57	47- 77	6.56	47- 77	68.6	6.5	4.26	47- 81	67.3	7.7	5.05
73 Drug Culture Orientation	12	.73	12- 72	5.20	12- 27	12.3	1.3	.68	12- 68	13.0	3.7	1.92
74 Personal Initiative on Church and Public Issues	18	.81	18- 98	4.36	20- 95	44.3	18.4	8.02	20- 76	23.7	5.7	2.48
75 Post World War II Presidential Voting	8	.76	12- 46	4.90	12- 46	20.3	8.5	4.16	12- 46	22.0	7.9	3.87
76 Republican Presidential Voting	6	.83	8- 40	4.12	8- 40	17.3	8.4	3.46	8- 40	14.2	6.4	2.64
77 Democratic Presidential Voting	8	.81	8- 51	4.36	8- 50	16.1	7.6	3.31	8- 51	18.0	10.0	4.36
78 Openness to Change Within the Church	12	.55	28- 82	6.71	36- 82	63.3	8.9	5.97	30- 82	56.2	8.1	5.43

the total to 78 scales (64 parent scales, and 14 subscales of which these quotients were the first four: Racial, Religious, Political, and Social Distance Quotients).

RELIABILITY AND STANDARD ERROR OF MEASUREMENT

As has been said earlier, the type of reliability sought in the process of extracting the scales was homogeneity (Loevinger, 1947, 1948) or internal consistency (Kuder–Richardson, 1937). Psychometric literature also uses other names for it; for example, Cronbach's (1951) alpha co-efficient, Hoyt's (1941) reliability by analysis of variance. All these approaches have a common property—that of giving reliability as a ratio and not as a correlation or measure of association. Data for a correlational approach, specifically test–retest reliability or stability, have not yet been collected.

Homogeneity of scales. The size of the 64 empirically derived parent scales averages 9.6 items. Their reliabilities range from .45 (only two scales under .50) to .90 with a median of .70. The size of the 10 empirically derived subscales averages 7.2 items. Their reliabilities range from .60 to .80 with a median of .74.

The naming of scales. Names and descriptions for scales 5-78 are the work of the four primary members of the research team and do not reflect identifications and insights from additional independent judges. They are based not only on item content but also on an awareness of the history of items and how the various scales behave in the context of each other and a wide variety of simple descriptive variables. Each researcher named the scales independently, then all four researchers reconciled differences in perception and perspective and came to a common terminology through lengthy discussion. Validation of scale names by blind matching of items to scales by independent judges must be part of future work.

Independence of scales. Since all of the items in subscales also occur in corresponding parent scales, subscales should and do intercorrelate highly with parent scales, but not so highly as to be identical. Otherwise scales should intercorrelate minimally, and thus each should make an independent contribution of information that no other scale makes. It is, of course, possible that two scales can correlate highly and yet be measuring two different properties, if the two properties are functionally related. For a fuller discussion of this issue, especially as it relates to the 64 parent scales of this survey, see the Introduction to Part II. It is sufficient here merely to notice that if two highly correlated scales are from the same general data set (e.g., all data concerning beliefs), they may be measuring somewhat the same dimension. By contrast if they have been derived from two different data sets (e.g., one from belief data, the other from attitudinal or self-reported behavior data), they likely measure two different but dependent or functionally related dimensions.

In keeping with an assumption that scales are best derived of data from the widest possible variety of subjects from the population under study, all scales were derived using half-samples of the combination of both clergy and lay samples. What was ultimately of consequence for this research was whether or not the parent scales were relatively independent measures for comparing subgroups of lay people with lay people, of clergy with clergy, or of lay people with clergy, but not mixed subgroups of lay people and clergy.

Therefore, using the reciprocal averages weights described earlier, scores of all *lay people only* on all scales were used to calculate all possible correlations among the 64 parent scales. A summary of those correlations is given in Table IV.8. Only 26 coefficients have an absolute value of .50 or higher, indicating that a common variance of 25% or more is limited to 1% of the possible number of correlations:

Table IV.8   Summary of Intercorrelations Among the 64 Parent Scales

Range of Correlation	Number of Intercorrelations
+ .700 through + .999	0
+ .600 through + .699	3
+ .500 through + .599	23
+ .400 through + .499	43
+ .300 through + .399	76
+ .200 through + .299	185
+ .100 through + .199	315
.000 through + .099	529
.000 through − .099	472
− .100 through − .199	244
− .200 through − .299	93
− .300 through − .399	30
− .400 through − .499	2
− .500 through − .599	1
− .600 through − .699	0
− .700 through − .999	0
	2,016

Careful study of the table also showed that roughly half of this apparent dependence among scales is likely due to functional relationships among different dimensions rather than overlap in measurement. This provides encouraging indication of success in developing independent scales.

Second-order factor analysis of all scales. Since scales were formed partially on the basis of factor analytic results, the later principal factor analysis (with normal varimax rotation) of the correlation matrix of all scales was a second-order factoring. As mentioned earlier, this analysis was partially for the purpose of investigating the possibility that the content of scales had been seriously limited due to a restriction of items to groups by number of response possibilities during scale derivation analysis. Results as reported in greater detail in the Introduction to Part II did *not* confirm the presence of such a problem.

In all, six factor analyses were performed, and with minor variations all produced basically the same factors. Three analyses were performed on each of two data sets of lay people alone, and lay people plus clergy (since the scales were developed out of this latter merger of two samples):

1. Intercorrelations of all 78 scales.
2. Intercorrelations of the 64 parent scales only.
3. Intercorrelations of the 56 unique scales; plus the 14 subscales without their 8 corresponding parent scales.

Complete factoring was performed, through all factors with eigenvalue ≥ 1.00.

Refactoring of items in the most cohesive second-order factor. Results of the above second-order factor analyses showed 28 scales loading most heavily in the first two most cohesive factors. As a final precaution against the possibility of item response restrictions having been too great in scale derivation analyses, the 196 items in the nine scales most highly related to the first factor, "The Heart of Lutheran Piety," were submitted both to principal factor analysis and to cluster analysis in two ways: (a) using the initial raw score weights, and (b) using the derived reciprocal averages weights. The sets of items so derived did *not* vary appreciably from those identified in the initial multivariate scale derivation analyses when restrictions of number of item responses were in force. Apparently, then, no significant variation in scale derivation resulted from the restrictions placed on the input item groups in the initial scale derivation analyses.

UNIVARIATE DATA ANALYSIS

Four levels of data analysis were planned prior to data collection. Results of these analyses were intended to be in the form of:

1. Descriptive statistics with comparisons of subgroups on a broad variety of variables such as age, education, sex, and region.
2. Tests of hypotheses that replicated or grew out of several previous scientific studies of religion and its relationship to certain attitudes and specific behaviors.
3. Typologies of belief, value, opinion, attitude, and self-reported life style.
4. World views (Weltanschauungen) that are composites of beliefs, values, and commensurate attitudes and frequent behaviors.

Each of these intended outcomes would require a combination of univariate and multivariate techniques of analysis, but as one moves from outcome 1 to 4 the multivariate techniques predominate progressively. Therefore, chronologically, if one views the multivariate scale derivation as preliminary for identification of major variables, the analyses proceeded from the univariate and simple to the more complex and multivariate.

The distinction between univariate and multivariate analyses is not a matter of how many variables are of interest or are analyzed; it is one of whether a single independent variable is being analyzed alone, as if no others existed (univariate), or whether the possible effects of two or more independent variables simultaneously are being analyzed (multivariate).

During the first four months of 1971 while the empirical scaling was being done, the following univariate analyses were also performed largely using single items and the four arbitrarily developed social distance scales:

1. Frequency distributions for all items, both single and multiple response, as well as subscales 1-4 and congregation descriptive variables for total lay sample, total clergy sample, and both combined, and for subgroups by a variety of age groupings, church body affiliation, region, sex, education, and a combination of education, sex, and clergy-lay status.

2. Subgroup graphs by education, sex, and age, developed by computer through use of a Cal-comp Plotter.

3. Expected frequencies, percentage distributions, chi-square tests of independence, and probabilities of the test results for every item, calculated with every frequency distribution.

4. Several double and triple joint distributions of interrelated items such as 721-722 concerning perceived level of church activity of father and mother during respondent's youth, and double response items such as 205 concerning perceived greatest influences upon one's life.

5. Frequency distributions, computer developed histograms, and measures of skewness, Kurtosis, and approximation to the normal curve for the distributions of the various empirically derived scales and subscales as they were identified.

Had multivariate analyses not been planned, they would have been compelled as a means of summarizing data because we found statistically significant differences among subgroups on most of the above-mentioned variables for one-half to three-fourths of the items even when a (Type I error) was set at .000001, due to the large sample size, instead of the conventional .05 to .001.

Preliminary findings, including the largest subgroup differences, were summarized and discussed in 400 pages of study documents by the end of April 1971. This reflected the researchers' conviction that good research includes involving potential users in the interpretation of findings, clarification of implications, and determination of the form of the report.

CONSULTING WITH CHURCH LEADERS

Inasmuch as the purpose of the study was to supply the kind of information that would be of help to a local parish pastor in carrying out his ministry, a special effort was made to organize the findings in a way that would speak to the needs of the parish situation. To secure counsel and reaction from churchmen and laymen at all levels of church responsibility, a series of conferences was held with church leaders. One was a February workshop with clergymen whose congregations participated in the survey, and the second was a series of regional conferences that involved pastors, congregational laymen, church executives, and educators. Inasmuch as the input from these people preceded the final stage of data analysis, an accounting will be given of the contribution of these consultations to the final outcome of what is reported.

February workshop. Twelve clergymen whose congregations had been drawn into the first stage sample were selected on the basis of region, size of church, and church body to participate in a three-day workshop in Minneapolis. The purpose of this workshop was to share the preliminary findings and to gain help in how to organize and interpret the results in a way that would provide the most benefit to parish life and ministry.

Tentative conclusions developed out of the pastors' workshop including the following:

1. A typical social science research report would not likely be used much by the churches.

2. A comprehensive report of findings, possibly in hard cover, would be helpful if it were only technical enough to be respected in the scientific community but were, nevertheless, written primarily in nontechnical language for the professional theologian, pastor, and somewhat sophisticated lay person, with focus on the parish.

3. A series of several popularly-written, interpretive paperbacks should be developed either around single, major issues or around the tasks and problems of several parish leadership roles, or around vignettes descriptive of "typical Lutherans" identified by the data.

4. A variety of media should be employed in dissemination of the findings.

Regional conferences. A series of seven regional conferences was held during the months of May and June in the following cities:

Atlanta, Georgia   Omaha, Nebraska
Chicago, Illinois   Philadelphia, Pennsylvania
Cleveland, Ohio   San Francisco, California
Minneapolis, Minnesota

In each location there was a conference for the parish pastor and one layman of each congregation that participated in A *Study of Generations.* Following the one and one-half day conference with these local representatives, a similar one and one-half day conference was devoted to sharing similar information with administrators and executives of the church as well as educational leaders of the colleges, universities, and seminaries of the church. A total of 678 persons registered and attended these 14 conferences. Prior to each conference one or more of the following five study documents were sent to each of the participants (one full set, including the Introduction, was given each participating congregation):

Document A: Youth of the Lutheran Church
Document B: Beliefs of Lutheranism
Document C: Mission and Ministry (Institutional Loyalty)
Document E: Who Are the Lutherans? (A Partial Descriptive Profile)

An oral presentation on "How Lutherans See Themselves and Others" replaced a projected Document D at each conference. These documents were based upon the initial findings of the study and hence were presented as a preliminary report.

Purposes of the conferences were:

1. Well in advance of any published material, to inform key leaders of what was being found and what likely would be found as a result of further analysis.
2. To test the reaction of these key Lutherans to what was being reported and how it was being stated.
3. To hear what these participants saw as implications of preliminary findings.
4. To secure their counsel concerning the importance and appropriate sequence of additional analyses.
5. To secure their counsel concerning most appropriate methods of dissemination and pertinent applications of findings.
6. To encourage them to take the necessary steps for involving their congregation, area, department, or institution in a study and application of the survey results.

Tape recordings were made of their questions and reactions, and written accounts were secured from all individuals. These conference data were funneled to appropriate members of the research team in preparation for this writing after:

1. Summary transcription of all conference tapes.
2. Reorganization of summaries by study document into questions, criticisms, suggestions for improvement, and alternative interpretations.
3. Collation of all clarifying questions written at the conferences with those secured by tape recording.

4. Isolation of requests for additional analyses for specifically stated purposes.
5. Isolation of technical questions and requests for clarification of research terminology and methodology.
6. Separate summarization of ideas and recommendations concerning communication of findings.
7. Condensation of written statements of what the participants felt should be done by whomever, how, and when, as a result of the preliminary findings available in study document form.

MULTIVARIATE DATA ANALYSIS

During June through October 1971 a depth analysis was made of the research data to establish the empirical base for the report given in this publication. Three methods of analysis that are pertinent here are factor analysis, analysis of variance, and the automatic interaction detection technique (AID).

Summary of factor analyses. The factor analytic techniques used in derivàtion of scales have already been described.

Chapter 1 reports the results of factoring the correlations among all persons by one-year age groups using data from all psychological and theological items. Full discussion of the four methods used for this identification of relatively discrete generations is available in an unpublished paper by Braun (1971), "On Finding the Generation Gap." *

Preliminary work was begun for a principal factor analysis of congregational descriptive data to isolate possible types of congregations. At this writing it has not been completed for lack of project resources and also because of disappointing results in later AID analyses aimed at discovery of significant differences among inner city, urban, suburban, and other congregations.

Second-order principal factor analyses of correlations of all scales have been described earlier in this section. Results are reported in the Introduction to Section II and provide the major framework for Chapters 4 through 9.

Analysis of variance. The plan for data analysis that was conceived before data collection included performing a series of two- to five-way factorial, fixed effects analyses of variance using scales as dependent variables with categorical and descriptive items and quartile versions of scales as independent variables. We anticipated identifying (1) significant interactions that might be developed into additive composite variables or, at least, explicated carefully, and (2) significant main effects that might identify sets of variables that could then be submitted to multiple regression analysis. All hypotheses were to be based on social scientific theory or theological systems. All higher analyses of variance above the order of two were abandoned because every early attempt apparently produced a matrix with such internal dependencies that there was no inverse.

Because they are so frequently claimed to be of major significance, a set of six variables was selected for analyses in relation to all scales, first with weighted then unweighted means, by all premutations of two (a total of 15). The six variables were age, sex, education, region, church body affiliation, and size of congregation. These analyses were completed and interpreted by late summer 1971. Though all six variables were found to be significantly related to some scales, and age and education most consistently and powerfully so (and in interaction), none were found to be accounting for more than 10% and often no more than negligible amounts of variance. These and other results that suggested the existence of other variables that each would account for much more variance, motivated the team first to make a drastic reduction of the number of dependent variables to be analyzed (later expanded again), and second to turn to a method of analysis not previously intended but obviously more efficient and better suited to the data—Automatic Interaction Detection which is described below. The clergy–lay variable and the five scales indicating subdimensions of committed and consensual religiosity were also analyzed as independent variables in relation to all of the scales. In all, more than 2700 analyses of variance were performed.

In an attempt to balance the probabilities of Type I and II error with such a large sample, a was set at .0001. For explication of interactions, Scheffé's correction (Winer, 1962, pp. 88-89) was applied to F-tests of comparisons of cell means, or the Newman–Keuls procedure (Winer, pp. 80-88) was used, again with $a = .0001$ and .001 respectively.

Automatic Interaction Detection (AID). Most multivariate procedures are based on the theoretical statistician's adages that both additivity and normality of distribution are good initial approximations to reality. Yet analyses of *A Study of Generations* data to this point had shown the presence of several variables with skewed distributions and obviously interactive relationships. The situation called for initial multivariate analytic procedures based on less rigid assumptions. What was needed was a technique by which a relatively large number of predictor or "effector" variables with a wide variety of relatively unknown characteristics and interrelationships could be analyzed in simultaneous relationship to one dependent or criterion variable after another. This did not mean that theory would not be taken into consideration in the selection of such data sets for analysis, but it did mean that we would be wise to make as few assumptions as possible about the statistical characteristics of our scales and leftover single items, and the dimensions and properties they represented. A good tool for work in the context of discovery—for mapping, describing, and for generating or fitting models implicit in the data—would likely serve better initially than any tool from the context of verification, based on assumptions about the data as rigorous as the assumptions for regression analysis or higher order analyses of variance. A large scale computer program for automatic interaction detection among as many as 39 predictors of one dependent variable was selected as the best tool with the least restrictions for the task (Sonquist and Morgan, 1964). Sonquist (1970) described the AID technique as an algorithm that: (1) involves the successive segregation of sample subgroups through the stepwise application of one-way analysis of variance techniques, (2) produces information for the analyst on whether to introduce additivity assumptions immediately or to develop and use interaction terms in an equation representing a possible predictive model implicit in the data, (3) gives a representation of interactive models that is clear and accurate, (4) discriminates between additive and interactive models even in the presence of noise in the data, and yet (5) cannot report main effects adjusted for intercorrelations. AID is especially fitted for the initial analysis of cross-sectional survey data, as in *A Study of Generations,* where the interrelationships among a multitude of variables are of interest but are neither known nor easily hypothesized because of the paucity of empirically based theory. Because of the fifth characteristic cited, which is really a limitation, AID is best used jointly, in the opinion of Sonquist (1970), with multiple classification analysis for careful and precise predictive model building. But AID is the best initial analysis.

A subset of the 78 scales, omitting most subscales and unique scales of lesser reliability, was used as the pool of dependent variables. A quartile version of every scale was developed for use of scales as independent (predictor) variables. Predictor variables were allowed to run free, i.e., any combination of levels of a variable, whether sequential or not, could be used in the formation of two subgroups of the sample at any stage of the analysis on the basis of maximizing the ratio of BSS (between sum of squares) to TSS (total sum of squares). The following parameters were arbitrarily set as limits on the process of partitioning the sample into subgroups that were progressively more homogeneous on the basis of the most powerful predictors:

1. A minimum value of 3.00 for Student's t for the difference between means of two subgroups created on the basis of a given predictor.
2. A minimum of 0.5% of the total sum of squares contained in any group before it becomes a candidate for splitting into two more subgroups.
3. A minimum of 0.1% of the remaining sum of squares explained by any split made on the basis of a given predictor.

4. A minimum of 25 persons in any subgroup.
5. A maximum of 30 subgroups.

Despite these restrictions that were placed on a rather automatic computer program, all results of AID analyses that are reported in the body of the book are about predictors that each controlled or explained a minimum of 2% of variance and sometimes as much as 20%. The ultimate criterion for identifying the significance of any predictor variable was neither the sequence in which sample subgroups were partitioned by various predictor variables, nor the t statistic from comparison of any two subgroup means, but rather the percentage of total variance explained by however many splits were made based on that variable.

Most AID analyses were based on the entire lay sample or the entire clergy sample with the exception of one series of approximately 15 analyses. There age was controlled by use of a subsample just of youth ages 15-28 because of the greater potential impact of educational programs upon them. In this subset of AID analyses concerning youth, predictor variables were introduced on the basis of theories and hypotheses derived from former research on youth performed at Youth Research Center and by others as summarized by Strommen (1971).

A variety of rationales were used to organize AID analyses based on the entire sample of lay people, but all were for the one purpose of providing as much meaningful, practically relevant, nonredundant explanations of variance as possible. Predictors were selected in each case with awareness of the following in varying proportions:

1. Social science theories and theological systems.
2. Intercorrelations among variables including results of previous second-order factoring of the scales. (When intercorrelated predictors compete in the same analysis, correlates tend to "wash out" after the one most highly related to the dependent variable subdivides the sample.)
3. Relationships of variables to conceptualization of the study in terms of beliefs and values that are hypothesized to influence attitudes and behaviors, and vice versa.
4. Results of previous AID analyses.

For the sake of brevity, results were reported where possible in terms of the ideal-type models of variable interrelationships identified by Sonquist (1970). If possession of characteristics is related to increase in a person's score on some criterion, the characteristics are advantages. If such possession is related to decrease in score, the characteristics are disadvantages. *Additive advantage* involves an upward push in score from the possession of multiple characteristics, which is equal to the sum of their separate effects. *Cumulative advantage* involves an upward push from possession of multiple characteristics, which is equal to more than the sum of their separate effects. In the case of *substitute advantage* the combined effects are less than the sum of the separate effects. One or more substitute advantages may raise criterion scores to a certain point, but no further, even with the addition of more advantages. Disadvantages may likewise be additive, cumulative, or substitutive. Three ideal-type models are:

AA where both advantages and disadvantages are additive

CS where advantages cumulate and disadvantages are substitutes

SC where advantages are substitutes and disadvantages cumulate

One can hypothesize 15 combinations of additivity, cumulation, and substitution in terms of advantage and disadvantage before one conceives of some of the truly complex situations likely to exist in reality.

One thing is sure. Though several hundred AID analyses were performed, there is no sense in which our multivariate data analyses have been exhaustive. There is much more to be done. What has been reported in this book represents only the time and resource limitations of *A Study of Generations*.

Future analyses might well include:

1. MANOVA (multivariate analysis of variance), toward identification of types, with tests for comparability of profiles.

2. Careful model building using a combination of AID and MCA (multiple classification analysis) for development of multiple linear regression prediction equations after development of additively related composite variables from defined interactions of single variables.

Several specific areas of practical and theoretical significance have already been set aside for continuing analysis.

REPORTING THE STUDY

During the summer of 1971 Dr. Arthur Johnson, a sociologist at the University of Minnesota, joined the research team. He became a part of the writing team that has produced this publication.

Since not all the implications of this study could be reported in this book, the Youth Research Center is developing a series of paperbacks for publication by Augsburg Publishing House. Each paperback will provide interpretation of data on a specific subject and will suggest implications for individuals and congregations.

Currently tests are being made which assess the validity of the data being reported here. The two primary approaches are those of establishing congruent and construct validity. It is outside of the scope of this book, however, to give an adequate account of the interlocking indices that establish the case for its validity. An illustration of what this can be, however, is found in a technical manual, produced by the Youth Research Center on Youth Research Survey Books I and II, that describes procedures similar to those reported in *A Study of Generations.* This technical manual is available upon request.

APPENDIX B

Dimension Names and Descriptions

Sixty-four scales and 10 subscales formed empirically from the data, as described in Chapter 3 and Appendix A. Additional subscales numbered 1 through 4 were formed arbitrarily, making a total of 78. Each scale is assumed to indicate an underlying property called a dimension as also described in Chapter 3.

Names and brief descriptions of the dimensions assumed by the research team to underlie the 64 scales are listed here by original number in the set of 78. Dimensions related to subscales have been omitted since they generally are not discussed in the body of the book.

Scale Number and Dimension Name	Content, or Assessment of:	High Score Indicates	Low Score Indicates
5. Humanity of Jesus	Agreement with statements describing the human characteristics of Jesus	Agreement	Nonagreement
6. Divinity of Jesus	Agreement with statements describing the divine characteristics of Jesus	Agreement	Nonagreement
8. Biblical Knowledge	Correct knowledge of the Bible at a rudimentary level	Elementary knowledge of Bible	Lack of elementary knowledge
9. Biblical Ignorance	Lack of knowledge or incorrect knowledge of the Bible	Considerable lack of knowledge or misinformation	Little or no elementary misinformation
Prior Denominational Membership			
10. Larger Church Bodies	Identification of persons who have had prior memberships in other Lutheran churches, as well as other church bodies. Dimension 10 includes prior membership in one of the three major Lutheran bodies and/or six other denominations. Dimension 11 includes prior membership in smaller Lutheran bodies and/or 12 other religious bodies	More than one church move	Lifelong membership in one's present Lutheran body
11. Smaller Church Bodies			
12. The Church, Me, and Social Justice	Desire for the church to be actively involved in issues of social justice including one's own willingness to be personally involved	Desire and willingness	Disagreement and unwillingness
13. Family and Congregational Caring Life	Perception of one's own family and congregation as open to caring for others	Perception of caring and openness to caring	Perception of not caring and lack of openness

359

Scale Number and Dimension Name	Content, or Assessment of:	High Score Indicates	Low Score Indicates
14. A Personal, Caring God	Belief in God as the wise and beneficent ruler of the world, and a feeling or awareness that God cares for you personally in Christ Jesus	Conviction, belief	Doubt or disbelief
15. Salvation by Works	Belief that I can influence God to think well of me by doing good things; this includes an achievement orientation to all of life	Belief in or uncertainty about salvation by works	Disbelief in salvation by works
16. The Exclusive Truth Claim of Christianity Exaggerated	Belief in one "True Church" and salvation only through Christ Jesus	Exaggeration: belief that the "True Church" is clearly known and, thus, its enemies are also clearly known. Distortion of the exclusive claims of Lutheran theology	Rejection of belief both in one "True Church" and salvation only in Christ
17. Feelings of Isolation and Pressure	One aspect of alienation: the feeling of being under strain and an outsider to the festival of life	Expression of a sense of aloneness and inner turmoil	Lack or denial of such feelings
18. Identification with Parents	Perception of self as alike or different from one's parents on a variety of values, opinions, and attitudes	Perception of considerable likeness	Perceived generation difference
19. Religious Experience	The degree and intensity of religious experience in one's life and the significance for salvation that one places on religious experience	Broad variety of intense religious experience, perhaps including faith healing and/or speaking in tongues	Limited, vague, or no religious experience
20. Supporting Others in Crises	Frequency during the last year of helping other people in emergency situations such as death, serious illness, severe financial hardship, and the like	Frequently helping in a variety of situations	Never helping due to lack of occasion or initiative
21. Personal Evangelism	Individual witnessing to one's faith and trying to draw others into Christian fellowship by a variety of means including both words and other actions	High activity during the past year	No specific or deliberate testimony or overtures to others during the past year
22. Neighborliness	Frequency of assisting friends and neighbors in a general spirit of helpfulness	Frequently assisting in a variety of ways during the past year	Never helping due to limited time, availability, or initiative
23. Questionable Personal Activities	Frequency of participation in a variety of activities for which there are varied ethical evaluations, such as swearing, lying, gambling, getting drunk, reading pornography, non-marital sexual expression, fighting, and attending X-rated movies	Frequent participation during the past year	Limited or no participation during the past year

Dimension Name	Content, or Assessment of:	High Score Indicates	Low Score Indicates
26. Mutual Support Among Church, Society, and Individuals	Composite opinion that I need the church to support my Christian life, society needs the church to support its life, and I willingly offer my support to the church at large	Agreement	Doubt or disagreement
27. Disappointment with the Church	Disappointment with one's congregation for its failure to accept me and its overemphasis on money, and with the larger church for its irrelevance and costly social service and education	Heavily negative or uncertain evaluation	Positive, at least not a negative evaluation
28. Transcendental Meaning in Life	Acceptance of a transcendental dimension to life, i.e., commitment to "another world" than the world immediately available through the senses, as well as to life in "this world" as involving acceptance of individual responsibility to build relationships with other persons upon certain values	Accepting, or placing a high value on these presuppositions	Rejecting, or at least placing a low value on these presuppositions
29. Values of Self-Development	Goals in life necessary for development of personal identity and gratification of personal needs such as personal power, adventure, money, appearance, recognition, pleasure	High ranking of these goals vs. "Transcendental Meaning in Life"	Low ranking of these goals
34. Generalized Prejudice	Proneness to make derogatory judgments about blacks and Jews as well as general stereotyped responses toward groups to which a person does not belong	Strong tendency toward negative judgment and stereotyping	Strong rejection of stereotypes and negative labeling
35. Pessimism	Alienation in terms of a negative or depressed quality of life that comes from turning in upon oneself	Alienation from hope and expectation	General optimism toward life and people
36. Christian Utopianism	Belief and opinion that religion, particularly every person becoming a Christian, will bring about the perfect life for individuals and will and should build the utopian society	Holding a nearly magical view of the power of religious faith	Rejection of overemphasis on the effectiveness of religion
37. Need for Unchanging Structure	Belief, attitude, and opinion that family and social life must be rigidly structured and unchanging in the face of perceived threat	Fear of change and low tolerance of diversity	Openness to change and role diversity
40. Congregational Activity	Frequency of participation and level of satisfaction in organized congregational life	Joy and satisfaction through high activity	Little involvement in organized congregational life, being either generally inactive in religious life or directing activities through noncongregational channels

Scale Number and Dimension Name	Content, or Assessment of:	High Score Indicates	Low Score Indicates
41. Personal Piety	Perception of oneself as a religious person	Orientation around religious beliefs, active participation in the church, and active devotional life	Rarely or never reading the Bible or other religious literature, giving low priority to religious matters, and giving little of themselves or their finances to church work
42. The Role of Pastors in Social Action	Attitudes toward the role of clergy in issues of social justice	Approval of highly activist pastors (including public demonstration and civil disobedience)	Rejection of the model of the social activist pastor
43. Need for Religious Absolutism	Appreciation of authoritative rituals and symbols that offer a sense of security	Strong need for such religious absolutism	Denial of the importance to ritual worship and rejection of authoritative symbols
44. Fundamentalism–Liberalism	Religious belief or stance from fundamentalism to liberalism on a variety of doctrines	Exaggerated exclusivism and commitment to fundamentalistic dogma	Rejection of Christian dogma in favor of liberalized attitudes toward truth claims
45. Organizational Memberships	Number of memberships in 13 varieties of organized groups such as unions, fraternal groups, and veterans, youth, civic, or charitable organizations other than the church	Many memberships	Noninvolvement in organized group life in the community
46. Importance of Christian Practices in My Life	Rough estimate of the importance a person attaches to prayer, communion, baptism, and faith	Very much importance	Little or no importance
47. Personal Involvement in Church and Community	Past service and leadership in church and community, as well as future willingness to serve	Great willingness and/or actual participation in congregational or community matters	Preference not to participate and/or never having been significantly involved in any church or community role requiring extra time or effort
49. Anxiety over My Faith	Personal concern over feelings of being distant and alienated from God, spiritually lonesome, unable to live up to one's religious convictions, and uncertain about one's relationship to God and one's state after death	Very much concern	Lack of concern due either to disinterest or having resolved this anxiety
50. Acceptance of Middle-Class Norms	Perception of the ease with which one accepts conventional standards of dress, respectability, law observance, and respect for authority	Perceived easy acceptance	Perceived rejection, or, at the very least, difficulty accepting

Scale Number and Dimension Name	Content, or Assessment of:	High Score Indicates	Low Score Indicates
51. Acceptance of Authority	Perception of the ease with which one accepts the societal prohibition of use of drugs and the authority of a "boss"	Perceived easy acceptance	Perceived repudiation, or, at the very least, difficulty accepting
52. Desire for a Dependable World	Liking for life in an orderly, predictable, stable world	Strong liking	Strong dislike
53. Desire for a Controllable World	Liking for a world that is subject to manipulation, where human actions make an impact	Strong liking	Strong dislike
54. Desire for Detachment from the World	Liking for a life of escape from a demanding, pushing, hostile world	Strong liking	Strong dislike
55. Family Level of Education	Composite level of formal education completed by oneself, one's spouse, and one's parents	Probably postgraduate training or degree; definitely college graduate	Eighth grade or less
56. Social Distance—Radical Life Styles	Openness to social interaction with persons who differ particularly in style of life or political ideology	Desire not to have close social interaction	Willingness to have close relationships
57. Social Distance—Racial and Religious Groups	Openness to social interaction with persons who differ particularly in religious belief or race	Desire not to have close social interaction	Willingness to have close relationships
58. Awareness of the Immanent Trinity	Belief in the Triune God as both transcendent and immanent	Sense of God as more close	Sense of God as more distant
59. Social Utility of Christianity	Opinion of the usefulness of the church and Christian faith in combatting attitudes that are detrimental to society	Evaluation of church and faith as useful in developing positive social attitudes	Rejection of such an evaluation
60. Individual Christian Responsibility	Belief and opinion concerning the responsibility of every Christian to question yet hold the faith, and to bear candid witness to Christ and the faith with openness and flexibility in relationships with other people	Respect for, and acceptance of, that personal responsibility	Rejection and lack of respect for such responsibility
61. Image of Lutherans as Different	Opinion that Lutherans are distinctive due to their beliefs and practices, ethnic background, or pronounced personality characteristics	Seeing Lutherans as different in negative ways	Rejection of any unique stereotype or labeling of Lutherans as different from other Christians
62. Service Without Proclamation	Preference for mission work that does not include proclamation of the gospel but rather service to human need only	Strong preference	Strong disagreement

Scale Number and Dimension Name	Content, or Assessment of:	High Score Indicates	Low Score Indicates
63. Peer Orientation	Taking one's signals from one's own age group. Questions are couched so as to be most meaningful to youth	Strong anti-adult feelings, or not so strong anti-youth feelings, if one is an adult. Person may be unaware of the influences he really follows	Orientation to learning and taking cues from people of widely varied ages
64. Power Orientation to Social Issues	Endorsement of social reform cliches that there is a generation gap, that church and society must change, and that conflicts over issues of social justice and reform are essentially power struggles	Strong endorsement, for whatever changes are desired	Strong disagreement
65. Church Involvement in Social Issues	Opinion that the mission of the church is to take a liberal position on social issues and actively to work against injustice, inequality, and cruelty	Desire that the church become more involved in resolving social issues	Rejection of social involvement and endorsement of a more traditional model of the church's role
66. Emotional Certainty of Faith	Personal evaluation of worship services, frequent family worship, talking about one's faith, and the certainty of one's faith in God versus doubt	Considerable positive feeling, positive evaluation, and certainty	Doubt with neither positive feelings nor evaluations
67. Self-Oriented Utilitarianism	Attitude that religious and social life are for the purpose of serving my self-interest; this is a rough measure of tendency toward unsophisticated instrumentalism—use of religion for one's own ends	Rather crass use of religion for one's own purposes and satisfaction	Rejection of such utilitarianism
68. Life Purpose	Whether my life has purpose and meaning	Sense of purpose, and view of life as meaningful and joyous	Little or no sense of purpose, and tendency to view life despairingly
69. Horatio Alger Orientation	Conviction that everybody has opportunity, and anybody can achieve if he tries	Firm opinion that life is for doing: work hard, conform to the system, and you're bound to make it	Opinion that hard work doesn't always pay off: life is more for "being" than "doing"
70. Gospel-Oriented Life	Application of the gospel in relationships with other people by responding in difficult situations with personal forgiving interaction rather than primarily with use of authority or attempts at being just or reasonable	Consistent gospel response	Response with authority, law, justice, or reason

Scale Number and Dimension Name	Content, or Assessment of:	High Score Indicates	Low Score Indicates
71. Attitudes Toward Life and Death	Attitude toward death, human nature, interpersonal relationships, and sources of major influence on one's life and personality	View of death that is calm and serene and a view of life tending toward pious optimism that recognizes God as the major influence	View of death as enemy, end, or unknown, a pessimistic view of human nature, and a tendency to control interpersonal relationships
72. Orientation to "Doing" Influenced by the Church	Evaluation of human activity in terms of external standards of how much one succeeds at doing; but in this case the church's emphasis on service to others is built into this evaluative stance	Evaluation of life not in terms of "being" but of "doing," including tendencies toward authoritarianism, pessimistic view of human nature, and respect for the influence of the church	Evaluation of life in terms of "being" with an optimistic view of human nature
73. Drug Culture Orientation	Attitudes and practices of a counterculture with special emphasis on use of drugs	Heavy use of drugs with accompanying attitudes	No use of drugs or no inclination toward participation in a drug culture
74. Personal Initiative on Church and Public Issues	Individual initiative in making one's views known to officials both in church and in public affairs	Having personally contacted officials, engaged in some public protest, circulated a petition or otherwise taken a public stand	No personal involvement in controversial issues
75. Post World War II Presidential Voting	Actual voting record for president from 1952 to 1968	Consistent voting for Democrats	Consistent voting for Republicans
76. Republican Presidential Voting	Voting for Republican presidential candidates between 1932 and 1956	Consistent voting for Republicans	Consistent voting for other than Republicans
77. Democratic Presidential Voting	Voting for Democratic presidential candidates between 1932 and 1964	Consistent voting for Democrats	Consistent voting for other than Democrats
78. Openness to Change Within the Church	Whether liberal social thought should effect changes in both society and the church	Agreement; it should	Disagreement

APPENDIX C

Selected Scales, Including Percentages of
Response by Item

The derivation of 78 scales including 14 subscales is described in Section IV, Appendix A. Table IV.7 of that appendix contains detailed characteristics of each scale, such as number of items, theoretic range, actual range, mean, standard deviation, and raw score standard error of measurement for both clergy and lay samples.

This appendix, C, includes 56 scales and no subscales of the total set of 78, each identified by its original scale number. They have been selected on the basis of additional understanding they may provide as one meets new concepts, arguments, and descriptions of dimensions thought to underlie scales mentioned in the body of the book.

All percentages are for laity and clergy combined. Though clergy are slightly oversampled by comparison with lay people, these percentages are the best estimates we have for Lutherans *as a whole*. As such they are better estimates than the percentages from either the lay or clergy samples *alone* would be. All percentages of response have been rounded to the nearest whole percent; therefore, a report of 0% always means less than half of 1%. The letters NR consistently mean "no response."

All scales except 52, 53, and 54 are used by permission of Youth Research Center. Copyright 1972 Youth Research Center. ("Ways of Life" instructions and items 147-159, which comprise Scales 52, 53, and 54, are from Morris, Charles. *Varieties of Human Value*. Chicago: University of Chicago Press, 1956. These items were used in the *A Study of Generations* questionnaire by permission. Copyright 1956 by the University of Chicago. All rights reserved. Published 1956. Third impression 1968. Printed in the United States of America.)

Scale 5 Humanity of Jesus (Reliability .61)

Fill in the numbers of characteristics that you think accurately describe Jesus. Leave all other spaces blank.

2. Strong physically: NR — 3%, No — 43%, Yes — 54%
6. Not necessarily attractive physically: NR — 3%, No — 62%, Yes — 35%
8. Told jokes: NR — 3%, No — 75%, Yes — 23%
11. Was afraid of dying: NR — 3%, No — 84%, Yes — 14%
13. Felt sexual attraction: NR — 3%, No — 81%, Yes — 16%
15. Struggled to discover who he really was: NR — 3%, No — 82%, Yes — 16%

Scale 6 Divinity of Jesus (Reliability .78)

Fill in the number of characteristics that you think accurately describe Jesus. Leave all other spaces blank.

3. Alive today: NR — 3%, No — 31%, Yes — 66%
4. Knew everything all of the time: NR — 3%, No — 47%, Yes — 51%
5. Perfect in every way: NR — 3%, No — 33%, Yes — 65%
7. In command of all powers of nature: NR — 3%, No — 32%, Yes — 65%
9. Able to be anywhere in an instant: NR — 3%, No — 56%, Yes — 42%
10. Created everything there is: NR — 3%, No — 54%, Yes — 44%
12. All-powerful over illness and death: NR — 3%, No — 30%, Yes — 68%
14. In constant, perfect communication with God: NR — 3%, No — 18%, Yes — 79%

Scale 8 Biblical Knowledge (Reliability .66)

Mark only those statements you think are from the Bible. Leave others blank.

92. For it is easier for a camel to go through a needle's eye, than for a rich man to enter into the Kingdom of God: NR — 3%, No — 29%, Yes — 68%
95. Let your women keep silence in the churches; for it is not permitted unto them to speak: NR — 3%, No — 72%, Yes — 25%
96. For I the Lord thy God am a jealous God, visiting the iniquity of the fathers upon the children unto the third and fourth generation of them that hate me: NR — 3%, No — 21%, Yes — 77%

Mark the spaces for the following which you think were Old Testament prophets. Leave all other spaces blank.

97. Elijah: NR — 3%, No — 31%, Yes — 66%
99. Jeremiah: NR — 3%, No — 32%, Yes — 66%
102. Ezekiel: NR — 3%, No — 35%, Yes — 62%

Scale 9 Biblical Ignorance (Reliability .60)

Mark only those statements you think are from the Bible. Leave others blank.

93. Blessed are the strong; for they shall be the sword of God: NR — 3%, No — 61%, Yes — 36%

Mark only those which you think are Old Testament prophets.

98. Deuteronomy: NR — 3%, No — 65%, Yes — 32%
101. Leviticus: NR — 3%, No — 59%, Yes — 38%

Scale 10 Prior Denominational Membership—Larger Church Bodies
(Reliability .53)

104. Before joining the Lutheran Church were you a member of any other denomination? Mark "Yes" if you were; otherwise leave blank: NR — 3%, No — 72%, Yes — 25%

If you answered "Yes" to Question 104, mark "Yes" to as many of the following denominations to which you once belonged:

106. Baptist: NR — 3%, No — 93%, Yes — 4%
109. Episcopal: NR — 3%, No — 96%, Yes — 1%
112. Lutheran (ALC): NR — 3%, No — 94%, Yes — 3%
113. Lutheran (LCA): NR — 3%, No — 95%, Yes — 2%
114. Lutheran (LC-MS): NR — 3%, No — 95%, Yes — 2%
117. Methodist: NR — 3%, No — 91%, Yes — 6%
121. Presbyterian: NR — 3%, No — 94%, Yes — 3%
122. Roman Catholic: NR — 3%, No — 94%, Yes — 4%
127. Other: NR — 3%, No — 94%, Yes — 3%

Scale 12   The Church, Me, and Social Justice   (Reliability .67)

553. For the most part, Lutheran congregations have been woefully inadequate in facing up to the civil rights issue: NR — 6%, No — 59%, Yes — 35%
555. Christian education needs to bring laymen face to face with urban problems, racial discrimination, and possible solutions to these matters: NR — 6%, No — 26%, Yes — 69%
557. The Christian layman should examine his business to make sure it does not discriminate against Negroes: NR — 6%, No — 23%, Yes — 72%
561. A congregation should cut off financial support from church institutions (hospitals, missions, etc.) that discriminate against Negroes: NR — 6%, No — 56%, Yes — 39%
562. I really enjoy the work that I do for the Church at large: NR — 6%, No — 25%, Yes — 69%
563. Clergymen have a responsibility to speak out as the moral conscience of this nation: NR — 6%, No — 30%, Yes — 65%
565. A Christian layman should work to make sure Negroes can buy property in the area of their choice: NR — 6%, No — 52%, Yes — 43%
566. If my congregation offered me a chance to be active in meaningful work that made a difference in something, I would gladly do it: NR — 6%, No — 26%, Yes — 69%
567. When the Church at any level gives me an opportunity to use my occupational skills and training in serving my Lord and the Church, I am pleased and happy to do so and generally find it very meaningful: NR — 6%, No — 22%, Yes — 73%

Scale 13   Family and Congregational Caring Life   (Reliability .75)

588. The congregation where I am a member is doing something about some problems of social concern (for example, injustice, racism, housing, civil rights): NR — 6%, No — 62%, Yes — 32%
589. The congregation where I am a member tries to meet the pressing personal problems of people like me: NR — 6%, No — 37%, Yes — 57%
590. (If you are an adult, answer this:) Some children in my congregation recognize me and call me by name: NR — 6%, No — 32%, Yes — 62%
592. Most members of my congregation would accept a family of another race or religion into their community: NR — 6%, No — 30%, Yes — 64%
593. Most members of my congregation are quick to help those who are sick or in need: NR — 6%, No — 17%, Yes — 76%
594. Most adults in my congregation are concerned about such world problems as starvation, poverty, war: NR — 6%, No — 28%, Yes — 66%
596. My congregation is trying to help families improve parent-child relationships: NR — 6%, No — 44%, Yes — 50%
597. My congregation brings young people and adult members together to share points of view: NR — 6%, No — 50%, Yes — 44%
598. People who are quite different (richer, poorer, of another race, different in dress and hair) are welcome in my congregation: NR — 6%, No — 20%, Yes — 74%
599. Most confirmed members in my congregation would be able to tell you what the purpose of our congregation is: NR — 6%, No — 38%, Yes — 56%
601. My congregation seems interested in my age group: NR — 6%, No — 34%, Yes — 59%
603. My family and I are willing to invite persons of other races into our home: NR — 6%, No — 35%, Yes — 59%
605. My family often helps someone in need: NR — 6%, No — 20%, Yes — 74%
606. I appreciate the example in caring for others that my parents set for me: NR — 6%, No — 19%, Yes — 75%
607. My family discusses the use of our money as it relates to sharing with others: NR — 6%, No — 43%, Yes — 51%

Scale 14   A Personal, Caring God   (Reliability .77)

16. Christ is a living reality: NR — 3%, Yes — 86%, No — 7%, ? — 4%
19. God is a Heavenly Father who cares for me and to whom I am accountable: NR — 2%, Yes — 95%, No — 2%, ? — 2%
20. I know that I need God's continual love and care: NR — 2%, Yes — 95%, No — 2%, ? — 2%
22. The Word of God is revealed through the Scriptures: NR — 2%, Yes — 95%, No — 2%, ? — 2%
23. The Church is the agency through which God accomplishes His saving work in the world: NR — 3%, Yes — 78%, No — 13%, ? — 6%

24. God answers my prayers: NR — 2%, Yes — 82%, No — 5%, ? — 11%
25. The Bible provides basic moral principles to guide every decision of my daily life: NR — 2%, Yes — 79%, No — 14%, ? — 5%
27. There is some kind of a hell where men are punished after death for rejecting God: NR — 2%, Yes — 64%, No — 18%, ? — 16%
29. I am forgiven by God even when I sin: NR — 2%, Yes — 85%, No — 8%, ? — 5%
33. Jesus is my personal Savior: NR — 2%, Yes — 86%, No — 8%, ? — 4%
49. There is a divine plan and purpose for every living person and thing: NR — 2%, Yes — 84%, No — 9%, ? — 5%
50. Property (house, automobile, money, investments, etc.) belongs to God; we only hold it in trust for him: NR — 2%, Yes — 69%, No — 24%, ? — 5%
52. No matter how unimportant the job may be, doing it well is important: NR — 2%, Yes — 95%, No — 3%, ? — 1%
57. I believe in salvation as release from sin and freedom for new life: NR — 3%, Yes — 84%, No — 8%, ? — 6%
58. God revealed himself to man in Jesus Christ: NR — 2%, Yes — 93%, No — 3%, ? — 2%

Scale 15   Salvation by Works   (Reliability .79)

17. The main emphasis of the Gospel is on God's rules for right living: NR — 4%, Yes — 59%, No — 34%, ? — 3%
18. Although there are many religions in the world, most of them lead to the same God: NR — 2%, Yes — 72%, No — 23%, ? — 3%
26. Hard work will always pay off if you have faith in yourself and stick to it: NR — 2%, Yes — 64%, No — 29%, ? — 5%
28. Being tolerant means that one accepts all religions—including Christianity—as equally important before God: NR — 3%, Yes — 41%, No — 44%, ? — 12%
30. Sin is whatever people (society) think is wrong behavior: NR — 3%, Yes — 16%, No — 78%, ? — 4%
31. The Bible teaches that God is like a friendly neighbor living upstairs: NR — 3%, Yes — 33%, No — 59%, ? — 6%
42. Hard work keeps people from getting into trouble: NR — 2%, Yes — 38%, No — 56%, ? — 5%
43. God is satisfied if a person lives the best life he can: NR — 2%, Yes — 50%, No — 43%, ? — 5%
44. A person at birth is neither good nor bad: NR — 2%, Yes — 50%, No — 42%, ? — 6%
45. Salvation depends upon being sincere in whatever you believe: NR — 2%, Yes — 44%, No — 49%, ? — 5%
51. There is nothing which science cannot eventually understand: NR — 2%, Yes — 14%, No — 75%, ? — 9%
53. A man should stand on his own two feet and not depend on others for help or favors: NR — 2%, Yes — 61%, No — 34%, ? — 3%
54. If I say I believe in God and do right, I will get to Heaven: NR — 2%, Yes — 31%, No — 57%, ? — 10%

Scale 16   The Exclusive Truth Claim of Christianity Exaggerated
(Reliability .68)

21. The Lutheran Church is the only true visible Church: NR — 3%, Yes — 8%, No — 84%, ? — 6%
36. The reason the Jews have so much trouble is because God is punishing them for rejecting Jesus: NR — 3%, Yes — 10%, No — 75%, ? — 12%
37. You can tell if a person is a true Christian or not: NR — 2%, Yes — 29%, No — 63%, ? — 6%
38. The only person who can do good works in the sight of God is the Christian because only the Christian has Christ living in him: NR — 2%, Yes — 29%, No — 63%, ? — 5%
39. The evil that we do, we do ourselves. The good that we do, Christ does in us: NR — 2%, Yes — 60%, No — 31%, ? — 7%
40. Unity among Christians can come only after complete doctrinal agreement: NR — 3%, Yes — 34%, No — 52%, ? — 12%
41. The Jews can never be forgiven for what they did to Jesus until they accept him as the true Saviour: NR — 3%, Yes — 38%, No — 45%, ? — 16%
46. The Pope is *the* Anti-Christ: NR — 3%, Yes — 6%, No — 75%, ? — 16%

56. God loves us only if we love him and believe in Christ: NR — 2%, Yes — 18%, No — 78%, ? — 2%
420. Do you think that belief in Jesus Christ as Saviour
   Is absolutely necessary for salvation — 74%
   Would probably help for salvation — 18%
   Probably has no influence for salvation — 4%
   No Response — 5%
421. Do you think that being a member of your particular religious faith
   Is absolutely necessary for salvation — 20%
   Would probably help for salvation — 40%
   Probably has no influence for salvation — 35%
   No Response — 5%
422. Do you think people being completely ignorant of Jesus, as might be the case for people living in other countries
   Will definitely prevent salvation — 13%
   May possibly prevent salvation — 39%
   Probably has no influence on salvation — 42%
   No Response — 6%

Scale 17   Feelings of Isolation and Pressure   (Reliability .68)

383. I often feel as if it would be good to get away from it all: NR — 6%, Yes — 65%, No — 28%, ? — 1%
385. There are so many problems to deal with today that sometimes I could just "blow up": NR — 5%, Yes — 48%, No — 44%, ? — 3%
388. Sometimes I feel God must hate me because there is so much misery in my life: NR — 4%, Yes — 8%, No — 85%, ? — 2%
397. I often feel left out of things that are going on around here: NR — 4%, Yes — 34%, No — 59%, ? — 2%
401. I feel all alone in the world fairly often: NR — 5%, Yes — 19%, No — 75%, ? — 2%
403. I often get the feeling that my ideas are out of date: NR — 8%, Yes — 35%, No — 56%, ? — 2%
405. I often feel people around here are not too friendly: NR — 7%, Yes — 26%, No — 67%, ? — 1%
During the past year I have . . .
631. Fought and argued within [my] immediate family circle: No Response — 5%, Frequently — 15%, Occasionally — 66%, Never — 15%
663. Thought of committing suicide: No Response — 6%, Frequently — 1%, Occasionally — 19%, Never — 74%

Scale 18   Identification with Parents   (Reliability .64)

384. In general, I respect and appreciate most of the adults I know: NR — 6%, Yes — 90%, No — 4%, ? — 1%
Choice of Responses: LM — More like me, S — About the same for both my parents and me, LP — More like my parents
408. Likely to compromise with things one doesn't like: NR — 6%, LM — 31%, S — 47%, LP — 15%
409. Respectful of people in positions of authority: NR — 6%, LM — 13%, S — 68%, LP — 14%
412. Have faith in the democratic process: NR — 6%, LM — 16%, S — 62%, LP — 17%
413. Tolerant of other people's views: NR — 6%, LM — 37%, S — 48%, LP — 9%
414. Honest with oneself: NR — 6%, LM — 24%, S — 61%, LP — 9%
415. Open to the world: NR — 7%, LM — 36%, S — 48%, LP — 9%
416. Optimistic about the future: NR — 6%, LM — 35%, S — 47%, LP — 13%
418. Concerned with what is happening to the country: NR — 6%, LM — 25%, S — 59%, LP — 11%

Scale 19   Religious Experience   (Reliability .69)

608. A feeling that you were somehow in the presence of God: No Response — 5%, Yes, I'm sure I have — 47%, Yes, I think I have — 36%, No — 12%
609. A sense of being saved in Christ: NR — 5%, Sure — 46%, Think — 38%, No — 12%
610. A feeling of being punished by God for something you had done: NR — 5%, Sure — 26%, Think — 36%, No — 33%

611. Assurance of having received the Holy Spirit: NR — 5%, Sure — 42%, Think — 39%, No — 14%
612. An experience of speaking in tongues: NR — 8%, Sure — 6%, Think — 12%, No — 75%
613. Evidence of having powers of healing or having been healed by faith: NR — 6%, Sure — 13%, Think — 21%, No — 60%
618. Do you think loving your neighbor . . .
    Is absolutely necessary for salvation — 36%
    Would probably help for salvation — 44%
    Probably has no influence for salvation — 15%
    No Response — 5%
619. Do you think doing good for others . . .
    Is absolutely necessary for salvation — 32%
    Would probably help for salvation — 47%
    Probably has no influence for salvation — 16%
    No Response — 5%

Scale 20 Supporting Others in Crises (Reliability .81)
During the past year I have . . .

636. Tried to offer comfort or support to a friend or neighbor in event of a death or tragedy either by talking or by action (e.g., taking a casserole dish to a family where the mother has been hospitalized): No Response — 5%, Frequently — 28%, Occasionally — 57%, Never — 9%
637. Expressed concern about a friend's (or neighbor's) welfare by sending a card in time of illness: NR — 5%, F — 40%, O — 49%, N — 6%
639. Visited a friend or neighbor in the hospital: NR — 5%, F — 32%, O — 57%, N — 6%
640. Attended a funeral of a friend or neighbor (non-family member): NR — 5%, F — 26%, O — 54%, N — 15%
641. Contributed to a special fund for aiding or helping a friend or neighbor: NR — 5%, F — 19%, O — 59%, N — 17%
664. Ran errands for someone who couldn't get them done either temporarily or permanently: NR — 6%, F — 13%, O — 75%, N — 6%

Scale 21 Personal Evangelism (Reliability .89)
During the past year I have . . .

632. Loaned religious books to others: No Response — 6%, Frequently — 9%, Occasionally — 41%, Never — 44%
633. Invited other Christians to your Church or Sunday School: NR — 6%, F — 14%, O — 59%, N — 22%
642. Invited non-Christians to your Church or Sunday School: NR — 6%, F — 9%, O — 43%, N — 42%
643. Shared the Gospel with others through home visitation: NR — 6%, F — 8%, O — 32%, N — 55%
649. Witnessed for Jesus through your actions or behavior but not by speaking about Jesus: NR — 7%, F — 17%, O — 65%, N — 11%
650. Distributed Christian tracts: NR — 8%, F — 5%, O — 30%, N — 57%
651. Witnessed for Jesus in any way to persons at work: NR — 8%, F — 9%, O — 49%, N — 34%
657. Successfully persuaded non-Christians to attend your Church or Sunday School: NR — 7%, F — 3%, O — 32%, N — 58%
659. Made a specific declaration of personal faith to friends or acquaintances: NR — 7%, F — 13%, O — 61%, N — 19%
661. Made a specific declaration of personal faith to strangers: NR — 7%, F — 4%, O — 33%, N — 57%
662. Participated in evangelistic rallies or meetings: NR — 7%, F — 2%, O — 31%, N — 59%
667. After assisting persons who were in trouble or needed help of some kind, was able to make a specific declaration of your faith: NR — 8%, F — 3%, O — 36%, N — 53%
668. Conducted Bible study in your home and/or helped to train and encourage fellow Christians to be better witnesses (with or without the active support of your congregation or pastor): NR — 7%, F — 4%, O — 21%, N — 68%

Scale 22   Neighborliness   (Reliability .80)

During the past year I have . . .

629. Helped a friend or neighbor with some building or repair project: No Response — 6%, Frequently — 22%, Occasionally — 56%, Never — 17%
630. Cared for a friend's (or neighbor's) children while the parent(s) were sick or required to be away: NR — 5%, F — 22%, O — 57%, N — 17%
646. Defended a friend or acquaintance who was being talked about when he wasn't there: NR — 6%, F — 18%, O — 73%, N — 3%
652. Contributed to a special fund for a person whom you did not know personally but had either read about or heard about who had had some tragic event occur: NR — 6%, F — 4%, O — 54%, N — 36%
653. Helped a friend or neighbor meet normal responsibilities in his life when he or she couldn't (helped get crops in when neighbor injured; on your own time helped finish a job at work when worker sick; done yard work for an elderly person, etc.): NR — 6%, F — 9%, O — 67%, N — 18%
658. Discussed religion with friends or acquaintances without making a specific declaration of personal faith: NR — 6%, F — 8%, O — 71%, N — 15%
665. Looked after a friend's (or neighbor's) home while he was gone: NR — 6%, F — 12%, O — 65%, N — 18%
671. Visited a friend in jail or helped in other ways when a friend or neighbor got in trouble with the law: NR — 6%, F — 2%, O — 24%, N — 67%
672. Took a friend or neighbor as guest in your home when some kind of difficulty had occurred: NR — 6%, F — 4%, O — 52%, N — 38%
675. Drove a friend somewhere when transportation wasn't available for him or her: NR — 6%, F — 24%, O — 63%, N — 8%
676. Loaned money to a friend or neighbor: NR — 6%, F — 10%, O — 64%, N — 21%
677. Welcomed a new family into your neighborhood by inviting them to your home or giving some token of your acceptance (e.g., cake or coffee): NR — 6%, F — 8%, O — 53%, N — 33%
678. Gave some aid or help to a total stranger whom you ran across who was in trouble of some sort (flat tire, sick, etc.): NR — 6%, F — 6%, O — 64%, N — 24%

Scale 23   Questionable Personal Activities   (Reliability .80)

During the past year I have . . .

634. Participated in heavy petting (with someone to whom you were not married): No Response — 6%, Frequently — 7%, Occasionally — 26%, Never — 61%
635. Had sexual intercourse with someone to whom you were not married: NR — 6%, F — 4%, O — 18%, N — 73%
638. Told a lie: NR — 6%, F — 12%, O — 76%, N — 7%
644. Masturbated: NR — 12%, F — 5%, O — 32%, N — 51%
647. Drank alcoholic beverages (other than at Communion): NR — 5%, F — 23%, O — 63%, N — 9%
648. Attended X-rated movies: NR — 6%, F — 4%, O — 39%, N — 51%
654. Had homosexual intercourse: NR — 7%, F — 1%, O — 3%, N — 90%
655. Attended movies: NR — 6%, F — 23%, O — 64%, N — 7%
656. Read pornographic literature: NR — 7%, F — 2%, O — 47%, N — 44%
660. Swore or used profanity or vulgar language: NR — 6%, F — 13%, O — 68%, N — 13%
669. Gambled (cards, dice, racing, sports events, etc.): NR — 6%, F — 4%, O — 50%, N — 40%
670. Fought (actual physical combat other than war, sports, or as part of job): NR — 7%, F — 1%, O — 20%, N — 73%
673. Was drunk: NR — 6%, F — 3%, O — 34%, N — 57%

Scale 26   Mutual Support Among Church, Society, and Individuals
         (Reliability .64)

679. A person who does not believe in God should not be permitted to teach in a church-related college: No Response — 6%, Agree — 64%, Disagree — 25%, ? — 5%
680. The campus minister, particularly on the state university campus, should seek to bring the students a program as nearly as possible like that of the student's home congregation: NR — 6%, A — 54%, D — 35%, ? — 5%
684. Church-supported welfare and service agencies do a better job than similar state or private agencies: NR — 7%, A — 43%, D — 33%, ? — 17%

685. Church-supported colleges do a better job than comparable state or private schools in teaching academic subjects like math, history, and biology: NR — 7%, A — 18%, D — 55%, ? — 20%

688. As far as the real questions that I wrestle with are concerned, the Church generally provides answers that are helpful: NR — 6%, A — 70%, D — 19%, ? — 5%

692. I enjoy giving money to the work of the Church as a national body (synodical or denominational budget): NR — 7%, A — 56%, D — 25%, ? — 12%

694. The more liberally I support my congregation financially, the closer I feel to it and to God: NR — 6%, A — 39%, D — 48%, ? — 7%

696. When I attend worship services I am among friends: NR — 6%, A — 77%, D — 11%, ? — 6%

698. Most of my friends would feel welcome at any service or meeting in my congregation: NR — 6%, A — 74%, D — 15%, ? — 6%

704. The Church as an institution is necessary to establish and preserve concepts of right and wrong in society: NR — 6%, A — 76%, D — 13%, ? — 4%

Scale 27   Disappointment with the Church   (Reliability .58)

686. In view of the increasing costs, our Lutheran churches as synods and denominations should seriously consider abandoning their social service work to competent private and public agencies: No Response — 7%, Agree — 16%, Disagree — 66%, ? — 11%

687. Either the Church as a whole doesn't know what is really going on, or it doesn't have answers for today's problems: NR — 7%, A — 31%, D — 54%, ? — 9%

690. Courses in school do not apply to the world I know: NR — 7%, A — 20%, D — 62%, ? — 11%

693. Congregations talk too much about money and not enough about what it means to be a Christian: NR — 6%, A — 45%, D — 44%, ? — 6%

695. Hardly anyone in my congregation would miss me if I stopped going: NR — 6%, A — 32%, D — 55%, ? — 7%

697. What the Lutheran Church teaches has little to say about life as it really is: NR — 6%, A — 14%, D — 75%, ? — 5%

703. With the increasing costs of higher education and the competition for qualified faculty, we Lutherans should seriously consider abandoning many of our private colleges: NR — 6%, A — 16%, D — 69%, ? — 9%

Scale 28   Transcendental Meaning in Life   (Reliability .73)

89. The Bible tells of many miracles, some credited to Christ, and some to other prophets and apostles. Generally speaking, which of the following statements comes closest to what you believe about Biblical miracles?
I am not sure whether these miracles really happened or not — 12%
I believe miracles are stories and never really happened — 1%
I believe the miracles happened, but can be explained by natural causes — 13%
I believe the miracles actually happened just as the Bible says they did — 71%
No Response — 3%

90. There is a life beyond death.
Completely true — 68%
Probably true — 24%
Probably not true — 4%
Definitely not true — 1%
No Response — 3%

91. The Devil actually exists.
Completely true — 53%
Probably true — 24%
Probably not true — 13%
Definitely not true — 6%
No Response — 3%

168. Service (devotion to the interests of others)
Extreme Importance — 20%
Quite Important — 28%
Some Importance — 28%
Least Importance — 15%
No Response — 9%

170. Ethical Life (responsible living toward others): NR — 9%, E — 17%, Q — 32%, S — 27%, L — 15%

178. Religion (religious belief, relationship with God, meaning in life): NR — 6%, E — 66%, Q — 18%, S — 7%, L — 2%
179. Love (warmth, caring, giving and receiving of love): NR — 6%, E — 71%, Q — 16%, S — 5%, L — 1%
185. Forgiveness (being willing to pardon others): NR — 8%, E — 31%, Q — 32%, S — 23%, L — 6%
186. Family Happiness (mutual caring among family members): NR — 8%, E — 54%, Q — 25%, S — 10%, L — 3%
187. Salvation (being saved, having eternal life): NR — 9%, E — 55%, Q — 18%, S — 12%, L — 7%

Scale 29 Values of Self-Development (Reliability .69)

167. Adventure (exploration, risks, danger)
    Extreme Importance — 7%
    Quite Important — 7%
    Some Importance — 12%
    Least Importance — 65%
    No Response — 9%
169. Recognition (being important, being well-liked): NR — 9%, E — 12%, Q — 19%, S — 24%, L — 36%
173. Pleasure (excitement, satisfaction, fun): NR — 9%, E — 12%, Q — 21%, S — 31%, L — 28%
175. Personal Freedom (independence, making own choices): NR — 9%, E — 20%, Q — 28%, S — 28%, L — 16%
176. Money (plenty of money for things I want): NR — 8%, E — 7%, Q — 18%, S — 25%, L — 42%
177. Personal Power (having influence and authority over others): NR — 8%, E — 2%, Q — 5%, S — 12%, L — 73%
180. Physical Appearance (attractiveness): NR — 8%, E — 7%, Q — 21%, S — 25%, L — 39%
181. Beauty (in the arts and in nature): NR — 9%, E — 4%, Q — 14%, S — 31%, L — 42%
184. Skill (being good at doing something important to me): NR — 9%, E — 13%, Q — 26%, S — 34%, L — 18%
188. Achievement (achieving one's desired goal): NR — 10%, E — 10%, Q — 24%, S — 36%, L — 21%

Scale 34 Generalized Prejudice (Reliability .86)

284. No punishment is too severe for those guilty of sex killings: No Response — 4%, Strongly Agree — 26%, Agree — 30%, Disagree — 33%, Strongly Disagree — 7%
295. Although there is no essential difference between blacks and whites, it is preferable for them not to mingle socially: NR — 3%, SA — 6%, A — 27%, D — 44%, SD — 20%
303. Conscientious objectors should be treated as traitors to their country: NR — 6%, SA — 5%, A — 18%, D — 56%, SD — 16%
305. Jews are just as honest as other businessmen: NR — 5%, SA — 16%, A — 64%, D — 14%, SD — 2%
307. I have no objection to Negroes and whites dating each other: NR — 3%, SA — 7%, A — 21%, D — 38%, SD — 31%
313. Jews have a lot of irritating faults: NR — 5%, SA — 3%, A — 25%, D — 60%, SD — 8%
327. Most people who live in poverty could do something about it if they really wanted to: NR — 4%, SA — 11%, A — 53%, D — 29%, SD — 3%
330. Jews don't care what happens to anyone but their own kind: NR — 5%, SA — 2%, A — 13%, D — 69%, SD — 12%
334. Jews always like to be at the head of things: NR — 5%, SA — 3%, A — 25%, D — 59%, SD — 8%
338. Jews are more willing than others to use shady practices to get what they want: NR — 6%, SA — 2%, A — 19%, D — 61%, SD — 12%
339. Poor people would be better off if they took advantage of the opportunities available to them rather than spending so much time protesting: NR — 4%, SA — 19%, A — 58%, D — 16%, SD — 2%
342. Negroes could solve many of their own problems if they would not be so irresponsible and carefree about life: NR — 4%, SA — 13%, A — 46%, D — 31%, SD — 6%
347. People (white or black) have a right to keep others out of their neighborhood if

they want to, and this right should be respected: NR — 5%, SA — 5%, A — 25%, D — 49%, SD — 16%

351. Jews are more loyal to Israel than to America: NR — 7%, SA — 3%, A — 23%, D — 58%, SD — 9%

356. The trouble with Jewish businessmen is that they are so shrewd and tricky that other people don't have a fair chance in competition: NR — 5%, SA — 2%, A — 17%, D — 61%, SD — 15%

Scale 35 Pessimism (Reliability .67)

286. These days a person must look out for himself since there is no one else to depend on for help: No Response — 3%, Strongly Agree — 5%, Agree — 21%, Disagree — 56%, Strongly Disagree — 15%

297. There is little one person can do to make the world a better place in which to live· NR — 3%, SA — 3%, A — 11%, D — 52%, SD — 31%

306. There is little chance to get ahead on a job unless a man gets a break: NR — 4%, SA — 2%, A — 17%, D — 65%, SD — 12%

315. Old people demand more consideration than they have any right to expect: NR — 3%, SA — 2%, A — 14%, D — 68%, SD — 13%

328. An experienced person knows that most people can't be trusted to be honest in their personal relationships: NR — 4%, SA — 2%, A — 20%, D — 67%, SD — 7%

350. You have to be a little bit bad to make money these days: NR — 4%, SA — 2%, A — 9%, D — 63%, SD — 22%

355. To get ahead today you sometimes have to be bad as well as good: NR — 4%, SA — 2%, A — 16%, D — 63%, SD — 16%

Scale 36 Christian Utopianism (Reliability .74)

301. It is wise to sacrifice now in order to have a better life in later years: No Response — 4%, Strongly Agree — 7%, Agree — 47%, Disagree — 39%, Strongly Disagree — 4%

304. Religious education in schools should be compulsory: NR — 5%, SA — 5%, A — 21%, D — 57%, SD — 12%

323. Worry to a Christian is really a sin because if he truly had faith in God he wouldn't worry about anything: NR — 5%, SA — 5%, A — 27%, D — 55%, SD — 8%

324. If a Christian truly believes in God's promises and takes God at his Word, he will tithe: NR — 8%, SA — 6%, A — 47%, D — 36%, SD — 3%

326. The only way to build an ideal world society is to convert everyone to Christianity: NR — 5%, SA — 9%, A — 39%, D — 42%, SD — 6%

331. The Church should have more evangelism programs that encourage church members to get out and visit others and witness: NR — 5%, SA — 12%, A — 55%, D — 27%, SD — 2%

333. The true Christian has the joy and peace which come from recognizing that he is a forgiven sinner: NR — 4%, SA — 30%, A — 57%, D — 8%, SD — 1%

335. If one will only grasp God's grace and trust in his love, all doors will be opened and all obstacles will melt away: NR — 5%, SA — 14%, A — 41%, D — 37%, SD — 4%

352. A person should make a public testimony about his religion before he becomes a church member: NR — 4%, SA — 3%, A — 20%, D — 61%, SD — 12%

353. Most Protestant churches need to have more revivals: NR — 6%, SA — 4%, A — 29%, D — 54%, SD — 7%

360. Knowing Christ as Lord brings complete happiness no matter what: NR — 4%, SA — 15%, A — 39%, D — 39%, SD — 3%

Scale 37 Need for Unchanging Structure (Reliability .78)

288. If a child is unusual in any way, his parents should get him to be more like other children: No Response — 3%, Strongly Agree — 2%, Agree — 17%, Disagree — 58%, Strongly Disagree — 19%

314. If children are told much about sex, they are likely to go too far in experimenting with it: NR — 3%, SA — 4%, A — 18%, D — 59%, SD — 16%

341. If a child is allowed to talk back to his parents, he will lose respect for them: NR — 4%, SA — 25%, A — 50%, D — 19%, SD — 2%

423. There is hardly anything lower than a person who does not feel a great love, gratitude, and respect for his parents: NR — 9%, SA — 19%, A — 37%, D — 32%, SD — 3%

427. A woman whose children are at all messy or rowdy has failed in her duties as a mother: NR — 6%, SA — 5%, A — 22%, D — 57%, SD — 11%
428. When you are young, you can afford to be an enthusiastic supporter of reform and change, but as you grow older, you learn that it is wiser to be cautious about making changes: NR — 6%, SA — 5%, A — 51%, D — 35%, SD — 4%
429. Some equality in marriage is a good thing, but by and large the husband ought to have the main say-so in family matters: NR — 5%, SA — 13%, A — 51%, D — 28%, SD — 4%
432. The world as it is is a pretty good place. We really don't need all this concern about change: NR — 5%, SA — 2%, A — 24%, D — 58%, SD — 11%
433. My first reaction when I think of the future is to be aware of its dangers: NR — 5%, SA — 5%, A — 51%, D — 37%, SD — 3%
434. The best way to improve world conditions is for each man to take care of his own corner of the vineyard: NR — 5%, SA — 7%, A — 43%, D — 39%, SD — 6%
435. A man should not be expected to have respect for a woman if they have sexual relations before they are married: NR — 5%, SA — 4%, A — 15%, D — 58%, SD — 18%
437. It is somehow unnatural to place women in positions of authority over men: NR — 5%, SA — 7%, A — 47%, D — 36%, SD — 5%
439. The facts on crime and sexual immorality show that we will have to crack down harder on young people if we are going to save our moral standards: NR — 5%, SA — 12%, A — 44%, D — 34%, SD — 5%
441. Women who want to remove the word *obey* from the marriage service don't understand what it means to be a wife: NR — 5%, SA — 8%, A — 47%, D — 36%, SD — 4%
443. We Christians have to exercise caution when we act in the local community, because it is so easy for those outside the Church to misinterpret what we are trying to do: NR — 11%, SA — 6%, A — 50%, D — 31%, SD — 3%
447. The most important qualities of a real man are determination and driving ambition: NR — 7%, SA — 6%, A — 32%, D — 49%, SD — 6%
448. The future is in God's hands. I will await what He sends and accept what comes as His will for me: NR — 6%, SA — 21%, A — 50%, D — 22%, SD — 3%
449. If I were to follow my deepest concern, I would concentrate on trying to preserve the very best of a long tradition. This seems to me to be a primary need today: NR — 6%, SA — 6%, A — 42%, D — 42%, SD — 4%

Scale 40   Congregational Activity   (Reliability .90)

452. How would you rate your activity in your congregation?
On a scale from 1 (Very active) to 4 (Inactive): 1 — 15%, 2 — 27%, 3 — 33%, 4 — 23%, No Response — 3%
453. How often do you spend evenings at church meetings or in church work?
On a scale from 1 (Regularly) to 4 (Never): 1 — 16%, 2 — 14%, 3 — 37%, 4 — 31%, NR — 3%
454. How often have you taken Communion during the past year?
On a scale from 1 (Regularly) to 4 (Never): 1 — 50%, 2 — 24%, 3 — 16%, 4 — 7%, NR — 3%
455. I keep pretty well informed about my congregation.
On a scale from 1 (Accurate Description of Me) to 4 (Inaccurate Description of Me): 1 — 28%, 2 — 32%, 3 — 24%, 4 — 13%, NR — 3%
456. Participating in congregational activities is a major source of satisfaction in my life.
On a scale from 1 (Accurate Description of Me) to 4 (Inaccurate Description of Me:) 1 — 19%, 2 — 23%, 3 — 29%, 4 — 26%, NR — 3%
457. I enjoy working in the activities of the congregation.
On a scale from 1 (Accurate Description of Me) to 4 (Inaccurate Description of Me): 1 — 29%, 2 — 26%, 3 — 26%, 4 — 16%, NR — 3%
465. Count the offices, special jobs, committees, etc., of either the congregation or denomination in which you served during the past year: 0 — 42%, 1 — 18%, 2 — 15%, 3 or more — 22%, NR — 3%

Scale 41   Personal Piety   (Reliability .89)

458. I try to cooperate with the pastor in his program for the congregation.
On a scale from 1 (Accurate Description of Me) to 4 (Inaccurate Description of Me): 1 — 46%, 2 — 29%, 3 — 16%, 4 — 6%, NR — 3%

459. All in all, how well do you think you fit in with the groups of people who make up your congregation?
On a scale from 1 (Very well) to 4 (Rather poorly): 1 — 26%, 2 — 41%, 3 — 21%, 4 — 11%, NR — 3%

460. In proportion to your income, do you consider that your contributions of money to all areas of the Church as a whole are . . .
On a scale from 1 (Generous) to 4 (Small): 1 — 17%, 2 — 38%, 3 — 24%, 4 — 18%, NR — 3%

461. I have some influence on the decisions made by my congregation.
On a scale from 1 (Accurate Description of Me) to 4 (Inaccurate Description of Me): 1 — 16%, 2 — 17%, 3 — 26%, 4 — 38%, NR — 3%

462. How often do you read the Bible? Daily — 12%, Weekly — 15%, Occasionally — 59%, Never — 12%, No Response — 2%

463. In talking with members of your family, how often do you yourself mention Christianity or church activities?
On a scale from 1 (Regularly) to 4 (Never): 1 — 28%, 2 — 33%, 3 — 32%, 4 — 4%, NR — 3%

467. Last year, approximately what percent of your total family income was contributed to any and all kinds of church work? 1% or less — 20%, 2-5% — 43%, 6-9% — 22%, 10% or more — 11%, No Response — 5%

470. When church activities conflict with your community responsibilities, how do you handle the situation?
I usually choose the church activities — 30%
I choose church activities more than half the time — 32%
I choose community activities more than half the time — 21%
I am usually faithful to my community responsibilities — 11%
No Response — 7%

473. I try hard to carry my religion over into all my other dealings in life.
I definitely disagree — 5%
I tend to disagree — 13%
I tend to agree — 49%
I definitely agree — 31%
No Response — 3%

475. Quite often I have been keenly aware of the presence of God.
Definitely not true — 4%
Tends not to be true — 12%
Tends to be true — 41%
Definitely true — 40%
No Response — 3%

477. My Christian beliefs are what really lie behind my whole approach to life. Definitely not so — 4%, Probably not so — 11%, Probably so — 43%, Definitely so — 40%, No Response — 3%

482. If I were to join a group within the congregation and had to choose between a Bible study and a social fellowship,
I would definitely prefer to join a Bible study — 25%
I probably would prefer a Bible study — 29%
I probably would prefer a social fellowship — 35%
I definitely would prefer to join a social fellowship — 7%
No Response — 3%

486. I read literature about my faith (or church): Frequently — 29%, Occasionally — 46%, Rarely — 19%, Never — 3%, No Response — 3%

487. It is important to me to spend periods of time in private religious thought and meditation: Frequently true — 30%, Occasionally true — 42%, Rarely true — 21%, Never true — 5%, No Response — 3%

507. If faith and science disagree on any issue, faith must be accepted rather than science: NR — 4%, Strongly Agree — 18%, Agree — 43%, Disagree — 31%, Strongly Disagree — 5%

Scale 42 The Role of Pastors in Social Action (Reliability .86)

Please indicate for each of the following how much you approve or disapprove of clergymen who take that action.

512. Publicly (not from the pulpit) take a stand on some political issue: No Response — 4%, Strongly Approve — 12%, Approve — 55%, Disapprove — 23%, Strongly Disapprove — 6%

513. Publicly (not from the pulpit) support a political candidate: NR — 4%, SA — 8%, A — 48%, D — 31%, SD — 8%
514. Take a stand from the pulpit on some political issue: NR — 4%, SA — 4%, A — 21%, D — 47%, SD — 24%
515. Deliver a sermon on a controversial political or social topic: NR — 4%, SA — 8%, A — 39%, D — 34%, SD — 16%
517. Organize study groups within their congregations to discuss public affairs: NR — 4%, SA — 16%, A — 51%, D — 24%, SD — 5%
518. Organize social action groups within their congregations to accomplish directly some political or social goal: NR — 4%, SA — 7%, A — 32%, D — 44%, SD — 13%
519. Participate in civil rights protest marches: NR — 4%, SA — 4%, A — 17%, D — 40%, SD — 36%
520. Participate in anti-war protest marches: NR — 4%, SA — 4%, A — 13%, D — 40%, SD — 39%
521. Participate in civil rights civil disobedience (risk arrest to symbolize protest): NR — 4%, SA — 2%, A — 8%, D — 39%, SD — 47%
522. Participate in anti-war civil disobedience (risk arrest). NR — 4%, SA — 2%, A — 8%, D — 38%, SD — 48%

Scale 43   Need for Religious Absolutism   (Reliability .70)

283. The true Christian is sure that his beliefs are correct: No Response — 4%, Strongly Agree — 30%, Agree — 49%, Disagree -- 15%, Strongly Disagree — 2%
292. The true Christian believes honestly and wholeheartedly in the doctrines of his church: NR — 3%, SA — 24%, A — 48%, D — 23%, SD — 2%
354. What is different about Lutherans is that they have pure and true doctrine: NR — 6%, SA — 4%, A — 35%, D — 50%, SD — 5%
523. An important purpose of worship is to find out what God wants us to do: NR — 4%, SA — 20%, A — 58%, D — 17%, SD — 2%
524. The essence of all religion is authority and obedience: NR — 5%, SA — 5%, A — 35%, D — 47%, SD — 8%
527. Christ is more real to me during my attendance at public worship services: NR — 4%, SA — 11%, A — 43%, D — 37%, SD — 5%
529. I am interested in the Church because of its efforts for moral and social reform in which I desire to share: NR — 5%, SA — 5%, A — 46%, D — 39%, SD — 5%
530. One of the most important aspects of Christianity is the liturgical service of public worship: NR — 5%, SA — 5%, A — 42%, D — 42%, SD — 6%
533. I like to think that Christians all over the world are going through nearly the same liturgical service in their public worship: NR — 5%, SA — 6%, A — 54%, D — 32%, SD — 4%
542. It is equally important to preach the Gospel and to work to improve the material well-being of people so that these two aims are kept in balance: NR — 5%, SA — 11%, A — 60%, D — 22%, SD — 2%
543. The more a worship service is formal and liturgical, the more it has meaning for me: NR — 4%, SA — 4%, A — 25%, D — 55%, SD — 12%
705. Every person needs to have the feeling of security given by belonging to a congregation: NR — 6%, A — 68%, D — 22%, ? — 4%

Scale 44   Fundamentalism-Liberalism   (Reliability .86)

76. The Bible is the Word of God. God inspired men to report verbally what he said. The Bible in the original text contained no errors.
No Response — 3%
I strongly agree. Persons who disbelieved this are not true to the Christian faith. — 24%
I agree. But exact agreement on this point is not necessary. There may have been mistranslations and slips in copying the original text of Scripture. — 35%
I agree in part. The Bible communicates the Word of God. But God spoke through fallible men. Therefore the Bible contains errors because of the human element, which we may judge by reason. — 34%
I disagree. The Bible is the record of the early moral and religious progress of Hebrews and Christians. It contains much wisdom from great men. But we cannot be sure of any "divine" element in it. — 4%
I strongly disagree. The Bible is only one of many collections of ancient religious writings. It is no more important for modern life than similar writings of other religions. — 1%

77. Jesus was conceived by the Holy Spirit and born of the Virgin Mary without a human father.
No Response — 3%
   I strongly agree. Persons who disbelieve this are not true to the Christian faith. — 40%
   I agree. But exact agreement is not essential. (As a case in point, St. Paul and the Gospel of John do not mention the virgin birth.) — 25%
   I agree in part. Jesus was divine, but his divinity is better explained by the Gospel of John (the Word of God became flesh) than by the virgin birth. — 22%
   I d:sagree. Jesus is the supreme revelation of God to men, but he was conceived like anyone else. In a sense any child is divinely conceived. — 8%
   I strongly disagree. If Jesus ever lived at all, he was conceived like everyone else. The "virgin birth" is just a great folk tale that grew up to explain a great man. — 2%

78. God raised Jesus from the dead. Jesus arose in his crucified body, left the tomb empty, appeared to his disciples and friends, and ascended into heaven.
No Response — 3%
   I strongly agree. Persons who disbelieve this are not true to the Christian faith. — 40%
   I agree. But exact agreement is not essential. The risen body of our Lord was a glorified body. It was different from his body before the crucifixion. — 41%
   I agree in part. Some great spiritual experience convinced Jesus' followers that he was alive and with them. But this did not necessarily involve Jesus' original body. — 13%
   I disagree. I believe in immortality and hope for it, but my belief does not depend solely upon the Bible stories of the resurrection. — 2%
   I strongly disagree. The New Testament reports of Jesus appearing to his disciples are stories growing out of the untrained imaginations of his followers. There is no after-life, and a bodily resurrection is impossible. — 1%

79. Today, just as at Pentecost, the gift of the Holy Spirit is evidenced by the person speaking in unknown tongues. This promise should be claimed in modern churches.
No Response — 5%
   I strongly agree. People who disbelieve this are not true to the Christian faith. — 12%
   I agree. But exact agreement is not essential. All the details of the original Pentecost need not be repeated today. — 15%
   I agree in part. Pentecost was the great spiritual experience by which the Holy Spirit empowered the Church. But we can have the Holy Spirit without "speaking in tongues." — 51%
   I disagree. If we ask him, God will give us spiritual power for Christ-like living. But religious emotion is not always a guarantee of Christ-like character. — 14%
   I strongly disagree. Pentecost was just a case of religious crowd psychology. "Speaking in unknown tongues" is just emotional nonsense. Sensible people drop such superstition. — 2%

80. Jesus will some day return from heaven in personal and visible form to rule the earth.
No Response — 3%
   I strongly agree. Persons who disbelieve this are not true to the Christian faith. — 19%
   I agree. But I do not believe that exact agreement on this point is essential. — 15%
   I agree in part. Jesus will return, but the method and character of his coming at some future date is unknown to us. This is not a proper way to talk about his return. — 42%
   I disagree. The return of Jesus to earth will be spiritual rather than in visible bodily form. He will come eventually to dwell and rule in every human heart. — 19%
   I strongly disagree. There is no heaven from which Jesus can return. To wait for his coming causes men to neglect their task of making life in this world better now. — 2%

81. Jesus Christ died for sinners. As a substitute, he suffered the just penalty due us for our sins in order to satisfy the wrath of God and to save guilty men from hell.
No Response — 3%
   I strongly agree. Persons who disbelieve this are not true to the Christian faith. — 37%
   I agree. But exact agreement is not required of Christians. One might say Jesus died to satisfy the justice of God. — 11%

I agree in part. One can use this language if it is understood that this is one of several ways to understand the meaning of Christ's death. Jesus died to soften the hearts of sinful men and reveal God's love for them. God saves men who repent, and he brings them to triumph over the powers of death and evil. — 43%

I disagree. Jesus was a great and good man who died a martyr in the struggle against evil. His martyrdom has been a powerful moral influence and is an example for us. — 6%

I strongly disagree. There is no such thing as "atonement" (a sacrificial death of one person for the sins of many). There is only a law of cause and effect in moral matters—so the death of Jesus also was a matter of cause and effect in a specific situation. — 1%

82. Today, just as in ancient times, God frequently intervenes to work miracles, especially in response to prayer, as for the healing of the sick.
No Response — 3%
I strongly agree. Persons who disbelieve this are not true to the Christian faith. — 15%
I agree. But exact agreement is not required of Christians. — 14%
I agree in part. Christians should pray for what they need. Prayer for the sick is good and may help in ways we do not understand. God wants us to use all means of help, including medical care. — 63%
I disagree. Natural laws have always been God's ways of working and healing. Some laws are physical, some spiritual, and they operate even if we do not pray. — 5%
I strongly disagree. We have no proof of any "higher power" which "intervenes" to help men. There is only natural law to which man must adjust. — 1%

83. The belief that human beings descended from some lower animal form is contrary to the Word of God and un-Christian.
No Response — 4%
I strongly agree. Persons who disbelieve this are not true to the Christian faith. — 27%
I agree. But exact agreement on this point is not essential. — 14%
I agree in part. But evolution can be harmonized with the Bible. Evolution is God's method of creation. — 29%
I disagree. The Biblical account is not a scientific account. The truth they saw was that God is the Creator. — 21%
I strongly disagree. Science has proved that man has evolved from sub-human forms of life. The Bible should not be used to decide what is an historical and biological question. — 5%

84. Baptism is a Holy Sacrament and is necessary for salvation.
No Response — 3%
I strongly agree. Persons who disbelieve this are not true to the Christian faith. — 34%
I agree. But exact agreement is not required of Christians. Others may believe that Baptism is a sacrament and is commanded by God but may not believe that it is necessary for salvation. — 15%
I agree in part. Baptism is a sacrament and it is commanded by God, but it is not required in order to be saved. A person may believe and not be able to be baptized but still is saved. — 43%
I disagree. Baptism is a ceremony which men do to confess their faith and does not affect salvation in any way. — 4%
I strongly disagree. Baptism is nothing more than a practice which makes families feel they are doing right by their children and which keeps the church membership growing. — 1%

85. In Holy Communion we are given the true Body and Blood of Jesus for the forgiveness of our sins.
No Response — 3%
I strongly agree. Persons who disbelieve this are not true to the Christian faith. — 28%
I agree, but I know that people can understand this statement in different ways. People may not be completely clear in their understanding of the relationship between bread and wine and body and blood but know that Jesus is really present. — 51%
I agree in part. The meaning of Holy Communion is that we are forgiven by God. However, we cannot make any definite assertions regarding the presence or absence of something like Christ's Body and Blood or the person of Christ. — 12%
I disagree. The real meaning of Communion is that we, as human beings, led by

love and brotherhood, mystically join together in unity, remembering the need for men to be one and to sacrifice self-interest for others as Jesus did. — 6%

I strongly disagree. There can be no such thing as the body and blood of a person (who may or may not have even lived) being given for men today to eat. The very idea of a cannibalistic feast on supposed human flesh and blood is repugnant to me. — 1%

86. The Ten Commandments are the Law of God and are God's rules for the way all men must live if they are to be good men.

No Response — 3%

I strongly agree. Persons who don't live by the Ten Commandments are not true to the Christian faith. — 19%

I agree. However, we must recognize that we can't keep all of the Commandments, even though they are the standard by which Christians must try to live. The Gospel tells us that God forgives us when we can't keep them. Hence they help us to understand and appreciate the Gospel. — 51%

I agree in part. The Ten Commandments are a part of God's Law but not by any means the whole of it. The Law of God is felt by men in the very nature of human existence with its demands and realities, including death. However, the Law of God cannot give us the power to live. Only the Gospel can give us life. — 25%

I disagree. The Ten Commandments are moral rules of an ancient people, and they have no more binding force upon us than any set of ethical rules that makes sense to us and helps us to live together peacefully. — 2%

I strongly disagree. There is no set of rules that can be applied universally to human life. We need to be free from all rules or standards. Only then will the full potential of humanity be recognized and will each man be free to develop himself as he chooses. — 0%

87. Pastors have the right and the power to forgive sins and to excommunicate the unrepentant sinner.

No Response — 3%

I strongly agree. Persons who disbelieve this are not true to the Christian faith. — 5%

I agree. But exact agreement is not essential. Congregations need to be able to exercise a spiritual discipline and to have the power to exclude people whose behavior is grossly sinful and who do not repent. However, it is more important to emphasize the forgiveness of God through the absolution which the pastor pronounces. — 33%

I agree in part. Pastors can only announce that God has forgiven sins. They don't really forgive sins themselves, and to claim to do so is presumptuous. As far as excommunication is concerned, it doesn't seem to do any good and should not be practiced even if it is in the Bible and has been a part of the Church's history. — 42%

I disagree. I don't need anybody to tell me that I'm personally forgiven, and I don't think that pastors have any right or duty to interfere in people's lives. If somebody is doing something wrong, that's his business and not the pastor's. The pastor's job is to preach and teach, not to judge me or anybody else. — 7%

I strongly disagree. The entire idea of anybody having priestly powers to magically erase sin or pronounce a curse upon a person is a superstitious relic of a primitive age that has no place in our modern world. — 10%

88. The nature of man is that he is absolutely and completely evil, totally depraved, and there is nothing good in him.

No Response — 5%

I strongly agree. Persons who disbelieve this are not true to the Christian faith. — 5%

I agree that it is correct to say that man is totally depraved, but this must be understood to be true in the sight of God. As far as men thinking about other men, we must recognize that men can be moral and decent and can accomplish things that are good at a human level. — 32%

I agree in part. The essence of man, namely his nature, is not evil. He has fallen from his nature and is now by custom and habit sinful. Therefore, it is his condition that is evil. — 28%

I disagree. Man is neither good nor evil but neutral. Whether he does good or bad things all depends on the way you look at it. What is good for one man may be evil for another, so ultimately it is foolish to wonder whether man is good or evil. It cannot be firmly decided either way. — 17%

I strongly disagree. Man is inherently good, and unless he is brutalized by savagery he will strive toward what is good. The whole history of mankind's development proves that he keeps progressing toward the good and the perfect. We can be quite confident that man's future will be one of steady progress toward perfection. — 13%

Scale 46 Importance of Christian Practices in My Life (Reliability .83)
192. How important is prayer in your life?
No Response — 5%, Very Important — 45%, Quite Important — 27%, Somewhat Important — 19%, Of Little Importance — 4%, Of No Importance — 1%
193. How Important is Communion (the Lord's Supper) in your life? NR — 5%, VI — 45%, QI — 30%, SI — 16%, LI — 4%, NI — 1%
194. How important is your Baptism in your life? NR — 5%, VI — 54%, QI — 22%, SI — 13%, LI — 5%, NI — 1%
195. How important is your faith to you? NR — 5%, VI — 68%, QI — 20%, SI — 6%, LI — 1%, NI — 0%

Scale 47 Personal Involvement in Church and Community (Reliability .90)
570. Serve as an officer or board member for my congregation:
NR — No Response — 7%
HR — Have been asked to do this but *have refused* — 5%
WR — Have never been asked but I *would refuse* if asked — 21%
HT — Have done this but really didn't want to. Felt I *had to* do it — 4%
WD — Have not been asked, but if I were I *would do* this — 35%
HD — Have been asked and I *have done* this willingly — 27%
571. Teach Sunday School or Bible Class: NR — 7%, HR — 10%, WR — 24%, HT — 5%, WD — 19%, HD — 36%
572. Serve on a committee to improve conditions at school or in the neighborhood: NR — 7%, HR — 3%, WR — 15%, HT — 4%, WD — 52%, HD — 21%
573. Conduct a small group Bible study program in my home or the home of someone else: NR — 8%, HR — 3%, WR — 39%, HT — 5%, WD — 31%, HD — 15%
575. Help in maintenance and repair tasks around the church building or parsonage: NR — 7%, HR — 3%, WR — 10%, HT — 4%, WD — 40%, HD — 36%
576. Attend a political party precinct caucus: NR — 8%, HR — 4%, WR — 38%, HT — 3%, WD — 36%, HD — 10%
577. Participate in politics as a campaign worker for a candidate: NR — 8%, HR — 4%, WR — 41%, HT — 3%, WD — 33%, HD — 12%
578. Help with planning and work for social or fellowship events in a congregation: NR — 7%, HR — 2%, WR — 14%, HT — 4%, WD — 35%, HD — 38%
579. Give a talk or layman's sermon before a church group or in worship: NR — 8%, HR — 3%, WR — 46%, HT — 4%, WD — 21%, HD — 18%
580. Participate in an effort to remove an incompetent or ineffective official in school, church, union, at work, or in government: NR — 8%, HR — 2%, WR — 28%, HT — 7%, WD — 48%, HD — 8%
581. Serve as delegate to a church conference or convention: NR — 7%, HR — 3%, WR — 30%, HT — 4%, WD — 36%, HD — 21%
582. Help in a stewardship drive by visiting fellow members to obtain pledges: NR — 7%, HR — 3%, WR — 27%, HT — 8%, WD — 28%, HD — 27%
583. Work for youth as a supporter of youth programs in the congregation or denomination: NR — 7%, HR — 2%, WR — 15%, HT — 3%, WD — 47%, HD — 26%
584. Serve on a citizens' review board to assess functions of public officials: NR — 9%, HR — 2%, WR — 44%, HT — 3%, WD — 39%, HD — 3%
585. Help in money-raising projects for some form of church work: NR — 7%, HR — 2%, WR — 13%, HT — 5%, WD — 38%, HD — 36%
586. Serve on congregational or denominational committees concerned with social issues: NR — 8%, HR — 2%, WR — 32%, HT — 3%, WD — 43%, HD — 12%
587. Join and work in congregational organizations (Ladies' Guilds, Youth Groups, Laymen's Leagues, etc.): NR — 7%, HR — 5%, WR — 16%, HT — 5%, WD — 25%, HD — 43%

Scale 49 Anxiety over My Faith (Reliability .82)
Respond to each of the statements by deciding how seriously you are bothered by them.
363. I do not know if I will go to heaven when I die.
NR — No Response — 6%
N   — Never — 23%

NL — No Longer — 20%
V — Very Much — 9%
Q — Quite a Bit — 11%
S — Somewhat — 20%
L — Very Little — 11%

364. It is hard for me to give a reason for my faith and convictions: NR — 6%, N — 28%, NL — 18%, V — 8%, Q — 9%, S — 20%, L — 13%
365. I do not feel I am close enough to Christ: NR — 5%, N — 12%, NL — 10%, V — 24%, Q — 16%, S — 26%, L — 8%
366. I am afraid I am losing my faith: NR — 5%, N — 42%, NL — 14%, V — 8%, Q — 5%, S — 12%, L — 15%
368. I cannot believe some things I have been taught in church: NR — 5%, N — 38%, NL — 13%, V — 5%, Q — 5%, S — 16%, L — 19%
369. I am not living up to my Christian convictions: NR — 5%, N — 13%, NL — 7%, V — 18%, Q — 17%, S — 30%, L — 10%
370. It's hard to share my religious faith in a natural way: NR — 5%, N — 23%, NL — 10%, V — 13%, Q — 12%, S — 24%, L — 13%
371. God does not seem to hear me when I pray: NR — 5%, N — 37%, NL — 14%, V — 8%, Q — 7%, S — 15%, L — 15%
372. I wish I could have a deep faith in God: NR — 5%, N — 25%, NL — 11%, V — 21%, Q — 12%, S — 17%, L — 10%

Scale 50 Acceptance of Middle-Class Norms (Reliability .69)

376. Conforming in matters of clothing and personal grooming:
On a scale from 1 (Accept most easily) to 6 (Impossible to accept): No Response — 5%, 1 — 31%, 2 — 23%, 3 — 21%, 4 — 11%, 5 — 6%, 6 — 4%
377. Outward respectability for the sake of career advancement: NR — 6%, 1 — 25%, 2 — 22%, 3 — 21%, 4 — 12%, 5 — 8%, 6 — 6%
378. Having little decision-making power in the first few years of a job: NR — 6%, 1 — 30%, 2 — 23%, 3 — 21%, 4 — 12%, 5 — 6%, 6 — 3%
379. Abiding by laws you don't agree with: NR — 5%, 1 — 16%, 2 — 22%, 3 — 22%, 4 — 18%, 5 — 13%, 6 — 6%
380. Being expected to show respect for all authority: NR — 5%, 1 — 34%, 2 — 28%, 3 — 14%, 4 — 10%, 5 — 6%, 6 — 4%
382. The assumption that leisure must be justified (earned): NR — 5%, 1 — 24%, 2 — 18%, 3 — 17%, 4 — 15%, 5 — 12%, 6 — 9%

Scale 51 Acceptance of Authority (Reliability .74)

On a scale from 1 (Accept most easily) to 6 (Impossible to accept):
373. Prohibitions of use of marijuana: No Response — 5%, 1 — 60%, 2 — 6%, 3 — 4%, 4 — 5%, 5 — 4%, 6 — 17%
374. Prohibitions of use of other mind-expanding drugs: NR — 5%, 1 — 64%, 2 — 5%, 3 — 3%, 4 — 3%, 5 — 4%, 6 — 17%
375. The power and authority of the "boss" in a work situation: NR — 5%, 1 — 42%, 2 — 27%, 3 — 15%, 4 — 7%, 5 — 2%, 6 — 2%

Scale 52 Desire for a Dependable World (Reliability .53)

147. WAY 1: In this "design for living" the individual actively participates in the social life of his community, not to change it primarily, but to understand, appreciate, and preserve the best that man has attained. Excessive desires should be avoided and moderation sought. One wants the good things of life but in an orderly way. Life is to have clarity, balance, refinement, control. Vulgarity, great enthusiasm, irrational behavior, impatience, indulgence are to be avoided. Friendship is to be esteemed but not easy intimacy with many people. Life is to have discipline, intelligibility, good manners, predictability. Social changes are to be made slowly and carefully, so that what has been achieved in human culture is not lost. The individual should be active physically and socially, but not in a hectic or radical way. Restraint and intelligence should give order to an active life.
No Response — 4%
1 — I like it *very much* — 29%
2 — I like it *quite a lot* — 32%
3 — I like it *slightly* — 17%
4 — I am *indifferent* to it — 7%

5 — I dislike it *slightly* — 6%
6 — I dislike it *quite a lot* — 4%
7 — I dislike it *very much* — 2%

149. WAY 3: This way of life makes central the sympathetic concern for other persons. Affection should be the main thing in life, affection that is free from all traces of the imposition of oneself upon others or of using others for one's own purposes. Greed in possessions, emphasis on sexual passion, the search for power over persons and things, excessive emphasis upon intellect, and undue concern for oneself are to be avoided. For these things hinder the sympathetic love among persons which alone gives significance to life. If we are aggressive we block our receptivity to the personal forces upon which we are dependent for genuine personal growth. One should accordingly purify oneself, restrain one's self-assertiveness, and become receptive, appreciative, and helpful with respect to other persons.
    NR — 6%, 1 — 10%, 2 — 23%, 3 — 24%, 4 — 13%, 5 — 11%, 6 — 9%, 7 — 5%

156. WAY 10: Self-control should be the keynote of life. Not the easy self-control which retreats from the world, but the vigilant, stern, manly control of a self which lives in the world, and knows the strength of the world and the limits of human power. The good life is rationally directed and holds firm to high ideals. It is not bent by the seductive voices of comfort and desire. It does not expect social utopias. It is distrustful of final victories. Too much cannot be expected. Yet one can with vigilance hold firm the reins to his self, control his unruly impulses, understand his place in the world, guide his actions by reason, maintain his self-reliant independence. And in this way, though he finally perish, man can keep his human dignity and respect, and die with cosmic good manners.
    NR — 6%, 1 — 9%, 2 — 16%, 3 — 21%, 4 — 17%, 5 — 14%, 6 — 12%, 7 — 5%

159. WAY 13: A person should let himself be used. Used by other persons in their growth, used by the great objective purposes in the universe which silently and irresistibly achieve their goal. For persons and the world's purposes are dependable at heart, and can be trusted. One should be humble, constant, faithful, uninsistent. Grateful for the affection and protection which one needs, but undemanding. Close to persons and to nature, and secure because close. Nourishing the good by devotion and sustained by the good because of devotion. One should be a serene, confident, quiet vessel and instrument of the great dependable powers which move to their fulfillment.
    NR — 7%, 1 — 9%, 2 — 14%, 3 — 16%, 4 — 13%, 5 — 12%, 6 — 15%, 7 — 14%

Scale 53 Desire for a Controllable World (Reliability .53)

151. WAY 5: A person should not hold on to himself, withdraw from people, keep aloof and self-centered. Rather merge oneself with a social group, enjoy cooperation and companionship, join with others in resolute activity for the realization of common goals. Persons are social and persons are active. Life should merge energetic group activity and cooperative group enjoyment. Meditation, restraint, concern for one's self-sufficiency, abstract intellectuality, solitude, stress on one's possessions all cut the roots which bind persons together. One should live outwardly with gusto, enjoying the good things of life, working with others to secure the things which make possible a pleasant and energetic social life. Those who oppose this ideal are not to be dealt with too tenderly.
    No Response — 6%
    1 — I like it *very much* — 8%
    2 — I like it *quite a lot* — 19%
    3 — I like it *slightly* — 22%
    4 — I am *indifferent* to it — 13%
    5 — I dislike it *slightly* — 16%
    6 — I dislike it *quite a lot* — 12%
    7 — I dislike it *very much* — 6%

152. WAY 6: Life continuously tends to stagnate, to become "comfortable," to become sicklied o'er with the pale cast of thought. Against these tendencies, a person must stress the need of constant activity—physical action, adventure, the realistic solution of specific problems as they appear, the improvement of techniques for controlling the world and society. Man's future depends primarily on what he does, not on what he feels or on his speculations. New problems constantly arise and always will arise. Improvements must always be made if man is to progress. We can't just follow the past or dream of what the future might be. We have to work resolutely and continually if control is to be gained over the forces which threaten us. Man should

rely on technical advances made possible by scientific knowledge. He should find his goal in the solution of his problems. The good is the enemy of the better.

NR — 6%, 1 — 8%, 2 — 22%, 3 — 24%, 4 — 16%, 5 — 12%, 6 — 9%, 7 — 3%

153. WAY 7: We should at various times and in various ways accept something from all other paths of life, but give no one our exclusive allegiance. At one moment one of them is the more appropriate; at another moment another is the most appropriate. Life should contain enjoyment and action and contemplation in about equal amounts. When either is carried to extremes we lose something important for our life. So we must cultivate flexibility, admit diversity in ourselves, accept the tension which this diversity produces, find a place for detachment in the midst of enjoyment and activity. The goal of life is found in the dynamic integration of enjoyment, action, and contemplation, and so in the dynamic interaction of the various paths of life. One should use all of them in building a life, and no one alone.

NR — 6%, 1 — 16%, 2 — 27%, 3 — 23%, 4 — 14%, 5 — 8%, 6 — 5%, 7 — 2%

154. WAY 8: Enjoyment should be the keynote of life. Not the hectic search for intense and exciting pleasures, but the enjoyment of the simple and easily obtainable pleasures: the pleasures of just existing, of savory food, of comfortable surroundings, of talking with friends, of rest and relaxation. A home that is warm and comfortable, chairs and a bed that are soft, a kitchen well stocked with food, a door open to the entrance of friends—this is the place to live. Body at ease, relaxed, calm in its movements, not hurried, breath slow, willing to nod and to rest, grateful to the world that is its food—so should the body be. Driving ambition and the fanaticism of ascetic ideals are the signs of discontented people who have lost the capacity to float in the stream of simple, carefree, wholesome enjoyment.

NR — 6%, 1 — 22%, 2 — 25%, 3 — 20%, 4 — 8%, 5 — 9%, 6 — 7%, 7 — 3%

158. WAY 12: The use of the body's energy is the secret of a rewarding life. The hands need material to make into something: lumber and stone for building, food to harvest, clay to mold. The muscles are alive to joy only in action, in climbing, running, skiing, and the like. Life finds its zest in overcoming, dominating, conquering some obstacle. It is the active deed which is satisfying, the deed adequate to the present, the daring and adventuresome deed. Not in cautious foresight, not in relaxed ease does life attain completion. Outward energetic action, the excitement of power in the tangible present—this is the way to live.

NR — 7%, 1 — 10%, 2 — 20%, 3 — 27%, 4 — 14%, 5 — 11%, 6 — 8%, 7 — 4%

Scale 54 Desire for Detachment from the World (Reliability .52)

148. WAY 2: The individual should for the most part "go it alone," assuring himself of privacy in living quarters, having much time to himself, attempting to control his own life. One should stress self-sufficiency, reflection and meditation, knowledge of himself. The direction of interest should be away from intimate associations with social groups, and away from the physical manipulation of objects or attempts at control of the physical environment. One should aim to simplify one's external life, to moderate those desires whose satisfaction is dependent upon physical and social forces outside of oneself, and to concentrate attention upon the refinement, clarification, and self-direction of oneself. Not much can be done or is to be gained by "living outwardly." One must avoid dependence upon persons or things; the center of life should be found within oneself.

No Response — 6%
1 — I like it *very much* — 3%
2 — I like it *quite a lot* — 7%
3 — I like it *slightly* — 13%
4 — I am *indifferent* to it — 11%
5 — I dislike it *slightly* — 14%
6 — I dislike it *quite a lot* — 26%
7 — I dislike it *very much* — 21%

150. WAY 4: Life is something to be enjoyed—sensuously enjoyed, enjoyed with relish and abandonment. The aim in life should not be to control the course of the world or society or the lives of others, but to be open and receptive to things and persons and to delight in them. Life is more a festival than a workshop or a school for moral discipline. To let oneself go, to let things and persons affect oneself, is more important than to do—or to do good. Such enjoyment, however, requires that one be self-centered enough to be keenly aware of what is happening and free for new happenings. So one should avoid entanglements, should not be too dependent on particular people or things, should not be self-sacrificing. One should be alone a lot, should have

time for meditation and awareness of oneself. Solitude and sociality together are both necessary in the good life.
NR — 5%, 1 — 6%, 2 — 13%, 3 — 18%, 4 — 11%, 5 — 14%, 6 — 20%, 7 — 12%

155. WAY 9: Receptivity should be the keynote of life. The good things of life come of their own accord, and come unsought. They cannot be found by resolute action. They cannot be found in the indulgence of the sensuous desires of the body. They cannot be gathered by participation in the turmoil of social life. They cannot be given to others by attempts to be helpful. They cannot be garnered by hard thinking. Rather do they come unsought when the bars of the self are down. When the self has ceased to make demands and waits in quiet receptivity, it becomes open to the powers which nourish it and work through it, and sustained by these powers it knows joy and peace. To sit alone under the trees and the sky, open to nature's voices, calm and receptive, then can the wisdom from without come within.
NR — 7%, 1 — 6%, 2 — 13%, 3 — 19%, 4 — 22%, 5 — 15%, 6 — 13%, 7 — 6%

157. WAY 11: The contemplative life is the good life. The external world is no fit habitat for man. It is too big, too cold, too pressing. Rather, it is the life turned inward that is rewarding. The rich internal world of ideals, of sensitive feelings, of reverie, of self-knowledge is man's true home. By the cultivation of the self within, man alone becomes human. Only then does there arise deep sympathy with all that lives, an understanding of the suffering inherent in life, a realization of the futility of aggressive action, the attainment of contemplative joy. Conceit then falls away and austerity is dissolved. In giving up the world one finds the larger and finer sea of the inner self.
NR — 7%, 1 — 4%, 2 — 8%, 3 — 16%, 4 — 19%, 5 — 17%, 6 — 17%, 7 — 12%

Scale 55   Family Level of Education   (Reliability .70)

Choice of Answers:

A — 8th grade or less
B — Some high school or trade school, but not enough to graduate
C — High school or trade school graduate
D — Some college, but not enough to graduate
E — College graduate
F — Some graduate or professional school, but not enough for an advanced degree
G — Graduate or professional degree

163. How much formal education have you had? NR — 4%, A — 7%, B — 15%, C — 37%, D — 16%, E — 7%, F — 5%, G — 9%

164. How much formal education has your spouse had? (Leave blank if not married.) NR — 24%, A — 7%, B — 9%, C — 30%, D — 14%, E — 9%, F — 3%, G — 4%

165. How much formal education did your father have? NR — 6%, A — 47%, B — 13%, C — 18%, D — 6%, E — 5%, F — 2%, G — 4%

166. How much formal education did your mother have? NR — 7%, A — 41%, B — 14%, C — 25%, D — 6%, E — 4%, F — 2%, G — 1%

Scale 56   Social Distance — Radical Life Styles   (Reliability .90)

Choice of Answers:

1 — Would marry into group
2 — Would have as close friends
3 — Would have as next door neighbors
4 — Would work in same office
5 — Would have as speaking acquaintances only
6 — Would not want in my community
7 — Would debar from my nation

258. Hippies: NR — 5%, 1 — 6%, 2 — 12%, 3 — 7%, 4 — 9%, 5 — 21%, 6 — 33%, 7 — 8%

259. Alcoholics: NR — 6%, 1 — 2%, 2 — 19%, 3 — 13%, 4 — 12%, 5 — 29%, 6 — 17%, 7 — 2%

260. Members of Students for Democratic Society (SDS): NR — 9%, 1 — 5%, 2 — 11%, 3 — 12%, 4 — 10%, 5 — 20%, 6 — 21%, 7 — 12%

261. Negroes: NR — 5%, 1 — 8%, 2 — 38%, 3 — 15%, 4 — 18%, 5 — 10%, 6 — 6%, 7 — 1%

262. Welfare mothers with illegitimate children: NR — 7%, 1 — 5%, 2 — 23%, 3 — 18%, 4 — 13%, 5 — 20%, 6 — 13%, 7 — 1%

264. Members of John Birch Society: NR — 11%, 1 — 7%, 2 — 14%, 3 — 17%, 4 — 10%, 5 — 20%, 6 — 15%, 7 — 6%

265. Mentally disturbed persons: NR — 8%, 1 — 2%, 2 — 33%, 3 — 17%, 4 — 7%, 5 — 22%, 6 — 11%, 7 — 0%
269. Communists: NR — 6%, 1 — 2%, 2 — 5%, 3 — 6%, 4 — 4%, 5 — 10%, 6 — 28%, 7 — 39%
271. Homosexuals: NR — 6%, 1 — 1%, 2 — 8%, 3 — 10%, 4 — 10%, 5 — 21%, 6 — 37%, 7 — 7%
272. Atheists: NR — 8%, 1 — 7%, 2 — 19%, 3 — 16%, 4 — 8%, 5 — 16%, 6 — 20%, 7 — 7%
274. Ex-convicts: NR — 6%, 1 — 10%, 2 — 24%, 3 — 17%, 4 — 16%, 5 — 16%, 6 — 11%, 7 — 1%
275. Drug addicts: NR — 6%, 1 — 2%, 2 — 13%, 3 — 8%, 4 — 9%, 5 — 20%, 6 — 38%, 7 — 5%

Scale 57 Social Distance — Racial and Religious Groups (Reliability .89)
Choice of Answers:
1 — Would marry into group
2 — Would have as close friends
3 — Would have as next door neighbors
4 — Would work in same office
5 — Would have as speaking acquaintances only
6 — Would not want in my community
7 — Would debar from my nation

263. Catholics: NR — 5%, 1 — 36%, 2 — 47%, 3 — 9%, 4 — 2%, 5 — 1%, 6 — 1%, 7 — 0%
266. Divorcees: NR — 6%, 1 — 26%, 2 — 39%, 3 — 14%, 4 — 7%, 5 — 7%, 6 — 2%, 7 — 0%
267. High school dropouts: NR — 6%, 1 — 21%, 2 — 40%, 3 — 14%, 4 — 6%, 5 — 6%, 6 — 2%, 7 — 0%
268. Jews: NR — 6%, 1 — 18%, 2 — 50%, 3 — 15%, 4 — 4%, 5 — 5%, 6 — 2%, 7 — 1%
270. American Indians: NR — 5%, 1 — 25%, 2 — 42%, 3 — 13%, 4 — 5%, 5 — 6%, 6 — 3%, 7 — 1%
273. Non-Lutheran Protestants: NR — 6%, 1 — 52%, 2 — 28%, 3 — 8%, 4 — 2%, 5 — 3%, 6 — 1%, 7 — 0%
276. Orientals: NR — 7%, 1 — 22%, 2 — 43%, 3 — 15%, 4 — 6%, 5 — 5%, 6 — 3%, 7 — 1%
277. Whites: NR — 5%, 1 — 75%, 2 — 14%, 3 — 4%, 4 — 1%, 5 — 1%, 6 — 0%, 7 — 0%

Scale 58 Awareness of the Immanent Trinity (Reliability .51)
221. Comes to me through other people: No Response — 5%, No — 51%, Yes — 43%
223. At work in my life: NR — 5%, N — 23%, Y — 72%
226. Three persons, yet one God: NR — 5%, N — 23%, Y — 72%
227. Met only in his Word and Sacraments: NR — 5%, N — 86%, Y — 9%
228. Makes things work out all right in the long run: NR — 5%, N — 51%, Y — 44%
230. Tests people through their suffering: NR — 5%, N — 55%, Y — 40%
231. Friendly and loving: NR — 5%, N — 21%, Y — 73%
233. Works in the world only through Christians: NR — 5%, N — 86%, Y — 8%
234. Revealed only by the Holy Spirit: NR — 5%, N — 68%, Y — 27%

Scale 59 Social Utility of Christianity (Reliability .62)
538. The Church is helping me to develop the social attitudes of understanding, sympathy, and cooperation: No Response — 4%, Strongly Agree — 10%, Agree — 68%, Disagree — 16%, Strongly Disagree — 2%
541. I believe the Church is absolutely needed to overcome the tendency to selfishness: NR — 4%, SA — 14%, A — 58%, D — 22%, SD — 2%
544. Unselfish love is the prerequisite for any real knowledge of Christianity: NR — 6%, SA — 12%, A — 60%, D — 21%, SD — 2%
546. Tender concern for others is a means of finding joy in one's Christian faith: NR — 4%, SA — 25%, A — 69%, D — 3%, SD — 0%

Scale 60 Individual Christian Responsibility (Reliability .65)
296. To be a Lutheran is to believe strongly in the Bible as God's Word: No Response — 3%, Strongly Agree — 38%, Agree — 48%, Disagree — 10%, Strongly Disagree — 1%
298. There should be a frank sharing of differences among people in a congregation: NR — 4%, SA — 17%, A — 68%, D — 10%, SD — 1%

309. If I were to become convinced that the resurrection never happened, I could no longer be a Christian: NR — 3%, SA — 4%, A — 25%, D — 61%, SD — 7%
337. If every Christian were a witness for Christ, we wouldn't have all the problems we have now: NR — 4%, SA — 20%, A — 53%, D — 21%, SD — 2%
340. All Christians, not just pastors, share the responsibility for being witnesses to Christ and the faith: NR — 4%, SA — 38%, A — 56%, D — 2%, SD — 0%
349. The true Christian is likely to have sincere and searching questions about the nature of a life of faith in God: NR — 4%, SA — 17%, A — 70%, D — 8%, SD — 1%
357. The family is a sacred institution, divinely ordained: NR — 5%, SA — 23%, A — 56%, D — 15%, SD — 1%
362. Christians should be willing to speak up and protest what is not right: NR — 4%, SA — 23%, A — 66%, D — 6%, SD — 1%

Scale 62   Service Without Proclamation   (Reliability .49)

320. Christians should leave other people alone and not try to change their religion: No Response — 4%, Strongly Agree — 5%, Agree — 35%, Disagree — 46%, Strongly Disagree — 11%
531. Missionaries should not proclaim God's Law too often to people suffering from poverty and sickness: NR — 5%, SA — 3%, A — 20%, D — 59%, SD — 15%
534. The Church's task to help eliminate physical sufferings of people is more important than proclaiming the Gospel by preaching and teaching: NR — 5%, SA — 2%, A — 17%, D — 60%, SD — 16%
539. A worship service must be beautiful to be readily meaningful to me: NR — 4%, SA — 3%, A — 16%, D — 66%, SD — 12%

Scale 63   Peer Orientation   (Reliability .62)

392. When making decisions, I listen primarily to my own age group: No Response — 4%, Yes — 27%, No — 65%, ? — 4%
394. (If you are a youth, answer this): I do not enjoy being with adults. (If you are an adult, answer this:) I do not enjoy being with young people: NR — 6%, Y — 14%, N — 78%, ? — 3%
396. The only ones I really trust are other people about my age: NR — 4%, Y — 3%, N — 91%, ? — 2%
399. I don't know a single adult whom I trust and enjoy: NR — 5%, Y — 6%, N — 88%, ? — 1%
404. (If you are a youth, answer this:) My first reaction to adults is to suspect their motives. I don't trust them. (If you are an adult, answer this:) My first reaction to youth is to suspect their motives. I don't trust them: NR — 8%, Y — 8%, N — 82%, ? — 2%
558. Much of the so-called church work today is just "busy work" that doesn't do a thing to or for anybody: NR — 6%, N — 72%, Y — 22%
560. Much of what my congregation asks me to do just doesn't seem meaningful at all: NR — 6%, N — 79%, Y — 15%
591. (If you are a youth, answer this:) Some adults in my congregation recognize me and call me by name: NR — 6%, N — 74%, Y — 20%
595. Older people in my congregation seem to be suspicious of what the young people do: NR — 6%, N — 52%, Y — 42%
600. The Christian faith has little effect on the actual lives of most members of my congregation: NR — 6%, N — 75%, Y — 19%
614. Choose the view which corresponds most closely with yours:
     No Response — 6%
     A. Life is unchanging and will continue largely as I know it now — 5%
     B. Though life is constantly changing, human nature and human ideals do not change — 56%
     C. Life has changed so radically that youth and adults cannot understand each other — 33%
615. Choose the view of education that corresponds most closely with yours.
     No Response — 6%
     A. The accumulated wisdom of the past should be one's primary source of learning 14%
     B. What is currently being discovered and what men have learned in the past are about equally important to learn — 78%
     C. The past is such a colossal failure that there is little or nothing from the past worth learning except "know how" — 3%

616. Which kind of person is most influential in what young people learn?
    No Response — 5%
    A. Young people learn primarily from their forefathers and elders — 11%
    B. Young people learn primarily from their own age group (peers) — 13%
    C. Young people learn primarily from participating with adults and youth together — 71%
617. Choose the statement that best describes your understanding of how you have learned what is most important to you.
    No Response — 6%
    A. I have accepted unquestioningly what was taught by my elders — 23%
    B. Conflict and change have forced me to rethink and restate ageless truths for myself — 55%
    C. I have questioned everything from the past, and together with my own age group, have sought new approaches to life — 17%
714. Pastors should be especially concerned with youth programs: No Response — 7%, Agree — 90%, Disagree — 4%
715. Young people should be able to serve on congregational boards and committees and hold offices in congregations: NR — 7%, A — 52%, D — 41%
716. In today's world young people know better than the older people what the Church should be doing: NR — 7%, A — 15%, D — 78%
717. The Church is doing a pretty good job of involving youth and teaching them about the Christian life: NR — 7%, A — 64%, D — 29%

Scale 64 Power Orientation to Social Issues (Reliability .45)

34. The doctrines of the Church need to grow and develop to keep up with the needs of the time: NR — 2%, Y — 70%, N — 23%, ? — 5%
398. My understanding of the central doctrines of the Church has changed considerably during the last several years: NR — 5%, Y — 39%, N — 51%, ? — 5%
419. Concerning the idea of a "generation gap" today, do you feel that
    No Response — 5%
    A. There is such a gap — 26%
    B. It exists but has been exaggerated — 64%
    C. It doesn't exist — 6%
436. In the last analysis, it's having the power that makes the difference: No Response — 7%, Strongly Agree — 2%, Agree — 26%, Disagree — 56%, Strongly Disagree — 10%
438. If I were to follow my deep convictions, I would devote much time to reform movements. This seems to me to be a primary need today: NR — 6%, SA — 4%, A — 31%, D — 54%, SD — 5%
450. The most important issues in the world today are issues of social justice: NR — 6%, SA — 5%, A — 42%, D — 44%, SD — 3%

Scale 65 Church Involvement in Social Issues (Reliability .65)

32. All war is basically wrong: No Response — 2%, Yes — 52%, No — 39%, ? — 7%
256. The primary role of the Church is . . .
    On a scale from 1 (No involvement in social issues but only preach the Gospel) to 4 (Neutral) to 7 (Work for social reform first): No Response — 3%, 1 — 11%, 2 — 10%, 3 — 21%, 4 — 17%, 5 — 21%, 6 — 9%, 7 — 8%
257. My present feeling is that the Church is now involved in social issues . . .
    On a scale from 1 (Far too much) to 4 (Neutral) to 7 (Far too little): No response — 4%, 1 — 9%, 2 — 6%, 3 — 16%, 4 — 20%, 5 — 20%, 6 — 10%, 7 — 16%
285. People in a congregation should accept those who differ radically in what they believe is the work of the Church: No Response — 5%, Strongly Agree — 11%, Agree — 49%, Disagree — 33%, Strongly Disagree — 3%
293. Lutheran Church bodies should attempt to get their congregations to adopt an "open church" policy of accepting persons as members who are from minority racial and nationality groups: NR — 4%, SA — 28%, A — 50%, D — 16%, SD — 3%
294. The elimination of all racial discrimination is a goal of Christianity: NR — 4%, SA — 31%, A — 49%, D — 14%, SD — 3%
310. The death penalty is barbaric and should be abolished: NR — 4%, SA — 9%, A — 27%, D — 46%, SD — 14%
312. Alcoholics and drug addicts should be regarded as victims of a disease: NR — 3%, SA — 28%, A — 59%, D — 8%, SD — 2%
316. Most people can be trusted: NR — 3%, SA — 8%, A — 74%, D — 13%, SD — 1%

346. Every person has a right to free medical care if he needs it but cannot afford it: NR — 4%, SA — 20%, A — 64%, D — 11%, SD — 2%
348. Every person has a right to adequate housing, even if he cannot afford it: NR — 4%, SA — 8%, A — 60%, D — 26%, SD — 3%
528. To present Christianity as one religion, missionaries should plan evangelism together with other missionaries representing various denominations: NR — 5%, SA — 11%, A — 63%, D — 19%, SD — 2%

Scale 66   Emotional Certainty of Faith   (Reliability .71)

161. Which of the following statements comes closest to expressing what you believe about God?
     No Response — 3%
     A. I know God really exists, and I have no doubts about it — 58%
     B. While I have doubts, I feel I do believe in God — 30%
     C. I find myself believing in God some of the time, but not at other times — 5%
     D. I don't believe in a personal God, but I do believe in a higher power of some kind — 2%
     E. I don't know whether there is a God, and I don't believe there is any way to find out — 1%
     F. I don't believe in God — 0%
     G. None of the above represents what I believe — 1%
391. Whenever I talk about my faith in God and what it means to me, I feel very good afterwards: No Response — 4%, Yes — 78%, No — 10%, ? — 7%
548. Which of the following best describes your participation in the act of prayer?
     No Response — 3%
     A. Prayer is a regular part of my behavior — 53%
     B. I pray primarily in times of stress and/or need, but not much otherwise — 27%
     C. My prayer is restricted pretty much to formal worship services — 11%
     D. I pray very rarely — 5%
     E. I never pray — 1%
728. To what extent are you inspired by the worship services in your church?
     No Response — 7%
     A. Never inspired, only bored — 2%
     B. No longer inspired, but I once was — 6%
     C. Very often inspired — 26%
     D. Quite often inspired — 31%
     E. Sometimes inspired — 24%
     F. Seldom inspired — 5%
729. Which of the following statements comes closest to expressing what you believe about Jesus?
     No Response — 6%
     A. Jesus is the Divine Son of God, and I have no doubts about it — 71%
     B. While I have some doubts, I believe that Jesus is Divine — 15%
     C. I believe that Jesus was a great man and very holy, but I don't believe him to be the Son of God any more than all of us are children of God — 2%
     D. I think Jesus was only a man, although an extraordinary one — 2%
     E. Frankly, I'm not entirely sure there really was such a person as Jesus — 1%
     F. None of the above represents what I believe — 3%
730. Frequent family worship in the home is (Read each statement carefully and *mark all* those you agree with.)
     No Response — 8%
     A. An ideal I would like to see my family carry out — 51%
     B. A source of strength that draws the family together — 26%
     C. A nice thing but difficult or impossible because there is never a time when the whole family is together — 9%
     D. Not beneficial because no group worship can meet the needs of the very young child and the mature adult — 1%
     E. Undesirable because it is often hypocritical or just dull routine — 3%
     F. Potentially harmful if children are sometimes forced into it and later rebel against the faith — 2%

Scale 67   Self-Oriented Utilitarianism   (Reliability .53)

325. A worthwhile goal in life is to find security and certainty: No Response — 4%, Strongly Agree — 9%, Agree — 68%, Disagree — 17%, Strongly Disagree — 1%

345. Sometimes it's all right to get around the law if you don't actually break it: NR — 5%, SA — 2%, A — 27%, D — 52%, SD — 15%

358. In times like these a person ought to enjoy what he can *now* and not wait: NR — 4%, SA — 5%, A — 44%, D — 43%, SD — 4%

381. Pressures to close one's eyes to dishonest behavior.
On a scale from 1 (Accept most easily) to 6 (Impossible to accept): No Response — 5%, 1 — 4%, 2 — 4%, 3 — 7%, 4 — 12%, 5 — 30%, 6 — 39%

472. What my religion offers me most is comfort when sorrows and misfortune strike: No Response — 3%, I definitely disagree — 10%, I tend to disagree — 17%, I tend to agree — 39%, I definitely agree — 32%

474. One reason for my being a church member is that such membership helps to establish a person in the community: No Response — 3%, Definitely not true — 51%, Tends not to be true — 17%, Tends to be true — 21%, Definitely true — 7%

476. The purpose of prayer is to secure a happy and peaceful life: No Response — 3%, I definitely disagree — 12%, I tend to disagree — 21%, I tend to agree — 37%, I definitely agree — 27%

526. We should be concerned with our own private welfare and stop trying to help others by butting into their private lives: No Response — 4%, Strongly Agree — 5%, Agree — 29%, Disagree — 50%, Strongly Disagree — 12%

559. Clergy should stick to religion and not concern themselves with social, economic, and political questions: No Response — 6%, No — 72%, Yes — 23%

Scale 68   Life Purpose   (Reliability .80)

244. If I could choose, I would . . .
On a scale from 1 (Prefer never to have been born) to 4 (Neutral) to 7 (Like nine more lives just like this one): No Response — 3%, 1 — 2%, 2 — 1%, 3 — 4%, 4 — 12%, 5 — 30%, 6 — 26%, 7 — 22%

245. In achieving life goals I have . . .
On a scale from 1 (Made no progress whatever) to 4 (Neutral) to 7 (Progressed to complete fulfillment): No Response — 3%, 1 — 2%, 2 — 2%, 3 — 9%, 4 — 12%, 5 — 45%, 6 — 18%, 7 — 8%

246. My life is . . .
On a scale from 1 (Empty, filled only with despair) to 4 (Neutral) to 7 (Running over with exciting good things): No Response — 3%, 1 — 3%, 2 — 2%, 3 — 7%, 4 — 9%, 5 — 33%, 6 — 26%, 7 — 16%

247. If I should die today, I would feel that my life has been . . .
On a scale from 1 (Completely worthless) to 4 (Neutral) to 7 (Very worthwhile): No Response — 2%, 1 — 2%, 2 — 1%, 3 — 5%, 4 — 7%, 5 — 24%, 6 — 24%, 7 — 35%

248. In thinking of my life, I . . .
On a scale from 1 (Often wonder why I exist) to 4 (Neutral) to 7 (Always see a reason for my being here): No Response — 2%, 1 — 6%, 2 — 2%, 3 — 8%, 4 — 7%, 5 — 23%, 6 — 21%, 7 — 31%

249. As I view the world in relation to my life, the world . . .
On a scale from 1 (Completely confuses me) to 4 (Neutral) to 7 (Fits meaningfully with my life): No response — 2%, 1 — 10%, 2 — 5%, 3 — 17%, 4 — 12%, 5 — 27%, 6 — 15%, 7 — 12%

250. I am a . . .
On a scale from 1 (Very irresponsible person) to 4 (Neutral) to 7 (Very responsible person): No Response — 3%, 1 — 3%, 2 — 2%, 3 — 3%, 4 — 8%, 5 — 20%, 6 — 31%, 7 — 31%

254. Facing my daily tasks is . . .
On a scale from 1 (A painful and boring experience) to 4 (Neutral) to 7 (A source of pleasure and satisfaction): No Response — 3%, 1 — 3%, 2 — 3%, 3 — 7%, 4 — 8%, 5 — 22%, 6 — 27%, 7 — 27%

255. I have discovered . . .
On a scale from 1 (No mission or purpose in life) to 4 (Neutral) to 7 (Clear-cut goals and a satisfying life purpose): No Response — 3%, 1 — 3%, 2 — 2%, 3 — 5%, 4 — 9%, 5 — 30%, 6 — 27%, 7 — 22%

Scale 69   Horatio Alger Orientation   (Reliability .64)

61. IDEAS ABOUT THE FUTURE: Here is what [two] people thought about their children's future. Which comes closest to your thoughts?
If my children work hard and plan right, they will have more than I have

had. There are always good chances for people who try: No Response — 2%, No — 48%, Yes — 51%

I don't know whether my children will be better off, worse off, or just the same. Things always go up and down, even if one works hard: No Response — 2%, No — 70%, Yes — 28%

62. HUMAN TROUBLES: Some people get into trouble and cause others trouble. Which explanation is most agreeable to you?

People have great possibilities for both good and bad and therefore must learn how to get along with others. If life teaches them to be selfish, they will be selfish. If it teaches them to be unselfish, they will be unselfish: No Response — 2%, No — 39%, Yes — 60%

People are basically much more good than bad. If they fail to develop their greatest possibilities for unselfish service, and they get into trouble, it is because they are surrounded by bad examples and are mistreated: No Response — 2%, No — 74%, Yes — 24%

64. CHANGE IN WORSHIP: People react in many different ways when worship services change from what they used to be. Which best describes your feeling?

You are unhappy with the changes. You feel that worship services should be kept as they were in the past: No Response — 2%, No — 86%, Yes — 13%

You like the old ways of worshiping but don't think you should hang onto them if they don't fit how people feel and think now: No Response — 2%, No — 49%, Yes — 50%

65. THE TEACHER'S JOB: There is disagreement about just what the main job of the teacher is. Which do you feel is the teacher's main job?

It is to decide, as a trained teacher, what the children need to learn and to see that it gets learned: No Response — 2%, No — 86%, Yes — 13%

66. CARE OF THE STORE: There were two men with small stores who lived very differently. Which of the two ways comes closest to how you might do it?

One took good care of his store but spent no more on it than he had to. He gave only the time needed to keep his business going, preferring to visit with friends and go on trips: No Response — 0%, No — 61%, Yes — 39%

One liked to work in his store, and he put in many hours fixing and improving things. This left little time for friends or going places, but to see the results of his work made him feel happy: No Response — 0%, No — 39%, Yes — 61%

68. NON-WORKING TIME: Two men spend their time in different ways when they are not working. Which of the two comes closer to the way you would use your leisure?

One man spends most of his time learning, doing, or trying out new things which interest him or will help him in his work: No Response — 2%, No — 42%, Yes — 56%

One man spends most of his non-working time talking, visiting or just being with his friends: No Response — 2%, No — 56%, Yes — 42%

73. DISOBEDIENCE: Assume you are a parent and for some time you have been concerned that your 13-year-old has been disobeying you and has now begun to talk back when you have tried to give direction. Which of the following comes closest to what you think would be the best course of action to take?

Make it clear to the child that you will not tolerate such disrespect because it is important for a child to learn to do what he ought, even though he doesn't like it, because there will always be someone to whom he is responsible. Besides that, God's Law says he ought to honor his parents. To help the child learn this important lesson, you let him know what punishments are likely to come: No Response — 2%, No — 66%, Yes — 32%

Scale 70   Gospel-Oriented Life   (Reliability .50)

160. If you were to move away from your present location, which one of the following would you consider most important when selecting a church?

A Lutheran church of the synod of which I am now a member: No Response — 3%, No — 70%, Yes — 27%

70. DISCIPLINE: Assume you are a teacher of an unruly class and that one day you have vented your anger toward the class on one child. Knowing that you have acted unfairly by severely punishing the one child, which of the following are you most likely to do?

Recognizing that this event creates a credibility-gap in leadership, you express your feelings to the class and try to guide them toward a class decision on appropriate student-teacher behavior: No Response — 1%, No — 67%, Yes — 32%

You go to the child privately and acknowledge that you wronged the child and ask his forgiveness for having been too harsh with him: No Response —1%, No — 60%, Yes — 39%

72. STEALING IN BUSINESS: Assume you are operating a small business with four employees. You become aware that one of the four is stealing from you. Which of the following is the best course of action to take?

Call the group together and reason with them about the need that all of you have for the business to keep going. For example, tell them the livelihood of all of you depends upon it. Or appeal to their sense of right and wrong, justice, and fair play: No Response — 2%, No — 79%, Yes — 19%

Go to the thief privately and let him understand that you know he has been stealing but that you willingly forgive him for this wrong to you and the others. Stress that you know and believe he is no worse than the rest, including yourself, so you're not going to hold this over his head but will continue to trust him: No Response — 2%, No — 49%, Yes — 49%

73. DISOBEDIENCE: Assume you are a parent and for some time you have been concerned that your 13-year-old has been disobeying you and has now begun to talk back when you have tried to give direction. Which of the following comes closest to what you think would be the best course of action to take?

Go to the child and let him know that you understand that this is very human behavior but that nevertheless you are bothered and offended by it. Tell the child that you are sorry if you have hurt him or provoked him in any way and that you forgive him for hurting you. Let him know that you will try not to hold this against him: No Response — 2%, No — 71%, Yes — 27%

74. ADULTERY: Assume that you are married and you become certain that your spouse has committed adultery recently with another married person. Which of the following is the closest to what you now think that you would do?

Try to be the best possible husband or wife you can be in the fullest sense, not denying your spouse any marital privileges or attempting any punishment. At the same time, let your spouse know that you have been hurt very much and that you forgive him/her. Also make it clear that you want to do all you can to bring the two of you closer together and that you want to continue to build your marriage together: No Response — 3%, No — 63%, Yes — 34%

Talk it through like two reasonable people, trying to understand how it happened, how you may have contributed to it, what it means, and where you go from here. Your goal is to try to keep the marriage together in view of the children who are hurt most by divorce, and because you know the social and financial problems that divorce creates: No Response — 3%, No — 48%, Yes — 49%

75. PREACHING FALSE DOCTRINE: Assume that you and several others in your congregation feel that your pastor is not preaching the truth. Which of the following is the closest to what you think ought to be done in such a situation?

See the pastor privately and try to show him from the Bible where he is wrong and be ready to forgive him when he admits his errors: No Response — 3%, No — 78%, Yes — 19%

Scale 73   Drug Culture Orientation   (Reliability .73)

160. If you were to move away from your present location, which one of the following would you consider most important when selecting a church?

* 7. Considerations other than these: No Response — 3%, No — 92%, Yes — 5%

---

* Other possible answers were: 1) A Lutheran church of the synod of which I am now a member; 2) A Lutheran church near my home; 3) A Lutheran church where I like the pastor and his preaching; 4) A Lutheran congregation where I feel there is a sense of mission; 5) Any Lutheran church that combines 2, 3, and 4; 6) Any Protestant church that combines 2, 3, and 4.

210. I think of myself as
°° K. Other: No Response — 6%, No — 93%, Yes — 1%
489. With which of the following have you experimented (tried once or twice)? Mark as many as apply.
    B. Marijuana (pot), hashish, peyote, or psilocybin, etc.: No Response — 15%, No — 81%, Yes — 5%
    C. LSD (acid) and/or other strong psychedelics: No Response — 15%, No — 84%, Yes — 1%
    D. Heroin and/or "speed," amphetamines or barbiturates: No Response — 15%, No — 84%, Yes — 1%
490. Which of the following do you use occasionally?
    B. Marijuana (pot), hashish, peyote, or psilocybin, etc.: No Response — 23%, No — 75%, Yes — 2%
    C. LSD (acid) and/or other strong psychedelics: No Response — 23%, No — 77%, Yes — 1%
    D. Heroin and/or "speed," amphetamines or barbiturates: No Response — 23%; No — 76%, Yes — 1%
491. Which of the following do you use regularly?
    B. Marijuana (pot), hashish, peyote or psilocybin, etc.: No Response — 74%, No — 25%, Yes — 1%
    C. LSD (acid) and/or other strong psychedelics: No Response — 74%, No — 26%, Yes — 0%
    D. Heroin and/or "speed," amphetamines or barbiturates: No Response — 74%, No — 26%, Yes — 1%
730. Frequent family worship in the home is
    E. Undesirable because it is often hypocritical or just dull routine. No Response — 8%, No — 88%, Yes — 4%

Scale 74 Personal Initiative on Church and Public Issues (Reliability .81)

200. Have you made your views on controversial religious issues in the Church (fellowship, doctrine, ministry and mission of the Church, etc.) known in any of the following ways? (Mark as many as you have done; if none, leave blank.)
    A. Spoken to a pastor personally: No Response — 53%, Not This Response — 11%, This Response — 36%
    B. Taken a public stand in your congregation: NR — 53%, NTR — 33%, TR — 14%
    C. Initiated or presented a discussion or study program among church members on such an issue: NR — 53%, NTR — 37%, TR — 10%
    D. Written a conference, district, or synodical official: NR — 53%, NTR — 43%, TR — 4%
    E. Personally contacted a conference, district, or synodical official: NR — 53%, NTR — 43% TR — 4%
    F. Taken a public stand in a conference, district, or synodical meeting: NR — 53%, NTR — 42%, TR — 5%
    G. Written a letter to an editor of a church publication: NR — 53%, NTR — 45%, TR — 2%
    H. Participated in efforts to remove offending officials: NR — 53%, NTR — 45%, TR — 2%
    I. Participated in an active protest against church policies: NR — 53%, NTR — 45%, TR — 2%
206. Have you made your views on public affairs known in any of the following ways? (Mark as many as you have done; if none, leave blank.)
    A. Signed a petition: No Response — 36%, Not This Response — 10%, This Response — 54%
    B. Written a public official: NR — 36%, NTR — 45%, TR — 19%
    C. Personally contacted a public official: NR — 36%, NTR — 50%, TR — 14%
    D. Written a letter to the editor of a newspaper: NR — 36%, NTR — 56%, TR — 7%
    E. Publicly took a stand on some public issue: NR — 36%, NTR — 53%, TR — 11%
    F. Publicly supported a political candidate: NR — 36%, NTR — 52%, TR — 12%
    G. Circulated a petition: NR — 36%, NTR — 54%, TR — 9%

°° Other possible answers were: a) A liberal Democrat; b) A moderate Democrat; c) A conservative Democrat; d) A liberal Republican; e) A moderate Republican; f) A conservative Republican; g) American Independent Party Member; h) An Independent; i) A Socialist; j) A Communist; l) Not interested in politics.

H. Taken a stand from the pulpit on some political issue: NR — 36%, NTR — 61%, TR — 3%

I. Run for public office: NR — 36%, NTR — 60%, TR — 3%

Scale 78 Openness to Change Within the Church (Reliability .55)

47. The Bible does not contain all of God's revelation of himself: No Response — 3%, Yes — 44%, No — 34%, ? — 19%

48. There are changeless truths (Absolutes) that can be known by men: No Response — 4%, Yes — 61%, No — 13%, ? — 22%

505. The Gospel rather than the Law of God is the only power which can actually produce a change in a person's life: No Response — 5%, Strongly Agree — 13%, Agree — 24%, Disagree — 48%, Strongly Disagree — 11%

506. The doctrines of the Lutheran Church, as I understand them, encourage active participation in social reform: NR — 7%, SA — 5%, A — 43%, D — 42%, SD — 1%

547. I like variety in the order of service rather than the same order every week: NR — 4%, SA — 14%, A — 43%, D — 35%, SD — 4%

682. Congregations should continue to support their liberal arts colleges: No Response — 7%, Agree — 67%, Disagree — 15%, ? — 11%

689. The protests of college students are a healthy sign for America: NR — 6%, A — 20%, D — 68%, ? — 6%

691. Students should have more to say about what is taught in high schools: NR — 6%, A — 30%, D — 60%, ? — 5%

701. Couples should be strongly encouraged to have no more than two natural children: NR — 6%, A — 44%, D — 44%, ? — 6%

707. Our Church as a national organization should take an official position and speak out on important social and political issues of the day: NR — 6%, A — 46%, D — 39%, ? — 9%

708. Women should be able to hold office and vote in congregations just as men do: No Response — 7%, Agree — 83%, Disagree — 11%

709. It should be possible for women to be ordained into the ministry: NR — 6%, A — 61%, D — 33%

BIBLIOGRAPHY

Albert, E. M., and Kluckhohn, C. K. M. 1960. *A selected bibliography on values, ethics, and esthetics in the behavioral sciences and philosophy.* New York: Free Press.

Allport, G. 1937. *Personality: a psychological interpretation.* New York: Holt.

————. 1954. *The nature of prejudice.* Reading, Mass.: Addison-Wesley.

Allport, G., and Ross, J. M. 1967. Personal religious orientation and prejudice. *Journal of personal social psychology,* 5: 432-443.

Anderson, T. W. 1958. *Introduction to multivariate statistical analysis.* New York: Wiley.

Backus, D. W. 1969. The seven deadly sins: their meaning and measurement. Unpublished doctoral dissertation, University of Minnesota.

Bakan, D. 1966. *The duality of human existence.* Chicago: Rand McNally.

Berger, P. L., and Luckmann, T. 1966. *The social construction of reality.* Garden City: Doubleday.

Bogardus, E. S. 1925. Measuring social distance. *Journal of applied sociology,* 9: 299-308.

————. 1933. Social distance scale. *Sociology of social research,* 17: 265-271.

————. 1967a. Measuring social distance. In *Readings in attitude theory and measurement,* ed. M. Fishbein, pp. 71-76. New York: Wiley.

————. 1967b. Intergroup relations, racial and ethnic: prejudice and social distance. In *Sociological measurement, an inventory of scales and indices,* by D. M. Bonjean, R. J. Hill, and S. D. McLemore, pp. 154-55. San Francisco: Chandler.

Britton, K. 1969. *Philosophy and the meaning of life.* Cambridge: Cambridge University Press.

Brown, L. B. 1962. A study of religious belief. *British journal of psychology,* 53: 259-272.

Chemnitz, M. Tr. 1971. *The two natures in Christ*. Translated by J. A. O. Preus. St. Louis: Concordia.

Chweh, C. Y. 1968. Factors related to varying conceptions of the modern missionary task held by professional leaders and laymen of the Lutheran Church—Missouri Synod. Unpublished doctoral dissertation.

Concordia Theological Seminary. 1958. *What, then, is man?* A symposium of theology, psychology, and psychiatry (graduate study number III), Paul Meehl, committee chairman. St. Louis: Concordia.

Cronbach, L. 1951. Coefficient alpha and the internal structure of tests. *Psychometrika*, 16: 297-334.

Crumbaugh, J. 1968. Cross-validation of purpose-in-life test based on Frankl's concepts. *Journal of individual psychology*, 24: 74-81.

Dittes, J. E. 1969. Psychology of religion. In *The handbook of social psychology*, eds., G. Lindzey and E. Aronson, 2nd ed. Vol. 5: Applied social psychology. Reading, Mass.: Addison-Wesley.

DuBois, P.; Loevinger, J.; and Gleser, G. 1952. The construction of homogeneous keys for a biographical inventory. *Research bulletin*, 52-18. U.S.A.F. Human Resources Center, Lackland Air Force Base, San Antonio.

Duncombe, D. C. 1969. *The shape of the Christian life*. Nashville: Abingdon.

Dynes, R. 1957. The consequences of sectarianism for social participation. *Social forces*, 35: 331-334.

Edwards, W. 1954. The theory of decision making. *Psychological bulletin*, 51: 380-417.

Elert, W. 1962. *The structure of Lutheranism*. St. Louis: Concordia.

Eysenck, H. J. 1947. Primary social attitudes: I. the organization and measurement of social attitudes. *International journal of opinion and attitude research*, 1: 49-84.

———. 1954. *The psychology of politics*. London: Routledge and Kegan.

Faulkner, J. and DeJong, G. 1966. Religiosity in 5-D: an empirical analysis. *Social forces*, 45: 246-254.

Feagin, J. 1964. Prejudice and religious types: a focused study of southern fundamentalists. *Journal for the scientific study of religion*, 4: 3-13.

Ferguson, L. W. 1944. Socio-psychological correlates of primary attitude scales: I. religionism, II. humanitarianism. *Journal of social psychology*, 19: 18-98.

Feucht, Oscar, ed. 1961. *Sex and the church: a sociological, historical, and theological investigation of sex attitudes*. Vol. 5. Marriage and Family research series. St. Louis: Concordia.

Festinger, L.; Riecken, W.; and Schachter, S. 1956. *When prophecy fails*. Minneapolis: University of Minnesota Press.

Forde, G. O. 1969. *The law-gospel debate*. Minneapolis: Augsburg.

Frank, J. D. 1962. The role of cognitions in illness and healing. In *Research in psychotherapy*, eds. H. Strupp and L. Luborsky. Washington, D.C.: American Psychological Association.

Gallup, George, Jr., and Davies, John O., III, eds. 1971. *Religion in America 1971*. (The Gallup Opinion Index, Report No. 70). Princeton: Gallup International.

Gilbert, A. 1967. A Jewish response. *Dialog*, 6: 176-183.

Glock, C. Y., and Stark, R. 1966. *Christian beliefs and anti-Semitism*. New York: Harper and Row.

Gupta, R. 1968a. Multivariate analyses of test responses as a prerequisite to item analyses. *Alberta journal of educational research*, 14: 95-100.

———. 1968b. Certain techniques of multivariate analysis applied to different measures of inter-item relationships for developing unifactor tests. *Journal of educational measurement,* 5: 223-230.

Gustafson, C. V. 1956. The sociology of fundamentalism: a typological analysis based on selected groups in Portland, Oregon, and vicinity. Unpublished doctoral dissertation. University of Chicago.

Hadden, J. K. 1969. *The gathering storm in the churches.* Garden City: Doubleday.

———.1967-68. "New Life" study conducted at House of Prayer Lutheran Church, Minneapolis.

Hammer, E. F., ed. 1968. *Use of interpretation in treatment: technique and art.* New York: Grune and Stratton.

Harman, H. H. 1967. *Modern factor analysis.* Chicago: University of Chicago Press.

Hathaway, S. R., and McKinley, J. C. 1951. *Minnesota multiphasic personality inventory.* Rev. ed. New York: Psychological Corporation.

Hays, W. L. 1963. *Statistics for Psychologists.* New York: Holt, Rinehart, & Winston.

Heider, F. 1958. *The psychology of international relations.* New York: Wiley.

Hepburn, R. W., 1966. Questions about the meaning of life. *Religious studies,* 1(2): 125-140.

Hotelling, H. 1933. Analysis of a complex of statistical variables into principal components. *Journal of educational psychology,* 24: 498-520.

Hoyt, C. 1941. Test reliability estimated by analysis of variance. *Psychometrika,* 6: 153-160.

Hussel, O. 1968. Religious education and research: an analysis of religious language theory use in a study of beliefs. Unpublished doctoral dissertation, Teachers College, Columbia University.

Jaspers, K. 1957. *Man in the modern age.* New York: Anchor Doubleday.

Jeeves, M. A. 1959. Contribution on prejudice and religion in symposium on problems of religious psychology. *Proceedings of the 15th international congress of psychology, Brussels.* Amsterdam: North Holland.

Kaiser, H. 1956. The varimax method of factor analysis. Unpublished doctoral dissertation, University of California.

———. 1958. The varimax criterion for analytic rotation in factor analysis. *Psychometrika,* 23: 187-200.

Kant, I. Tr. 1956. *Critique of practical reason.* Translated by L. W. Beck. New York: Bobbs-Merrill.

Katz, D., and Stotland, E. 1959. A preliminary statement to a theory of attitude structure and change. In *Psychology: a study of a science,* ed. S. Koch. Vol. 3: Formulations of the person and the social context. New York: McGraw-Hill.

Kelley, G. A. 1955. *The psychology of personal constructs.* Two volumes. New York: W. W. Norton.

Kersten, L. K. 1968. The Lutheran ethic and social change. Unpublished doctoral dissertation, Wayne State University. See also Kersten 1970. *Lutheran ethics: the impact of religion on laymen and clergy.* Detroit: Wayne State University Press.

King, M. 1967. Measuring the religious variable: nine proposed dimensions. *Journal for the scientific study of religion,* 6: 173-190.

Kirkpatrick, C. 1949. Religion and humanitarianism. A study of institutional implications. *Psychology monographs,* 63: No. 9 (Whole No. 304).

Kluckhohn, C. K. M. 1954. Culture and behavior. In *The handbook of social psychology,* ed. G. Lindzey. Cambridge: Addison-Wesley.

Kluckhohn, F. R., and Strodtbeck, F. L. 1961. *Variations in value orientations.* Evanston: Row, Peterson, and Co.

Kuder, G., and Richardson, M. 1937. The theory of the estimation of test reliability. *Psychometrika,* 2: 151-160.
Kuhn, T. S. 1962. *Structure of scientific revolutions.* Chicago: University of Chicago Press.

Lakatos, I., and Musgrave, A., eds. 1970. *Criticism and the growth of knowledge.* Cambridge: Cambridge University Press.
Levinson, D. J., and Huffmann, P. 1955. Traditional family ideology and its relation to personality. *Journal of personality,* 23: 251-273.
Littell, F. 1971. Christians and Jews and ecumenism. *Dialog,* 10: 249-255.
Loevinger, J. 1947. A systematic approach to the construction and evaluation of tests of ability. *Psychological monograph,* 61(4): iii, 49.
———. 1948. The technique of homogeneous tests compared with some aspects of scale analysis and factor analysis. *Psychological bulletin,* 45: 507-529.
Loevinger, J.; Gleser, B.; and DuBois, P. 1953. Maximizing the discriminating power of a multiple-score test. *Psychometrika,* 18: 309-317.
Lutheran World Federation. 1957. Messages of the Third Assembly, p. 114. Minneapolis: Augsburg.
Maranell, G. M. 1966. Some preliminary studies of religious attitudes. *Kansas journal of sociology,* 2: 81-90.
———. 1967. An examination of some religious and political attitude correlates of bigotry. *Social forces,* 45: 356-362.

Marty, M. 1964. *Varieties of unbelief.* New York: Holt, Rinehart, & Winston.
Mead, M. 1970. *Culture and commitment.* New York: Natural History Press.
Metz, D. L. 1967. *New congregations: security and mission in conflict.* Philadelphia: Westminster.
Milton, J. 1963. *Complete English poetry of John Milton,* ed. J. Shawcross. New York: New York University Press.
Moore, W. E. 1969. Social Structure and behavior. In *The handbook of social psychology,* eds. G. Lindzey and E. Aronson. 2nd ed. Vol. 4. Reading, Mass.: Addison-Wesley.
Morris, C. M. 1956. *Varieties of human value.* Chicago: University of Chicago Press.
Mosier, C. 1946. Machine methods of scaling by reciprocal averages. *Proceedings of the research forum.* International Business Machines Corporation.
Myrdal, G. 1968. *Asian drama.* Three volumes. New York: Pantheon.

Neal, M. A. 1965. *Values and interests in social change.* Englewood Cliffs: Prentice-Hall.

Polanyi, M. 1958. *Personal knowledge towards a post-critical philosophy.* London: Routledge and Kegan.
Popper, K. R. 1959. *The logic of scientific discovery.* New York: Basic Books.
Preus, R. D. 1970. *The theology of post-Reformation Lutheranism.* St. Louis: Concordia.
Putney, S., and Middleton, R. 1961. Dimensions and correlates of religious ideologies. *Social forces,* 39: 285-290.

Quinley, H. 1968. Clergymen and public affairs (questionnaire). Stanford: Institute of Political Studies.

Rand Corporation. 1955. *A million random digits with 100,000 normal deviates.* Glencoe, Ill.: Free Press.
Reich, C. A. 1970. *The greening of America.* New York: Random House.

Roberts, A., and Donaldson, J., eds. 1963. *The ante-Nicene fathers.* Vol. III: Latin Christianity: its founder, Tertullian. Grand Rapids: Wm. B. Eerdmans.

Robinson, J. P., and Shaver, P. R. 1969. *Measures of social psychological attitudes.* Ann Arbor: University of Michigan Publications Division, Institute for Social Research.

Rokeach, M. 1969. The H. Paul Douglass lectures for 1969. *Review of religious research,* 11(1): 3-39.

Schneiderman, L. 1963. The culture of poverty. Unpublished doctoral dissertation, University of Minnesota.

Selznick, G., and Steinberg, S. 1969. *The tenacity of prejudice.* New York: Harper and Row.

Skinner, B. F. 1971. *Beyond freedom and dignity.* New York: Alfred A. Knopf.

Smith, M. B. 1961. "Mental health" reconsidered. *American Psychologist,* 16: 299-306.

Sommerfeld, R. J. 1968. Conceptions of the ultimate and the social organization of religious bodies. *Journal for the scientific study of religion,* 7(2): 178-196.

Sonquist, J. A. 1970. *Multivariate model building.* Ann Arbor: University of Michigan.

Sonquist, J. A., and Morgan, J. N. 1964. *The detection of interaction effects.* Ann Arbor: Cushing-Malloy.

Spilka, B. 1969. Unpublished report of six factor analyses of data on alienation scales using 1600 high school age Indians and whites. University of Denver.

————. 1971. Unpublished personal correspondence.

Spranger, E. 1928. *Types of men.* Translated by P. J. W. Pigors. Halle: Niemeyer.

Stark, R., and Glock, C. Y. 1968. *American piety: the nature of religious commitment.* Berkeley: University of California Press.

————. 1969. Chapter Three: Prejudice and the churches. In *Prejudice, U.S.A.,* eds. C. Glock and E. Siegelman. New York: Frederick A. Praeger.

Statistical Abstract of the United States. 1971. U.S. Department of Commerce, Bureau of the Census.

Stone-Brandel Center. 1968. Achievement Motivation Program. Values Preference Scale. Chicago.

Strommen, M. P. 1963. *Profiles of church youth.* St. Louis: Concordia.

Strommen, M. P., ed. 1971. *Research on religious development: a comprehensive handbook.* New York: Hawthorn Books.

Wahlberg, R. 1971. Is Lent exaggerated? *Lutheran Witness,* 90: 93-96.

Westie, F. R. 1953. A technique for the measurement of race attitudes. *American sociological review,* 18: 73-78.

————. 1967. Intergroup relations, racial and ethnic: prejudice and social distance. In *Sociological measurement, an inventory of scales and indices* by D. M. Bonjean, R. J. Hill, and S. D. McLemore, pp. 160-162. San Francisco: Chandler.

Winer, B. J. 1962. *Statistical principles in experimental design.* New York: McGraw-Hill.

Wrenn, C. G. 1969. Unpublished lecture delivered at American Professional Guidance Association annual meeting in Las Vegas.

Yankelovich, D. 1969. What they believe: a *Fortune* survey. Chapter Three in *Youth in Turmoil.* New York: Time-Life.

INDEX

Absolutism, need for religious (Scale 43), 72, 83, 90, 123, 125, 133, 135-137, 146, 148, 204, 208, 210, 212-213, 225-226, 233, 252, 260, 267, 271, 276-277, 292

Achievement, 91, 95, 126

Activity: in church and community, 191; community, 44, 177; congregational indicators of, 177; helping, 182, in life of congregation, See Participation; questionable personal (Scale 23), 74-75, 187-189, 191, 225-226

Addiction, drug, 204

Additivity, test of, 66, 354

Affiliation: congregational, 38-39; organizational, 74, 145; political party, 46, 75; prior denominational, 75

Agape, 236, 319

Age: 47, 50, 83, 93, 113, 135, 137, 142, 143, 146, 156, 181, 198, 200, 201, 209, 219-262, 265, 279, 281; groupings used in study, 23; differences among lay people by church body, region, congregation size, sex, and education, 49

Ages: fifteen through eighteen, 23, 31, 33, 37, 38, 39, 40, 41, 42, 43, 44, 45, 50, 51, 229, 230, 245, 247-248, 258, 293; fifteen through twenty-three, 232, 240, 246, 249, 250, 251, 255, 258, 259; fifteen through twenty-nine, 21, 23, 49, 50, 221, 225, 236, 243, 247, 254, 257, 258, 259, 293; fifteen through forty-one, 236, 247; fifteen through forty-nine, 238; nineteen through twenty-three, 23, 31, 33, 34, 37, 38, 41, 42, 43, 44, 45, 50, 51, 55, 56, 225, 229, 245, 247, 248, 258, 293; nineteen through twenty-nine, 38, 45, 240; twenty-four through twenty-nine, 23, 31, 33, 34, 37, 38, 39, 40, 41, 42, 43, 44, 45, 50, 55, 230, 232, 247, 248, 249, 258, 279, 293; twenty-four through sixty-five, 259; thirty through forty-one, 23, 31, 33, 37, 38, 41, 42, 43, 44, 45, 49, 232, 248, 258, 279, 293; thirty through sixty-five, 230, 232, 236, 249, 259; forty through forty-nine, 23, 31, 33, 37, 38, 41, 42, 43, 44, 45, 49, 248, 258, 293; forty-two through sixty-five, 238; fifty through sixty-five, 21, 23, 31, 33, 34, 37, 38, 40, 41, 42, 43, 44, 45, 49, 50, 221, 225, 236, 240, 243, 246, 248, 250, 258, 259, 260, 293; over sixty-five, 40

AID: *See* Automatic Interaction Detection

ALC (American Lutheran Church): *See* Church: Lutheran bodies

Alcohol: use of, 189-190; attitude toward alcoholics, 206

Alienation: 125, 147, 222, 225, 253, 318; from the church, 255; from God, 253; from life, 256; of youth, 229, 259. *See also* Pessimism, Isolation, Purposelessness

Alpha coefficient, 336

Altruism, 182-185, 191, 318

American Indians, 206

Analysis: cluster (homogeneous keying), 59, 336; content, 328; factor, 21-22, 336-340; multivariate, 353-357; multivariate for scale derivation, 335-349; univariate, 349-351; of variance, 66, 353, 355-356

Anomie, 141

Anti-adult feelings, 223, 240-241, 245, 295

Anti-church feelings, 240, 256, 295

Anti-Semitism, 208, 216, 247, 319

Anxiety, over one's faith (Scale 49), 75, 195-199, 225, 227, 235-236, 254

Aristotle, 219

Assent, creedal, 318

Assistants, research, 25-26, 28, 325-326

Assumptions, 20, 310

Assurance, of personal salvation (Scale 66), 95, 105-106, 113, 119, 127, 143, 180, 185, 197, 211, 226, 235-236, 270, 274-275

Atheism, 131, 132, 206, 247

Attendance, church, 44-46, 175-176, 178-179, 197. *See also* Liturgy

Attitude, definition of: 311; *See also* Death, attitude toward; *etc.*

Authority: acceptance of, (Scale 51), 74-75, 189, 228; resistance to, 301; of Scripture, 111, 304

Automatic Interaction Detection (AID), 67, 96-98, 354-357

Averages, reciprocal, 339-340

Baptism, 111-112

Behavior: 174-193, financial, 319; moral, 185-191; predictors of, 287

Belief: 101, 105-106, 113, 115, 132, 136, 153, 168, 274, 100-151; crisis in, 172; definition of, 311; in Devil, 82; in God (Scale 14), 72, 103-105, 113, 127,

401